Dalton's TABLES *of* HOUSES

SPHERICAL BASIS of ASTROLOGY

FOR LATITUDES 22° TO 59° 0' N.

MACOY PUBLISHING & MASONIC SUPPLY CO., INC.

Richmond, Virginia 23228

MACOY PUBLISHING & MASONIC SUPPLY CO., INC.
Richmond, Virginia 23228

ISBN-0-88053-750-7

Printed in the United States of America

F O R E W O R D by the Publishers

DO READ the author's *Views and Suggestions* along with his *Explanations and Instructions.*

In addition to the valuable data given, there will be a chuckle or two as well. You will enjoy his candid statements about writers of his day and the "orthodox mental strut" of the scientists. The unsympathetic attitude toward astrology has not been entirely erased, but certainly great forward strides have been made since the author wrote. We wonder about his statement that "astrology is a curious and seductive rather than a useful study." Would he change that statement were he writing at the present time? We think so. He would be pleasantly surprised to find that astrology is being widely used for "useful" purposes in many fields and offered in college courses of study.

After more than 60 years, Dalton's *Table of Houses* are considered to be among the very best and are widely used by professional astrologers as well as being basic requirement in many astrological classes. Yes, Mr. Dalton was correct in his belief that his *Tables* were so accurate that they would be as useful for a hundred and more years as when first published in 1893. (In more than 40 years, we have had only one error called to our attention – and that being one degree short for Aquarius 8°, Latitude 35°!)

Mr. Dalton's hopes for an "invigorating infusion of modern thought" and students of "the right kind" who would bring "intellectual respectability" to the aims and methods of astrology have been realized. It was for such of you that he undertook the laborious task (in the days without computers) of compiling these *Tables*, which required more than a thousand operations in trigonometry by seven or ten logarithms each, so as to "diminish errors" for the work of future astrologers.

In the words of the author – "Tarry not in the dim region of fallible conjecture, but proceed to mathematic certainties."

Mr. Dalton stated in his *Explanations and Instructions* that his original compilations covered from 10° to 60°, but limited the published Tables to 22° to 56° because they would serve for the "whole civilized globe." Little did he realize how our world would expand! We gratefully acknowledge with appreciation the courtesy of the publishers of *Raphael's Tables of Houses* to permit us to include the Tables for Latitudes 57° to 59° N.

1975 THE PUBLISHERS

VIEWS and SUGGESTIONS by the AUTHOR

THERE appears to be a wide and increasing interest in regard to Astrology in this country, and perhaps there are some who wish to study it with as much exactness and thoroughness as the peculiar subject is capable of in its principal branch, the doctrine of nativities. If such are very few as yet, the spirit of this age now inclining to submit the occult and elusive to scientific scrutiny is likely to breed them ere long.

The present writer has studied it in quite a private way from a rational point of view and with careful induction for many years, taking the fundamental ideas as probable hypotheses and using a strict mathematical method according to the best works on spherical astronomy, with the intent particularly of testing with scientific caution what correspondence there is between "arcs of direction" and the events of a person's life when the data are known to be correct.

As geometrical laws shape everything, this is the part that can probably be made nearly an exact science. The rest of it – after rejecting the mouldy old nonsense and jargon, the figments and lies of the books – is mostly deductions from general and ambiguous symbols which yield little definite meaning to the intellect, though often read wonderfully by some persons who have the fine divining faculty. But this insight, however real in its way, is a raw poetry – not science, and is unreliable, especially as to times of events.

I have reached numerous confident conclusions on the subject by a long inquisitorial search. Some are negative ones, indeed, yet valuable. But many are drawn from positive proof of close accord between planetary movements and personal events, disclosing to view the main points and lines in the geometrical plan of life, though giving no clear picture of anything.

Astrology is far from being a baseless and refuted pretension, as the cyclopædias and scientists, with "orthodox and mental strut," generally assert. They condemn it without a trial, without examination and experiment, confounding its essential truth with the error and folly that corrupt it.

Genteel scholarship and formal intellects are naturally content to abide in ignorance and aversion concerning these ancient ideas of "spherical predominance," which the unsophisticated multitude treat with innate sympathy and which many great poets and thinkers have entertained as easily credible in a universe so full of wonders and mystery. Its coarser aspect is conspicuous in the saleable books and almanacs of the elusory charlatans who commonly lurk concealed under the name of some angel or star to prey upon the credulous, and in whose hands it has made no progress for hundreds of years. They "hitch" their wagon to a star, but remain in the mire and the mist.

As practised for gain and gammon, Astrology is eternal truth in distress and demoralized, disgraced by its friends, despised by its foes, and thus ever in deserved ill-repute with sensible people. It was in the same dismal plight in Bacon's time who said that it "is so full of superstition that scarce anything sound can be discovered in it, though we judge it should rather be purged than absolutely rejected."

Bacon also looked for what he calles "*Astronomia viva*, a living astronomy, an astronomy that should set forth the nature, the motion, and the influences of the heavenly bodies as they really are." Here is the hint of a wise ideal which, after three centuries, modern astronomy, in all its extreme excellent of material means, does not fulfil. It is a vast and complex growth of declared exact science, but all mechanical and soulless, empty of divine reason and human meaning. It has been wanting in the very precision which is its chief pride.

That the tabular positions of planets were erroneous, and getting more and more wide of their observed places, was seldom mentioned except in official documents. In 1882, Prof. Newcomb said: "the increasing discordance between theory and observation is a field which greatly needs to be investigated." The showy astronomy was mainly devoted to solar gas and meteors and exact places of millions of the minutest stars. Since then the American astronomers have perfected new tables of the planets.

Astrology is a curious and seductive rather than a useful study; yet, is a legitimate subject for research, with the attraction of general interest, but has its own perplexities and hindrances like any other scientific inquiry. It needs an invigorating infusion of modern thought, students of the right kind to give intellectual respectability to its aims and methods, minds with the true soular elevation and openness, "not regarding of any one's mocks," and able to emulate the patient and severe sagacity that has reached the admirable results of the established sciences. It requires no high mathematical ability, but such as will be enamoured of much dry ciphering if it lead to a real advance by gradual steps.

For the sake of such students, to furnish them a new and ample instrument, and to diminish their liability to error, this volume is issued. Drink deep, or taste not, the Uranian cup of mystical science; the empty froth and dubious flavor are mostly on the surface. Tarry not in the dim region of fallible conjecture, but proceed to mathematic certainties.

Ars vera est, sed pauci artifices reperiuntur.

1893 THE AUTHOR

EXPLANATIONS and INSTRUCTIONS with USEFUL TABLES

THE twelve astrological Houses are formed by trisecting each of the four natural divisions of the heavens made by the meridian and horizon. It is as if the eastern horizon were tilted up to one third and to two thirds the distance, and then down in like manner.

This makes six equal sections on the east of the meridian, the others being directly opposite. The celestial equator is equally divided by these into arcs of 30° each. The ecliptic on account of its obliquity is unequally divided. Hence the present Table which gives for each latitude the intersecting points of the ecliptic with the eastern horizon and those other great circles, to each degree of ecliptic longitude on the meridian and its proper sidereal time.

It is the only general one of the kind ever made. The original MS. covers from 10° to 60° of latitude, but the limits here, 22° to 56°, include the whole civilized globe. Hitherto all such tables have been for some one latitude and they but rudely serve within narrow bounds. Its usefulness therefore is very obvious in making a diagram of the heavens at a given date and locality to get the mundane positions of planets and stars for astrological purposes or any questions that require such a figure.

An immense amount of laborious calculation has been necessary, and systematic method and the utmost care was used to insure its correctness.

The ascendant, or first house, was strictly computed to the nearest tenth of a minute at a sufficient number of points (according to the more or less uniform variation), and then interpolated downward and across the page by second, third and often fourth differences, insuring general accuracy to the nearest minute. The other and minor houses were similarly fixed at many points to the nearest hundredth of a degree and interpolated for accuracy to the nearest tenth. More than a thousand operations in trigonometry, by seven or ten logarithms each, were performed, between which to fill in by the quicker but correct process of interpolation. The ecliptic obliquity used was 23° 27′ 15″, its mean value in 1885. On account of the very slow decrease in this angle, I find that for dates at least sixty years before and after that year, the Table will hardly err anywhere more than 1′ on the horizon, and this mostly in the highest latitudes. It will serve still for a century more either way and be but a trifle wrong sometimes.

The formula used in the computation was adapted from that for getting the longitude of "the nonagesimal," or ecliptic point 90° from the horizon, as given in the appendix to Bowditch's *Navigator, Problem IV* (old editions). It is substantially the same as that by which the ordinary tables are made for single latitudes. But I have examined many of these and find them erroneous in several ways, and they betray a defective method in not showing the exact recurrence of the series of differences and the consequent agreements of one quadrant with another. Some give the sidereal time to the nearest minute only, which is often an error of seven minutes of arc, to start with!

That the simple mathematical facts of these conformities appear in the present Table is a means of *detecting any copying* from it, on pretence of original work, by that sort of persons who make the usual tables. These plainly show the incapacity of the computers, who do more than is needful, and worse than is endurable.

The astrological books are so erroneous and various in the rules for making a figure, that it is well to have here some instructions and cautions for getting the true sidereal time in any case with which to use this Table.

Hardly a single one of those books mentions the correction to be applied for distance in longitude from Greenwich! and most of them ignore also the correction of mean time to sidereal. Neglect of the first one makes an error of 47^s at Boston and of $1^m\ 20^s$ on the Pacific coast, which in arc equals 12^m to 20^m, a difference of four months in directions to the "angles." To neglect the other correction may cause a further error of 57^m – about a whole year.

I give the usual Table here for making these corrections, and the entire process is as follows:

To the Greenwich sidereal time at the previous mean noon, add the correction for longitude of the place, taken from Table A, and you have the sidereal time of the same noon at the given place. (East of Greenwich this correction is *minus.*) To this add the interval between that noon and the given time, and by the same Table, its correction. The sum is the sidereal time, or right ascension, of the midheaven for the given place and time.

It is to enable students to be accurate, when necessary, that these details of precision are given, as otherwise they must be gathered from several sources. Of course, they can be omitted in making a rough figure for general consideration and then the rule is: Gr. sid. t. at previous noon + time from same local noon = approx. sid. t. required. Add 2 or 3 minutes, and it will be nearer right on the average.

There is, however, of late a liability to fall into much larger errors. On Nov. 18, 1883, Standard Time was adopted in this country, and time-pieces no longer indicate mean solar time, though they measure it. Any given standard time must therefore first be corrected to mean time. Boston, for example, is in the Eastern Division, the central meridian of which is five hours west longitude, and the new time throughout that division is fixed at five hours earlier than Greenwich time. As Boston is east of the centre, with longitude or time-difference of $4^h\ 44^m\ 15^s$, its standard time is too slow by $15^m\ 45^s$. Therefore, add that amount to get the mean time.

At New York it is too slow by $3^m\ 58^s$. Philadelphia is in the same division, but a little *west* of the centre, in longitude $5^h\ 0^m\ 36^s$; hence standard time there is 36^s too *fast.* So of any place in either of the five hourly divisions: the long.-diff. of cent. merid. and place = corr. to mean t. and is *plus* if the place be east, and *minus* if west of the meridian.

This correction must be made with care, as it amounts to about *half an hour* near the border of a division, and if applied wrongly may make an error of double that!

Practically, there are many exceptions and uncertainties in the use of our standard time, also liabilities to large error for such places as many in Maine, Ohio and Pennsylvania, where it was not fully adopted until several years after. In *The Pathfinder Railway Guide* of Boston, there has been much information as to its local use with a map.

As to the various systems of standard time in foreign countries, information is not easy to obtain; the astrologians know little of it and say nothing, for they always prefer to evade difficulties.

Now with the sidereal time and the *geographic*, or the *geocentric*, latitude (as you may think proper), the Table is used like any table of double entry.

The calculations were made from the exact R.A. in arc, but it is here given to the nearest tenth of a minute as best for getting proportional parts in the Table.

Sid. T., with its equivalent arc, to each degree on the meridian, or 10th house, heads each main column. "H" below indicates the other houses, and on the side is the Latitude. Intermediate values are got generally by simple proportion between the two nearest ones, in doing which between columns, it is easier to use the arc than the time.

Time can be changed into arc by Table C. To save needless repetition, many figures and decimal points are omitted where they are readily seen above. On each left-hand page a column is duplicated from the previous page to escape the awkwardness of reckoning between columns so situated.

There is hardly any obvious use in having the minor houses so closely calculated, but it might be needed for some purposes, and their columns would not look well if they differed too much in that respect from the ascendant.

These Explanations, etc., are now much amended, 1903.

The geographical latitude is certainly not to be used for primary directions, for all such calculations as are affected by the earth's rotation will be wrong except when the equinoctial points are near the horizon. For those purposes, therefore, the latitude must be corrected for the spheroidal shape of the earth by Table B, to convert it into the *geocentric* latitude by "the angle of the vertical," as astronomers do in computing eclipses, for which fact see the same chapter in Bowditch, before referred to, and the reductions of latitude in British and the American Ephemeris with the list of observatories. This correction often alters very much all semi-arcs, especially in high latitudes; hence a main cause of the monstrous errors constantly made by those who attempt to calculate primary directions is their use of the geographic latitude.

The matter of the "poles" of the minor houses is unsound in the astrological books, and their tables of them are wrong. It should be understood, therefore, that those houses in the present Table are calculated by a strictly correct method, which, for some parts in high latitudes, gives results that differ, sometimes more than half a degree, from those got by using the common table of poles. I found it necessary to examine the whole question thoroughly. These poles are angles analogous to the pole of a place, its latitude, and while the ascendant is obtained directly from that, the other houses can be had precisely only by a trial-and-error process from a mean or approximate pole to begin with, because the poles are factors in the operation that depend upon the very thing sought for.

Now, the usual table of poles is not made for an average case, but for the extreme one, that is when 0 or 0 is on the cusp – the blunder of some one about a century ago, and has been blindly copied ever since. The errors therein are large for high latitudes.

The proper average poles are a mean between those of ♈ 0 on the cusp of a house, and those when ♋ 0 is there. I find that a near average is had when ♉ 22, or any point of same declination, is on the cusps. The Table D is made accordingly.

The formula for 11th and 3d houses is:

$$\tan \text{pole} = \frac{\text{sine } \frac{1}{3} \text{ asc. diff.}}{\tan \text{decl.}}$$

For the 12th and 2d, 2/3 is put instead of 1/3. Ecliptic obliquity is taken at $23^{\circ}\ 27^{m}\ 15^{s}$, but its variation for many years has little effect. This Table will give in all cases nearly true results directly by the usual formula, especially if account be made of 2d differences between the tabular latitudes.

The test of exactness in such point is, that 1/3 (or 2/3) its semi-arc should equal its meridian distance by right ascension.

OF FIGURES for SOUTH LATITUDES

THOUGH the Table, as it stands, is for North latitudes only, it is equally and easily available for Sourthern ones, as follows:

Obtain the R.A. and longitude of the midheaven as usual. Then, instead of getting the other houses from the same page, ADD 180°, and in *that* part of the Table, with the latitude, find the values for those houses, but *substitute the opposite signs* for the ones found there. (This very necessary problem is left out of all the old books, and recent writers have mostly ignored or befogged it.)

Make the figure with ascendant on the left as usual. To reverse it, though correct in idea, causes endless confusion to one accustomed to the common position. Only bear in mind that the equator and zodiacal ring above the earth are now behind you, to the North. In calculations from a Southern figure, the only change is that the plus-or-minus rule for ascensional difference is reversed.

If the geographical latitude be proper for figures, then the English tables of houses are tolerable correct except some inaccuracies in making, and by taking ecliptic obliquity at $23^{\circ}\ 28^{m}$, its amount more than a century ago. But the whole system of primary direction has been confused and falsified owing to ignorance of that essential factor, the Geocentric latitude.

These pages rectify all that and provide means for correct figures at any point in two wide belts around the world at any date for about two centuries before or after our assumed Obliquity of 1885.

Of course, there can be no really scientific and thorough treatment of nativities unless the factors for all operations are complete and correct. The present work is "well calculated" to facilitate that; and our *Sixteen Principal Stars* repairs many glaring omissions in all writers on the subject.

The working of nativities has always been utterly chaotic, and is worse than ever now that they falsely equate arcs by that vain scheme of *a degree for a year.* It can never be otherwise without the full astronomical basis and a right mathematical method, in place of the scant system and excessive error of the sordid Sidrophels who debase the real astrology by their confusions and deceit, and whose spurious teaching is the worst obstacle to the development of what exact science in it is possible.

O curvæ animæ, et mathesis inanis.

TABLE A.

Correction of Mean to Sidereal Time.

Mean time.	Correction. +	Mean time.	Correction. +	Mean time.	Correction. +	Mean time.	Correc. +	Mean time.	Correc. +
H.	M. S.	M.	S.	M.	S.	S.	S.	S.	S.
1	0 9.86	1	0.16	31	5.09	1	.00	31	.09
2	0 19.71	2	0.33	32	5.26	2	.00	32	.09
3	0 29.57	3	0.49	33	5.42	3	.01	33	.09
4	0 39.43	4	0.66	34	5.58	4	.01	34	.09
5	0 49.28	5	0.82	35	5.75	5	.01	35	.10
6	0 59.14	6	0.99	36	5.91	6	.02	36	.10
7	1 9.00	7	1.15	37	6.08	7	.02	37	.10
8	1 18.85	8	1.31	38	6.24	8	.02	38	.10
9	1 28.71	9	1.48	39	6.41	9	.02	39	.11
10	1 38.57	10	1.64	40	6.57	10	.03	40	.11
11	1 48.42	11	1.81	41	6.73	11	.03	41	.11
12	1 58.28	12	1.97	42	6.90	12	.03	42	.11
13	2 8.13	13	2.14	43	7.06	13	.04	43	.12
14	2 17.99	14	2.30	44	7.23	14	.04	44	.12
15	2 27.85	15	2.46	45	7.39	15	.04	45	.12
16	2 37.70	16	2.63	46	7.56	16	.04	46	.13
17	2 47.56	17	2.79	47	7.72	17	.05	47	.13
18	2 57.42	18	2.96	48	7.88	18	.05	48	.13
19	3 7.27	19	3.12	49	8.05	19	.05	49	.13
20	3 17.13	20	3.28	50	8.21	20	.05	50	.14
21	3 26.99	21	3.45	51	8.38	21	.06	51	.14
22	3 36.84	22	3.61	52	8.54	22	.06	52	.14
23	3 46.70	23	3.78	53	8.71	23	.06	53	.15
		24	3.94	54	8.87	24	.07	54	.15
		25	4.11	55	9.03	25	.07	55	.15
		26	4.27	56	9.20	26	.07	56	.15
		27	4.43	57	9.36	27	.07	57	.16
		28	4.60	58	9.53	28	.08	58	.16
		29	4.76	59	9.69	29	.08	59	.16
		30	4.93	60	9.86	30	.08	60	.16

The sum of correct's will be taken to nearest second.

TABLE B.

Correction of Latitude.

Always *minus.*

Lat.	Correction.	Lat.	Correction.
°	′ ″	°	′ ″
22	8 8	41	11 37
23	8 25	42	11 40
24	8 42	43	11 42
25	8 58	44	11 43
26	9 14	45	11 44
27	9 29	46	11 44
28	9 43	47	11 43
29	9 56	48	11 40
30	10 9	49	11 38
31	10 21	50	11 34
32	10 32	51	11 29
33	10 42	52	11 24
34	10 52	53	11 17
35	11 1	54	11 10
36	11 9	55	11 2
37	11 16	56	10 54
38	11 23	57	10 44
39	11 28	58	10 34
40	11 33	59	10 23
41	11 37	60	10 11

N. B. This table is newly calculated from the latest determination of the ellipticity, E, by the formula,

tan geoc. Lat. $= (1-E)^2$ tan Lat.

Log. of $(1-E)^2$ is 9.9970351.

TABLE C.

To Convert Sidereal Time into R. A. in Arc.

Time	Arc.	Time	Arc.	Time	Arc.
H.	°	M. S.	° ′ ′ ″	M. S.	° ′ ′ ″
1	15	1	0 15	31	7 45
2	30	2	0 30	32	8 0
3	45	3	0 45	33	8 15
4	60	4	1 0	34	8 30
5	75	5	1 15	35	8 45
6	90	6	1 30	36	9 0
7	105	7	1 45	37	9 15
8	120	8	2 0	38	9 30
9	135	9	2 15	39	9 45
10	150	10	2 30	40	10 0
11	165	11	2 45	41	10 15
12	180	12	3 0	42	10 30
13	195	13	3 15	43	10 45
14	210	14	3 30	44	11 0
15	225	15	3 45	45	11 15
16	240	16	4 0	46	11 30
17	255	17	4 15	47	11 45
18	270	18	4 30	48	12 0
19	285	19	4 45	49	12 15
20	300	20	5 0	50	12 30
21	315	21	5 15	51	12 45
22	330	22	5 30	52	13 0
23	345	23	5 45	53	13 15
24	360	24	6 0	54	13 30
		25	6 15	55	13 45
		26	6 30	56	14 0
		27	6 45	57	14 15
		28	7 0	58	14 30
		29	7 15	59	14 45
		30	7 30	60	15 0

This table is merely to multiply by 15, as the units of time are that larger than those of arc.

TABLE D.

Approximate Poles.

Lat.	11th and 3d H.	12th and 2d H.
°	° ′	°
10	3 21.9	6 42.4
13	4 24.3	8 45.3
16	5 28.0	10 49.8
19	6 33.5	12 56.5
22	7 41.4	15 5.9
25	8 52.0	17 18.3
28	10 5.8	19 34.2
31	11 23.5	21 54.1
34	12 45.8	24 18.7
37	14 13.7	26 48.6
40	15 48.1	29 24.1
42	16 55.1	31 11.3
44	18 6.3	33 1.7
46	19 22.1	34 55.5
48	20 42.8	36 52.8
50	22 9.0	38 53.6
51	22 54.6	39 55.5
52	23 41.9	40 58.6
53	24 31.2	42 2.8
54	25 22.6	43 8.1
55	26 16.1	44 14.5
56	27 12.0	45 22.1
57	28 10.5	46 31.0
58	29 11.8	47 41.2
59	30 16.3	48 52.7
60	31 24.1	50 5.7

This table is only for use in making figures without a table of houses, or to form such a one.

For LATITUDES from EQUATOR to 22°

As the tabular spherical basis here built fails to cover a considerable zone near the equator, and figures are often wanted for latitudes less than 22°, the formula for their calculation is added and can be used by any one a little versed in trigonometry; and any part of the Table may also be tested thereby.

(1) To the R. A.* of the M. C. add 30°, 60°, or 90°, or so on, according to the place of the house in order from the meridian, which will give the oblique ascension of its cusp. Express this in distance, forward or backward, from ♈ 0 or ♎ 0, whichever be the nearer, and call it d. Call the ecliptic obliquity O.

Then, cos d cot pole = cot A.

And the sum, or difference, of A and O (according as d measures from ♈ or ♎) = B.

Then, sec B cos A tan d = tan long. required, to be reckoned from ♈ or ♎ as d was; unless B exceed 90°, when the longitude is reckoned from the opposite equinox, reversely.

For South latitude, first add 180° to the R. A. of the M. C., and proceed as above; but in the final result put opposite zodiacal signs for those found on the minor houses.

The poles below latitude 10° are given in the annexed extension to the equator of table D.

Lat.	11th and 3d H.	12th and 2d H.
°	° ′	° ′
0	0 0	0 0
1	0 20.0	0 40.0
4	1 20.1	2 40.2
7	2 20.7	4 40.8
10	3 21.9	6 42.4

(2) On the equator the previous formula becomes simply $\frac{\tan d}{\cos O} = \tan$ long., to be reckoned as above. Hence a better method than the other would be to compute the longitude for latitude 0, and then interpolate by trial between that and 22°, by aid of the tabular differences in each column. It can often be done by mere inspection. In this way any part of the Table can be completed to the equator with sufficient accuracy, as interpolation in that interval is easy.

For latitudes from 56° to 60°, follow precepts and formula of Art. (1). Interpolation for such high latitudes is not so simple, but should allow for second differences in using table D.

For latitude more than 60° special calculations must be made.

J. G. D.

July, 1903.

* To convert ecliptic longitude into R. A., express the long. in distance (forward) from the nearest cardinal point; then, if from ♈ or ♎, tan R. A. = tan long. cos O; if from ♋ or ♑, use cot instead of tan.

UPPER MERIDIAN, CUSP OF 10th H.

SID. T. 0 0 0 (H. M. S.), ARC 0° 0′.0 — ♈ 0°

Lat.	11 ♉ °	12 ♊ °	1 ♋ ° ′	2 ♌ °	3 ♌ °
22	4.0	7.9	9 8	3.2	29.4
23	1	8.2	9 35	4	5
24	2	6	10 3	7	6
25	3	9	10 31	9	7
26	4	9.2	10 59	4.2	29.8
27	4.5	6	11 27	5	8
28	6	9	11 56	7	9
29	7	10.2	12 26	5.0	♍
30	8	6	12 56	3	0.1
31	4.9	11.0	13 26	6	2
32	5.0	3	13 57	8	3
33	2	7	14 29	6.1	4
34	3	12.1	15 1	4	5
35	4	5	15 34	7	0.6
36	5.6	13.0	16 8	7.0	7
37	7	4	16 42	3	8
38	9	9	17 16	7	9
39	6.1	14.4	17 52	8.0	1.0
40	3	9	18 28	3	1
41	4	15.4	19 5	7	2
42	6	9	19 43	9.0	4
43	8	16.5	20 22	3	5
44	7.0	17.1	21 1	6	1.6
45	2	7	21 42	10.0	7
46	5	18.3	22 24	4	8
47	7	19.0	23 7	8	9
48	9	7	23 51	11.2	2.1
49	8.1	20.4	24 36	6	2
50	3	21.2	25 22	12.0	3
51	6	22.0	26 10	4	4
52	9	9	26 59	8	6
53	9.2	23.8	27 50	13.3	8
54	5	24.8	28 43	8	3.0
55	8	25.8	29 37	14.3	1
56	10.1	27.0	♌ 0 32	8	3

SID. T. 0 3 40, ARC 0° 55′.0 — ♈ 1°

Lat.	11 ♉ °	12 ♊ °	1 ♋ ° ′	2 ♌ °	3 ♍ °
22	5.0	8.8	9 57	4.0	0.3
23	1	9.1	10 24	2	4
24	2	5	10 52	5	5
25	3	8	11 20	8	6
26	4	10.1	11 48	5.0	0.7
27	5.5	5	12 16	3	7
28	6	8	12 45	6	8
29	7	11.1	13 15	8	9
30	8	5	13 44	6.1	1.0
31	6.0	9	14 15	4	1
32	1	12.2	14 45	7	2
33	2	6	15 17	9	3
34	4	13.0	15 49	7.2	4
35	6.5	4	16 21	5	1.5
36	7	9	16 54	8	6
37	8	14.3	17 28	8.1	7
38	7.0	8	18 2	4	8
39	1	15.3	18 37	7	9
40	3	8	19 13	9.0	2.0
41	4	16.3	19 50	3	1
42	6	9	20 28	7	2
43	8	17.4	21 6	10.0	4
44	8.0	18.0	21 45	4	5
45	2	6	22 26	8	2.6
46	4	19.3	23 7	11.1	7
47	6	9	23 50	5	8
48	8	20.6	24 33	9	9
49	9.1	21.3	25 18	12.3	3.0
50	4	22.1	26 4	7	2
51	6	9	26 51	13.1	4
52	9	23.7	27 40	5	5
53	10.2	24.6	28 30	14.0	3.6
54	6	25.6	29 22	5	7
55	9	26.7	♌ 0 15	15.0	9
56	11.3	27.8	1 10	5	4.1

SID. T. 0 7 20, ARC 1° 50′.1 — ♈ 2°

Lat.	11 ♉ °	12 ♊ °	1 ♋ ° ′	2 ♌ °	3 ♍ °
22	6.0	9.7	10 46	4.8	1.3
23	1	10.0	11 13	5.1	4
24	2	4	11 41	3	4
25	3	7	12 8	6	5
26	4	11.0	12 36	8	6
27	6.5	4	13 5	6.1	1.7
28	7	7	13 34	4	7
29	8	12.1	14 3	6	8
30	9	4	14 32	9	9
31	7.0	8	15 2	7.2	2.0
32	2	13.2	15 33	5	1
33	3	6	16 4	8	2
34	4	14.0	16 36	8.0	3
35	7.6	4	17 8	3	4
36	7	9	17 41	6	2.5
37	9	15.3	18 14	9	6
38	8.1	8	18 48	9.2	7
39	2	16.3	19 23	5	8
40	4	8	19 59	9	9
41	6	17.3	20 35	10.2	3.0
42	8	8	21 12	5	1
43	9	18.4	21 50	9	2
44	9.1	19.0	22 29	11.2	3
45	3	6	23 9	5	3.4
46	5	20.3	23 50	8	5
47	7	9	24 32	12.2	6
48	9	21.6	25 15	6	7
49	10.2	22.3	25 59	13.0	9
50	5	23.0	26 45	4	4.0
51	8	8	27 31	8	2
52	11.1	24.6	28 20	14.2	3
53	4	25.5	29 9	7	4
54	7	26.5	♌ 0 0	15.2	5
55	12.0	27.5	0 53	7	7
56	4	28.6	1 47	16.2	8

SID. T. 0 11 1, ARC 2° 45′.2 — ♈ 3°

Lat.	11 ♉ °	12 ♊ °	1 ♋ ° ′	2 ♌ °	3 ♍ °
22	7.0	10.6	11 35	5.7	2.2
23	1	9	12 2	9	3
24	2	11.3	12 29	6.2	3
25	3	6	12 57	4	4
26	4	9	13 25	7	5
27	7.5	12.3	13 53	9	2.6
28	7	6	14 22	7.2	7
29	8	13.0	14 51	5	7
30	9	3	15 20	7	8
31	8.0	7	15 50	8.0	9
32	2	14.1	16 20	3	3.0
33	3	5	16 51	5	1
34	5	9	17 22	8	2
35	8.6	15.3	17 54	9.1	3
36	8	8	18 27	4	4
37	9	16.2	19 0	7	3.5
38	9.1	7	19 34	10.0	6
39	3	17.2	20 8	3	7
40	4	7	20 44	6	8
41	6	18.2	21 20	11.0	9
42	8	7	21 56	3	4.0
43	10.0	19.3	22 34	6	1
44	1	9	23 13	12.0	2
45	3	20.5	23 52	3	3
46	5	21.1	24 33	6	4.4
47	7	8	25 15	9	5
48	9	22.5	25 57	13.3	6
49	11.2	23.2	26 41	7	7
50	5	9	27 26	14.1	9
51	8	24.7	28 12	5	5.0
52	12.1	25.5	28 59	9	1
53	4	26.4	29 48	15.4	2
54	8	27.4	♌ 0 39	9	4
55	13.2	28.4	1 31	16.4	6
56	6	29.5	2 25	9	7

SID. T. 0 14 41, ARC 3° 40′.2 — ♈ 4°

Lat.	11 ♉ °	12 ♊ °	1 ♋ ° ′	2 ♌ °	3 ♍ °
22	8.0	11.5	12 24	6.5	3.1
23	1	8	12 51	7	2
24	2	12.2	13 18	7.0	3
25	3	5	13 45	2	4
26	4	8	14 13	5	3.4
27	8.5	13.2	14 41	7	5
28	7	5	15 10	8.0	6
29	8	9	15 38	3	7
30	9	14.2	16 7	5	3.7
31	9.0	6	16 37	8	8
32	2	15.0	17 7	9.1	9
33	3	4	17 38	3	4.0
34	5	8	18 9	6	1
35	9.6	16.2	18 41	9	2
36	8	7	19 13	10.2	3
37	9	17.1	19 46	5	4.4
38	10.1	6	20 20	8	4
39	3	18.1	20 54	11.0	5
40	5	6	21 29	3	6
41	7	19.1	22 4	6	4.7
42	9	6	22 41	12.0	8
43	11.1	20.2	23 18	3	9
44	3	8	23 56	7	5.0
45	4	21.4	24 35	13.0	1
46	6	22.0	25 16	4	2
47	8	7	25 57	7	3
48	12.0	23.4	26 39	14.1	4
49	3	24.0	27 22	5	5.6
50	6	7	28 6	9	7
51	9	25.5	28 52	15.3	8
52	13.2	26.3	29 39	7	9
53	5	27.2	♌ 0 27	16.1	6.1
54	9	28.2	1 17	5	2
55	14.3	29.3	2 9	17.0	4
56	6	♋ 0.4	3 2	5	5

SID. T. 0 18 21, ARC 4° 35′.3 — ♈ 5°

Lat.	11 ♉ °	12 ♊ °	1 ♋ ° ′	2 ♌ °	3 ♍ °
22	9.0	12.4	13 13	7.3	4.1
23	1	7	13 40	6	1
24	2	13.1	14 7	8	2
25	3	4	14 34	8.1	3
26	4	7	15 1	3	4.3
27	9.5	14.1	15 29	6	4
28	7	4	15 57	8	5
29	8	8	16 26	9.1	6
30	9	15.1	16 55	3	4.7
31	10.0	5	17 25	6	7
32	2	9	17 54	9	8
33	3	16.3	18 25	10.1	9
34	5	7	18 56	4	5.0
35	6	17.1	19 27	7	1
36	8	6	19 59	11.0	2
37	11.0	18.0	20 32	3	2
38	1	5	21 5	6	5.3
39	3	19.0	21 39	8	4
40	5	5	22 14	12.1	5
41	7	20.0	22 49	4	6
42	9	5	23 25	7	5.7
43	12.1	21.1	24 2	13.1	8
44	4	7	24 40	4	9
45	6	22.3	25 19	8	6.0
46	8	9	25 58	14.1	1
47	13.0	23.6	26 39	4	2
48	2	24.3	27 20	8	3
49	5	9	28 3	15.2	4
50	7	25.6	28 47	6	6.5
51	14.0	26.4	29 32	16.0	6
52	3	27.2	♌ 0 19	4	7
53	6	28.1	1 7	8	8
54	15.0	29.1	1 56	17.2	7.0
55	4	♋ 0.1	2 47	7	2
56	8	1.2	3 39	18.2	3

UPPER MERIDIAN, CUSP OF 10th H.

SID. T. 0 H. 22 M. 2 S. — ARC 5° 30′.4 — ♈ 6°

H. / Lat.	11 ♉	12 ♊	1 ♋	2 ♌	3 ♍
°	°	°	° ′	°	°
22	10.0	13.3	14 2	8.2	5.0
23	1	6	14 29	4	1
24	2	14.0	14 55	7	1
25	3	3	15 22	9	2
26	4	6	15 50	9.1	3
27	10.5	15.0	16 17	4	5.3
28	7	3	16 45	6	4
29	8	7	17 14	9	5
30	9	16.0	17 43	10.2	6
31	11.1	4	18 12	4	5.6
32	2	8	18 41	7	7
33	3	17.2	19 12	11.0	8
34	5	6	19 42	2	9
35	7	18.0	20 14	5	6.0
36	8	5	20 45	8	0
37	12.0	9	21 18	12.1	1
38	2	19.4	21 51	4	2
39	3	9	22 24	6	6.3
40	5	20.4	22 58	9	4
41	7	9	23 33	13.2	5
42	9	21.4	24 9	5	6
43	13.2	22.0	24 46	8	6.7
44	4	6	25 23	14.1	8
45	6	23.2	26 2	5	9
46	8	8	26 41	8	7.0
47	14.0	24.5	27 21	15.1	1
48	3	25.1	28 2	5	2
49	5	8	28 45	9	3
50	8	26.5	29 28	16.3	4
51	15.1	27.3	♌ 0 13	7	7.5
52	4	28.1	0 58	17.1	6
53	7	29.0	1 46	5	7
54	16.1	9	2 34	9	8
55	5	♋ 0.9	3 24	18.4	8.0
56	9	2.0	4 16	9	1

0 H. 25 M. 42 S. — 6° 25′.6 — ♈ 7°

H. / Lat.	11 ♉	12 ♊	1 ♋	2 ♌	3 ♍
°	°	°	° ′	°	°
22	10.9	14.2	14 51	9.0	5.9
23	11.1	5	15 17	3	6.0
24	2	8	15 44	5	0
25	3	15.2	16 11	7	1
26	4	5	16 38	10.0	2
27	11.5	9	17 5	2	3
28	7	16.2	17 33	5	6.3
29	8	6	18 1	7	4
30	9	9	18 30	11.0	5
31	12.1	17.3	18 59	2	5
32	2	7	19 29	5	6.6
33	4	18.1	19 59	8	7
34	5	5	20 29	12.0	8
35	7	9	21 0	3	9
36	8	19.3	21 31	6	7.0
37	13.0	8	22 3	9	1
38	2	20.3	22 36	13.1	2
39	4	7	23 9	4	3
40	5	21.2	23 43	7	7.4
41	7	8	24 18	14.1	4
42	14.0	22.3	24 53	4	5
43	2	9	25 30	7	5
44	4	23.5	26 7	15.0	7.6
45	6	24.1	26 44	3	7
46	8	7	27 23	6	8
47	15.0	25.3	28 3	16.0	9
48	2	26.0	28 44	4	8.0
49	5	7	29 26	7	1
50	8	27.4	♌ 0 9	17.1	2
51	16.1	28.2	0 53	5	3
52	4	29.0	1 38	9	8.4
53	8	8	2 25	18.3	5
54	17.2	♋ 0.8	3 13	7	6
55	6	1.8	4 2	19.1	8
56	18.0	2.9	4 53	6	9

0 H. 29 M. 23 S. — 7° 20′.8 — ♈ 8°

H. / Lat.	11 ♉	12 ♊	1 ♋	2 ♌	3 ♍
°	°	°	° ′	°	°
22	11.9	15.1	15 40	9.9	6.8
23	12.0	4	16 6	10.1	9
24	2	8	16 32	3	7.0
25	3	16.1	16 59	6	0
26	4	4	17 26	8	1
27	12.5	8	17 54	11.0	2
28	7	17.1	18 21	3	2
29	8	5	18 49	5	7.3
30	9	8	19 17	8	4
31	13.0	18.2	19 46	12.0	5
32	2	5	20 16	3	5
33	3	9	20 45	6	6
34	5	19.3	21 15	8	7.7
35	7	8	21 46	13.1	7
36	8	20.2	22 17	4	8
37	14.0	7	22 49	7	9
38	2	21.1	23 21	9	8.0
39	4	6	23 54	14.2	1
40	6	22.1	24 28	5	1
41	8	6	25 2	8	2
42	15.0	23.2	25 37	15.1	8.3
43	2	7	26 13	4	4
44	4	24.3	26 50	7	5
45	6	9	27 27	16.0	6
46	8	25.5	28 6	3	8.7
47	16.1	26.2	28 45	6	8
48	4	8	29 25	17.0	9
49	6	27.5	♌ 0 7	4	9.0
50	9	28.2	0 49	8	1
51	17.2	29.0	1 33	18.2	2
52	5	8	2 18	6	3
53	9	♋ 0.7	3 4	19.0	9.4
54	18.3	1.6	3 51	4	5
55	7	2.6	4 40	8	6
56	19.1	3.7	5 30	20.2	7

0 H. 33 M. 4 S. — 8° 16′.0 — ♈ 9°

H. / Lat.	11 ♉	12 ♊	1 ♋	2 ♌	3 ♍
°	°	°	° ′	°	°
22	12.9	16.0	16 29	10.7	7.8
23	13.0	3	16 55	9	8
24	1	6	17 21	11.2	9
25	2	17.0	17 47	4	8.0
26	4	3	18 14	6	0
27	13.5	6	18 41	9	1
28	6	18.0	19 9	12.1	1
29	8	3	19 37	3	2
30	9	7	20 5	6	8.3
31	14.0	19.1	20 33	8	4
32	2	4	21 3	13.1	4
33	3	8	21 32	4	5
34	5	20.2	22 2	6	6
35	7	6	22 32	9	8.6
36	8	21.1	23 3	14.2	7
37	15.0	5	23 34	4	8
38	2	22.0	24 7	6	9
39	4	5	24 39	9	9
40	6	23.0	25 13	15.2	9.0
41	8	5	25 47	5	1
42	16.0	24.1	26 21	8	2
43	2	6	26 57	16.1	3
44	5	25.2	27 33	5	9.4
45	7	8	28 10	8	4
46	9	26.4	28 48	17.1	5
47	17.1	27.1	29 27	4	6
48	4	7	♌ 0 7	7	9.7
49	7	28.4	0 48	18.1	8
50	18.0	29.1	1 30	5	9
51	3	9	2 12	9	10.0
52	6	♋ 0.7	2 57	19.3	1
53	9	1.5	3 42	7	2
54	19.3	2.4	4 29	20.1	3
55	7	3.4	5 17	5	4
56	20.2	4.5	6 7	9	5

0 H. 36 M. 45 S. — 9° 11′.3 — ♈ 10°

H. / Lat.	11 ♉	12 ♊	1 ♋	2 ♌	3 ♍
°	°	°	° ′	°	°
22	13.9	16.9	17 18	11.6	8.7
23	14.0	17.2	17 44	8	8
24	1	5	18 10	12.0	8
25	2	8	18 36	2	9
26	3	18.2	19 2	4	9
27	14.5	5	19 29	7	9.0
28	6	9	19 57	9	1
29	7	19.2	20 24	13.2	1
30	9	6	20 52	4	2
31	15.0	9	21 20	7	3
32	2	20.3	21 49	9	9.3
33	3	7	22 18	14.2	4
34	5	21.1	22 48	4	5
35	7	5	23 18	7	5
36	8	22.0	23 49	15.0	6
37	16.0	4	24 20	2	9.7
38	2	9	24 52	5	8
39	4	23.4	25 24	7	8
40	6	9	25 57	16.0	9
41	8	24.4	26 31	3	10.0
42	17.0	9	27 5	6	1
43	2	25.5	27 40	9	1
44	5	26.1	28 16	17.2	2
45	7	7	28 53	5	10.3
46	9	27.3	29 30	8	4
47	18.2	9	♌ 0 9	18.1	5
48	5	28.6	0 48	5	6
49	7	29.2	1 29	8	10.7
50	19.0	9	2 10	19.2	8
51	3	♋ 0.7	2 52	6	9
52	6	1.5	3 36	20.0	11.0
53	20.0	2.3	4 21	4	1
54	4	3.2	5 7	8	2
55	8	4.2	5 55	21.2	3
56	21.3	5.2	6 44	6	4

0 H. 40 M. 27 S. — 10° 6′.6 — ♈ 11°

H. / Lat.	11 ♉	12 ♊	1 ♋	2 ♌	3 ♍
°	°	°	° ′	°	°
22	14.8	17.7	18 7	12.4	9.6
23	15.0	18.1	18 32	6	7
24	1	4	18 58	8	8
25	2	7	19 24	13.1	8
26	3	19.1	19 50	3	9
27	15.5	4	20 17	5	9
28	6	8	20 44	8	10.0
29	7	20.1	21 12	14.0	1
30	9	5	21 39	2	1
31	16.0	8	22 7	5	2
32	2	21.2	22 36	7	2
33	3	6	23 5	15.0	10.3
34	5	22.0	23 34	2	4
35	7	4	24 4	5	4
36	8	8	24 35	8	5
37	17.0	23.3	25 5	16.0	6
38	2	7	25 37	2	10.6
39	4	24.2	26 9	5	7
40	6	8	26 42	8	8
41	8	25.3	27 15	17.1	9
42	18.0	8	27 49	4	9
43	3	26.4	28 24	7	11.0
44	5	9	28 59	18.0	1
45	7	27.5	29 36	3	2
46	9	28.1	♌ 0 13	6	3
47	19.1	8	0 51	19.0	11.3
48	4	29.4	1 30	3	4
49	7	♋ 0.1	2 9	7	5
50	20.0	8	2 50	20.0	6
51	3	1.5	3 32	3	11.7
52	7	2.3	4 15	7	8
53	21.1	3.2	5 0	21.1	9
54	5	4.1	5 45	5	12.0
55	9	5.1	6 32	9	1
56	22.4	6.1	7 21	22.3	2

	SID. T. 0 40 27 (H. M. S.) ARC 10° 6′.6 ♈ 11°					0 44 8 (H. M. S.) 11° 2′.0 ♈ 12°					0 47 50 (H. M. S.) 11° 57′.5 ♈ 13°				
H.	11	12	1	2	3	11	12	1	2	3	11	12	1	2	3
Lat.	♉	♊	♋	♌	♍	♉	♊	♋	♌	♍	♉	♊	♋	♌	♍
°	°	°	° ′	°	°	°	°	° ′	°	°	°	°	° ′	°	°
22	14.8	17.7	18 7	12.4	9.6	15.8	18.6	18 55	13.3	10.6	16.8	19.5	19 44	14.1	11.5
23	15.0	18.1	18 32	6	7	9	9	19 21	5	6	9	8	20 9	3	6
24	1	4	18 58	8	8	16.1	19.3	19 46	7	7	17.0	20.2	20 35	5	6
25	2	7	19 24	13.1	8	2	6	20 12	9	7	2	5	21 1	8	7
26	3	19.1	19 50	3	9	3	9	20 38	14.1	10.8	3	8	21 27	15.0	7
27	15.5	4	20 17	5	9	4	20.3	21 5	4	8	4	21.2	21 53	2	11.8
28	6	8	20 44	8	10.0	16.6	6	21 32	6	9	17.6	5	22 20	4	8
29	7	20.1	21 12	14.0	1	7	21.0	21 59	8	11.0	7	9	22 46	7	9
30	9	5	21 39	2	1	9	4	22 26	15.1	0	8	22.2	23 14	9	9
31	16.0	8	22 7	5	2	17.0	7	22 54	3	1	18.0	6	23 41	16.1	12.0
32	2	21.2	22 36	7	2	2	22.1	23 23	6	1	1	23.0	24 9	4	1
33	3	6	23 5	15.0	10.3	3	5	23 51	8	2	3	3	24 38	6	1
34	5	22.0	23 34	2	4	5	9	24 21	16.1	11.3	5	7	25 7	9	2
35	7	4	24 4	5	4	6	23.3	24 50	3	3	6	24.2	25 36	17.1	2
36	8	8	24 35	8	5	8	7	25 20	6	4	8	6	26 6	4	12.3
37	17.0	23.3	25 5	16.0	6	18.0	24.2	25 51	8	5	19.0	25.0	26 36	6	4
38	2	7	25 37	2	10.6	2	6	26 22	17.1	5	2	5	27 7	9	4
39	4	24.2	26 9	5	7	4	25.1	26 54	4	11.6	4	26.0	27 39	18.2	5
40	6	8	26 42	8	8	6	6	27 26	6	7	6	5	28 11	4	6
41	8	25.3	27 15	17.1	9	8	26.1	27 59	9	7	8	27.0	28 43	7	12.6
42	18.0	8	27 49	4	9	19.0	7	28 33	18.2	8	20.0	5	29 17	19.0	7
43	3	26.4	28 24	7	11.0	3	27.2	29 7	5	9	3	28.1	29 51	3	8
44	5	9	28 59	18.0	1	5	8	29 42	8	12.0	5	7	♌ 0 25	6	8
45	7	27.5	29 36	3	2	7	28.4	♌ 0 18	19.1	1	7	29.3	1 1	8	9
46	9	28.1	♌ 0 13	6	3	9	29.0	0 55	4	2	9	9	1 37	20.1	13.0
47	19.1	8	0 51	19.0	11.3	20.2	6	1 32	7	2	21.2	♋ 0.5	2 14	4	0
48	4	29.4	1 30	3	4	5	♋ 0.3	2 11	20.0	12.3	5	1.1	2 52	7	1
49	7	♋ 0.1	2 9	7	5	8	9	2 50	3	4	8	8	3 31	21.0	2
50	20.0	8	2 50	20.0	6	21.1	1.6	3 31	7	5	22.1	2.5	4 11	4	3
51	3	1.5	3 32	3	11.7	4	2.4	4 12	21.0	5	4	3.2	4 52	7	13.4
52	7	2.3	4 15	7	8	8	3.2	4 55	4	12.6	8	4.0	5 34	22.1	4
53	21.1	3.2	5 0	21.1	9	22.2	4.1	5 38	8	7	23.2	9	6 17	5	5
54	5	4.1	5 45	5	12.0	6	5.0	6 23	22.2	8	6	5.8	7 2	9	6
55	9	5.1	6 32	9	1	23.0	5.9	7 10	6	9	24.0	6.7	7 47	23.3	7
56	22.4	6.1	7 21	22.3	2	5	6.9	7 57	23.0	13.0	5	7.7	8 34	7	8

	0 51 32 (H. M. S.) 12° 53′.0 ♈ 14°					0 55 14 (H. M. S.) 13° 48′.6 ♈ 15°					0 58 57 (H. M. S.) 14° 44′.3 ♈ 16°				
H.	11	12	1	2	3	11	12	1	2	3	11	12	1	2	3
Lat.	♉	♊	♋	♌	♍	♉	♊	♋	♌	♍	♉	♊	♋	♌	♍
°	°	°	° ′	°	°	°	°	° ′	°	°	°	°	° ′	°	°
22	17.7	20.4	20 33	15.0	12.4	18.7	21.2	21 22	15.8	13.4	19.7	22.1	22 10	16.7	14.3
23	9	7	20 58	2	5	8	6	21 47	16.0	4	8	4	22 35	9	4
24	18.0	21.0	21 23	4	5	19.0	9	22 12	2	5	9	8	23 0	17.1	4
25	1	4	21 49	6	6	1	22.2	22 37	4	5	20.0	23.1	23 25	3	5
26	2	7	22 15	8	6	2	6	23 3	6	13.6	2	4	23 51	5	5
27	4	22.0	22 41	16.0	12.7	4	9	23 29	9	6	3	8	24 17	7	14.6
28	18.5	4	23 7	3	7	19.5	23.3	23 55	17.1	7	5	24.1	24 43	9	6
29	7	7	23 34	5	8	6	6	24 21	3	7	20.6	5	25 9	18.1	6
30	8	23.1	24 1	7	9	8	24.0	24 48	5	13.8	8	8	25 35	4	7
31	19.0	5	24 28	9	9	20.0	3	25 15	8	8	9	25.2	26 2	6	7
32	1	8	24 56	17.2	13.0	1	7	25 43	18.0	9	21.1	6	26 30	8	14.8
33	3	24.2	25 24	4	0	3	25.1	26 11	2	9	3	26.0	26 57	19.0	8
34	5	6	25 53	7	1	5	5	26 39	5	14.0	4	4	27 25	3	9
35	6	25.0	26 22	9	1	6	9	27 8	7	0	6	8	27 54	5	9
36	8	5	26 52	18.2	2	8	26.3	27 37	19.0	1	8	27.2	28 23	8	15.0
37	20.0	9	27 22	4	13.3	21.0	8	28 7	2	1	22.0	6	28 53	20.0	0
38	2	26.4	27 52	7	3	2	27.2	28 37	5	14.2	2	28.1	29 23	2	1
39	4	9	28 23	9	4	4	7	29 8	7	3	4	6	29 53	4	2
40	6	27.4	28 55	19.2	4	6	28.2	29 39	20.0	3	6	29.1	♌ 0 24	7	15.2
41	8	9	29 27	5	5	8	7	♌ 0 11	3	4	8	6	0 55	21.0	3
42	21.0	28.4	♌ 0 0	8	13.6	22.0	29.2	0 44	5	14.4	23.0	♋ 0.1	1 28	2	3
43	3	9	0 34	20.0	6	3	8	1 17	8	5	3	6	2 1	5	4
44	5	29.5	1 8	3	7	5	♋ 0.3	1 51	21.1	6	5	1.2	2 34	8	15.5
45	7	♋ 0.1	1 43	6	8	8	9	2 26	4	7	8	8	3 8	22.1	5
46	9	7	2 19	9	9	23.0	1.5	3 1	7	14.7	24.0	2.4	3 44	4	6
47	22.2	1.3	2 56	21.2	14.0	3	2.1	3 38	22.0	8	3	3.0	4 19	7	7
48	5	2.0	3 34	5	0	6	8	4 15	3	9	6	6	4 56	23.0	15.8
49	8	6	4 12	8	1	9	3.5	4 53	6	9	9	4.3	5 33	3	8
50	23.1	3.3	4 51	22.2	2	24.2	4.1	5 32	9	15.0	25.2	5.0	6 12	6	9
51	5	4.1	5 32	5	3	6	8	6 11	23.2	1	6	7	6 51	9	9
52	9	9	6 13	9	14.3	9	5.6	6 52	6	1	26.0	6.5	7 32	24.3	16.0
53	24.3	5.7	6 56	23.2	4	25.3	6.4	7 34	9	2	4	7.3	8 13	6	1
54	7	6.6	7 40	6	5	7	7.3	8 18	24.3	15.3	8	8.1	8 56	25.0	2
55	25.1	7.5	8 25	24.0	6	26.1	8.2	9 2	7	4	27.2	9.0	9 40	4	2
56	6	8.5	9 11	4	7	6	9.2	9 48	25.1	5	7	10.0	10 25	8	3

SID. T. 1 2 40 (H. M. S.) ♈ 17° — ARC 15° 40′.0

H.	11	12	1	2	3
Lat.	♉	♊	♋	♌	♍
°	°	°	° ′	°	°
22	20.6	23.0	22 59	17.5	15.3
23	7	3	23 24	7	3
24	9	6	23 49	9	4
25	21.0	24.0	24 14	18.1	4
26	1	3	24 39	3	4
27	3	6	25 5	6	15.5
28	4	25.0	25 30	8	5
29	21.6	3	25 56	19.0	6
30	7	7	26 23	2	6
31	9	26.1	26 49	4	7
32	22.1	4	27 16	6	15.7
33	2	8	27 44	9	8
34	4	27.2	28 12	20.1	8
35	6	6	28 40	4	9
36	8	28.0	29 9	6	9
37	23.0	5	29 38	8	16.0
38	2	9	♌ 0 7	21.0	0
39	4	29.4	0 38	2	1
40	6	9	1 8	5	1
41	8	♋ 0.4	1 40	7	2
42	24.0	9	2 11	22.0	16.2
43	3	1.5	2 44	3	3
44	5	2.0	3 17	6	4
45	7	6	3 51	9	4
46	25.0	3.2	4 26	23.2	16.5
47	3	8	5 1	5	6
48	6	4.4	5 37	8	6
49	9	5.1	6 14	24.1	7
50	26.2	8	6 52	4	16.7
51	6	6.5	7 31	7	8
52	27.0	7.3	8 11	25.0	8
53	4	8.1	8 52	3	9
54	8	9	9 34	7	17.0
55	28.2	9.8	10 17	26.1	1
56	7	10.7	11 2	5	1

1 6 23 (H. M. S.) ♈ 18° — 16° 35′.9

H.	11	12	1	2	3
Lat.	♉	♊	♋	♌	♍
°	°	°	° ′	°	°
22	21.6	23.8	23 49	18.4	16.2
23	7	24.2	24 13	6	3
24	8	5	24 38	8	3
25	22.0	8	25 2	19.0	3
26	1	25.2	25 27	2	4
27	2	5	25 53	4	16.4
28	4	8	26 18	6	5
29	22.5	26.2	26 44	8	5
30	7	6	27 10	20.1	6
31	9	9	27 36	3	16.6
32	23.0	27.3	28 3	5	6
33	2	7	28 30	7	7
34	4	28.1	28 58	9	7
35	6	5	29 26	21.2	16.8
36	8	9	29 54	4	8
37	24.0	29.3	♌ 0 23	6	9
38	2	8	0 53	8	9
39	4	♋ 0.3	1 22	22.0	17.0
40	6	8	1 53	3	0
41	8	1.3	2 24	5	1
42	25.0	8	2 55	8	1
43	3	2.3	3 27	23.1	2
44	5	9	4 0	3	17.2
45	7	3.5	4 33	6	3
46	26.0	4.1	5 8	9	4
47	3	7	5 43	24.2	4
48	6	5.3	6 18	5	17.5
49	9	9	6 55	8	5
50	27.2	6.6	7 32	25.1	6
51	6	7.3	8 11	4	7
52	28.0	8.1	8 50	7	17.7
53	4	9	9 31	26.1	8
54	8	9.7	10 12	4	8
55	29.3	10.6	10 55	8	9
56	8	11.5	11 39	27.2	9

1 10 7 (H. M. S.) ♈ 19° — 17° 31′.8

H.	11	12	1	2	3
Lat.	♉	♊	♋	♌	♍
°	°	°	° ′	°	°
22	22.5	24.7	24 38	19.3	17.2
23	7	25.0	25 2	5	2
24	8	4	25 26	7	3
25	9	7	25 51	9	3
26	23.1	26.0	26 16	20.1	3
27	2	4	26 41	3	17.4
28	4	7	27 6	5	4
29	5	27.1	27 32	7	4
30	7	4	27 57	9	5
31	8	8	28 24	21.1	5
32	24.0	28.1	28 50	3	17.6
33	2	5	29 17	6	6
34	3	9	29 44	8	7
35	5	29.3	♌ 0 12	22.0	7
36	7	7	0 40	2	7
37	9	♋ 0.2	1 9	4	17.8
38	25.1	6	1 38	6	8
39	3	1.1	2 7	8	9
40	6	6	2 37	23.1	9
41	8	2.1	3 8	3	18.0
42	26.0	6	3 39	6	0
43	2	3.2	4 11	9	1
44	5	7	4 43	24.1	1
45	7	4.3	5 16	4	2
46	27.0	9	5 50	7	18.2
47	3	5.5	6 24	9	3
48	6	6.1	7 0	25.2	3
49	9	7	7 36	5	4
50	28.2	7.4	8 13	8	4
51	6	8.1	8 51	26.1	18.5
52	29.0	9	9 29	4	5
53	4	9.7	10 9	8	6
54	8	10.5	10 50	27.1	7
55	♊ 0.3	11.4	11 32	5	8
56	8	12.3	12 15	9	9

1 13 51 (H. M. S.) ♈ 20° — 18° 27′.8

H.	11	12	1	2	3
Lat.	♉	♊	♋	♌	♍
°	°	°	° ′	°	°
22	23.5	25.6	25 27	20.1	18.1
23	6	9	25 51	3	2
24	7	26.2	26 15	5	2
25	9	5	26 39	7	2
26	24.0	9	27 4	9	3
27	2	27.2	27 29	21.1	18.3
28	3	6	27 54	3	3
29	5	9	28 19	5	4
30	6	28.3	28 45	7	4
31	8	6	29 11	9	18.4
32	25.0	29.0	29 37	22.1	5
33	2	4	♌ 0 4	4	5
34	4	8	0 31	6	6
35	5	♋ 0.2	0 58	8	18.6
36	7	6	1 26	23.0	6
37	9	1.0	1 54	2	7
38	26.1	5	2 23	4	7
39	3	2.0	2 52	6	18.8
40	5	5	3 22	9	8
41	8	3.0	3 52	24.1	9
42	27.0	5	4 22	4	9
43	2	4.0	4 54	6	19.0
44	5	6	5 26	9	0
45	7	5.1	5 58	25.2	1
46	9	7	6 32	5	1
47	28.2	6.3	7 6	7	2
48	5	9	7 41	26.0	19.2
49	8	7.6	8 16	3	3
50	29.2	8.2	8 53	6	3
51	6	9	9 30	9	4
52	♊	9.6	10 8	27.2	19.4
53	0.4	10.4	10 48	5	5
54	8	11.2	11 28	8	5
55	1.3	12.1	12 10	28.2	6
56	8	13.0	12 53	6	7

1 17 36 (H. M. S.) ♈ 21° — 19° 24′.0

H.	11	12	1	2	3
Lat.	♉	♊	♋	♌	♍
°	°	°	° ′	°	°
22	24.4	26.4	26 16	21.0	19.1
23	6	8	26 40	2	1
24	7	27.1	27 4	4	2
25	8	4	27 28	6	2
26	25.0	7	27 52	8	2
27	1	28.1	28 17	22.0	19.3
28	3	4	28 42	2	3
29	5	8	29 7	4	3
30	6	29.1	29 32	6	4
31	8	5	29 58	8	4
32	26.0	9	♌ 0 24	23.0	19.4
33	1	♋ 0.2	0 50	2	5
34	3	6	1 17	4	5
35	5	1.0	1 44	6	5
36	7	5	2 12	8	6
37	9	9	2 40	24.0	19.6
38	27.1	2.4	3 8	2	7
39	3	8	3 37	4	7
40	5	3.3	4 6	7	7
41	7	8	4 36	9	19.8
42	28.0	4.3	5 7	25.2	8
43	2	9	5 38	4	9
44	5	5.4	6 9	7	9
45	7	6.0	6 41	9	20.0
46	9	5	7 14	26.2	0
47	29.2	7.1	7 48	4	1
48	5	7	8 22	7	1
49	8	8.3	8 57	27.0	1
50	♊ 0.2	9.0	9 33	3	20.2
51	6	7	10 10	6	2
52	1.0	10.4	10 48	9	3
53	4	11.2	11 27	28.2	3
54	8	12.0	12 6	5	20.4
55	2.3	9	12 47	9	4
56	8	13.8	13 29	29.3	5

1 21 21 (H. M. S.) ♈ 22° — 20° 20′.2

H.	11	12	1	2	3
Lat.	♉	♊	♋	♌	♍
°	°	°	° ′	°	°
22	25.4	27.3	27 5	21.9	20.1
23	5	6	27 29	22.1	1
24	7	9	27 53	3	1
25	8	28.3	28 17	5	2
26	26.0	6	28 41	7	2
27	1	9	29 5	8	20.2
28	3	29.3	29 30	23.0	2
29	4	6	29 55	2	3
30	26.6	♋	♌ 0 20	4	3
31	7	0.4	0 45	6	3
32	9	7	1 11	8	20.4
33	27.1	1.1	1 37	24.0	4
34	3	5	2 4	2	4
35	5	9	2 30	4	5
36	7	2.4	2 58	6	5
37	9	8	3 25	8	20.5
38	28.1	3.2	3 53	25.0	6
39	3	7	4 22	2	6
40	5	4.2	4 51	5	6
41	7	6	5 20	7	20.7
42	9	5.1	5 50	26.0	7
43	29.2	7	6 21	2	7
44	4	6.2	6 52	5	8
45	6	8	7 24	7	20.8
46	9	7.3	7 56	27.0	8
47	♊ 0.2	9	8 29	3	9
48	5	8.5	9 3	5	9
49	8	9.2	9 38	8	21.0
50	1.2	8	10 14	28.1	0
51	6	10.5	10 50	4	1
52	2.0	11.2	11 27	7	1
53	4	12.0	12 6	29.0	21.2
54	9	8	12 45	3	3
55	3.4	13.7	13 25	6	3
56	9	14.6	14 6	♍	4

SID. T. / ARC	H. M. S. 1 21 21, 20° 20′.2, ♈ 22°					H. M. S. 1 25 6, 21° 16′.6, ♈ 23°					H. M. S. 1 28 52, 22° 13′, ♈ 24°					H. M. S. 1 32 38, 23° 9′.6, ♈ 25°					H. M. S. 1 36 25, 24° 6′.3, ♈ 26°					H. M. S. 1 40 12, 25° 3′.2, ♈ 27°				
H.	11	12	1	2	3	11	12	1	2	3	11	12	1	2	3	11	12	1	2	3	11	12	1	2	3	11	12	1	2	3
Lat.	♉	♊	♋	♌	♍	♉	♊	♋	♌	♍	♉	♊	♋	♌	♍	♉	♊	♋	♌	♍	♉	♋	♌	♌	♍	♊	♋	♌	♌	♍
°	°	°	° ′	°	°	°	°	° ′	°	°	°	°	° ′	°	°	°	°	° ′	°	°	°	°	° ′	°	°	°	°	° ′	°	°
22	25.4	27.3	27 5	21.9	20.1	26.3	28.2	27 55	22.8	21.0	27.3	29.0	28 45	23.7	22.0	28.2	29.9	29 34	24.5	23.0	29.1	0.8	0 24	25.4	24.0	0.1	1.6	1 14	26.3	24.9
23	5	6	27 29	22.1	1	5	5	28 18	9	1	4	4	29 8	8	0	3	♋ 0.2	29 57	7	0	3	1.1	0 46	6	0	2	9	1 36	5	9
24	7	9	27 53	3	1	6	8	28 42	23.1	1	5	7	29 31	24.0	1	5	5	♌ 0 20	9	0	4	4	1 9	8	0	4	2.3	1 59	7	25.0
25	8	28.3	28 17	5	2	8	29.1	29 6	3	1	7	♋	29 54	2	1	6	9	0 43	25.1	1	6	7	1 32	9	0	5	6	2 22	8	0
26	26.0	6	28 41	7	2	9	5	29 30	5	1	8	0.3	♌ 0 18	4	1	8	1.2	1 7	3	1	7	2.1	1 56	26.1	0	7	9	2 45	27.0	0
27	1	9	29 5	8	20.2	27.1	8	29 54	7	21.2	28.0	7	0 42	6	22.1	29.0	5	1 31	4	23.1	9	4	2 19	3	24.0	9	3.2	3 8	2	0
28	3	29.3	29 30	23.0	2	2	♋ 0.1	♌ 0 18	9	2	1	1.0	1 6	7	1	1	9	1 54	6	1	♊ 0.1	7	2 43	5	1	1.0	6	3 31	4	0
29	4	6	29 55	2	3	4	5	0 43	24.1	2	3	4	1 31	9	2	3	2.2	2 19	8	1	2	3.1	3 7	7	1	2	9	3 55	5	25.0
30	26.6	♋	♌ 0 20	4	3	5	9	1 8	3	3	5	7	1 55	25.1	2	4	6	2 43	26.0	2	4	4	3 31	8	1	4	4.3	4 19	7	1
31	7	0.4	0 45	6	3	7	1.2	1 33	5	3	7	2.1	2 20	3	2	6	9	3 8	2	2	6	8	3 55	27.0	1	5	7	4 43	9	1
32	9	7	1 11	8	20.4	9	6	1 58	7	21.3	8	4	2 45	5	22.2	8	3.3	3 32	4	23.2	8	4.2	4 20	2	24.1	7	5.0	5 7	28.1	1
33	27.1	1.1	1 37	24.0	4	28.1	2.0	2 24	9	3	29.0	8	3 11	7	3	♊	7	3 58	6	2	1.0	5	4 45	4	2	9	4	5 32	2	1
34	3	5	2 4	2	4	2	4	2 50	25.1	4	2	3.2	3 37	9	3	0.2	4.1	4 23	7	2	1	9	5 10	6	2	2.1	8	5 57	4	25.1
35	5	9	2 30	4	5	4	8	3 17	3	4	4	6	4 3	26.1	3	4	5	4 49	9	3	3	5.3	5 36	8	2	3	6.2	6 22	6	1
36	7	2.4	2 58	6	5	6	3.2	3 43	5	4	6	4.0	4 30	3	3	6	9	5 16	27.1	3	5	7	6 2	28.0	2	5	6	6 48	8	2
37	9	8	3 25	8	20.5	8	6	4 11	6	21.5	8	4	4 57	5	22.4	8	5.3	5 42	3	23.3	7	6.1	6 28	2	24.2	7	7.0	7 14	29.0	2
38	28.1	3.2	3 53	25.0	6	29.0	4.1	4 38	8	5	♊	9	5 24	7	4	1.0	7	6 9	6	3	9	6	6 55	4	3	9	4	7 40	2	2
39	3	7	4 22	2	6	2	5	5 7	26.0	5	0.2	5.4	5 52	9	4	2	6.2	6 37	8	4	2.1	7.1	7 22	6	3	3.1	9	8 7	4	25.2
40	5	4.2	4 51	5	6	5	5.0	5 35	3	6	4	8	6 20	27.1	5	4	7	7 5	28.0	4	4	5	7 49	8	3	3	8.4	8 34	6	2
41	7	6	5 20	7	20.7	7	5	6 5	5	6	7	6.3	6 49	3	5	6	7.1	7 33	2	4	6	8.0	8 18	29.0	3	6	8	9 2	8	3
42	9	5.1	5 50	26.0	7	9	6.0	6 34	8	21.6	9	8	7 18	5	22.5	9	6	8 2	4	23.4	8	5	8 46	2	24.4	8	9.3	9 30	♍	3
43	29.2	7	6 21	2	7	♊ 0.2	5	7 4	27.0	7	1.1	7.4	7 48	8	6	2.1	8.1	8 32	7	5	3.1	9.0	9 15	4	4	4.1	8	9 59	0.2	3
44	4	6.2	6 52	5	8	4	7.0	7 35	3	7	4	9	8 18	28.0	6	4	7	9 2	9	5	4	5	9 45	6	4	3	10.4	10 28	4	25.3
45	6	8	7 24	7	20.8	6	6	8 6	5	7	6	8.5	8 49	3	6	7	9.2	9 32	29.1	5	7	10.1	10 15	8	4	6	9	10 58	6	3
46	9	7.3	7 56	27.0	8	9	8.1	8 38	7	8	9	9.0	9 21	5	7	9	8	10 3	3	5	9	7	10 46	♍ 0.1	5	9	11.5	11 28	8	4
47	♊ 0.2	9	8 29	3	9	1.2	7	9 11	9	21.8	2.2	6	9 53	7	22.7	3.2	10.4	10 35	5	23.6	4.2	11.2	11 17	3	24.5	5.2	12.0	11 59	1.0	4
48	5	8.5	9 3	5	9	5	9.3	9 45	28.2	8	5	10.2	10 26	29.0	7	5	11.0	11 8	7	6	5	8	11 49	6	5	5	6	12 31	3	25.4
49	8	9.2	9 38	8	21.0	8	10.0	10 19	5	9	8	8	11 0	3	8	9	6	11 41	♍	6	9	12.4	12 22	9	5	8	13.2	13 3	5	4
50	1.2	8	10 14	28.1	0	2.2	6	10 54	8	9	3.2	11.4	11 35	6	8	4.2	12.2	12 15	0.3	6	5.2	13.0	12 56	1.1	5	6.2	8	13 36	8	4
51	6	10.5	10 50	4	1	6	11.3	11 30	29.1	9	6	12.1	12 10	9	22.8	6	9	12 50	6	7	6	7	13 30	4	6	6	14.5	14 10	2.1	5
52	2.0	11.2	11 27	7	1	3.0	12.0	12 7	4	22.0	4.0	8	12 46	♍ 0.2	9	5.0	13.6	13 26	9	23.7	6.0	14.4	14 5	6	24.6	7.0	15.2	14 45	3	25.5
53	4	12.0	12 6	29.0	21.2	4	8	12 44	7	0	4	13.6	13 23	5	9	4	14.4	14 2	1.2	7	4	15.1	14 41	9	6	4	9	15 20	6	5
54	9	8	12 45	3	3	9	13.6	13 23	♍	1	9	14.4	14 1	8	23.0	9	15.2	14 40	5	8	9	9	15 18	2.2	7	9	16.7	15 57	9	5
55	3.4	13.7	13 25	6	3	4.4	14.5	14 3	0.3	1	5.4	15.2	14 40	1.1	0	6.4	16.0	15 17	8	8	7.4	16.7	15 56	5	7	8.4	17.5	16 34	3.2	5
56	9	14.6	14 6	♍	4	9	15.4	14 43	7	2	9	16.1	15 21	4	1	9	9	15 58	2.1	9	8.0	17.5	16 35	8	7	9.0	18.4	17 13	5	6

SID. T. H. M. S. 1 44 0 ARC 26° 0′.1 ♈ 28°						H. M. S. 1 47 49 26° 57′.2 ♈ 29°					H. M. S. 1 51 38 27° 54′.5 ♉ 0°					H. M. S. 1 55 27 28° 51′.9 ♉ 1°					H. M. S. 1 59 18 29° 49′.4 ♉ 2°					H. M. S. 2 3 8 30° 47′.1 ♉ 3°				
H.	11	12	1	2	3	11	12	1	2	3	11	12	1	2	3	11	12	1	2	3	11	12	1	2	3	11	12	1	2	3
Lat.	♊	♋	♌	♌	♍	♊	♋	♌	♌	♍	♊	♋	♌	♌	♍	♊	♋	♌	♍	♍	♊	♋	♌	♍	♍	♊	♋	♌	♍	♎
°	°	°	° ′	°	°	°	°	° ′	°	°	°	°	° ′	°	°	°	°	° ′	°	°	°	°	° ′	°	°	°	°	° ′	°	°
22	1.0	2.5	2 4	27.2	25.9	1.9	3.4	2 54	28.1	26.9	2.9	4.2	3 44	29.0	27.9	3.8	5.1	4 35	0.0	28.9	4.8	6.0	5 25	0.9	29.8	5.7	6.8	6 16	1.8	0.8
23	2	8	2 26	4	9	2.1	7	3 16	3	9	3.0	5	4 6	2	9	4.0	4	4 56	1	9	9	3	5 47	1.0	8	8	7.1	6 37	9	8
24	3	3.1	2 48	5	9	2	4.0	3 38	5	9	2	9	4 28	4	9	1	7	5 18	3	9	5.1	6	6 8	2	8	6.0	5	6 58	2.1	8
25	5	5	3 11	7	9	4	3	4 0	6	9	3	5.2	4 50	5	9	3	6.0	5 40	4	9	2	9	6 30	3	8	2	8	7 20	2	8
26	7	8	3 34	9	26.0	6	7	4 23	8	9	5	5	5 12	7	27.9	4	4	6 2	0.6	9	4	7.2	6 51	5	8	3	8.1	7 41	3	8
27	8	4.1	3 56	28.1	0	7	5.0	4 45	9	9	6	8	5 35	8	9	4.6	7	6 24	7	28.9	5	6	7 13	1.6	29.8	6.5	4	8 3	5	0.8
28	2.0	5	4 20	2	0	9	3	5 8	29.1	27.0	8	6.2	5 57	♍	9	8	7.0	6 46	9	9	7	9	7 35	7	8	6	8	8 25	2.6	8
29	1	8	4 43	4	0	3.0	7	5 31	3	0	4.0	5	6 20	0.1	9	9	4	7 9	1.0	9	9	8.2	7 58	9	8	8	9.1	8 47	8	8
30	3	5.2	5 7	6	0	2	6.0	5 55	4	0	2	9	6 43	3	27.9	5.1	7	7 32	2	9	6.1	6	8 20	2.0	8	7.0	5	9 9	9	8
31	5	5	5 31	7	26.0	4	4	6 18	6	0	3	7.2	7 6	5	9	3	8.1	7 55	3	9	2	9	8 43	2	8	2	8	9 31	3.1	8
32	7	9	5 55	9	0	6	7	6 42	8	0	5	6	7 30	6	9	5	4	8 18	5	28.9	4	9.3	9 6	4	29.8	4	10.2	9 54	2	0.8
33	9	6.2	6 19	29.1	1	8	7.1	7 6	9	27.0	7	8.0	7 54	8	28.0	7	8	8 41	6	9	6	7	9 29	5	8	6	5	10 17	4	8
34	3.1	6	6 44	3	1	4.0	5	7 31	♍ 0.1	0	9	3	8 18	1.0	0	9	9.2	9 5	8	9	8	10.0	9 52	7	8	8	9	10 40	5	8
35	3	7.0	7 9	5	1	2	9	7 55	3	0	5.1	7	8 42	1	0	6.1	6	9 29	2.0	9	7.0	4	10 16	8	8	8.0	11.3	11 3	7	8
36	5	4	7 34	7	26.1	4	8.3	8 20	5	0	3	9.1	9 7	3	0	3	10.0	9 54	2	9	2	8	10 40	3.0	8	2	7	11 27	9	8
37	7	8	8 0	9	1	6	7	8 46	6	0	5	5	9 32	4	0	5	4	10 18	3	28.9	4	11.2	11 4	2	29.8	4	12.1	11 51	4.0	0.8
38	9	8.3	8 26	♍	1	8	9.1	9 12	8	27.1	7	10.0	9 57	6	28.0	7	8	10 43	5	9	6	7	11 29	4	8	6	5	12 15	1	8
39	4.1	7	8 52	0.2	1	5.0	6	9 38	1.0	1	6.0	4	10 23	8	0	9	11.3	11 9	7	9	9	12.1	11 54	5	8	8	9	12 40	3	8
40	3	9.2	9 19	4	2	2	10.0	10 4	2	1	2	9	10 49	2.0	0	7.1	7	11 34	9	9	8.1	5	12 20	7	8	9.0	13.3	13 5	5	8
41	5	7	9 47	6	26.2	5	4	10 31	4	1	4	11.3	11 16	2	0	4	12.2	12 1	3.1	9	4	13.0	12 46	9	8	3	7	13 31	7	8
42	8	10.2	10 14	8	2	7	9	10 59	6	1	7	8	11 43	4	0	7	7	12 27	2	28.9	6	5	13 12	4.1	29.8	6	14.2	13 57	8	0.8
43	5.0	7	10 43	1.0	2	6.0	11.4	11 26	8	27.1	7.0	12.3	12 10	6	28.0	9	13.2	12 55	4	9	9	14.0	13 39	3	8	9	7	14 23	5.0	8
44	3	11.2	11 12	2	2	3	9	11 55	2.0	1	3	9	12 38	8	0	8.2	7	13 22	6	9	9.2	5	14 6	4	8	10.1	15.2	14 50	2	8
45	5	7	11 41	4	2	5	12.5	12 24	2	1	5	13.4	13 7	3.0	0	5	14.2	13 50	8	9	4	15.0	14 33	6	8	4	7	15 17	4	8
46	8	12.3	12 11	6	26.2	8	13.0	12 53	4	1	8	9	13 36	2	0	8	7	14 19	4.0	9	7	5	15 2	8	8	7	16.3	15 45	6	8
47	6.1	9	12 41	8	3	7.1	6	13 23	7	2	8.1	14.5	14 6	4	0	9.1	15.3	14 48	3	28.9	10.0	16.1	15 30	5.0	29.8	11.0	9	16 13	8	0.7
48	4	13.4	13 12	2.0	3	4	14.2	13 54	9	27.2	4	15.1	14 36	6	28.0	4	9	15 18	5	9	3	7	16 0	2	8	3	17.5	16 42	6.0	7
49	7	14.0	13 44	3	3	7	8	14 26	3.2	2	8	6	15 7	8	0	7	16.4	15 48	7	9	6	17.2	16 30	4	8	6	18.0	17 11	2	7
50	7.1	6	14 17	6	3	8.1	15.4	14 58	4	2	9.1	16.2	15 39	4.1	0	10.1	17.0	16 19	9	9	11.0	8	17 0	6	8	12.0	6	17 41	4	7
51	5	15.3	14 50	8	26.3	5	16.1	15 31	6	2	5	8	16 11	3	1	5	7	16 51	5.1	29.0	4	18.5	17 32	8	8	4	19.2	18 12	6	7
52	9	16.0	15 25	3.0	4	9	8	16 4	8	27.2	9	17.5	16 44	5	28.1	9	18.4	17 24	3	0	8	19.2	18 4	6.0	29.8	8	9	18 44	8	0.7
53	8.3	7	16 0	3	4	9.3	17.5	16 39	4.0	2	10.3	18.2	17 18	7	1	11.3	19.1	17 57	6	0	12.3	9	18 37	2	8	13.2	20.6	19 16	7.0	7
54	8	17.5	16 35	6	4	8	18.2	17 14	3	2	8	19.0	17 52	5.0	1	8	8	18 31	8	0	8	20.6	19 10	5	8	7	21.3	19 49	2	7
55	9.3	18.3	17 12	9	4	10.3	19.0	17 50	6	2	11.3	8	18 28	3	1	12.3	20.5	19 6	6.1	0	13.3	21.3	19 45	8	8	14.2	22.1	20 23	5	7
56	9	19.1	17 50	4.2	5	9	8	18 27	9	3	9	20.6	19 5	6	2	9	21.3	19 42	4	0	9	22.1	20 20	7.0	8	8	9	20 58	7	7

SID. T. (H. M. S.) / ARC	2 3 8 / 30° 47′.1 } ♉ 3°					2 7 0 / 31° 44′.9 } ♉ 4°					2 10 52 / 32° 42′.9 } ♉ 5°					2 14 44 / 33° 41′ } ♉ 6°					2 18 37 / 34° 39′.4 } ♉ 7°					2 22 31 / 35° 37′.8 } ♉ 8°				
H.	11	12	1	2	3	11	12	1	2	3	11	12	1	2	3	11	12	1	2	3	11	12	1	2	3	11	12	1	2	3
Lat.	♊	♋	♌	♍	♎	♊	♋	♌	♍	♎	♊	♋	♌	♍	♎	♊	♋	♌	♍	♎	♊	♋	♌	♍	♎	♊	♋	♌	♍	♎
°	°	°	° ′	°	°	°	°	° ′	°	°	°	°	° ′	°	°	°	°	° ′	°	°	°	°	° ′	°	°	°	°	° ′	°	°
22	5.7	6.8	6 16	1.8	0.8	6.7	7.7	7 7	2.7	1.8	7.6	8.6	7 58	3.6	2.8	8.6	9.5	8 49	4.5	3.8	9.5	10.4	9 41	5.5	4.8	10.4	11.2	10 33	6.4	5.8
23	8	7.1	6 37	9	8	8	8.0	7 28	8	8	8	9	8 19	8	8	7	8	9 10	7	8	6	7	10 1	6	8	6	5	10 53	5	8
24	6.0	5	6 58	2.1	8	7.0	3	7 49	3.0	8	9	9.2	8 40	9	8	9	10.1	9 30	8	8	8	11.0	10 21	7	8	7	8	11 12	6	8
25	2	8	7 20	2	8	2	6	8 10	1	8	8.1	5	9 0	4.0	8	9.0	4	9 51	9	8	10.0	3	10 42	8	8	9	12.1	11 32	8	8
26	3	8.1	7 41	3	8	3	9.0	8 31	2	8	2	8	9 21	1	8	2	7	10 12	5.1	8	1	6	11 2	6.0	7	11.1	5	11 53	9	7
27	6.5	4	8 3	5	0.8	5	3	8 53	4	1.8	4	10.2	9 43	3	2.8	4	11.0	10 32	2	3.7	3	9	11 23	1	4.7	2	8	12 13	7.0	5.7
28	6	8	8 25	2.6	8	6	6	9 14	3.5	8	6	5	10 4	4	8	5	4	10 53	3	7	5	12.2	11 43	2	7	4	13.1	12 33	1	7
29	8	9.1	8 47	8	8	8	10.0	9 36	7	8	8	8	10 25	4.6	8	7	7	11 14	5	7	6	6	12 4	3	7	6	4	12 54	2	7
30	7.0	5	9 9	9	8	8.0	3	9 58	8	8	9	11.2	10 47	7	7	9	12.0	11 36	5.6	7	8	9	12 25	6.5	7	8	8	13 14	4	7
31	2	8	9 31	3.1	8	2	7	10 20	9	8	9.1	5	11 9	8	7	10.1	4	11 57	7	7	11.0	13.2	12 46	6	7	9	14.1	13 35	7.5	6
32	4	10.2	9 54	2	0.8	4	11.0	10 42	4.1	1.8	3	9	11 31	5.0	2.7	2	7	12 19	9	3.7	2	6	13 8	7	4.7	12.1	4	13 56	6	5.6
33	6	5	10 17	4	8	5	4	11 5	2	8	5	12.2	11 53	1	7	4	13.1	12 41	6.0	7	4	9	13 29	9	6	3	8	14 18	8	6
34	8	9	10 40	5	8	7	8	11 28	4	8	7	6	12 15	3	7	6	5	13 3	1	7	6	14.3	13 51	7.0	6	5	15.2	14 39	9	6
35	8.0	11.3	11 3	7	8	9	12.2	11 51	6	7	9	13.0	12 38	4	7	8	9	13 25	3	6	8	7	14 13	2	6	7	6	15 1	8.0	6
36	2	7	11 27	9	8	9.1	6	12 14	7	7	10.1	4	13 1	5.6	7	11.0	14.3	13 48	4	6	12.0	15.1	14 35	3	6	9	9	15 23	2	5
37	4	12.1	11 51	4.0	0.8	3	13.0	12 38	9	1.7	3	8	13 24	7	2.7	2	7	14 11	6.6	3.6	2	5	14 58	5	4.6	13.1	16.3	15 45	3	5.5
38	6	5	12 15	1	8	6	4	13 2	5.0	7	5	14.2	13 48	9	7	5	15.1	14 34	8	6	4	9	15 21	7.6	6	3	7	16 8	4	5
39	8	9	12 40	3	8	8	8	13 26	2	7	7	6	14 12	6.1	7	7	5	14 58	9	6	6	16.3	15 44	8	5	6	17.2	16 31	8.5	5
40	9.0	13.3	13 5	5	8	10.0	14.2	13 51	4	7	11.0	15.1	14 36	2	7	9	9	15 22	7.0	6	9	7	16 8	9	5	8	6	16 54	7	5
41	3	7	13 31	7	8	3	7	14 16	6	7	2	5	15 1	4	6	12.2	16.3	15 46	1	6	13.1	17.2	16 32	8.1	5	14.1	18.0	17 17	8	4
42	6	14.2	13 57	8	0.8	5	15.1	14 41	8	1.7	5	16.0	15 26	6	2.6	4	8	16 11	3	3.5	4	6	16 56	2	4.5	3	5	17 41	9.0	5.4
43	9	7	14 23	5.0	8	8	6	15 7	9	7	8	4	15 52	8	6	7	17.3	16 36	5	5	7	18.1	17 21	4	5	6	9	18 5	1	4
44	10.1	15.2	14 50	2	8	11.1	16.1	15 34	6.1	7	12.1	9	16 18	9	6	13.0	7	17 2	7	5	14.0	6	17 46	5	4	9	19.4	18 30	3	4
45	4	7	15 17	4	8	4	6	16 0	2	7	4	17.4	16 44	7.0	6	3	18.2	17 28	8	5	3	19.1	18 12	6	4	15.2	9	18 55	5	3
46	7	16.3	15 45	6	8	7	17.1	16 28	4	7	7	9	17 11	2	6	6	7	17 54	8.0	5	6	6	18 38	7	4	5	20.4	19 21	6	3
47	11.0	9	16 13	8	0.7	12.0	7	16 56	6	1.7	13.0	18.5	17 38	4	2.6	9	19.3	18 21	1	3.5	9	20.1	19 4	9	4.4	8	9	19 47	8	5.3
48	3	17.5	16 42	6.0	7	3	18.2	17 24	8	6	3	19.0	18 6	5	6	14.2	8	18 48	3	4	15.2	7	19 31	9.1	3	16.1	21.5	20 14	10.0	3
49	6	18.0	17 11	2	7	6	8	17 53	7.0	6	6	6	18 35	7	5	5	20.4	19 16	5	4	5	21.2	19 58	3	3	4	22.0	20 41	2	2
50	12.0	6	17 41	4	7	13.0	19.4	18 22	2	6	9	20.2	19 4	9	5	9	21.0	19 45	7	4	8	8	20 27	5	3	8	6	21 8	3	2
51	4	19.2	18 12	6	7	4	20.0	18 53	4	6	14.3	8	19 33	8.1	5	15.3	6	20 14	9	4	16.2	22.4	20 55	7	3	17.2	23.2	21 36	4	2
52	8	9	18 44	8	0.7	8	7	19 24	6	1.6	7	21.5	20 4	3	2.5	7	22.3	20 44	9.1	3.4	6	23.0	21 25	9	4.2	6	8	22 5	6	5.2
53	13.2	20.6	19 16	7.0	7	14.2	21.4	19 55	8	6	15.2	22.2	20 35	5	5	16.1	9	21 15	3	3	17.1	7	21 55	10.1	2	18.0	24.4	22 35	8	1
54	7	21.3	19 49	2	7	7	22.1	20 28	8.0	6	7	9	21 7	7	5	6	23.6	21 47	5	3	6	24.4	22 26	3	2	4	25.1	23 5	11.0	1
55	14.2	22.1	20 23	5	7	15.2	8	21 1	3	6	16.2	23.6	21 40	9.0	4	17.1	24.3	22 19	7	3	18.1	25.1	22 58	5	2	19.0	8	23 36	2	1
56	8	9	20 58	7	7	8	23.6	21 36	5	6	8	24.4	22 14	2	4	7	25.0	22 52	9	3	7	8	23 30	8	1	5	26.5	24 8	4	1

H.	SID. T. 2 H. 26 M. 26 S. ARC 36° 36′.5 ♉ 9°					2 H. 30 M. 21 S. 37° 35′.3 ♉ 10°					2 H. 34 M. 17 S. 38° 34′.3 ♉ 11°					2 H. 38 M. 14 S. 39° 33′.4 ♉ 12°					2 H. 42 M. 11 S. 40° 32′.8 ♉ 13°					2 H. 46 M. 9 S. 41° 32′.3 ♉ 14°				
H.	11	12	1	2	3	11	12	1	2	3	11	12	1	2	3	11	12	1	2	3	11	12	1	2	3	11	12	1	2	3
Lat.	♊	♋	♌	♍	♎	♊	♋	♌	♍	♎	♊	♋	♌	♍	♎	♊	♋	♌	♍	♎	♊	♋	♌	♍	♎	♊	♋	♌	♍	♎
°	°	°	° ′	°	°	°	°	° ′	°	°	°	°	° ′	°	°	°	°	° ′	°	°	°	°	° ′	°	°	°	°	° ′	°	°
22	11.3	12.1	11 25	7.3	6.8	12.3	13.0	12 17	8.3	7.8	13.2	13.9	13 9	9.2	8.8	14.1	14.8	14 1	10.2	9.8	15.1	15.7	14 54	11.1	10.8	16.0	16.5	15 47	12.1	11.8
23	5	4	11 44	4	8	4	3	12 36	4	8	4	14.2	13 28	3	8	3	15.1	14 20	3	8	2	16.0	15 12	2	8	2	8	16 5	1	8
24	7	7	12 4	6	7	6	6	12 55	5	7	5	5	13 47	4	8	5	4	14 39	4	7	4	3	15 30	3	7	3	17.1	16 23	2	7
25	8	13.0	12 23	7	7	8	9	13 14	6	7	7	8	14 6	5	7	6	7	14 57	5	7	5	6	15 49	4	7	5	4	16 41	3	7
26	12.0	3	12 43	8	7	9	14.2	13 34	8.7	7	9	15.1	14 25	9.6	7	8	16.0	15 16	10.6	7	7	9	16 8	5	7	6	7	16 59	4	7
27	2	6	13 3	9	6.7	13.1	5	13 54	8	7.7	14.0	4	14 44	8	8.7	15.0	3	15 35	7	9.7	9	17.2	16 26	11.6	10.7	8	18.0	17 18	12.5	11.6
28	3	14.0	13 23	8.0	7	3	8	14 13	9	7	2	7	15 4	9	6	1	6	15 54	8	6	16.1	5	16 45	7	6	17.0	4	17 36	6	6
29	5	3	13 43	2	6	4	15.2	14 33	9.1	6	4	16.0	15 23	10.0	6	3	9	16 14	9	6	2	8	17 4	8	6	2	7	17 55	7	6
30	7	6	14 4	3	6	6	5	14 53	2	6	6	4	15 43	1	6	5	17.2	16 33	11.0	6	4	18.1	17 23	9	5	3	19.0	18 13	8	5
31	9	15.0	14 24	4	6	8	8	15 14	3	6	7	7	16 3	2	6	7	6	16 53	1	5	6	4	17 42	12.0	5	5	3	18 32	9	5
32	13.1	3	14 45	8.5	6.6	14.0	16.2	15 34	4	7.6	9	17.0	16 23	3	8.5	9	9	17 13	2	9.5	8	8	18 2	1	10.5	7	7	18 52	13.0	11.4
33	3	7	15 6	7	6	2	5	15 55	9.5	5	15.1	4	16 43	4	5	16.1	18.3	17 33	3	5	17.0	19.1	18 21	2	4	9	20.0	19 11	1	4
34	5	16.0	15 27	8	5	4	9	16 16	6	5	3	7	17 4	10.5	5	3	6	17 53	4	4	2	5	18 41	3	4	18.1	3	19 30	2	4
35	7	4	15 49	9	5	6	17.3	16 37	8	5	5	18.1	17 25	7	4	5	19.0	18 13	11.5	4	4	9	19 1	4	4	3	7	19 50	3	3
36	9	8	16 10	9.1	5	8	6	16 58	9	5	7	5	17 46	8	4	7	4	18 34	7	9.4	6	20.2	19 22	12.5	3	5	21.1	20 10	4	3
37	14.1	17.2	16 32	2	6.5	15.0	18.0	17 20	10.0	7.4	9	9	18 7	9	8.4	9	7	18 55	8	3	8	6	19 42	7	10.3	8	5	20 30	13.5	11.2
38	3	6	16 55	3	4	2	4	17 41	1	4	16.2	19.3	18 29	11.0	3	17.1	20.1	19 16	9	3	18.0	21.0	20 3	8	2	19.0	9	20 51	6	2
39	5	18.0	17 17	5	4	5	8	18 4	2	4	4	7	18 50	2	3	3	5	19 37	12.0	3	3	4	20 24	9	2	2	22.3	21 12	8	2
40	8	4	17 40	9.6	4	7	19.3	18 26	4	3	6	20.1	19 12	3	3	6	9	19 59	2	9.2	5	8	20 45	13.0	2	5	7	21 33	9	1
41	15.0	9	18 3	8	4	16.0	7	18 49	10.5	7.3	9	5	19 35	4	8.2	8	21.4	20 21	3	2	8	22.2	21 7	1	1	7	23.1	21 54	14.0	11.1
42	3	19.3	18 26	9	6.3	2	20.1	19 12	6	3	17.2	21.0	19 58	11.6	2	18.1	8	20 43	4	1	19.0	6	21 29	3	10.1	20.0	5	22 15	1	0
43	5	8	18 50	10.1	3	5	6	19 36	8	2	4	4	20 21	7	2	4	22.2	21 6	12.5	1	3	23.1	21 51	4	0	2	9	22 37	2	0
44	8	20.2	19 15	2	3	8	21.1	19 59	9	2	7	9	20 44	8	1	7	7	21 29	6	9.1	6	5	22 14	13.5	0	5	24.4	22 59	3	0
45	16.1	7	19 39	3	2	17.1	6	20 24	11.1	7.2	18.0	22.4	21 8	9	8.1	19.0	23.2	21 52	7	0	9	24.0	22 37	6	0	8	9	23 22	4	10.9
46	4	21.2	20 5	4	2	4	22.1	20 48	2	1	3	9	21 32	12.1	1	3	7	22 16	9	0	20.2	5	23 0	7	9.9	21.1	25.3	23 45	14.5	9
47	8	8	20 30	10.6	6.2	7	6	21 13	4	1	6	23.4	21 57	2	0	6	24.2	22 40	13.0	0	5	25.0	23 24	8	9	4	8	24 8	6	8
48	17.1	22.3	20 56	8	2	18.0	23.1	21 39	6	1	19.0	9	22 22	4	0	9	7	23 5	2	8.9	8	4	23 48	14.0	9	8	26.2	24 32	8	8
49	4	9	21 23	9	1	3	6	22 5	7	7.1	3	24.4	22 48	5	7.9	20.3	25.2	23 30	3	9	21.1	9	24 13	1	8	22.1	7	24 56	9	10.7
50	7	23.4	21 50	11.1	1	7	24.2	22 32	9	0	6	9	23 14	7	9	6	7	23 56	5	9	5	26.5	24 38	3	8	5	27.3	25 21	15.1	7
51	18.1	24.0	22 18	3	1	19.1	8	22 59	12.1	0	20.0	25.5	23 41	9	9	21.0	26.3	24 23	13.6	8	9	27.1	25 4	4	9.7	9	9	25 46	2	6
52	5	6	22 46	4	6.1	5	25.4	23 27	2	0	4	26.1	24 8	13.0	8	4	9	24 50	7	8.8	22.4	7	25 30	14.5	7	23.3	28.5	26 12	3	6
53	19.0	25.2	23 15	6	0	9	26.0	23 56	3	6.9	9	7	24 36	1	7.8	9	27.5	25 17	8	7	8	28.3	25 57	6	6	7	29.1	26 38	4	10.5
54	5	9	23 45	8	0	20.4	6	24 25	5	9	21.4	27.4	25 5	3	8	22.3	28.1	25 45	14.0	7	23.3	9	26 25	8	6	24.2	7	27 5	6	5
55	20.0	26.6	24 16	12.0	0	9	27.3	24 55	7	9	9	28.1	25 34	5	7	8	8	26 13	2	6	8	29.6	26 53	15.0	5	7	♌ 0.3	27 33	8	4
56	6	27.3	24 47	2	5.9	21.5	28.0	25 25	9	8	22.4	8	26 4	7	7	23.4	29.5	26 43	4	5	24.4	♌ 0.3	27 22	2	5	25.3	1.0	28 1	16.0	4

	SID. T. 2 46 9 (H. M. S.) ARC 41° 32′.3 ♉ 14°					2 50 8 (H. M. S.) 42° 32′.0 ♉ 15°					2 54 7 (H. M. S.) 43° 31′.8 ♉ 16°					2 58 7 (H. M. S.) 44° 31′.9 ♉ 17°					3 2 8 (H. M. S.) 45° 32′.1 ♉ 18°					3 6 10 (H. M. S.) 46° 32′.5 ♉ 19°				
H.	11	12	1	2	3	11	12	1	2	3	11	12	1	2	3	11	12	1	2	3	11	12	1	2	3	11	12	1	2	3
Lat.	♊	♋	♌	♍	♎	♊	♋	♌	♍	♎	♊	♋	♌	♍	♎	♊	♋	♌	♍	♎	♊	♋	♌	♍	♎	♊	♋	♌	♍	♎
°	°	°	° ′	°	°	°	°	° ′	°	°	°	°	° ′	°	°	°	°	° ′	°	°	°	°	° ′	°	°	°	°	° ′	°	°
22	16.0	16.5	15 47	12.1	11.8	16.9	17.4	16 40	13.0	12.8	17.9	18.3	17 33	14.0	13.8	18.8	19.2	18 27	14.9	14.9	19.7	20.1	19 20	15.9	15.9	20.7	21.0	20 14	16.9	16.9
23	2	8	16 5	1	8	17.1	7	16 57	1	8	18.0	6	17 51	1	8	19.0	5	18 44	15.0	8	9	4	19 37	16.0	8	8	3	20 31	9	8
24	3	17.1	16 23	2	7	2	18.0	17 15	2	8	2	9	18 8	1	8	1	8	19 1	1	8	20.1	7	19 54	0	8	21.0	6	20 48	17.0	8
25	5	4	16 41	3	7	4	3	17 33	3	7	3	19.2	18 26	2	7	3	20.1	19 18	2	7	2	21.0	20 11	1	7	2	9	21 4	1	7
26	6	7	16 59	4	7	6	6	17 51	13.4	7	5	5	18 43	14.3	7	4	4	19 35	3	7	4	3	20 28	2	7	3	22.2	21 21	1	7
27	8	18.0	17 18	12.5	11.6	7	9	18 9	4	12.6	7	8	19 1	4	13.6	6	7	19 53	15.3	14.6	6	6	20 45	3	15.6	5	5	21 38	2	16.6
28	17.0	4	17 36	6	6	9	19.2	18 27	5	6	9	20.1	19 19	5	6	8	21.0	20 10	4	6	7	9	21 2	16.3	6	7	8	21 55	17.3	6
29	2	7	17 55	7	6	18.1	6	18 46	6	6	19.0	4	19 37	6	5	20.0	3	20 28	5	5	9	22.2	21 20	4	5	9	23.1	22 12	4	5
30	3	19.0	18 13	8	5	3	9	19 4	13.7	5	2	8	19 55	14.7	5	2	6	20 46	6	5	21.1	5	21 37	5	5	22.0	4	22 29	4	5
31	5	3	18 32	9	5	5	20.2	19 23	8	12.5	4	21.1	20 13	7	13.5	3	22.0	21 4	15.7	4	3	8	21 55	6	4	2	7	22 46	5	4
32	7	7	18 52	13.0	11.4	7	5	19 41	9	4	6	4	20 32	8	4	5	3	21 22	7	14.4	5	23.2	22 12	16.7	15.4	4	24.1	23 3	6	16.4
33	9	20.0	19 11	1	4	9	9	20 0	14.0	4	8	7	20 50	9	4	7	6	21 40	8	3	7	5	22 30	7	3	6	4	23 21	17.7	3
34	18.1	3	19 30	2	4	19.1	21.2	20 20	1	4	20.0	22.1	21 9	15.0	3	9	23.0	21 59	9	3	9	8	22 48	8	3	8	7	23 38	7	3
35	3	7	19 50	3	3	3	6	20 39	2	12.3	2	5	21 28	1	13.3	21.1	3	22 17	16.0	2	22.1	24.2	23 7	9	2	23.0	25.1	23 56	8	2
36	5	21.1	20 10	4	3	5	22.0	20 59	3	3	4	8	21 47	2	2	3	7	22 36	1	2	3	5	23 25	17.0	15.2	2	4	24 14	9	16.1
37	8	5	20 30	13.5	11.2	7	3	21 18	4	2	6	23.2	22 7	3	2	5	24.0	22 55	2	14.1	5	9	23 44	1	1	4	8	24 32	18.0	1
38	19.0	9	20 51	6	2	9	7	21 38	14.5	2	8	6	22 26	4	1	8	3	23 14	3	1	7	25.3	24 3	2	1	6	26.2	24 51	1	0
39	2	22.3	21 12	8	2	20.1	23.1	21 59	6	12.1	21.1	24.0	22 46	15.5	13.1	22.0	7	23 34	4	0	9	7	24 22	3	0	9	5	25 10	1	0
40	5	7	21 33	9	1	4	4	22 20	7	1	3	4	23 7	6	0	2	25.1	23 54	16.5	0	23.2	26.1	24 41	17.3	14.9	24.1	9	25 29	2	15.9
41	7	23.1	21 54	14.0	11.1	6	8	22 40	9	0	6	8	23 27	7	0	5	5	24 14	6	13.9	4	5	25 1	4	9	4	27.3	25 48	18.3	8
42	20.0	5	22 15	1	0	9	24.3	23 1	15.0	0	8	25.2	23 48	8	0	8	9	24 34	7	9	7	9	25 21	5	8	6	7	26 7	4	8
43	2	9	22 37	2	0	21.2	7	23 23	1	11.9	22.1	6	24 9	9	12.9	23.0	26.3	24 54	8	8	24.0	27.3	25 41	6	8	9	28.1	26 27	5	7
44	5	24.4	22 59	3	0	5	25.2	23 44	2	9	4	26.1	24 30	16.0	9	3	8	25 15	9	8	2	7	26 1	17.7	14.7	25.2	6	26 47	6	7
45	8	9	23 22	4	10.9	8	7	24 6	3	9	7	5	24 51	1	8	6	27.2	25 37	17.0	7	5	28.2	26 22	7	7	5	29.0	27 7	18.7	15.6
46	21.1	25.3	23 45	14.5	9	22.1	26.1	24 29	15.4	8	23.0	27.0	25 13	2	8	9	7	25 58	1	13.7	8	6	26 43	8	6	8	4	27 28	8	6
47	4	8	24 8	6	8	4	6	24 52	5	8	3	5	25 36	3	7	24.2	28.2	26 21	1	6	25.2	29.1	27 5	9	6	26.1	8	27 49	9	5
48	8	26.2	24 32	8	8	7	27.0	25 15	6	11.7	6	9	25 59	4	12.7	6	7	26 42	2	6	5	5	27 26	18.0	14.5	5	♌ 0.3	28 10	9	5
49	22.1	7	24 56	9	10.7	23.1	5	25 39	7	7	24.0	28.4	26 22	16.5	6	9	29.2	27 5	3	5	8	♌	27 49	1	5	9	8	28 32	19.0	4
50	5	27.3	25 21	15.1	7	4	28.1	26 3	9	6	4	9	26 46	7	6	25.3	7	27 28	17.5	5	26.2	0.5	28 11	3	4	27.2	1.3	28 54	1	15.4
51	9	9	25 46	2	6	8	7	26 28	16.0	6	7	29.4	27 10	8	5	7	♌ 0.2	27 52	6	13.4	6	1.0	28 34	4	3	6	8	29 17	2	3
52	23.3	28.5	26 12	3	6	24.2	29.3	26 53	1	11.5	25.1	♌	27 35	9	12.5	26.1	8	28 16	7	3	27.0	6	28 58	18.5	14.2	28.0	2.3	29 40	3	2
53	7	29.1	26 38	4	10.5	6	9	27 19	2	5	6	0.6	28 0	17.0	4	5	4	28 41	8	3	4	2.2	29 22	6	2	4	9	♍ 0 3	19.4	1
54	24.2	7	27 5	6	5	25.1	♌ 0.5	27 45	16.3	4	26.1	1.2	28 26	1	3	27.0	2.0	29 6	9	2	9	8	29 47	7	1	9	3.5	0 28	5	0
55	7	♌ 0.3	27 33	8	4	6	1.1	28 12	5	3	6	9	28 52	3	2	5	6	29 32	18.1	1	28.4	3.4	♍ 0 12	9	0	29.4	4.1	0 52	6	14.9
56	25.3	1.0	28 1	16.0	4	26.2	8	28 40	7	3	27.1	2.6	29 19	4	1	28.0	3.3	29 58	3	0	29.0	4.0	0 38	19.0	13.9	9	8	1 18	8	8

SID. T. 3h 10m 12s — ARC 47° 33′.1 — ♉ 20°

H.	11	12	1	2	3
° Lat.	♊ °	♋ °	♌ ° ′	♍ °	♎ °
22	21.6	21.9	21 9	17.8	17.9
23	8	22.2	21 25	9	9
24	9	5	21 41	18.0	8
25	22.1	8	21 57	0	8
26	3	23.1	22 14	1	7
27	4	4	22 30	2	17.7
28	6	7	22 47	2	6
29	8	24.0	23 3	3	5
30	23.0	3	23 20	18.4	5
31	2	6	23 37	4	17.4
32	4	9	23 54	5	4
33	5	25.2	24 11	6	3
34	7	6	24 29	6	2
35	9	9	24 46	18.7	17.2
36	24.2	26.3	25 4	8	1
37	4	6	25 21	9	1
38	6	27.0	25 39	9	0
39	8	4	25 58	19.0	16.9
40	25.1	7	26 16	1	9
41	3	28.1	26 35	2	8
42	6	5	26 54	3	7
43	8	29.0	27 13	19.3	7
44	26.1	4	27 33	4	16.6
45	4	8	27 53	5	6
46	7	♌ 0.3	28 13	6	5
47	27.0	7	28 33	19.7	5
48	4	1.1	28 54	8	4
49	7	6	29 15	8	16.3
50	28.1	2.1	29 37	9	3
51	4	6	29 59	20.0	2
52	8	3.1	♍ 0 22	1	1
53	29.3	7	0 45	2	0
54	7	4.3	1 9	3	15.9
55	♋ 0.3	9	1 33	4	8
56	8	5.5	1 57	5	7

SID. T. 3h 14m 16s — ARC 48° 33′.9 — ♉ 21°

H.	11	12	1	2	3
° Lat.	♊ °	♋ °	♌ ° ′	♍ °	♎ °
22	22.6	22.8	22 3	18.8	18.9
23	7	23.1	22 19	9	9
24	9	4	22 35	9	8
25	23.0	7	22 51	19.0	8
26	2	24.0	23 7	1	7
27	4	3	23 23	1	18.7
28	6	6	23 39	2	6
29	7	9	23 56	2	5
30	9	25.2	24 12	19.3	5
31	24.1	5	24 29	4	18.4
32	3	8	24 45	4	4
33	5	26.1	25 2	5	3
34	7	5	25 19	6	2
35	9	8	25 36	19.6	18.2
36	25.1	27.2	25 53	7	1
37	3	5	26 11	8	0
38	5	9	26 28	8	0
39	8	28.2	26 46	9	17.9
40	26.0	6	27 4	20.0	8
41	3	29.0	27 23	0	8
42	5	4	27 41	1	7
43	8	8	28 0	2	6
44	27.1	♌ 0.2	28 19	3	17.6
45	4	7	28 38	20.4	5
46	7	1.1	28 58	4	5
47	28.0	5	29 18	5	4
48	3	2.0	29 39	6	3
49	7	4	29 59	20.7	17.2
50	29.1	9	♍ 0 20	8	2
51	5	3.4	0 42	9	1
52	9	9	1 4	9	0
53	♋ 0.3	4.5	1 26	21.0	16.9
54	7	5.1	1 49	1	8
55	1.2	7	2 13	2	7
56	7	6.3	2 37	3	6

SID. T. 3h 18m 19s — ARC 49° 34′.8 — ♉ 22°

H.	11	12	1	2	3
° Lat.	♊ °	♋ °	♌ ° ′	♍ °	♎ °
22	23.5	23.7	22 58	19.8	20.0
23	7	24.0	23 13	8	19.9
24	8	3	23 29	9	9
25	24.0	6	23 45	20.0	8
26	1	9	24 0	0	7
27	3	25.2	24 16	1	19.7
28	5	5	24 32	1	6
29	7	8	24 48	2	6
30	9	26.1	25 4	20.2	5
31	25.0	4	25 20	3	19.4
32	2	7	25 36	4	4
33	4	27.0	25 53	4	3
34	6	3	26 9	5	2
35	8	7	26 26	5	19.2
36	26.0	28.0	26 43	20.6	1
37	2	4	27 0	7	0
38	5	7	27 17	7	0
39	7	29.1	27 34	8	18.9
40	9	5	27 52	8	8
41	27.2	9	28 10	9	7
42	5	♌ 0.3	28 28	21.0	6
43	7	7	28 47	1	6
44	28.0	1.1	29 5	1	18.5
45	3	5	29 24	2	4
46	6	9	29 43	3	4
47	9	2.3	♍ 0 3	21.4	3
48	29.2	8	0 23	4	18.3
49	6	3.3	0 43	5	2
50	♋	7	1 4	6	1
51	0.3	4.2	1 25	21.7	0
52	7	7	1 46	8	17.9
53	1.1	5.2	2 8	9	8
54	6	8	2 31	22.0	7
55	2.1	6.4	2 54	0	6
56	6	7.0	3 17	1	5

SID. T. 3h 22m 24s — ARC 50° 36′.0 — ♉ 23°

H.	11	12	1	2	3
° Lat.	♊ °	♋ °	♌ ° ′	♍ °	♎ °
22	24.4	24.7	23 53	20.8	21.0
23	6	25.0	24 8	8	20.9
24	8	2	24 23	9	9
25	9	5	24 39	9	8
26	25.1	8	24 54	21.0	7
27	3	26.1	25 9	0	7
28	4	4	25 25	1	20.6
29	6	7	25 40	1	6
30	8	27.0	25 56	2	5
31	26.0	3	26 12	21.2	4
32	2	6	26 28	3	4
33	4	9	26 44	3	20.3
34	6	28.2	27 0	4	2
35	8	6	27 16	4	2
36	27.0	9	27 33	21.5	1
37	2	29.3	27 49	6	0
38	4	6	28 6	6	19.9
39	6	♌	28 23	7	9
40	9	0.3	28 40	21.7	8
41	28.1	7	28 58	8	7
42	4	1.1	29 15	9	6
43	7	5	29 33	9	19.5
44	9	9	29 52	22.0	5
45	29.2	2.4	♍ 0 10	1	4
46	5	8	0 29	1	4
47	9	3.2	0 48	2	3
48	♋ 0.2	6	1 7	22.3	19.2
49	5	4.0	1 27	3	2
50	9	5	1 47	4	1
51	1.2	5.0	2 8	5	0
52	6	5	2 29	6	18.9
53	2.0	6.0	2 50	22.7	8
54	5	6	3 12	7	7
55	3.1	7.2	3 35	8	5
56	6	8	3 57	9	4

SID. T. 3h 26m 29s — ARC 51° 37′.3 — ♉ 24°

H.	11	12	1	2	3
° Lat.	♊ °	♋ °	♌ ° ′	♍ °	♎ °
22	25.4	25.6	24 48	21.8	22.0
23	5	9	25 3	8	0
24	7	26.2	25 18	9	21.9
25	9	4	25 33	9	8
26	26.0	7	25 48	22.0	8
27	2	27.0	26 3	0	7
28	4	3	26 18	0	7
29	6	6	26 33	1	21.6
30	7	9	26 48	1	5
31	9	28.2	27 4	2	4
32	27.1	5	27 19	22.2	4
33	3	8	27 35	3	3
34	5	29.1	27 51	3	21.2
35	7	5	28 7	4	2
36	9	8	28 23	4	1
37	28.1	♌ 0.1	28 39	5	0
38	3	5	28 55	22.5	20.9
39	6	9	29 12	6	8
40	8	1.2	29 29	6	8
41	29.1	6	29 46	7	7
42	3	2.0	♍ 0 3	22.7	6
43	6	4	0 20	8	20.5
44	9	8	0 38	9	5
45	♋ 0.2	3.2	0 56	9	4
46	5	7	1 14	23.0	4
47	8	4.1	1 33	0	20.3
48	1.1	5	1 52	1	2
49	5	9	2 11	2	1
50	9	5.4	2 31	2	0
51	2.3	9	2 51	23.3	19.9
52	7	6.4	3 11	4	8
53	3.1	9	3 32	4	7
54	5	7.4	3 54	5	6
55	4.0	8.0	4 15	6	4
56	5	5	4 38	7	3

SID. T. 3h 30m 35s — ARC 52° 38′.8 — ♉ 25°

H.	11	12	1	2	3
° Lat.	♊ °	♋ °	♌ ° ′	♍ °	♎ °
22	26.3	26.5	25 43	22.8	23.1
23	5	8	25 58	8	0
24	6	27.1	26 12	8	22.9
25	8	4	26 27	9	9
26	27.0	6	26 42	9	8
27	2	9	26 56	23.0	7
28	3	28.2	27 11	0	7
29	5	5	27 26	0	22.6
30	7	8	27 41	1	5
31	9	29.1	27 56	1	5
32	28.1	4	28 11	23.2	4
33	3	7	28 26	2	3
34	5	♌	28 42	2	22.2
35	7	0.4	28 57	3	2
36	9	7	29 13	3	1
37	29.1	1.0	29 29	23.4	0
38	3	4	29 45	4	21.9
39	5	7	♍ 0 1	5	8
40	8	2.1	0 17	5	8
41	♋	5	0 34	23.6	7
42	0.3	9	0 51	6	6
43	5	3.3	1 8	7	21.5
44	8	7	1 25	7	5
45	1.1	4.1	1 43	23.8	4
46	4	4	2 0	8	3
47	7	8	2 18	9	21.2
48	2.1	5.3	2 37	9	1
49	4	7	2 56	24.0	1
50	8	6.2	3 15	1	0
51	3.1	7	3 34	1	20.9
52	5	7.2	3 54	2	8
53	9	7	4 15	24.2	7
54	4.4	8.2	4 35	3	6
55	9	7	4 57	4	4
56	5.4	9.3	5 18	4	3

SID. T. 3 h 30 m 35 s, ARC 52° 38′.8 — ♉ 25°

Lat.	H. 11 ♊	12 ♋	1 ♌	2 ♍	3 ♎
°	°	°	° ′	°	°
22	26.3	26.5	25 43	22.8	23.1
23	5	8	25 58	8	0
24	6	27.1	26 12	8	22.9
25	8	4	26 27	9	9
26	27.0	6	26 42	9	8
27	2	9	26 56	23.0	7
28	3	28.2	27 11	0	7
29	5	5	27 26	0	22.6
30	7	8	27 41	1	5
31	9	29.1	27 56	1	5
32	28.1	4	28 11	23.2	4
33	3	7	28 26	2	3
34	5	♌	28 42	2	22.2
35	7	0.4	28 57	3	2
36	9	7	29 13	3	1
37	29.1	1.0	29 29	23.4	0
38	3	4	29 45	4	21.9
39	5	7	♍ 0 1	5	8
40	8	2.1	0 17	5	8
41	♋	5	0 34	23.6	7
42	0.3	9	0 51	6	6
43	5	3.3	1 8	7	21.5
44	8	7	1 25	7	5
45	1.1	4.1	1 43	23.8	4
46	4	4	2 0	8	3
47	7	8	2 18	9	21.2
48	2.1	5.3	2 37	9	1
49	4	7	2 56	24.0	1
50	8	6.2	3 15	1	0
51	3.1	7	3 34	1	20.9
52	5	7.2	3 54	2	8
53	9	7	4 15	24.2	7
54	4.4	8.2	4 35	3	6
55	9	7	4 57	4	4
56	5.4	9.3	5 18	4	3

SID. T. 3 h 34 m 42 s, ARC 53° 40′.5 — ♉ 26°

Lat.	H. 11 ♊	12 ♋	1 ♌	2 ♍	3 ♎
°	°	°	° ′	°	°
22	27.3	27.5	26 39	23.7	24.1
23	4	7	26 53	8	0
24	6	28.0	27 7	8	0
25	8	3	27 21	9	23.9
26	9	6	27 36	9	8
27	28.1	8	27 50	9	8
28	3	29.1	28 5	24.0	7
29	5	4	28 19	0	6
30	6	7	28 34	0	23.6
31	8	♌	28 48	1	5
32	29.0	0.3	29 3	1	4
33	2	6	29 18	24.1	3
34	4	9	29 33	2	23.2
35	6	1.2	29 48	2	2
36	8	6	♍ 0 3	2	1
37	♋	9	0 19	3	0
38	0.2	2.2	0 34	24.3	22.9
39	5	5	0 50	4	8
40	7	9	1 6	4	8
41	1.0	3.2	1 22	5	7
42	2	6	1 38	5	22.6
43	5	4.0	1 55	24.6	5
44	8	4	2 12	6	4
45	2.1	8	2 29	6	3
46	4	5.2	2 46	7	22.3
47	7	7	3 4	7	2
48	3.0	6.1	3 22	24.8	1
49	3	6	3 40	8	0
50	7	7.0	3 59	9	21.9
51	4.0	5	4 18	9	8
52	4	8.0	4 37	25.0	7
53	8	5	4 57	0	6
54	5.3	9.0	5 17	1	5
55	8	5	5 38	2	3
56	6.3	10.1	5 59	2	2

SID. T. 3 h 38 m 49 s, ARC 54° 42′.3 — ♉ 27°

Lat.	H. 11 ♊	12 ♋	1 ♌	2 ♍	3 ♎
°	°	°	° ′	°	°
22	28.2	28.4	27 35	24.8	25.1
23	4	7	27 48	8	1
24	5	9	28 2	8	0
25	7	29.2	28 16	8	24.9
26	9	5	28 30	24.9	9
27	29.0	8	28 44	9	8
28	2	♌	28 58	9	7
29	4	0.3	29 12	25.0	7
30	6	6	29 26	0	24.6
31	8	9	29 41	0	5
32	♋	1.2	29 55	0	4
33	0.2	5	♍ 0 9	1	3
34	3	8	0 24	25.1	24.3
35	5	2.1	0 39	1	2
36	7	5	0 54	2	1
37	1.0	8	1 9	2	0
38	2	3.1	1 24	2	23.9
39	4	5	1 39	25.3	8
40	6	8	1 55	3	8
41	9	4.2	2 11	3	7
42	2.2	6	2 26	4	23.6
43	4	5.0	2 43	25.4	5
44	7	4	2 59	5	4
45	3.0	7	3 16	5	4
46	3	6.1	3 33	5	23.3
47	6	5	3 50	25.6	1
48	9	9	4 7	6	0
49	4.3	7.3	4 25	7	22.9
50	7	8	4 43	7	8
51	5.0	8.3	5 1	25.8	7
52	4	8	5 20	8	6
53	8	9.3	5 39	8	22.5
54	6.2	8	5 59	9	4
55	7	10.3	6 19	26.0	2
56	7.2	9	6 40	0	1

SID. T. 3 h 42 m 57 s, ARC 55° 44′.4 — ♉ 28°

Lat.	H. 11 ♊	12 ♋	1 ♌	2 ♍	3 ♎
°	°	°	° ′	°	°
22	29.2	29.4	28 31	25.7	26.2
23	3	6	28 44	8	1
24	5	9	28 58	8	1
25	7	♌ 0.2	29 11	8	0
26	8	4	29 25	8	25.9
27	♋	7	29 38	25.9	9
28	0.2	1.0	29 52	9	8
29	4	3	♍ 0 6	9	7
30	5	5	0 20	9	25.6
31	7	8	0 33	26.0	5
32	9	2.1	0 47	0	5
33	1.1	4	1 1	0	4
34	3	7	1 16	0	25.3
35	5	3.0	1 30	1	2
36	7	4	1 44	26.1	1
37	9	7	1 59	1	0
38	2.1	4.0	2 14	1	24.9
39	4	4	2 29	2	8
40	6	7	2 44	26.2	7
41	8	5.1	2 59	2	6
42	3.1	5	3 15	3	24.5
43	4	8	3 30	3	4
44	7	6.2	3 46	26.3	4
45	9	5	4 2	4	3
46	4.2	9	4 19	4	24.2
47	6	7.3	4 35	4	1
48	9	7	4 52	26.5	0
49	5.2	8.1	5 10	5	23.9
50	6	6	5 27	6	8
51	9	9.1	5 45	6	7
52	6.3	6	6 3	26.6	6
53	7	10.1	6 22	7	23.4
54	7.2	6	6 41	7	3
55	7	11.1	7 0	8	1
56	8.2	6	7 20	8	0

SID. T. 3 h 47 m 6 s, ARC 56° 46′.6 — ♉ 29°

Lat.	H. 11 ♋	12 ♌	1 ♌	2 ♍	3 ♎
°	°	°	° ′	°	°
22	0.1	0.3	29 27	26.8	27.3
23	3	5	29 40	8	2
24	4	8	29 53	8	1
25	6	1.1	♍ 0 6	8	1
26	8	3	0 19	26.8	0
27	1.0	6	0 33	9	26.9
28	1	9	0 46	9	8
29	3	2.1	0 59	9	7
30	5	4	1 13	26.9	7
31	7	7	1 26	9	26.6
32	9	3.0	1 40	9	5
33	2.1	3	1 54	27.0	4
34	2	6	2 7	0	3
35	4	9	2 21	0	26.2
36	6	4.2	2 36	0	1
37	9	6	2 50	0	0
38	3.1	9	3 4	27.1	0
39	3	5.2	3 18	1	25.9
40	5	6	3 33	1	8
41	8	9	3 48	1	7
42	4.1	6.3	4 3	2	6
43	3	7	4 18	27.2	4
44	6	7.0	4 34	2	25.3
45	9	4	4 49	2	3
46	5.2	8	5 5	3	2
47	5	8.2	5 21	3	1
48	8	6	5 38	27.3	0
49	6.1	9.0	5 55	3	24.8
50	5	4	6 12	4	7
51	8	9	6 29	4	6
52	7.2	10.4	6 47	27.4	5
53	6	9	7 5	5	24.3
54	8.1	11.4	7 23	5	2
55	6	9	7 42	6	0
56	9.1	12.4	8 1	6	23.9

SID. T. 3 h 51 m 16 s, ARC 57° 48′.9 — ♊ 0°

Lat.	H. 11 ♋	12 ♌	1 ♍	2 ♍	3 ♎
°	°	°	° ′	°	°
22	1.1	1.2	0 23	27.8	28.3
23	2	5	0 36	8	3
24	4	7	0 49	8	2
25	6	2.0	1 2	8	1
26	7	3	1 15	8	0
27	9	5	1 27	27.8	27.9
28	2.1	8	1 40	8	9
29	2	3.1	1 53	9	8
30	4	4	2 6	9	7
31	6	6	2 19	9	27.6
32	8	9	2 33	27.9	5
33	3.0	4.2	2 46	9	4
34	2	5	2 59	9	3
35	4	8	3 13	9	27.2
36	6	5.1	3 26	28.0	2
37	8	4	3 40	0	1
38	4.0	7	3 54	0	0
39	3	6.0	4 8	0	26.9
40	5	4	4 22	0	8
41	7	8	4 37	28.0	7
42	5.0	7.1	4 51	1	6
43	3	5	5 6	1	5
44	6	9	5 21	1	26.4
45	8	8.3	5 36	1	3
46	6.1	7	5 52	28.1	2
47	4	9.1	6 7	2	1
48	8	5	6 23	2	0
49	7.1	9	6 39	2	25.9
50	5	10.3	6 56	2	7
51	8	7	7 13	28.2	6
52	8.1	11.1	7 30	3	5
53	5	6	7 48	3	25.4
54	9.0	12.1	8 5	3	2
55	5	6	8 24	4	0
56	10.0	13.1	8 42	4	24.9

SID. T. 3 h 55 m 26 s, ARC 58° 51′.5 } ♊ 1°

H.	11	12	1	2	3
Lat.	♋	♌	♍	♍	♎
°	°	°	° ′	°	°
22	2.0	2.1	1 20	28.8	29.4
23	2	4	1 33	8	3
24	4	7	1 45	8	2
25	5	9	1 57	8	1
26	7	3.2	2 10	8	1
27	9	5	2 22	28.8	0
28	3.0	7	2 35	8	28.9
29	2	4.0	2 47	8	8
30	4	3	3 0	8	7
31	6	5	3 13	8	6
32	8	8	3 26	28.8	28.5
33	4.0	5.1	3 38	9	5
34	1	4	3 51	9	4
35	3	7	4 4	9	3
36	5	6.0	4 18	9	28.2
37	8	3	4 31	28.9	1
38	5.0	6	4 44	9	0
39	2	9	4 58	9	27.9
40	4	7.3	5 12	9	8
41	7	6	5 26	9	7
42	6.0	8.0	5 40	29.0	5
43	2	4	5 54	0	4
44	5	7	6 9	0	27.3
45	8	9.1	6 23	0	2
46	7.1	5	6 38	0	1
47	4	8	6 53	29.0	0
48	7	10.2	7 9	0	26.9
49	8.0	6	7 25	1	7
50	4	11.1	7 41	1	6
51	7	5	7 57	1	5
52	9.1	9	8 13	29.1	26.4
53	5	12.4	8 30	1	2
54	9	9	8 48	1	1
55	10.4	13.4	9 5	2	25.9
56	9	9	9 23	2	8

3 h 59 m 37 s, 59° 54′.2 } ♊ 2°

H.	11	12	1	2	3
Lat.	♋	♌	♍	♍	♏
°	°	°	° ′	°	°
22	3.0	3.1	2 17	29.8	0.4
23	2	3	2 29	8	3
24	3	6	2 41	8	3
25	5	9	2 53	8	2
26	6	4.1	3 5	8	1
27	8	4	3 17	29.8	0
28	4.0	6	3 30	8	♎ 29.9
29	2	9	3 42	8	8
30	3	5.2	3 54	8	8
31	5	5	4 6	8	7
32	7	7	4 19	29.8	29.6
33	9	6.0	4 31	8	5
34	5.1	3	4 44	8	4
35	3	6	4 56	8	3
36	5	9	5 9	8	29.2
37	7	7.2	5 22	29.8	1
38	9	5	5 35	8	0
39	6.2	8	5 48	8	28.9
40	4	8.2	6 2	8	8
41	6	5	6 15	29.8	7
42	9	9	6 29	8	5
43	7.2	9.2	6 43	9	4
44	5	6	6 57	9	28.3
45	7	10.0	7 11	29.9	2
46	8.0	4	7 25	9	1
47	3	7	7 40	9	0
48	6	11.1	7 55	9	27.9
49	9.0	5	8 10	29.9	8
50	3	9	8 25	9	6
51	6	12.3	8 41	9	5
52	10.0	7	8 57	9	27.3
53	4	13.2	9 13	♎	2
54	9	7	9 30	0.0	0
55	11.3	14.2	9 47	0	26.8
56	9	7	10 5	0	7

4 h 3 m 48 s, 60° 57′.1 } ♊ 3°

H.	11	12	1	2	3
Lat.	♋	♌	♍	♎	♏
°	°	°	° ′	°	°
22	3.9	4.1	3 14	0.8	1.5
23	4.1	3	3 26	8	4
24	3	6	3 37	8	3
25	4	8	3 49	8	2
26	6	5.1	4 1	8	1.1
27	8	3	4 13	0.8	1
28	9	6	4 24	8	0
29	5.1	8	4 36	8	0.9
30	3	6.1	4 48	8	8
31	5	4	5 0	8	7
32	7	7	5 12	0.8	6
33	9	9	5 24	8	5
34	6.0	7.2	5 36	8	0.4
35	2	5	5 48	8	3
36	4	8	6 1	8	2
37	7	8.1	6 13	0.8	1
38	9	4	6 26	8	0
39	7.1	7	6 38	8	♎ 29.9
40	3	9.1	6 51	8	8
41	6	4	7 4	8	7
42	9	8	7 18	0.8	5
43	8.1	10.1	7 31	8	4
44	4	5	7 44	8	29.3
45	7	8	7 58	8	2
46	9.0	11.2	8 12	8	1
47	3	5	8 26	0.8	0
48	6	9	8 41	8	28.8
49	10.0	12.3	8 55	8	7
50	3	7	9 10	8	5
51	6	13.1	9 25	8	4
52	11.0	5	9 41	0.8	2
53	4	14.0	9 57	8	1
54	8	5	10 13	8	27.9
55	12.2	15.0	10 29	8	7
56	7	5	10 46	8	6

4 h 8 m 1 s, 62° 0′.1 } ♊ 4°

H.	11	12	1	2	3
Lat.	♋	♌	♍	♎	♏
°	°	°	° ′	°	°
22	4.9	5.0	4 11	1.8	2.5
23	5.1	3	4 23	8	4
24	2	5	4 34	8	3
25	4	8	4 45	8	3
26	6	6.0	4 57	8	2.2
27	7	3	5 8	1.8	1
28	9	5	5 19	8	0
29	6.1	8	5 31	8	1.9
30	3	7.0	5 42	8	8
31	4	3	5 54	8	7
32	6	6	6 5	1.8	6
33	8	9	6 17	7	5
34	7.0	8.1	6 29	7	1.4
35	2	4	6 41	7	3
36	4	7	6 53	7	2
37	6	9.0	7 5	1.7	1
38	8	3	7 17	7	0
39	8.1	7	7 29	7	0.9
40	3	10.0	7 41	7	8
41	5	3	7 54	7	6
42	8	7	8 7	1.7	5
43	9.1	11.0	8 20	7	0.4
44	3	4	8 33	7	3
45	6	7	8 46	6	1
46	9	12.1	8 59	6	0
47	10.2	5	9 13	1.6	♎ 29.9
48	5	8	9 27	6	8
49	8	13.2	9 41	6	6
50	11.2	6	9 55	6	5
51	5	14.0	10 10	6	29.3
52	9	4	10 25	1.6	2
53	12.3	8	10 40	6	0
54	7	15.3	10 56	6	28.9
55	13.2	8	11 11	6	7
56	7	16.3	11 28	5	5

4 h 12 m 13 s, 63° 3′.3 } ♊ 5°

H.	11	12	1	2	3
Lat.	♋	♌	♍	♎	♏
°	°	°	° ′	°	°
22	5.9	6.0	5 9	2.9	3.6
23	6.0	3	5 20	9	5
24	2	5	5 31	9	4
25	4	8	5 42	8	3
26	5	7.0	5 53	8	3.2
27	7	3	6 4	2.8	1
28	9	5	6 15	8	0
29	7.0	8	6 26	8	2.9
30	2	8.0	6 37	7	8
31	4	3	6 48	7	7
32	6	6	6 59	2.7	6
33	8	8	7 10	7	5
34	8.0	9.1	7 22	7	2.4
35	2	4	7 33	7	3
36	4	7	7 44	7	2
37	6	10.0	7 56	2.7	1
38	8	3	8 8	6	0
39	9.0	6	8 19	6	1.9
40	2	9	8 31	6	8
41	5	11.3	8 44	6	6
42	8	6	8 56	2.6	5
43	10.0	12.0	9 8	6	1.4
44	3	3	9 21	6	2
45	6	6	9 34	6	1
46	9	9	9 47	5	0
47	11.2	13.3	10 0	2.5	0.9
48	5	6	10 13	5	7
49	8	14.0	10 27	5	6
50	12.1	4	10 41	5	4
51	4	8	10 55	5	0.3
52	8	15.2	11 9	2.4	1
53	13.2	6	11 24	4	0
54	6	16.1	11 39	4	♎ 29.8
55	14.1	6	11 54	4	6
56	6	17.1	12 10	3	4

4 h 16 m 27 s, 64° 6′.7 } ♊ 6°

H.	11	12	1	2	3
Lat.	♋	♌	♍	♎	♏
°	°	°	° ′	°	°
22	6.8	7.0	6 7	3.9	4.6
23	7.0	2	6 17	9	5
24	2	5	6 28	9	4
25	3	7	6 38	9	3
26	5	8.0	6 49	8	4.2
27	7	2	6 59	3.8	1
28	8	5	7 10	8	1
29	8.0	7	7 21	8	0
30	2	9.0	7 31	7	3.9
31	4	2	7 42	7	8
32	5	5	7 53	3.7	7
33	7	8	8 4	7	6
34	9	10.0	8 14	6	5
35	9.1	3	8 25	6	3.4
36	3	6	8 37	6	2
37	5	9	8 48	3.6	1
38	7	11.2	8 59	6	0
39	10.0	5	9 10	5	2.9
40	2	8	9 22	5	8
41	4	12.2	9 33	5	6
42	7	5	9 45	3.5	5
43	11.0	8	9 57	4	2.4
44	2	13.1	10 9	4	2
45	5	4	10 21	4	1
46	8	8	10 34	4	0
47	12.1	14.2	10 46	3.3	1.9
48	4	5	10 59	3	7
49	7	8	11 12	3	5
50	13.1	15.2	11 26	3	4
51	4	6	11 39	3	3
52	8	16.0	11 53	3.2	1
53	14.2	4	12 7	2	0.9
54	6	9	12 22	2	7
55	15.0	17.4	12 36	2	5
56	5	9	12 51	1	3

SID. T. 4 h 16 m 27 s, ARC 64° 6′.7 — ♊ 6°

H. Lat.	11 ♋ °	12 ♌ °	1 ♍ ° ′	2 ♎ °	3 ♏ °
22	6.8	7.0	6 7	3.9	4.6
23	7.0	2	6 17	9	5
24	2	5	6 28	9	4
25	3	7	6 38	9	3
26	5	8.0	6 49	8	4.2
27	7	2	6 59	3.8	1
28	8	5	7 10	8	1
29	8.0	7	7 21	8	0
30	2	9.0	7 31	7	3.9
31	4	2	7 42	7	8
32	5	5	7 53	3.7	7
33	7	8	8 4	7	6
34	9	10.0	8 14	6	5
35	9.1	3	8 25	6	3.4
36	3	6	8 37	6	2
37	5	9	8 48	3.6	1
38	7	11.2	8 59	6	0
39	10.0	5	9 10	5	2.9
40	2	8	9 22	5	8
41	4	12.2	9 33	5	6
42	7	5	9 45	3.5	5
43	11.0	8	9 57	4	2.4
44	2	13.1	10 9	4	2
45	5	4	10 21	4	1
46	8	8	10 34	4	0
47	12.1	14.2	10 46	3.3	1.9
48	4	5	10 59	3	7
49	7	8	11 12	3	5
50	13.1	15.2	11 26	3	4
51	4	6	11 39	3	3
52	8	16.0	11 53	3.2	1
53	14.2	4	12 7	2	0.9
54	6	9	12 22	2	7
55	15.0	17.4	12 36	2	5
56	5	9	12 51	1	3

SID. T. 4 h 20 m 41 s, ARC 65° 10′.2 — ♊ 7°

H. Lat.	11 ♋ °	12 ♌ °	1 ♍ ° ′	2 ♎ °	3 ♏ °
22	7.8	7.9	7 5	5.0	5.6
23	8.0	8.2	7 15	4.9	5
24	1	4	7 25	9	5
25	3	7	7 35	9	4
26	4	9	7 45	8	5.3
27	6	9.2	7 55	8	2
28	8	4	8 6	4.8	1
29	9.0	7	8 16	8	0
30	1	9	8 26	7	4.9
31	3	10.2	8 36	7	8
32	5	4	8 47	7	7
33	7	7	8 57	4.6	6
34	9	11.0	9 8	6	5
35	10.1	2	9 18	6	4.4
36	3	5	9 29	6	2
37	5	8	9 40	6	1
38	7	12.1	9 50	4.6	0
39	9	4	10 1	5	3.9
40	11.1	7	10 12	5	8
41	4	13.1	10 23	5	6
42	7	4	10 35	5	5
43	9	7	10 46	4.5	3.3
44	12.2	14.0	10 58	4	2
45	5	3	11 10	4	0
46	8	7	11 22	4	2.9
47	13.0	15.0	11 34	3	8
48	3	3	11 46	4.3	7
49	7	7	11 58	3	5
50	14.0	16.1	12 11	2	2.3
51	3	5	12 24	2	2
52	7	9	12 37	4.1	1
53	15.1	17.3	12 51	1	1.9
54	5	7	13 5	0	7
55	9	18.2	13 19	0	5
56	16.4	7	13 33	3.9	3

SID. T. 4 h 24 m 55 s, ARC 66° 13′.8 — ♊ 8°

H. Lat.	11 ♋ °	12 ♌ °	1 ♍ ° ′	2 ♎ °	3 ♏ °
22	8.8	8.9	8 3	6.0	6.7
23	9	9.2	8 13	0	6
24	9.1	4	8 22	5.9	5
25	3	6	8 32	9	4
26	4	9	8 42	9	6.3
27	6	10.1	8 52	8	2
28	8	4	9 1	8	1
29	9	6	9 11	5.8	0
30	10.1	8	9 21	7	5.9
31	3	11.1	9 31	7	8
32	5	3	9 41	7	7
33	6	6	9 51	6	6
34	8	9	10 1	5.6	5
35	11.0	12.2	10 11	6	5.4
36	2	4	10 21	5	3
37	4	7	10 31	5	1
38	7	13.0	10 42	4	0
39	9	3	10 52	5.4	4.9
40	12.1	6	11 3	4	7
41	4	14.0	11 13	3	6
42	6	3	11 24	3	5
43	9	6	11 35	5.3	4.3
44	13.1	9	11 46	2	2
45	4	15.2	11 58	2	0
46	7	5	12 9	1	3.9
47	14.0	9	12 21	5.1	7
48	3	16.2	12 32	1	5
49	6	5	12 44	0	4
50	9	9	12 57	0	2
51	15.2	17.3	13 9	4.9	0
52	6	7	13 22	9	2.8
53	9	18.1	13 35	8	6
54	16.3	5	13 48	8	4
55	8	19.0	14 1	7	1
56	17.3	4	14 15	6	1.9

SID. T. 4 h 29 m 11 s, ARC 67° 17′.6 — ♊ 9°

H. Lat.	11 ♋ °	12 ♌ °	1 ♍ ° ′	2 ♎ °	3 ♏ °
22	9.8	9.9	9 2	7.0	7.7
23	9	10.1	9 11	0	6
24	10.1	4	9 20	0	5
25	2	6	9 29	6.9	4
26	4	8	9 39	9	7.3
27	5	11.1	9 48	8	2
28	7	3	9 57	8	1
29	9	5	10 7	8	0
30	11.1	8	10 16	6.7	6.9
31	2	12.0	10 25	7	8
32	4	3	10 35	6	7
33	6	5	10 44	6	6
34	8	8	10 54	6	5
35	12.0	13.1	11 4	6.5	6.4
36	2	3	11 13	5	3
37	4	5	11 23	4	1
38	6	8	11 33	4	0
39	8	14.1	11 43	3	5.9
40	13.1	4	11 53	6.3	7
41	3	8	12 4	3	6
42	6	15.1	12 14	2	5
43	8	4	12 24	2	5.3
44	14.1	7	12 35	1	2
45	4	16.1	12 46	6.1	0
46	6	4	12 57	0	4.9
47	9	7	13 8	0	8
48	15.2	17.0	13 19	0	6
49	5	4	13 31	5.9	4
50	9	8	13 42	9	2
51	16.2	18.2	13 54	9	1
52	5	6	14 6	8	3.9
53	9	19.0	14 19	5.7	7
54	17.3	4	14 31	7	5
55	7	8	14 44	6	3
56	18.2	20.2	14 57	5	1

SID. T. 4 h 33 m 26 s, ARC 68° 21′.6 — ♊ 10°

H. Lat.	11 ♋ °	12 ♌ °	1 ♍ ° ′	2 ♎ °	3 ♏ °
22	10.7	10.9	10 0	8.1	8.8
23	9	11.1	10 9	1	7
24	11.0	3	10 18	0	6
25	2	6	10 27	0	5
26	4	8	10 36	7.9	4
27	5	12.0	10 44	9	8.3
28	7	3	10 53	8	2
29	9	5	11 2	8	1
30	12.0	7	11 11	7	0
31	2	13.0	11 20	7.7	7.9
32	4	2	11 29	6	7
33	6	5	11 38	6	6
34	8	8	11 48	5	5
35	13.0	14.0	11 57	5	7.4
36	2	3	12 6	7.4	3
37	4	5	12 16	4	1
38	6	7	12 25	3	0
39	8	15.0	12 35	3	6.9
40	14.0	3	12 44	7.3	7
41	3	6	12 54	2	6
42	5	16.0	13 4	2	4
43	8	3	13 14	2	6.3
44	15.0	6	13 24	7.1	1
45	3	9	13 34	1	0
46	6	17.3	13 45	0	5.8
47	9	6	13 55	0	7
48	16.2	9	14 6	6.9	6
49	5	18.2	14 17	9	4
50	8	6	14 28	8	2
51	17.1	19.0	14 39	7	1
52	5	4	14 51	6.7	4.9
53	9	8	15 3	6	7
54	18.3	20.2	15 15	6	5
55	7	6	15 27	5	3
56	19.1	21.0	15 40	4	1

SID. T. 4 h 37 m 42 s, ARC 69° 25′.6 — ♊ 11°

H. Lat.	11 ♋ °	12 ♌ °	1 ♍ ° ′	2 ♎ °	3 ♏ °
22	11.7	11.8	10 59	9.2	9.8
23	9	12.1	11 8	1	7
24	12.0	3	11 16	1	6
25	2	5	11 24	0	5
26	3	7	11 33	8.9	4
27	5	13.0	11 41	9	9.3
28	7	2	11 50	8	2
29	8	4	11 58	8	1
30	13.0	7	12 7	7	0
31	2	9	12 15	8.7	8.9
32	3	14.2	12 24	6	8
33	5	4	12 33	6	6
34	7	7	12 41	5	5
35	9	9	12 50	5	8.4
36	14.1	15.2	12 59	8.4	3
37	3	5	13 8	3	1
38	5	7	13 17	3	0
39	8	9	13 26	2	7.9
40	15.0	16.2	13 35	8.2	7
41	2	5	13 44	1	6
42	5	8	13 54	1	4
43	7	17.1	14 3	0	3
44	16.0	5	14 13	7.9	1
45	3	8	14 23	9	6.9
46	6	18.1	14 33	8	8
47	8	4	14 43	8	6
48	17.1	7	14 53	7.7	4
49	4	19.1	15 3	7	6.2
50	7	4	15 14	6	1
51	18.1	8	15 25	6	0
52	4	20.2	15 36	7.5	5.8
53	7	6	15 47	4	6
54	19.1	21.0	15 58	4	4
55	6	4	16 10	3	2
56	20.1	8	16 22	3	0

H.	SID. T. 4 41 59 (H. M. S.) ARC 70° 29′.8 ♊ 12°					4 46 16 (H. M. S.) 71° 34′.1 ♊ 13°				
H.	11	12	1	2	3	11	12	1	2	3
Lat. °	♋ °	♌ °	♍ ° ′	♎ °	♏ °	♋ °	♌ °	♍ ° ′	♎ °	♏ °
22	12.7	12.8	11 58	10.2	10.9	13.7	13.8	12 57	11.3	11.9
23	8	13.0	12 6	2	8	8	14.0	13 5	2	8
24	13.0	3	12 14	1	7	14.0	2	13 12	1	7
25	1	5	12 22	0	6	1	5	13 20	1	6
26	3	7	12 30	0	5	3	7	13 27	0	5
27	5	9	12 38	9.9	10.3	4	9	13 35	10.9	11.4
28	6	14.2	12 46	8	2	14.6	15.1	13 43	9	2
29	8	4	12 54	8	1	8	4	13 50	8	1
30	14.0	6	13 2	7	0	9	6	13 58	7	0
31	1	9	13 10	9.7	9.9	15.1	8	14 6	7	10.9
32	3	15.1	13 18	6	8	3	16.1	14 13	10.6	8
33	5	4	13 27	5	7	5	3	14 21	5	7
34	7	6	13 35	5	5	6	5	14 29	5	5
35	9	9	13 43	9.4	9.4	8	8	14 37	4	10.4
36	15.1	16.1	13 52	4	3	16.0	17.1	14 45	4	3
37	3	4	14 0	3	1	2	3	14 53	10.3	1
38	5	6	14 9	2	0	5	5	15 1	2	0
39	7	9	14 17	9.2	8.9	7	8	15 9	1	9.9
40	9	17.1	14 26	1	7	9	18.1	15 17	1	7
41	16.2	4	14 35	1	6	17.1	3	15 26	0	6
42	4	7	14 44	0	4	4	6	15 34	9.9	4
43	7	18.0	14 53	8.9	3	7	9	15 43	9	3
44	17.0	4	15 2	8	1	9	19.2	15 51	8	1
45	2	7	15 11	8	7.9	18.2	5	16 0	7	8.9
46	5	19.0	15 21	7	8	5	9	16 9	6	8
47	8	3	15 30	7	7	7	20.2	16 18	9.6	6
48	18.0	6	15 40	8.6	5	19.0	5	16 27	5	5
49	3	9	15 50	6	3	3	8	16 37	5	3
50	6	20.3	16 0	5	1	6	21.1	16 46	4	1
51	9	6	16 10	4	6.9	9	5	16 56	9.3	7.9
52	19.3	21.0	16 21	8.3	7	20.2	8	17 6	2	7
53	7	4	16 31	3	5	6	22.2	17 16	1	5
54	20.1	8	16 42	2	3	21.0	6	17 26	0	3
55	5	22.2	16 53	1	1	4	23.0	17 36	8.9	0
56	21.0	6	17 4	0	5.9	9	4	17 47	8	6.8

H.	4 50 34 (H. M. S.) 72° 38′.5 ♊ 14°					4 54 52 (H. M. S.) 73° 43′.1 ♊ 15°				
H.	11	12	1	2	3	11	12	1	2	3
Lat. °	♋ °	♌ °	♍ ° ′	♎ °	♏ °	♋ °	♌ °	♍ ° ′	♎ °	♏ °
22	14.6	14.8	13 57	12.4	12.9	15.6	15.8	14 56	13.4	13.9
23	8	15.0	14 4	3	8	8	16.0	15 3	4	8
24	9	2	14 11	2	7	9	2	15 9	3	7
25	15.1	4	14 18	1	6	16.1	4	15 16	2	6
26	3	7	14 25	1	5	2	6	15 23	1	5
27	4	9	14 32	0	12.4	4	8	15 29	0	13.4
28	6	16.1	14 39	11.9	3	6	17.1	15 36	12.9	3
29	7	3	14 46	8	2	7	3	15 43	9	2
30	9	5	14 54	8	0	9	5	15 50	8	1
31	16.1	8	15 1	7	11.9	17.1	7	15 56	7	12.9
32	2	17.0	15 8	6	8	2	18.0	16 3	6	8
33	4	2	15 16	11.5	7	4	2	16 10	12.5	7
34	6	5	15 23	5	6	6	4	16 17	5	6
35	8	7	15 30	4	11.4	8	7	16 24	4	12.4
36	17.0	9	15 38	3	3	18.0	9	16 31	3	3
37	2	18.1	15 45	11.2	1	2	19.1	16 38	12.2	2
38	4	4	15 53	2	0	4	3	16 45	1	0
39	6	7	16 1	1	10.9	6	6	16 53	1	11.9
40	9	19.0	16 9	0	7	8	9	17 0	0	7
41	18.1	2	16 17	10.9	6	19.1	20.2	17 7	11.9	5
42	4	5	16 25	9	4	3	4	17 15	8	4
43	6	8	16 33	8	2	6	7	17 23	7	2
44	9	20.1	16 41	7	1	8	21.0	17 30	6	0
45	19.1	4	16 49	10.6	9.9	20.1	3	17 38	11.5	10.9
46	4	7	16 58	5	8	4	6	17 46	4	8
47	6	21.0	17 6	4	6	6	9	17 54	4	6
48	9	3	17 15	3	4	9	22.2	18 2	3	4
49	20.2	6	17 24	10.2	2	21.2	5	18 10	11.2	2
50	5	22.0	17 32	2	0	5	8	18 19	1	0
51	8	3	17 41	1	8.8	8	23.2	18 27	0	9.8
52	21.1	6	17 51	0	6	22.1	5	18 36	10.9	6
53	5	23.0	18 0	9.9	4	4	8	18 45	8	4
54	9	4	18 10	8	2	8	24.2	18 54	7	2
55	22.3	8	18 20	7	0	23.2	6	19 3	6	8.9
56	8	24.2	18 30	6	7.8	7	25.0	19 12	5	7

H.	4 59 11 (H. M. S.) 74° 47′.7 ♊ 16°					5 3 30 (H. M. S.) 75° 52′.5 ♊ 17°				
H.	11	12	1	2	3	11	12	1	2	3
Lat. °	♋ °	♌ °	♍ ° ′	♎ °	♏ °	♋ °	♌ °	♍ ° ′	♎ °	♏ °
22	16.6	16.8	15 56	14.5	15.0	17.6	17.8	16 55	15.6	16.0
23	8	17.0	16 2	4	14.9	7	18.0	17 1	5	15.9
24	9	2	16 8	3	8	9	2	17 7	4	8
25	17.1	4	16 14	2	7	18.0	4	17 13	3	7
26	2	6	16 21	14.1	5	2	6	17 19	15.2	6
27	4	8	16 27	1	4	4	8	17 24	1	5
28	5	18.0	16 33	0	14.3	5	19.0	17 30	0	15.3
29	7	2	16 39	13.9	2	7	2	17 36	14.9	2
30	9	5	16 46	8	1	8	4	17 42	8	1
31	18.0	7	16 52	7	0	19.0	6	17 48	7	0
32	2	9	16 59	6	13.8	2	9	17 54	6	14.8
33	4	19.1	17 5	13.5	7	4	20.1	18 0	14.5	7
34	6	4	17 11	5	6	5	3	18 6	4	6
35	8	6	17 18	4	4	7	5	18 12	3	4
36	9	8	17 25	3	13.3	9	7	18 18	3	14.3
37	19.1	20.0	17 31	13.3	2	20.1	9	18 24	14.2	1
38	4	3	17 38	2	0	3	21.2	18 30	1	0
39	6	5	17 45	1	12.9	6	4	18 37	0	13.9
40	8	8	17 52	0	7	8	7	18 43	13.9	7
41	20.0	21.1	17 58	12.9	5	21.0	22.0	18 50	8	5
42	3	3	18 5	9	4	2	2	18 56	7	4
43	5	6	18 13	8	2	5	5	19 3	6	2
44	8	9	18 20	7	0	8	8	19 9	5	0
45	21.1	22.2	18 27	6	11.9	22.0	23.1	19 16	13.4	12.9
46	3	4	18 34	12.5	8	3	3	19 23	3	7
47	5	7	18 42	3	6	5	6	19 30	2	5
48	8	23.0	18 50	2	4	7	9	19 37	1	3
49	22.1	3	18 57	1	2	23.0	24.2	19 44	0	1
50	4	7	19 5	0	10.9	3	5	19 51	12.9	11.9
51	7	24.0	19 13	11.9	7	6	9	19 59	8	7
52	23.0	3	19 21	8	5	9	25.2	20 6	6	5
53	4	6	19 29	6	3	24.3	5	20 14	5	3
54	8	25.0	19 38	5	1	7	8	20 22	12.3	1
55	24.2	4	19 46	4	9.8	25.1	26.2	20 30	2	10.8
56	6	8	19 55	2	6	5	6	20 38	1	5

SID. T. H. M. S. 5 3 30 ARC 75° 52′.5 ♊ 17°						H. M. S. 5 7 49 76° 57′.3 ♊ 18°					H. M. S. 5 12 9 78° 2′.2 ♊ 19°					H. M. S. 5 16 29 79° 7′.2 ♊ 20°					H. M. S. 5 20 49 80° 12′.3 ♊ 21°					H. M. S. 5 25 10 81° 17′.4 ♊ 22°				
H.	11	12	1	2	3	11	12	1	2	3	11	12	1	2	3	11	12	1	2	3	11	12	1	2	3	11	12	1	2	3
Lat.	♋	♌	♍	♎	♏	♋	♌	♍	♎	♏	♋	♌	♍	♎	♏	♋	♌	♍	♎	♏	♋	♌	♍	♎	♏	♋	♌	♍	♎	♏
°	°	°	° ′	°	°	°	°	° ′	°	°	°	°	° ′	°	°	°	°	° ′	°	°	°	°	° ′	°	°	°	°	° ′	°	°
22	17.6	17.8	16 55	15.6	16.0	18.6	18.8	17 55	16.6	17.1	19.6	19.8	18 55	17.7	18.1	20.6	20.8	19 55	18.7	19.1	21.6	21.8	20 55	19.8	20.2	22.6	22.8	21 55	20.8	21.2
23	7	18.0	17 1	5	15.9	7	19.0	18 1	5	0	7	20.0	19 0	6	0	7	21.0	20 0	6	0	7	22.0	20 59	6	0	7	9	21 59	7	1
24	9	2	17 7	4	8	9	2	18 6	4	16.8	9	2	19 5	5	17.9	9	1	20 4	5	18.9	9	2	21 3	5	19.9	9	23.1	22 2	6	20.9
25	18.0	4	17 13	3	7	19.0	4	18 11	3	7	20.0	4	19 10	4	7	21.0	3	20 9	4	8	22.0	3	21 7	4	8	23.0	3	22 6	5	8
26	2	6	17 19	15.2	6	2	6	18 17	16.2	6	2	6	19 15	17.3	6	2	5	20 13	18.3	6	2	5	21 12	19.3	7	2	5	22 10	20.3	7
27	4	8	17 24	1	5	3	8	18 22	1	5	3	8	19 20	1	5	3	7	20 18	2	5	3	7	21 16	2	6	3	7	22 14	2	6
28	5	19.0	17 30	0	15.3	5	20.0	18 27	0	16.4	5	21.0	19 25	0	17.4	5	9	20 22	1	18.4	5	9	21 20	1	19.4	5	9	22 17	1	20.4
29	7	2	17 36	14.9	2	7	2	18 33	15.9	2	7	2	19 30	16.9	3	6	22.1	20 27	0	3	6	23.1	21 24	0	3	23.6	24.1	22 21	0	3
30	8	4	17 42	8	1	8	4	18 38	8	1	8	4	19 35	8	1	8	3	20 31	17.8	1	8	3	21 28	18.9	2	8	3	22 25	19.9	2
31	19.0	6	17 48	7	0	20.0	6	18 44	7	0	21.0	6	19 40	7	0	22.0	5	20 36	7	0	23.0	5	21 32	7	0	9	5	22 28	7	0
32	2	9	17 54	6	14.8	2	8	18 49	6	15.9	2	8	19 45	6	16.9	1	8	20 41	6	17.9	1	7	21 36	6	18.9	24.1	7	22 32	6	19.9
33	4	20.1	18 0	14.5	7	3	21.0	18 55	15.5	7	3	22.0	19 50	5	7	3	23.0	20 45	5	7	3	9	21 40	5	8	3	9	22 36	5	8
34	5	3	18 6	4	6	5	3	19 0	4	6	5	2	19 55	16.4	6	5	2	20 50	4	6	5	24.1	21 45	18.4	6	5	25.1	22 39	19.4	6
35	7	5	18 12	3	4	7	5	19 6	3	4	7	4	20 0	3	4	7	4	20 55	17.3	4	7	3	21 49	3	5	6	3	22 43	3	5
36	9	7	18 18	3	14.3	9	7	19 12	3	15.3	9	6	20 5	2	16.3	9	5	20 59	2	17.3	8	5	21 53	2	18.3	8	5	22 47	1	19.3
37	20.1	9	18 24	14.2	1	21.1	9	19 17	15.2	1	22.1	8	20 11	1	1	23.1	7	21 4	1	1	24.0	7	21 57	0	1	25.0	7	22 51	0	1
38	3	21.2	18 30	1	0	3	22.1	19 23	1	0	3	23.0	20 16	0	0	3	24.0	21 9	0	0	2	9	22 2	17.9	0	2	9	22 55	18.9	0
39	6	4	18 37	0	13.9	5	4	19 29	0	14.8	5	3	20 21	15.9	15.8	5	2	21 14	16.9	16.8	4	25.1	22 6	8	17.8	4	26.1	22 59	8	18.8
40	8	7	18 43	13.9	7	7	6	19 35	14.9	7	7	5	20 27	8	7	7	5	21 19	8	7	6	4	22 10	7	7	6	3	23 2	7	6
41	21.0	22.0	18 50	8	5	22.0	9	19 41	8	5	9	8	20 32	7	5	9	7	21 23	7	5	9	6	22 15	6	5	8	5	23 6	6	5
42	2	2	18 56	7	4	2	23.1	19 47	7	3	23.2	24.0	20 38	6	3	24.1	25.0	21 28	6	3	25.1	9	22 19	17.4	3	26.1	8	23 10	18.5	3
43	5	5	19 3	6	2	5	4	19 53	6	2	4	3	20 43	4	1	4	2	21 34	16.5	1	3	26.1	22 24	3	1	3	27.0	23 14	3	1
44	8	8	19 9	5	0	7	7	19 59	14.5	0	7	6	20 49	15.3	0	6	5	21 39	3	15.9	6	4	22 29	2	16.9	6	3	23 19	2	17.9
45	22.0	23.1	19 16	13.4	12.9	23.0	24.0	20 5	4	13.9	9	9	20 55	2	14.9	9	7	21 44	2	8	9	6	22 33	0	8	8	5	23 23	0	8
46	3	3	19 23	3	7	2	2	20 12	2	7	24.1	25.1	21 0	1	7	25.1	26.0	21 49	1	6	26.1	9	22 38	16.9	6	27.0	7	23 27	17.8	6
47	5	6	19 30	2	5	4	4	20 18	0	5	3	3	21 6	0	5	3	2	21 55	15.9	4	3	27.2	22 43	7	4	2	28.0	23 31	6	4
48	7	9	19 37	1	3	7	7	20 25	13.9	3	6	6	21 12	14.9	2	6	5	22 0	8	2	5	5	22 48	6	2	4	2	23 35	5	1
49	23.0	24.2	19 44	0	1	24.0	25.1	20 31	8	1	9	9	21 18	8	0	9	8	22 5	7	0	8	7	22 53	4	0	7	5	23 40	3	16.9
50	3	5	19 51	12.9	11.9	3	4	20 38	7	12.9	25.2	26.2	21 24	6	13.8	26.2	27.1	22 11	5	14.8	27.1	28.0	22 58	16.3	15.8	28.0	8	23 44	2	7
51	6	9	19 59	8	7	6	7	20 45	5	7	5	5	21 31	5	6	5	4	22 17	15.4	6	4	3	23 3	2	6	3	29.1	23 49	0	5
52	9	25.2	20 6	6	5	9	26.0	20 52	13.4	5	8	8	21 37	14.3	4	8	7	22 23	2	4	7	6	23 8	1	4	6	4	23 54	16.9	3
53	24.3	5	20 14	5	3	25.2	3	20 59	3	3	26.1	27.1	21 44	2	2	27.1	28.0	22 29	0	2	28.0	9	23 13	15.9	1	9	7	23 58	8	1
54	7	8	20 22	12.3	1	6	7	21 6	2	0	5	5	21 50	0	12.9	5	3	22 35	14.9	13.9	4	29.2	23 19	7	14.8	29.3	♍	24 3	6	15.8
55	25.1	26.2	20 30	2	10.8	26.0	27.1	21 13	0	11.7	9	9	21 57	13.9	6	9	7	22 41	7	6	8	5	23 24	5	5	7	0.3	24 8	4	5
56	5	6	20 38	1	5	4	5	21 21	12.9	4	27.3	28.3	22 4	7	3	28.3	29.1	22 47	5	3	29.2	9	23 30	3	2	♌ 0.1	7	24 13	2	2

SID. T. (H. M. S.)	5 29 30	5 33 51	5 38 12	5 42 34	5 46 55	5 51 17
ARC	82° 22′.6	83° 27′.8	84° 33′.1	85° 38′.5	86° 43′.8	87° 49′.2
10th H.	♊ 23°	♊ 24°	♊ 25°	♊ 26°	♊ 27°	♊ 28°

H.	11	12	1	2	3	11	12	1	2	3	11	12	1	2	3	11	12	1	2	3	11	12	1	2	3	11	12	1	2	3
Lat.	♋	♌	♍	♎	♏	♋	♌	♍	♎	♏	♋	♌	♍	♎	♏	♋	♌	♍	♎	♏	♋	♌	♍	♎	♏	♋	♌	♍	♎	♏
°	°	°	° ′	°	°	°	°	° ′	°	°	°	°	° ′	°	°	°	°	° ′	°	°	°	°	° ′	°	°	°	°	° ′	°	°
22	23.6	23.8	22 56	21.8	22.2	24.6	24.8	23 56	22.8	23.2	25.6	25.8	24 57	23.8	24.3	26.6	26.8	25 57	24.8	25.3	27.6	27.8	26 58	25.9	26.3	28.6	28.9	27 58	26.9	27.3
23	7	24.0	22 59	7	1	7	25.0	23 59	6	1	7	26.0	24 59	8	1	7	27.0	25 59	7	2	7	28.0	26 59	8	2	7	29.0	27 59	8	2
24	9	1	23 2	6	0	8	2	24 2	5	0	9	1	25 1	6	0	9	2	26 1	6	0	9	2	27 1	6	0	9	2	28 0	6	1
25	24.0	3	23 5	5	21.8	25.0	3	24 4	4	22.9	26.0	3	25 3	5	23.9	27.0	3	26 3	5	24.9	28.0	3	27 2	5	25.9	29.0	4	28 1	5	26.9
26	2	5	23 9	21.4	7	1	5	24 7	22.3	7	2	5	25 6	23.3	8	2	5	26 4	24.3	8	2	5	27 3	25.4	8	2	5	28 2	26.4	8
27	3	7	23 12	2	6	3	7	24 10	2	6	3	7	25 8	2	6	3	7	26 6	2	6	3	7	27 5	2	6	3	7	28 3	2	7
28	5	9	23 15	1	5	4	9	24 13	0	5	5	9	25 10	1	5	5	9	26 8	1	5	5	8	27 6	1	5	5	8	28 4	1	5
29	24.6	25.1	23 18	0	21.3	25.6	26.1	24 15	21.9	22.3	26.6	27.0	25 13	22.9	23.3	27.6	28.0	26 10	23.9	24.4	28.6	29.0	27 7	24.9	25.4	29.6	♍	28 5	25.9	26.4
30	8	2	23 21	20.9	2	8	2	24 18	8	2	8	2	25 15	8	2	8	2	26 12	8	2	8	2	27 9	8	2	8	0.2	28 6	8	2
31	9	4	23 25	8	0	9	4	24 21	7	1	9	4	25 17	7	1	9	4	26 14	7	1	9	3	27 10	7	1	9	3	28 7	7	1
32	25.1	6	23 28	6	20.9	26.1	6	24 24	6	21.9	27.1	6	25 20	5	22.9	28.1	6	26 16	5	23.9	29.1	5	27 12	5	24.9	♌ 0.1	5	28 8	5	25.9
33	3	8	23 31	5	8	3	8	24 27	21.4	8	3	8	25 22	22.4	8	3	7	26 17	23.4	8	2	7	27 13	24.4	8	2	7	28 9	25.4	8
34	4	26.0	23 34	20.4	6	4	27.0	24 29	3	6	4	28.0	25 24	3	6	4	9	26 19	2	6	4	9	27 14	3	6	4	8	28 10	2	6
35	6	2	23 38	3	5	6	2	24 32	2	5	6	1	25 27	1	5	6	29.1	26 21	1	5	6	♍ 0.1	27 16	1	5	6	1.0	28 11	1	4
36	8	4	23 41	1	20.3	8	4	24 35	0	21.3	8	3	25 29	0	22.3	8	3	26 23	0	23.3	8	3	27 17	0	3	8	2	28 11	24.9	3
37	26.0	7	23 44	0	1	27.0	6	24 38	20.9	1	28.0	5	25 31	21.9	1	0	5	26 25	22.8	1	9	4	27 19	23.9	1	9	4	28 12	7	1
38	2	9	23 48	19.9	0	2	8	24 41	8	0	2	7	25 34	7	0	29.2	7	26 27	7	0	♌ 0.1	6	27 20	8	23.9	1.1	5	28 13	6	24.9
39	4	27.1	23 51	7	19.8	4	28.0	24 44	7	20.8	4	9	25 36	6	21.8	3	9	26 29	5	22.8	3	8	27 22	6	8	3	7	28 14	4	7
40	6	3	23 54	6	6	6	2	24 47	6	6	6	29.1	25 39	4	6	5	♍ 0.1	26 31	4	6	5	1.0	27 23	4	6	5	9	28 15	2	6
41	8	5	23 58	5	4	8	5	24 50	20.5	4	8	3	25 41	21.3	4	8	3	26 33	2	4	7	2	27 25	3	4	7	2.1	28 16	1	4
42	27.1	7	24 1	19.3	3	28.0	7	24 53	3	2	29.0	5	25 44	1	2	♌	5	26 35	0	2	9	4	27 26	1	2	9	3	28 17	23.9	2
43	3	9	24 5	2	1	2	9	24 56	2	0	2	7	25 46	0	0	0.2	8	26 37	21.9	0	1.2	7	27 28	22.9	0	2.1	5	28 18	7	0
44	5	28.2	24 9	0	18.9	4	29.2	24 59	0	19.8	5	9	25 49	20.8	20.9	4	1.0	26 39	7	21.8	4	9	27 29	8	22.8	3	7	28 19	6	23.8
45	8	4	24 12	18.9	7	6	4	25 2	19.8	6	7	♍ 0.1	25 51	6	7	6	2	26 41	5	6	6	2.1	27 31	6	6	5	9	28 20	4	6
46	28.0	7	24 16	7	5	8	6	25 5	7	5	9	4	25 54	5	5	8	4	26 43	4	4	8	3	27 32	4	4	7	3.1	28 21	3	4
47	2	9	24 20	5	3	29.0	8	25 8	5	3	♌ 0.1	6	25 57	3	2	1.0	6	26 45	3	2	2.0	5	27 34	2	2	9	4	28 22	1	2
48	4	29.1	24 23	4	1	3	♍ 0.1	25 11	3	1	3	9	25 59	1	0	2	8	26 47	1	0	2	7	27 35	0	0	3.2	6	28 24	22.9	0
49	7	4	24 27	18.2	17.9	6	3	25 15	2	18.9	6	1.1	26 2	19.9	19.8	5	2.1	26 50	20.9	20.8	5	9	27 37	21.8	21.8	4	8	28 25	7	22.8
50	29.0	7	24 31	1	7	9	6	25 18	0	6	9	4	26 5	8	6	8	3	26 52	7	6	8	3.2	27 39	6	5	7	4.1	28 26	5	5
51	3	9	24 35	0	5	♌ 0.2	9	25 21	18.8	4	1.2	6	26 8	7	4	2.1	6	26 54	5	3	3.1	5	27 40	4	3	4.0	3	28 27	3	2
52	6	♍ 0.2	24 39	17.8	3	5	1.1	25 25	6	2	5	9	26 11	5	1	4	8	26 56	3	1	4	7	27 42	2	0	3	5	28 28	1	21.9
53	9	5	24 43	6	0	8	4	25 29	4	17.9	8	2.2	26 14	3	18.8	7	3.0	26 59	1	19.8	7	9	27 44	0	20.7	6	7	28 29	21.9	6
54	♌ 0.2	8	24 48	4	16.7	1.1	7	25 32	2	6	2.1	5	26 17	1	5	3.0	3	27 1	19.9	5	4.0	4.2	27 46	20.8	4	9	5.0	28 31	7	3
55	6	1.1	24 52	2	4	5	2.0	25 36	0	3	5	8	26 20	18.9	2	4	6	27 4	7	2	3	5	27 48	6	1	5.2	3	28 32	4	0
56	1.0	4	24 56	0	1	9	3	25 40	17.8	0	9	3.1	26 23	7	17.9	8	9	27 6	5	18.9	7	8	27 50	4	19.8	6	6	28 33	1	20.7

SID. T. 5 51 17 (H. M. S.) — ARC 87° 49′.2 — ♊ 28°

H.	11	12	1	2	3
° Lat.	♋	♌	♍	♎	♏
	°	°	° ′	°	°
22	28.6	28.9	27 58	26.9	27.3
23	7	29.0	27 59	8	2
24	9	2	28 0	6	1
25	29.0	4	28 1	5	26.9
26	2	5	28 2	26.4	8
27	3	7	28 3	2	7
28	5	8	28 4	1	5
29	29.6	♍	28 5	25.9	26.4
30	8	0.2	28 6	8	2
31	9	3	28 7	7	1
32	♌ 0.1	5	28 8	5	25.9
33	2	7	28 9	25.4	8
34	4	8	28 10	2	6
35	6	1.0	28 11	1	4
36	8	2	28 11	24.9	3
37	9	4	28 12	7	1
38	1.1	5	28 13	6	24.9
39	3	7	28 14	4	7
40	5	9	28 15	2	6
41	7	2.1	28 16	1	4
42	9	3	28 17	23.9	2
43	2.1	5	28 18	7	0
44	3	7	28 19	6	23.8
45	5	9	28 20	4	6
46	7	3.1	28 21	3	4
47	9	4	28 22	1	2
48	3.2	6	28 24	22.9	0
49	4	8	28 25	7	22.8
50	7	4.1	28 26	5	5
51	4.0	3	28 27	3	2
52	3	5	28 28	1	21.9
53	6	7	28 29	21.9	6
54	9	5.0	28 31	7	3
55	5.2	3	28 32	4	0
56	6	6	28 33	1	20.7

5 55 38 (H. M. S.) — 88° 54′.6 — ♊ 29°

H.	11	12	1	2	3
° Lat.	♋	♌	♍	♎	♏
	°	°	° ′	°	°
22	29.6	29.9	28 59	28.0	28.4
23	7	♍	29 0	27.8	2
24	9	2	29 0	7	1
25	♌	4	29 1	6	0
26	0.2	5	29 1	4	27.8
27	3	7	29 1	27.3	7
28	4	8	29 2	1	5
29	0.6	1.0	29 2	0	4
30	7	1	29 3	26.8	2
31	9	3	29 3	7	1
32	1.1	5	29 4	5	26.9
33	2	7	29 4	3	8
34	4	8	29 5	2	6
35	6	2.0	29 5	0	4
36	7	2	29 6	25.9	3
37	9	3	29 6	8	1
38	2.1	5	29 7	6	25.9
39	3	7	29 7	5	7
40	5	9	29 8	25.3	6
41	7	3.1	29 8	1	4
42	9	3	29 9	0	2
43	3.1	5	29 9	24.8	24.9
44	3	7	29 10	6	7
45	6	9	29 10	4	5
46	8	4.1	29 11	2	3
47	4.0	3	29 11	23.9	1
48	2	5	29 12	7	23.9
49	5	7	29 12	5	7
50	7	9	29 13	3	4
51	5.0	5.1	29 13	1	2
52	3	3	29 14	22.9	22.9
53	6	5	29 15	7	6
54	9	8	29 15	5	3
55	6.2	6.1	29 16	2	0
56	5	3	29 16	0	21.7

6 0 0 (H. M. S.) — 90° 0′.0 — ♋ 0°

H.	11	12	1	2	3
° Lat.	♌	♍	♎	♎	♏
	°	°	° ′	°	°
22	0.6	1.0	0 0	29.0	29.4
23	7	1	0 0	28.9	3
24	9	3	0 0	7	1
25	1.0	4	0 0	6	0
26	2	1.6	0 0	4	28.8
27	3	7	0 0	28.3	7
28	4	9	0 0	1	6
29	1.6	2.0	0 0	0	4
30	8	2	0 0	27.8	2
31	9	4	0 0	6	1
32	2.1	5	0 0	5	27.9
33	2	7	0 0	3	8
34	4	9	0 0	1	6
35	5	3.0	0 0	0	5
36	7	2	0 0	26.8	3
37	9	4	0 0	6	1
38	3.1	5	0 0	5	26.9
39	3	7	0 0	3	7
40	5	8	0 0	2	5
41	7	4.0	0 0	0	3
42	9	2	0 0	25.8	1
43	4.1	4	0 0	6	25.9
44	3	5	0 0	5	7
45	5	7	0 0	3	5
46	7	9	0 0	1	3
47	9	5.1	0 0	24.9	1
48	5.1	3	0 0	7	24.9
49	3	6	0 0	4	7
50	6	8	0 0	2	4
51	9	6.0	0 0	0	1
52	6.2	2	0 0	23.8	23.8
53	5	4	0 0	6	5
54	8	7	0 0	3	2
55	7.1	7.0	0 0	0	22.9
56	4	2	0 0	22.8	6

6 4 22 (H. M. S.) — 91° 5′.4 — ♋ 1°

H.	11	12	1	2	3
° Lat.	♌	♍	♎	♏	♐
	°	°	° ′	°	°
22	1.6	2.0	1 1	0.1	0.4
23	8	2	1 0	0	3
24	9	3	1 0	♎ 29.8	1
25	2.0	4	0 59	6	0
26	2	2.6	0 59	5	♏ 29.8
27	3	7	0 59	3	7
28	5	9	0 58	2	6
29	2.6	3.0	0 58	0	4
30	8	2	0 57	28.9	3
31	9	3	0 57	7	1
32	3.1	5	0 56	5	28.9
33	2	7	0 56	3	8
34	4	8	0 55	2	6
35	6	4.0	0 55	0	4
36	7	1	0 54	27.8	3
37	9	2	0 54	7	1
38	4.1	4	0 53	5	27.9
39	3	4.5	0 53	3	7
40	4	7	0 52	1	5
41	6	9	0 52	26.9	3
42	8	5.0	0 51	7	1
43	5.1	2	0 51	5	26.9
44	3	4	0 50	3	7
45	5	6	0 50	1	4
46	7	8	0 49	25.9	2
47	9	6.1	0 49	7	0
48	6.1	3	0 48	5	25.8
49	3	5	0 48	3	5
50	6	7	0 47	1	3
51	8	9	0 47	24.9	0
52	7.1	7.1	0 46	7	24.7
53	4	3	0 45	5	4
54	7	5	0 45	2	1
55	8.0	8	0 44	23.9	23.8
56	3	8.0	0 44	7	5

6 8 43 (H. M. S.) — 92° 10′.8 — ♋ 2°

H.	11	12	1	2	3
° Lat.	♌	♍	♎	♏	♐
	°	°	° ′	°	°
22	2.7	3.1	2 2	1.1	1.4
23	8	2	2 1	0	3
24	9	4	2 0	0.8	1
25	3.1	5	1 59	6	0
26	2	3.6	1 58	5	0.8
27	3	8	1 57	3	7
28	5	9	1 56	2	5
29	3.6	4.1	1 55	0	4
30	8	2	1 54	♎ 29.8	2
31	9	3	1 53	7	1
32	4.1	5	1 52	5	♏ 29.9
33	2	4.6	1 51	3	8
34	4	8	1 50	2	6
35	6	9	1 49	0	4
36	7	5.1	1 49	28.8	2
37	9	3	1 48	6	1
38	5.1	4	1 47	5	28.9
39	3	6	1 46	3	7
40	4	8	1 45	1	5
41	6	9	1 44	27.9	3
42	8	6.1	1 43	7	1
43	6.0	3	1 42	5	27.9
44	2	4	1 41	3	7
45	4	6	1 40	1	5
46	6	7	1 39	26.9	3
47	8	9	1 38	6	1
48	7.0	7.1	1 36	4	26.8
49	2	3	1 35	2	6
50	5	5	1 34	25.9	3
51	8	7	1 33	7	0
52	8.1	9	1 32	5	25.7
53	4	8.1	1 31	3	4
54	7	3	1 29	0	1
55	9.0	6	1 28	24.7	24.8
56	3	9	1 27	4	4

6 13 5 (H. M. S.) — 93° 16′.2 — ♋ 3°

H.	11	12	1	2	3
° Lat.	♌	♍	♎	♏	♐
	°	°	° ′	°	°
22	3.7	4.1	3 2	2.2	2.4
23	8	2	3 1	0	3
24	4.0	4	2 59	1.8	1
25	1	5	2 58	7	0
26	2	4.6	2 57	5	1.8
27	4	8	2 55	3	7
28	4.5	9	2 54	2	5
29	6	5.1	2 53	0	4
30	8	2	2 51	0.8	2
31	9	3	2 50	7	1
32	5.1	5	2 48	5	0.9
33	2	5.6	2 47	3	8
34	4	7	2 46	1	6
35	5	9	2 44	♎ 29.9	4
36	7	6.0	2 43	7	2
37	9	1	2 41	6	1
38	6.1	2	2 40	4	♏ 29.9
39	2	4	2 38	2	7
40	4	6.6	2 37	0	5
41	6	7	2 35	28.8	3
42	8	9	2 34	6	1
43	7.0	7.1	2 32	3	28.8
44	2	2	2 31	1	6
45	4	4	2 29	27.9	4
46	6	6	2 28	7	2
47	8	8	2 26	5	0
48	8.0	8.0	2 25	3	27.8
49	2	2	2 23	1	5
50	5	4	2 21	26.8	2
51	7	6	2 20	5	26.9
52	9.0	8	2 18	3	6
53	3	9.0	2 16	1	3
54	6	2	2 14	25.8	0
55	9	4	2 12	5	25.7
56	10.2	6	2 10	2	3

SID. T. 6 h 17 m 26 s, ARC 94° 21′.5 — ♋ 4°

H.	11	12	1	2	3
Lat.	♌	♍	♎	♏	♐
°	°	°	° ′	°	°
22	4.7	5.2	4 3	3.2	3.4
23	8	3	4 1	0	3
24	5.0	4	3 59	2.8	1
25	1	5	3 57	7	0
26	2	5.7	3 56	5	2.8
27	4	8	3 54	3	7
28	5.5	9	3 52	1	5
29	6	6.1	3 50	0	4
30	8	2	3 48	1.8	2
31	9	3	3 46	6	1
32	6.1	5	3 44	4	1.9
33	2	6.6	3 43	3	7
34	4	8	3 41	1	6
35	5	9	3 39	0.9	4
36	7	7.0	3 37	7	2
37	9	2	3 35	5	0
38	7.0	3	3 33	3	0.8
39	2	5	3 31	1	7
40	4	6	3 29	♎ 29.9	5
41	6	8	3 27	7	2
42	8	8.0	3 25	5	0
43	8.0	1	3 23	2	♏ 29.8
44	2	3	3 21	0	6
45	4	5	3 19	28.8	4
46	6	8.6	3 17	6	2
47	8	7	3 15	4	0
48	9.0	9	3 13	2	28.8
49	2	9.1	3 10	27.9	5
50	4	3	3 8	7	2
51	7	5	3 6	4	27.9
52	9	7	3 4	2	6
53	10.2	9	3 1	0	3
54	5	10.1	2 59	26.7	0
55	8	3	2 56	4	26.6
56	11.1	5	2 54	1	2

6 h 21 m 47 s, 95° 26′.9 — ♋ 5°

H.	11	12	1	2	3
Lat.	♌	♍	♎	♏	♐
°	°	°	° ′	°	°
22	5.7	6.2	5 3	4.2	4.4
23	9	3	5 1	0	3
24	6.0	4	4 59	3.9	1
25	1	5	4 57	7	0
26	2	6.7	4 54	5	3.8
27	4	8	4 52	3	7
28	6.5	9	4 50	1	5
29	7	7.1	4 47	0	4
30	8	2	4 45	2.8	2
31	9	3	4 43	6	1
32	7.1	5	4 40	4	2.9
33	2	7.6	4 38	2	7
34	4	7	4 36	0	6
35	5	9	4 33	1.9	4
36	7	8.0	4 31	7	2
37	9	1	4 29	5	0
38	8.0	3	4 26	3	1.8
39	2	4	4 24	1	6
40	4	8.6	4 21	0.9	4
41	6	7	4 19	7	2
42	8	9	4 16	5	0
43	9.0	9.0	4 14	3	0.8
44	2	2	4 11	1	5
45	4	4	4 9	♎ 29.9	3
46	6	5	4 6	6	1
47	8	7	4 3	4	♏ 29.9
48	10.0	9	4 1	1	7
49	2	10.1	3 58	28.9	4
50	4	2	3 55	6	1
51	6	3	3 52	4	28.8
52	9	5	3 49	1	5
53	11.2	7	3 46	27.8	2
54	5	9	3 43	5	27.9
55	8	11.1	3 40	2	5
56	12.1	3	3 37	26.9	1

6 h 26 m 9 s, 96° 32′.2 — ♋ 6°

H.	11	12	1	2	3
Lat.	♌	♍	♎	♏	♐
°	°	°	° ′	°	°
22	6.8	7.2	6 4	5.2	5.4
23	9	4	6 1	0	3
24	7.0	5	5 58	4.8	2
25	1	6	5 56	7	0
26	3	7	5 53	5	4.9
27	4	8	5 50	3	7
28	7.5	8.0	5 47	1	6
29	7	1	5 45	3.9	4
30	8	2	5 42	8	2
31	9	3	5 39	6	1
32	8.1	8.4	5 36	4	3.9
33	2	6	5 33	2	7
34	4	7	5 31	0	6
35	5	8	5 28	2.8	4
36	7	9.0	5 25	6	2
37	9	1	5 22	4	0
38	9.0	2	5 19	2	2.8
39	2	3	5 16	0	6
40	4	9.4	5 13	1.8	4
41	6	5	5 10	5	2
42	8	7	5 7	3	0
43	10.0	8	5 4	1	1.8
44	2	10.0	5 1	0.8	6
45	4	2	4 58	6	4
46	5	3	4 55	4	2
47	7	5	4 52	2	0
48	9	7	4 49	♎ 29.9	0.7
49	11.1	8	4 45	7	4
50	4	11.0	4 42	4	1
51	6	2	4 39	1	♏ 29.8
52	8	4	4 35	28.9	5
53	12.1	6	4 31	6	2
54	4	8	4 28	3	28.9
55	7	12.0	4 24	0	5
56	13.0	2	4 20	27.7	1

6 h 30 m 30 s, 97° 37′.4 — ♋ 7°

H.	11	12	1	2	3
Lat.	♌	♍	♎	♏	♐
°	°	°	° ′	°	°
22	7.8	8.3	7 4	6.2	6.4
23	9	4	7 1	0	3
24	8.0	5	6 58	5.9	1
25	2	6	6 55	7	0
26	3	7	6 51	5	5.8
27	4	8	6 48	3	7
28	8.5	9.0	6 45	1	5
29	7	1	6 42	4.9	4
30	8	2	6 39	8	2
31	9.0	3	6 35	6	1
32	1	4	6 32	4	4.9
33	2	9.6	6 29	2	7
34	4	7	6 26	0	6
35	9.5	8	6 22	3.8	4
36	7	9	6 19	6	2
37	9	10.1	6 16	3	0
38	10.0	2	6 12	1	3.8
39	2	3	6 9	2.9	6
40	4	5	6 6	7	4
41	6	10.6	6 2	5	2
42	7	7	5 59	3	2.9
43	9	9	5 55	1	7
44	11.1	11.0	5 51	1.8	5
45	3	2	5 48	6	2
46	5	3	5 44	3	0
47	7	5	5 40	1	1.8
48	9	11.7	5 37	0.9	6
49	12.1	8	5 33	6	3
50	3	9	5 29	3	0
51	5	12.0	5 25	1	0.7
52	7	2	5 21	♎ 29.8	4
53	13.0	4	5 17	5	1
54	3	6	5 12	2	♏ 29.8
55	6	8	5 8	28.9	4
56	9	13.0	5 3	6	0

6 h 34 m 50 s, 98° 42′.6 — ♋ 8°

H.	11	12	1	2	3
Lat.	♌	♍	♎	♏	♐
°	°	°	° ′	°	°
22	8.8	9.2	8 5	7.2	7.4
23	9	3	8 1	1	3
24	9.1	4	7 58	6.9	1
25	2	5	7 54	7	0
26	3	9.7	7 50	5	6.8
27	4	8	7 47	3	7
28	9.6	9	7 43	1	5
29	7	10.0	7 39	5.9	4
30	8	1	7 35	7	2
31	10.0	3	7 32	5	1
32	1	4	7 28	3	5.9
33	2	10.5	7 24	1	7
34	4	6	7 21	4.9	5
35	10.5	7	7 17	7	4
36	7	9	7 13	5	2
37	9	11.0	7 9	3	0
38	11.0	1	7 5	1	4.8
39	2	2	7 1	3.9	6
40	4	3	6 58	7	4
41	5	11.4	6 54	5	2
42	7	5	6 50	2	3.9
43	9	7	6 46	0	7
44	12.1	8	6 41	2.7	4
45	2	12.0	6 37	5	2
46	4	2	6 33	3	0
47	6	4	6 29	0	2.8
48	9	5	6 25	1.8	6
49	13.1	7	6 20	5	3
50	3	8	6 16	2	0
51	5	13.0	6 11	0.9	1.7
52	7	1	6 6	6	4
53	9	2	6 2	3	1
54	14.2	4	5 57	0	0.7
55	5	6	5 52	♎ 29.7	3
56	8	8	5 47	3	♏ 29.9

6 h 39 m 11 s, 99° 47′.7 — ♋ 9°

H.	11	12	1	2	3
Lat.	♌	♍	♎	♏	♐
°	°	°	° ′	°	°
22	9.8	10.2	9 5	8.2	8.4
23	10.0	4	9 1	0	3
24	1	5	8 57	7.8	1
25	2	6	8 53	7	0
26	3	10.7	8 48	5	7.8
27	10.4	8	8 44	3	7
28	6	9	8 40	1	5
29	7	11.0	8 36	6.9	4
30	8	1	8 32	7	2
31	11.0	3	8 28	5	0
32	1	4	8 24	3	6.9
33	2	11.5	8 20	1	7
34	4	6	8 15	5.9	5
35	11.5	7	8 11	7	3
36	7	8	8 7	5	2
37	9	12.0	8 3	3	0
38	12.0	1	7 58	1	5.8
39	2	2	7 54	4.9	6
40	3	3	7 50	6	4
41	5	12.4	7 45	4	1
42	7	6	7 41	1	4.9
43	9	7	7 36	3.9	7
44	13.1	8	7 31	6	4
45	2	13.0	7 27	4	1
46	4	1	7 22	1	3.9
47	6	3	7 17	2.8	7
48	8	4	7 12	5	5
49	14.0	13.6	7 7	3	2
50	2	7	7 2	0	2.9
51	4	8	6 57	1.7	6
52	6	9	6 52	4	3
53	9	14.1	6 47	1	0
54	15.2	3	6 41	0.8	1.6
55	5	5	6 36	5	2
56	8	7	6 30	1	0.8

SID. T. / ARC	H. M. S. 6 39 11 — 99° 47′.7 ♋ 9°					H. M. S. 6 43 31 — 100° 52′.8 ♋ 10°					H. M. S. 6 47 51 — 101° 57′.8 ♋ 11°					H. M. S. 6 52 11 — 103° 2′.7 ♋ 12°					H. M. S. 6 56 30 — 104° 7′.5 ♋ 13°					H. M. S. 7 0 49 — 105° 12′.3 ♋ 14°				
H.	11	12	1	2	3	11	12	1	2	3	11	12	1	2	3	11	12	1	2	3	11	12	1	2	3	11	12	1	2	3
Lat.	♌	♍	♎	♏	♐	♌	♍	♎	♏	♐	♌	♍	♎	♏	♐	♌	♍	♎	♏	♐	♌	♍	♎	♏	♐	♌	♍	♎	♏	♐
°	°	°	° ′	°	°	°	°	° ′	°	°	°	°	° ′	°	°	°	°	° ′	°	°	°	°	° ′	°	°	°	°	° ′	°	°
22	9.8	10.2	9 5	8.2	8.4	10.9	11.3	10 5	9.2	9.4	11.9	12.3	11 5	10.2	10.4	12.9	13.4	12 5	11.2	11.4	14.0	14.4	13 5	12.2	12.4	15.0	15.5	14 4	13.2	13.4
23	10.0	4	9 1	0	3	11.0	4	10 0	0	3	12.0	4	11 0	0	3	13.0	5	11 59	0	3	1	5	12 59	0	3	1	6	13 58	0	2
24	1	5	8 57	7.8	1	1	5	9 56	8.9	1	1	5	10 55	9.8	1	2	6	11 54	10.8	1	2	6	12 53	11.8	1	2	7	13 52	12.8	1
25	2	6	8 53	7	0	2	6	9 51	7	0	3	6	10 50	6	0	3	7	11 49	6	0	3	7	12 47	6	0	3	8	13 46	6	12.9
26	3	10.7	8 48	5	7.8	4	11.7	9 47	5	8.8	4	7	10 45	4	9.8	4	8	11 43	4	10.8	4	8	12 41	4	11.8	5	9	13 39	4	8
27	10.4	8	8 44	3	7	11.5	8	9 42	3	7	12.5	9	10 40	2	7	13.5	9	11 38	2	7	14.5	9	12 36	2	6	15.6	9	13 33	2	6
28	6	9	8 40	1	5	6	9	9 38	1	5	6	13.0	10 35	0	5	6	14.0	11 33	0	5	7	15.0	12 30	0	5	7	16.0	13 27	0	5
29	7	11.0	8 36	6.9	4	7	12.0	9 33	7.9	4	7	1	10 30	8.8	3	8	1	11 27	9.8	3	8	1	12 24	10.8	3	8	1	13 21	11.8	12.3
30	8	1	8 32	7	2	9	2	9 29	7	2	9	2	10 25	6	2	9	2	11 22	6	2	9	2	12 18	6	2	9	2	13 14	5	1
31	11.0	3	8 28	5	0	12.0	3	9 24	5	0	13.0	3	10 20	4	0	14.0	3	11 16	4	0	15.0	3	12 12	4	0	16.0	3	13 8	3	0
32	1	4	8 24	3	6.9	1	4	9 19	2	7.9	1	4	10 15	2	8.8	1	14.4	11 11	2	9.8	2	15.4	12 6	1	10.8	2	16.4	13 1	1	11.8
33	2	11.5	8 20	1	7	3	5	9 15	0	7	3	13.5	10 10	0	7	3	5	11 5	0	7	3	5	12 0	9.9	6	3	5	12 55	10.9	6
34	4	6	8 15	5.9	5	4	12.6	9 10	6.8	5	4	6	10 5	7.8	5	4	6	11 0	8.7	5	4	6	11 54	7	5	4	5	12 49	6	4
35	11.5	7	8 11	7	3	12.6	7	9 5	6	3	13.6	7	10 0	6	3	14.6	7	10 54	5	3	15.6	7	11 48	5	3	16.6	6	12 42	4	2
36	7	8	8 7	5	2	7	8	9 1	5	1	7	8	9 55	4	1	7	14.7	10 48	3	1	7	15.7	11 42	3	1	7	16.7	12 35	2	1
37	9	12.0	8 3	3	0	9	9	8 56	3	6.9	9	9	9 49	2	7.9	9	8	10 43	1	8.9	9	8	11 36	1	9.9	8	7	12 29	0	10.9
38	12.0	1	7 58	1	5.8	13.0	13.0	8 51	0	7	14.0	14.0	9 44	0	7	15.0	9	10 37	7.9	7	16.0	9	11 30	8.8	7	17.0	8	12 22	9.7	6
39	2	2	7 54	4.9	6	2	1	8 46	5.8	5	2	1	9 39	6.7	5	2	15.0	10 31	6	5	1	16.0	11 23	6	4	1	9	12 15	5	4
40	3	3	7 50	6	4	3	2	8 41	5	3	3	2	9 33	5	3	3	1	10 25	4	3	3	1	11 17	3	2	3	17.0	12 8	2	2
41	5	12.4	7 45	4	1	5	3	8 37	3	1	5	3	9 28	2	1	5	2	10 19	1	0	5	2	11 10	0	0	5	1	12 2	8.9	0
42	7	6	7 41	1	4.9	7	13.4	8 32	0	5.9	7	4	9 22	0	6.8	7	3	10 13	6.9	7.8	6	3	11 4	7.8	8.8	6	1	11 55	7	9.7
43	9	7	7 36	3.9	7	9	5	8 26	4.8	6	9	14.6	9 17	5.7	6	8	15.4	10 7	6	5	8	4	10 57	5	5	8	2	11 47	4	5
44	13.1	8	7 31	6	4	14.1	7	8 21	5	4	15.0	7	9 11	4	3	16.0	5	10 1	3	3	17.0	16.5	10 51	2	2	18.0	3	11 40	1	2
45	2	13.0	7 27	4	1	2	8	8 16	3	1	1	8	9 5	1	1	1	6	9 55	0	0	1	6	10 44	6.9	0	1	17.4	11 33	7.8	8.9
46	4	1	7 22	1	3.9	4	9	8 11	0	4.9	3	9	9 0	4.9	5.9	3	8	9 48	5.8	6.8	3	7	10 37	7	7.7	2	5	11 26	6	7
47	6	3	7 17	2.8	7	6	14.1	8 5	3.8	7	5	15.0	8 54	7	7	5	16.0	9 42	6	6	5	8	10 30	4	5	4	7	11 18	3	5
48	8	4	7 12	5	5	8	2	8 0	5	4	8	1	8 48	4	4	7	1	9 35	3	3	7	9	10 23	1	3	6	8	11 10	0	2
49	14.0	13.6	7 7	3	2	15.0	3	7 55	2	1	16.0	2	8 42	1	1	9	2	9 29	4.9	0	9	17.0	10 16	5.8	0	8	9	11 3	6.7	7.9
50	2	7	7 2	0	2.9	2	14.5	7 49	2.9	3.8	2	4	8 36	3.8	4.8	17.1	3	9 22	6	5.7	18.1	1	10 9	5	6.7	19.1	18.0	10 55	3	6
51	4	8	6 57	1.7	6	4	6	7 43	6	5	4	15.5	8 29	5	5	3	16.5	9 15	3	4	3	2	10 1	1	4	3	1	10 47	0	3
52	6	9	6 52	4	3	6	8	7 37	3	2	6	7	8 23	2	2	5	6	9 8	0	1	5	4	9 54	4.8	1	5	2	10 39	5.7	0
53	9	14.1	6 47	1	0	8	15.0	7 31	0	2.9	8	8	8 16	2.9	3.9	7	7	9 1	3.7	4.8	7	17.5	9 46	5	5.7	7	18.4	10 31	4	6.6
54	15.2	3	6 41	0.8	1.6	16.1	1	7 25	1.7	5	17.1	16.0	8 10	5	5	18.0	8	8 54	3	4	9	7	9 38	2	3	9	5	10 22	0	2
55	5	5	6 36	5	2	4	3	7 19	3	1	4	1	8 3	1	1	3	17.0	8 47	2.9	0	19.2	8	9 30	3.8	4.9	20.2	6	10 14	4.6	5.8
56	8	7	6 30	1	0.8	7	5	7 13	0.9	1.7	7	3	7 56	1.7	2.7	6	1	8 39	5	3.6	5	9	9 22	4	5	4	8	10 5	2	4

SID. T. H. M. S. 7 5 8 ARC 106° 16′.9 ♋ 15°						7 9 26 107° 21′.5 ♋ 16°					7 13 44 108° 25′.9 ♋ 17°					7 18 1 109° 30′.2 ♋ 18°					7 22 18 110° 34′.4 ♋ 19°					7 26 34 111° 38′.4 ♋ 20°				
H.	11	12	1	2	3	11	12	1	2	3	11	12	1	2	3	11	12	1	2	3	11	12	1	2	3	11	12	1	2	3
Lat. °	♌ °	♍ °	♎ ° ′	♏ °	♐ °	♌ °	♍ °	♎ ° ′	♏ °	♐ °	♌ °	♍ °	♎ ° ′	♏ °	♐ °	♌ °	♍ °	♎ ° ′	♏ °	♐ °	♌ °	♍ °	♎ ° ′	♏ °	♐ °	♌ °	♍ °	♎ ° ′	♏ °	♐ °
22	16.1	16.6	15 4	14.2	14.4	17.1	17.6	16 3	15.2	15.4	18.1	18.7	17 3	16.2	16.3	19.1	19.8	18 2	17.2	17.3	20.2	20.8	19 1	18.2	18.3	21.2	21.9	20 0	19.1	19.3
23	2	6	14 57	0	2	2	7	15 56	0	2	2	8	16 55	0	2	2	8	17 54	0	2	3	9	18 52	17.9	1	3	9	19 51	18.9	1
24	3	7	14 51	13.8	1	3	8	15 49	14.8	1	3	9	16 48	15.8	0	3	9	17 46	16.7	0	4	9	18 44	7	0	4	22.0	19 42	7	0
25	4	8	14 44	6	13.9	4	9	15 42	6	14.9	4	9	16 40	5	15.9	4	20.0	17 38	5	16.9	5	21.0	18 36	5	17.8	5	0	19 33	4	18.8
26	5	9	14 37	4	8	17.5	9	15 35	3	7	18.5	19.0	16 33	3	7	19.5	0	17 30	3	7	20.6	1	18 27	3	7	21.6	1	19 24	2	6
27	16.6	17.0	14 31	2	6	6	18.0	15 28	1	6	6	1	16 25	1	6	7	1	17 22	1	5	7	1	18 19	0	5	7	1	19 16	0	5
28	7	1	14 24	12.9	4	7	1	15 21	13.9	4	8	1	16 18	14.9	4	8	2	17 14	15.8	4	8	2	18 10	16.8	3	8	2	19 7	17.7	3
29	8	1	14 17	7	3	8	2	15 14	7	3	9	2	16 10	6	2	9	2	17 6	6	2	9	2	18 2	6	2	9	22.2	18 58	5	1
30	9	2	14 10	5	1	18.0	2	15 6	5	1	19.0	3	16 2	4	1	20.0	20.3	16 58	4	0	21.0	21.3	17 53	3	0	22.0	3	18 49	3	0
31	17.1	3	14 4	3	12.9	1	3	14 59	2	13.9	1	19.3	15 54	2	14.9	1	3	16 50	1	15.9	1	3	17 45	1	16.8	1	3	18 40	0	17.8
32	2	17.4	13 57	0	8	2	18.4	14 52	0	8	2	4	15 47	13.9	7	2	4	16 42	14.9	7	2	4	17 36	15.8	7	3	4	18 31	16.8	6
33	3	5	13 50	11.8	6	3	5	14 44	12.8	6	3	5	15 39	7	5	3	5	16 33	6	5	4	4	17 27	6	5	4	4	18 22	5	4
34	4	5	13 43	6	4	18.4	5	14 37	5	4	19.5	5	15 31	5	4	20.5	20.5	16 25	4	3	21.5	5	17 19	3	3	22.5	22.5	18 12	2	2
35	17.6	6	13 36	3	2	6	6	14 30	3	2	6	6	15 23	2	2	6	6	16 17	1	1	6	21.5	17 10	1	1	6	5	18 3	0	0
36	7	17.7	13 29	1	0	7	18.7	14 22	1	0	7	19.6	15 15	12.9	0	7	6	16 8	13.9	14.9	7	6	17 1	14.8	15.9	7	6	17 54	15.7	16.8
37	8	8	13 22	10.9	11.8	9	8	14 15	11.9	12.8	9	7	15 7	7	13.8	9	7	16 0	6	7	9	7	16 52	5	7	9	6	17 44	5	6
38	18.0	9	13 15	7	6	19.0	8	14 7	6	6	20.0	8	14 59	5	5	21.0	20.8	15 51	4	5	22.0	7	16 43	3	5	23.0	22.7	17 35	3	4
39	1	9	13 7	4	4	1	9	13 59	3	4	1	9	14 51	2	3	1	8	15 43	1	3	1	21.8	16 34	1	2	1	7	17 25	0	2
40	3	18.0	13 0	1	2	3	19.0	13 51	0	1	3	9	14 43	11.9	1	3	9	15 34	12.9	1	3	8	16 25	13.8	0	3	7	17 16	14.7	0
41	5	1	12 53	9.8	10.9	4	1	13 43	10.8	11.9	4	20.0	14 34	7	12.9	4	9	15 25	6	13.8	4	9	16 16	5	14.8	4	8	17 6	4	15.7
42	6	2	12 45	6	7	19.6	1	13 35	5	6	20.6	1	14 26	4	6	21.6	21.0	15 16	3	6	22.6	9	16 6	2	5	23.6	22.8	16 56	0	5
43	8	3	12 37	3	4	8	2	13 27	2	4	7	1	14 17	1	3	7	1	15 7	0	3	7	22.0	15 57	12.9	3	7	8	16 46	13.7	2
44	19.0	18.4	12 30	0	2	9	19.3	13 19	9.9	1	9	2	14 9	10.8	1	9	2	14 58	11.6	0	9	1	15 47	5	0	9	9	16 36	4	0
45	1	5	12 22	8.7	9.9	20.1	4	13 11	6	10.9	21.1	3	14 0	5	11.8	22.1	2	14 49	3	12.8	23.1	1	15 37	2	13.7	24.0	9	16 26	1	14.7
46	2	6	12 14	4	6	2	5	13 2	3	6	2	20.4	13 51	1	5	2	3	14 39	0	5	2	2	15 27	11.9	4	2	23.0	16 15	12.7	4
47	4	6	12 6	1	4	4	6	12 54	0	4	4	4	13 42	9.8	3	3	21.3	14 30	10.7	2	4	2	15 17	6	2	3	0	16 5	4	1
48	6	18.7	11 58	7.8	1	6	19.7	12 45	8.7	1	5	5	13 33	5	0	5	4	14 20	4	0	6	22.3	15 7	3	12.9	4	1	15 54	1	13.8
49	8	8	11 50	5	8.8	8	8	12 36	4	9.8	7	5	13 23	2	10.7	7	4	14 10	1	11.7	8	3	14 57	10.9	6	24.6	1	15 43	11.8	5
50	20.0	9	11 41	2	5	21.0	8	12 28	0	5	9	20.6	13 14	8.9	4	9	5	14 0	9.7	4	9	4	14 46	6	3	8	2	15 32	4	2
51	2	19.0	11 33	6.8	2	2	9	12 19	7.7	2	22.1	7	13 4	5	1	23.1	6	13 50	4	1	24.0	4	14 35	2	11.9	9	23.3	15 21	0	12.9
52	4	1	11 24	5	7.9	4	20.0	12 9	4	8.9	3	8	12 54	2	9.8	3	21.7	13 39	0	10.7	2	22.5	14 24	9.8	6	25.1	3	15 9	10.6	5
53	6	2	11 15	2	6	6	1	12 0	0	5	5	9	12 44	7.8	4	5	7	13 29	8.6	3	4	6	14 13	4	3	3	4	14 57	2	1
54	8	3	11 6	5.8	2	8	2	11 50	6.6	1	7	21.0	12 34	4	0	7	8	13 18	2	9.9	6	6	14 2	0	10.9	5	4	14 45	9.8	11.7
55	21.1	4	10 57	4	6.8	22.0	3	11 40	2	7.7	23.0	1	12 24	0	8.6	9	9	13 7	7.8	5	8	7	13 50	8.6	4	7	5	14 33	4	3
56	3	5	10 48	0	3	2	4	11 30	5.8	2	2	2	12 13	6.6	1	24.1	22.0	12 56	4	0	25.0	7	13 38	2	9.9	9	6	14 20	0	10.9

H.	11	12	1	2	3	11	12	1	2	3
	SID. T. H. M. S. 7 26 34 ARC 111° 38′.4 ♋ 20°					H. M. S. 7 30 49 112° 42′.4 ♋ 21°				
Lat.	♌	♍	♎	♏	♐	♌	♍	♎	♏	♐
°	°	°	° ′	°	°	°	°	° ′	°	°
22	21.2	21.9	20 0	19.1	19.3	22.3	23.0	20 58	20.1	20.2
23	3	9	19 51	18.9	1	4	0	20 49	19.9	1
24	4	22.0	19 42	7	0	5	0	20 40	6	19.9
25	5	0	19 33	4	18.8	6	1	20 31	4	8
26	21.6	1	19 24	2	6	22.7	1	20 21	2	6
27	7	1	19 16	0	5	8	23.2	20 12	18.9	5
28	8	2	19 7	17.7	3	9	2	20 3	7	3
29	9	22.2	18 58	5	1	23.0	2	19 53	5	1
30	22.0	3	18 49	3	0	1	3	19 44	2	18.9
31	1	3	18 40	0	17.8	2	3	19 35	0	8
32	3	4	18 31	16.8	6	3	23.4	19 25	17.7	6
33	4	4	18 22	5	4	4	4	19 16	5	4
34	22.5	22.5	18 12	2	2	23.5	4	19 6	2	2
35	6	5	18 3	0	0	6	5	18 56	16.9	0
36	7	6	17 54	15.7	16.8	7	5	18 47	7	17.8
37	9	6	17 44	5	6	9	23.6	18 37	5	6
38	23.0	22.7	17 35	3	4	24.0	6	18 27	2	4
39	1	7	17 25	0	2	1	7	18 17	15.9	2
40	3	7	17 16	14.7	0	3	7	18 7	6	16.9
41	4	8	17 6	4	15.7	4	7	17 56	2	7
42	23.6	22.8	16 56	0	5	24.5	23.8	17 46	14.9	4
43	7	8	16 46	13.7	2	7	8	17 36	6	2
44	9	9	16 36	4	0	8	9	17 25	3	15.9
45	24.0	9	16 26	1	14.7	25.0	9	17 14	13.9	6
46	2	23.0	16 15	12.7	4	1	24.0	17 3	6	4
47	3	0	16 5	4	1	2	0	16 52	3	1
48	4	1	15 54	1	13.8	4	0	16 41	0	14.8
49	24.6	1	15 43	11.8	5	25.6	1	16 29	12.6	5
50	8	2	15 32	4	2	8	1	16 18	2	1
51	9	23.3	15 21	0	12.9	9	24.1	16 6	11.8	13.8
52	25.1	3	15 9	10.6	5	26.1	2	15 54	4	5
53	3	4	14 57	2	1	3	3	15 41	0	1
54	5	4	14 45	9.8	11.7	5	3	15 29	10.6	12.7
55	7	5	14 33	4	3	7	4	15 16	2	3
56	9	6	14 20	0	10.9	9	5	15 3	9.8	11.8

H.	11	12	1	2	3	11	12	1	2	3
	H. M. S. 7 35 5 113° 46′.2 ♋ 22°					H. M. S. 7 39 19 114° 49′.8 ♋ 23°				
Lat.	♌	♍	♎	♏	♐	♌	♍	♎	♏	♐
°	°	°	° ′	°	°	°	°	° ′	°	°
22	23.3	24.0	21 57	21.1	21.2	24.4	25.0	22 55	22.1	22.2
23	4	0	21 47	20.8	1	5	1	22 45	21.8	0
24	5	1	21 38	6	20.9	5	1	22 35	6	21.9
25	6	1	21 28	4	7	6	1	22 25	3	7
26	23.7	1	21 18	1	6	24.7	2	22 15	1	6
27	8	24.2	21 9	19.9	4	8	25.2	22 5	20.8	4
28	9	2	20 59	6	2	9	2	21 54	6	2
29	24.0	2	20 49	4	1	25.0	2	21 44	3	0
30	1	3	20 39	2	19.9	1	3	21 34	1	20.9
31	2	3	20 29	18.9	7	2	3	21 24	19.8	7
32	3	24.3	20 19	7	5	3	25.3	21 13	6	5
33	4	4	20 9	4	4	4	4	21 3	3	3
34	24.5	4	19 59	1	2	25.5	4	20 52	0	1
35	6	4	19 49	17.8	0	6	4	20 42	18.8	19.9
36	7	5	19 39	6	18.8	8	4	20 31	5	7
37	9	24.5	19 28	3	6	9	25.4	20 21	2	5
38	25.0	6	19 18	0	3	26.0	4	20 10	17.9	3
39	1	6	19 8	16.7	1	1	5	19 59	6	1
40	3	6	18 57	4	17.9	2	5	19 48	3	18.9
41	4	7	18 47	0	6	4	5	19 37	16.9	6
42	25.5	24.7	18 36	15.7	4	26.5	25.5	19 25	6	3
43	7	7	18 25	4	1	7	5	19 14	3	1
44	8	8	18 14	1	16.9	8	6	19 2	0	17.8
45	26.0	8	18 2	14.8	6	27.0	6	18 50	15.7	5
46	1	8	17 51	5	3	1	25.6	18 38	3	2
47	2	24.9	17 39	1	0	2	7	18 26	0	0
48	4	9	17 28	13.8	15.7	3	7	18 14	14.7	16.7
49	26.5	9	17 16	5	4	27.5	7	18 2	3	3
50	7	9	17 3	1	1	7	25.8	17 49	13.9	0
51	8	25.0	16 51	12.7	14.8	8	8	17 36	5	15.7
52	27.0	0	16 38	3	4	9	9	17 23	1	3
53	2	1	16 25	11.9	1	28.1	9	17 9	12.7	14.9
54	4	1	16 12	5	13.7	3	26.0	16 55	3	5
55	6	2	15 59	0	2	5	0	16 41	11.8	1
56	8	3	15 45	10.6	12.7	7	1	16 27	3	13.6

H.	11	12	1	2	3	11	12	1	2	3
	H. M. S. 7 43 33 115° 53′.3 ♋ 24°					H. M. S. 7 47 47 116° 56′.7 ♋ 25°				
Lat.	♌	♍	♎	♏	♐	♌	♍	♎	♏	♐
°	°	°	° ′	°	°	°	°	° ′	°	°
22	25.4	26.1	23 53	23.0	23.2	26.4	27.1	24 51	24.0	24.1
23	5	1	23 43	22.8	0	5	1	24 40	23.7	0
24	6	1	23 32	5	22.8	6	1	24 29	5	23.8
25	7	1	23 22	3	7	7	2	24 18	2	6
26	25.8	2	23 11	0	5	8	2	24 7	0	5
27	9	26.2	23 1	21.8	3	9	27.2	23 56	22.7	3
28	9	2	22 50	5	2	27.0	2	23 45	5	1
29	26.0	2	22 39	3	0	1	2	23 34	2	0
30	1	3	22 29	0	21.8	2	3	23 23	0	22.8
31	2	3	22 18	20.8	6	3	3	23 12	21.7	6
32	3	26.3	22 7	5	5	4	27.3	23 1	4	4
33	4	3	21 56	2	3	27.5	3	22 50	2	2
34	26.5	4	21 46	0	1	6	3	22 38	20.9	0
35	6	4	21 35	19.7	20.9	7	3	22 27	6	21.8
36	8	4	21 23	4	7	8	3	22 15	3	6
37	9	26.4	21 12	1	5	9	27.3	22 4	0	4
38	27.0	4	21 1	18.8	3	28.0	4	21 52	19.7	2
39	1	5	20 50	5	0	1	4	21 41	4	0
40	2	5	20 38	2	19.8	2	4	21 29	1	20.8
41	4	5	20 27	17.8	6	4	4	21 17	18.7	5
42	27.5	26.5	20 15	5	3	28.5	27.4	21 4	4	2
43	6	6	20 3	2	0	6	4	20 52	0	0
44	8	6	19 51	16.9	18.8	8	4	20 39	17.7	19.7
45	9	6	19 39	6	5	9	4	20 26	4	4
46	28.0	6	19 26	2	2	29.0	5	20 13	1	1
47	1	26.7	19 14	15.8	17.9	1	27.5	20 0	16.7	18.8
48	3	7	19 1	5	6	3	5	19 47	4	5
49	5	7	18 48	2	3	4	5	19 33	0	2
50	28.6	7	18 34	14.8	16.9	29.6	5	19 19	15.6	17.9
51	7	7	18 21	4	6	7	5	19 5	2	6
52	9	26.8	18 7	0	2	9	27.6	18 51	14.8	2
53	29.1	8	17 53	13.6	15.8	♍	6	18 36	4	16.8
54	3	8	17 38	1	4	0.2	6	18 21	13.9	4
55	5	8	17 24	6	0	4	6	18 6	4	15.9
56	7	9	17 9	12.1	14.5	6	7	17 50	12.9	4

	SID. T. 7 51 59 (H. M. S.) ARC 117° 59′.9 ♋ 26°					7 56 12 (H. M. S.) 119° 2′.9 ♋ 27°					8 0 23 (H. M. S.) 120° 5′.8 ♋ 28°					8 4 34 (H. M. S.) 121° 8′.5 ♋ 29°					8 8 44 (H. M. S.) 122° 11′.1 ♌ 0°					8 12 54 (H. M. S.) 123° 13′.4 ♌ 1°				
H.	11	12	1	2	3	11	12	1	2	3	11	12	1	2	3	11	12	1	2	3	11	12	1	2	3	11	12	1	2	3
Lat.	♌	♍	♎	♏	♐	♌	♍	♎	♏	♐	♌	♎	♎	♏	♐	♍	♎	♎	♏	♐	♍	♎	♎	♏	♐	♍	♎	♏	♏	♐
°	°	°	° ′	°	°	°	°	° ′	°	°	°	°	° ′	°	°	°	°	° ′	°	°	°	°	° ′	°	°	°	°	° ′	°	°
22	27.5	28.2	25 49	25.0	25.1	28.5	29.2	26 46	25.9	26.1	29.6	0.2	27 43	26.9	27.0	0.6	1.2	28 40	27.9	28.0	1.7	2.2	29 37	28.8	28.9	2.7	3.2	0 33	29.7	29.9
23	6	2	25 37	24.7	24.9	6	2	26 34	7	25.9	7	2	27 31	7	26.8	7	2	28 27	6	27.8	7	2	29 24	5	8	8	2	0 20	5	7
24	7	2	25 26	5	8	7	2	26 22	4	7	7	2	27 19	4	7	8	2	28 15	3	6	8	2	29 11	3	6	9	2	0 7	2	6
25	7	2	25 14	2	6	8	2	26 10	2	6	8	2	27 7	1	5	9	2	28 3	1	5	9	2	28 58	0	4	9	2	♎ 29 54	28.9	4
26	8	2	25 3	0	4	9	2	25 59	24.9	4	9	2	26 55	25.9	4	9	2	27 50	26.8	3	2.0	2	28 45	27.7	3	3.0	3.2	29 41	7	2
27	9	28.2	24 52	23.7	3	9	29.2	25 47	7	2	♍	0.2	26 43	6	2	1.0	1.2	27 38	5	1	1	2.2	28 33	5	1	1	1	29 27	4	0
28	28.0	2	24 41	5	1	29.0	2	25 36	4	1	0.1	2	26 30	4	0	1	2	27 25	3	0	1	2	28 20	2	27.9	2	1	29 14	1	28.9
29	1	2	24 29	2	23.9	1	2	25 24	2	24.9	2	2	26 18	1	25.8	2	2	27 13	0	26.8	2	1	28 7	26.9	7	3	1	29 1	27.9	7
30	2	2	24 18	0	7	2	2	25 12	23.9	7	2	2	26 6	24.8	7	3	2	27 0	25.7	6	2.3	1	27 54	6	6	3.3	3.1	28 47	6	5
31	3	2	24 6	22.7	6	3	2	25 0	6	5	3	2	25 54	5	5	1.4	2	26 47	5	4	4	1	27 41	4	4	4	1	28 34	3	3
32	4	28.2	23 55	4	4	4	29.2	24 48	3	3	4	0.2	25 41	3	3	5	1.2	26 34	2	2	5	2.1	27 27	1	2	5	1	28 20	0	1
33	28.5	3	23 43	1	2	29.5	2	24 36	1	1	0.5	2	25 29	0	1	5	1	26 22	24.9	0	6	1	27 14	25.8	0	6	0	28 6	26.7	27.9
34	6	3	23 31	21.9	0	6	2	24 24	22.8	0	6	2	25 16	23.7	24.9	6	1	26 9	6	25.9	2.7	1	27 1	5	26.8	3.7	3.0	27 53	4	8
35	7	3	23 19	6	22.8	7	2	24 12	5	23.8	7	2	25 4	4	7	1.7	1	25 56	3	7	8	1	26 47	2	6	8	0	27 39	1	6
36	8	3	23 7	3	6	8	2	23 59	2	6	8	2	24 51	1	5	8	1	25 42	0	5	8	0	26 34	24.9	4	9	0	27 24	25.8	4
37	9	28.3	22 55	0	4	9	29.2	23 47	21.9	3	9	0.2	24 38	22.8	3	9	1.1	25 29	23.7	2	9	2.0	26 20	6	2	4.0	0	27 10	4	1
38	29.0	3	22 43	20.7	2	♍	2	23 34	6	1	1.0	2	24 25	5	1	2.0	1	25 16	4	0	3.0	0	26 6	3	0	0	2.9	26 56	1	26.9
39	1	3	22 31	3	21.9	0.1	2	23 22	3	22.9	1	2	24 12	2	23.8	1	1	25 2	1	24.8	1	0	25 52	0	25.7	1	9	26 42	24.8	7
40	2	3	22 19	0	7	2	2	23 9	20.9	7	2	2	23 58	21.8	6	2	1	24 48	22.7	6	2	0	25 38	23.6	5	2	9	26 27	4	5
41	4	3	22 6	19.7	5	3	2	22 56	6	4	3	2	23 45	5	4	3	1.1	24 34	4	3	3	0	25 23	2	3	4.3	9	26 12	1	2
42	29.5	28.3	21 53	3	2	5	29.2	22 42	2	1	5	0.2	23 31	1	1	5	0	24 20	0	0	4	1.9	25 9	22.9	0	4	8	25 57	23.7	25.9
43	6	3	21 40	0	20.9	0.6	2	22 29	19.9	21.9	1.6	1	23 17	20.8	22.8	2.6	0	24 6	21.6	23.8	3.5	9	24 54	5	24.7	6	2.8	25 42	3	7
44	7	3	21 27	18.6	7	7	2	22 16	5	6	7	1	23 3	4	5	7	0	23 51	3	5	6	9	24 39	1	4	7	8	25 26	0	4
45	9	4	21 14	3	4	8	2	22 2	2	3	8	1	22 49	0	3	8	1.0	23 37	20.9	2	7	9	24 24	21.7	2	4.7	8	25 11	22.6	1
46	♍	4	21 1	17.9	1	9	2	21 48	18.8	0	9	1	22 35	19.6	0	9	0	23 22	5	22.9	8	9	24 8	3	23.9	8	7	24 55	2	24.8
47	0.1	28.4	20 47	5	19.8	1.0	29.2	21 34	5	20.7	2.0	0.1	22 20	3	21.7	3.0	0	23 7	2	6	9	1.8	23 53	20.9	6	9	7	24 39	21.8	5
48	2	4	20 33	2	5	2	2	21 19	1	4	1	1	22 5	18.9	4	1	0	22 51	19.8	3	4.0	8	23 37	5	2	5.0	2.7	24 22	4	2
49	4	4	20 19	16.8	2	3	2	21 5	17.7	0	2	1	21 50	5	0	3	0.9	22 35	4	0	1	8	23 21	1	22.9	2	7	24 5	0	23.9
50	5	4	20 5	4	18.8	5	2	20 50	3	19.7	4	1	21 35	1	20.7	4	9	22 19	18.9	21.6	3	8	23 4	19.7	5	3	6	23 49	20.6	5
51	7	4	19 50	0	5	1.6	2	20 35	16.9	4	2.5	1	21 19	17.7	4	3.5	9	22 3	5	3	4	8	22 47	3	2	4	6	23 31	1	2
52	8	28.4	19 35	15.6	1	8	29.2	20 19	5	0	7	0.1	21 3	3	0	6	9	21 47	1	20.9	4.5	1.7	22 30	18.9	21.9	5.5	2.6	23 13	19.6	22.8
53	1.0	4	19 20	2	17.7	9	2	20 3	0	18.6	8	0	20 47	16.8	19.6	8	0.9	21 30	17.6	5	6	7	22 12	4	5	7	5	22 55	1	4
54	1	4	19 4	7	3	2.1	2	19 47	15.5	2	3.0	0	20 30	3	1	9	9	21 12	1	1	8	7	21 55	17.9	0	8	5	22 37	18.6	21.9
55	3	4	18 49	14.2	16.8	3	2	19 31	0	17.8	2	0	20 13	15.8	18.7	4.1	8	20 55	16.6	19.6	5.0	6	21 36	4	20.5	6.0	4	22 18	1	4
56	5	5	18 32	13.7	3	4	2	19 14	14.5	3	3	0	19 55	3	1	2	8	20 37	1	1	1	6	21 18	16.9	0	1	4	21 59	17.6	20.9

	♌ 1°					♌ 2°					♌ 3°					♌ 4°					♌ 5°					♌ 6°				
	SID. T. H. M. S. 8 12 54		ARC 123° 13′.4			H. M. S. 8 17 3		124° 15′.6			H. M. S. 8 21 11		125° 17′.7			H. M. S. 8 25 18		126° 19′.5			H. M. S. 8 29 25		127° 21′.2			H. M. S. 8 33 31		128° 22′.7		
H.	11	12	1	2	3	11	12	1	2	3	11	12	1	2	3	11	12	1	2	3	11	12	1	2	3	11	12	1	2	3
Lat.	♍	♎	♏	♏	♐	♍	♎	♏	♐	♑	♍	♎	♏	♐	♑	♍	♎	♏	♐	♑	♍	♎	♏	♐	♑	♍	♎	♏	♐	♑
°	°	°	° ′	°	°	°	°	° ′	°	°	°	°	° ′	°	°	°	°	° ′	°	°	°	°	° ′	°	°	°	°	° ′	°	°
22	2.7	3.2	0 33	29.7	29.9	3.8	4.3	1 29	0.6	0.8	4.9	5.2	2 25	1.6	1.8	5.9	6.3	3 21	2.5	2.7	6.9	7.2	4 17	3.5	3.7	8.0	8.2	5 12	4.4	4.6
23	8	2	0 20	5	7	9	2	1 16	4	7	9	2	2 12	3	6	6.0	2	3 7	3	6	7.0	2	4 2	2	5	0	2	4 57	1	5
24	9	2	0 7	2	6	9	2	1 2	1	5	5.0	2	1 58	1	5	0	2	2 53	0	4	1	2	3 48	2.9	4	1	1	4 42	3.8	3
25	9	2	♎ 29 54	28.9	4	4.0	2	0 49	♏ 29.8	3	1	2	1 44	0.8	3	1	1	2 39	1.7	2	1	1	3 33	6	2	2	1	4 27	6	1
26	3.0	3.2	29 41	7	2	1	2	0 35	6	2	1	5.1	1 30	5	1	2	1	2 24	4	1	2	7.1	3 18	4	0	2	8.0	4 12	3	0
27	1	1	29 27	4	0	1	4.1	0 22	3	0	2	1	1 16	2	0	2	6.1	2 10	2	1.9	3	0	3 4	1	2.8	8.3	0	3 57	0	3.8
28	2	1	29 14	1	28.9	2	1	0 8	0	♐ 29.8	3	1	1 2	0	0.8	6.3	0	1 55	0.9	7	7.3	0	2 49	1.8	7	3	0	3 42	2.7	6
29	3	1	29 1	27.9	7	4.3	1	♎ 29 54	28.7	6	5.3	0	0 48	♏ 29.7	6	4	0	1 41	6	5	4	0	2 34	5	5	4	7.9	3 27	4	4
30	3.3	3.1	28 47	6	5	4	1	29 40	5	5	4	5.0	0 34	4	4	4	0	1 26	3	4	5	6.9	2 19	2	3	5	9	3 12	1	3
31	4	1	28 34	3	3	5	4.0	29 27	2	3	5	0	0 19	1	2	5	5.9	1 12	0	2	5	9	2 4	0.9	1	6	8	2 56	1.8	1
32	5	1	28 20	0	1	5	0	29 13	27.9	1	6	0	0 5	28.8	0	6	9	0 57	♏ 29.7	0	6	8	1 49	6	1.9	8.6	8	2 41	5	2.9
33	6	0	28 6	26.7	27.9	4.6	0	28 59	6	28.9	5.7	4.9	♎ 29 51	5	♐ 29.8	6.7	9	0 42	4	0.8	7.7	8	1 34	3	7	7	7	2 25	2	7
34	3.7	3.0	27 53	4	8	7	0	28 44	3	7	7	9	29 36	2	7	8	8	0 27	1	6	8	8	1 18	0	5	8	7.7	2 9	0.9	5
35	8	0	27 39	1	6	8	3.9	28 30	0	5	8	9	29 21	27.9	5	8	8	0 12	28.8	4	8	6.7	1 3	♏ 29.6	3	8	6	1 53	5	3
36	9	0	27 24	25.8	4	9	9	28 16	26.6	3	9	8	29 6	5	3	9	5.8	♎ 29 57	4	2	9	7	0 47	3	1	9	6	1 37	2	1
37	4.0	0	27 10	4	1	5.0	9	28 1	3	1	6.0	8	28 51	2	0	7.0	7	29 41	1	0	8.0	6	0 31	0	0.9	9.0	5	1 21	♏ 29.9	1.9
38	0	2.9	26 56	1	26.9	1	9	27 46	0	27.9	1	4.8	28 36	26.9	28.8	1	7	29 26	27.8	♐ 29.8	1	6	0 15	28.6	7	1	5	1 5	5	7
39	1	9	26 42	24.8	7	2	8	27 31	25.6	6	2	7	28 21	5	6	2	6	29 10	5	5	2	5	♎ 29 59	3	5	2	7.4	0 48	1	4
40	2	9	26 27	4	5	3	3.8	27 16	3	4	2	7	28 5	2	4	2	6	28 54	1	3	2	6.5	29 43	27.9	2	2	4	0 31	28.8	2
41	4.3	9	26 12	1	2	5.4	8	27 1	24.9	2	6.3	7	27 49	25.8	1	7.3	5.5	28 38	26.8	0	3	4	29 26	5	0	3	3	0 14	4	0.9
42	4	8	25 57	23.7	25.9	5	7	26 45	5	26.9	4	6	27 34	4	27.8	4	5	28 22	4	28.8	8.4	4	29 9	1	♐ 29.7	9.4	3	♎ 29 57	0	7
43	6	2.8	25 42	3	7	6	7	26 30	2	6	5	4.6	27 17	0	6	5	4	28 5	0	5	5	3	28 52	26.7	5	5	2	29 40	27.6	4
44	7	8	25 26	0	4	6	7	26 14	23.8	3	6	5	27 1	24.6	3	6	4	27 48	25.6	2	5	3	28 35	3	2	5	7.1	29 22	2	1
45	4.7	8	25 11	22.6	1	5.7	3.6	25 58	5	1	6.6	5	26 44	3	0	7.7	4	27 31	2	27.9	6	6.2	28 17	25.9	28.9	6	1	29 4	26.8	♐ 29.8
46	8	7	24 55	2	24.8	8	6	25 41	1	25.8	7	5	26 27	23.9	26.7	7	5.3	27 14	24.8	6	8.7	2	28 0	6	6	9.6	0	28 46	3	5
47	9	7	24 39	21.8	5	9	6	25 25	22.7	4	9	4	26 10	5	4	8	3	26 56	3	3	8	1	27 42	2	3	7	0	28 27	25.9	2
48	5.0	2.7	24 22	4	2	6.0	5	25 8	3	1	7.0	4.4	25 53	1	1	9	2	26 38	23.9	0	9	1	27 23	24.7	27.9	8	6.9	28 8	5	28.9
49	2	7	24 5	0	23.9	1	3.5	24 50	21.9	24.8	1	3	25 35	22.7	25.7	8.0	2	26 20	4	26.7	9	0	27 4	3	6	9	8	27 49	1	5
50	3	6	23 49	20.6	5	2	5	24 33	4	4	2	3	25 17	2	3	1	5.1	26 1	0	3	9.0	5.9	26 45	23.8	2	10.0	8	27 29	24.6	1
51	4	6	23 31	1	2	3	4	24 15	20.9	1	3	2	24 59	21.7	0	2	1	25 42	22.5	0	1	9	26 26	3	26.9	1	7	27 9	1	27.7
52	5.5	2.6	23 13	19.6	22.8	6.4	4	23 57	4	23.7	7.4	4.2	24 40	2	24.6	3	0	25 23	0	25.6	2	8	26 6	22.8	5	2	6.6	26 49	23.6	3
53	7	5	22 55	1	4	6	3.3	23 38	19.9	3	5	2	24 21	20.7	2	8.4	0	25 3	21.5	2	3	8	25 45	3	1	3	6	26 28	1	26.9
54	8	5	22 37	18.6	21.9	7	3	23 19	4	22.8	6	1	24 1	2	23.8	5	4.9	24 43	0	24.7	9.4	5.7	25 25	21.8	25.6	10.4	5	26 6	22.6	5
55	6.0	4	22 18	1	4	9	2	23 0	18.9	3	8	0	23 41	19.7	3	7	8	24 22	20.5	2	6	6	25 3	3	1	6	4	25 45	0	0
56	1	4	21 59	17.6	20.9	7.0	2	22 40	4	21.8	9	0	23 20	1	22.8	8	8	24 1	19.9	23.7	7	6	24 42	20.7	24.6	7	3	25 22	21.4	25.5

H. M. S. SID. T. 8 37 36 ARC 129° 24′.0 ♌ 7°					
H.	11	12	1	2	3
Lat. °	♍ °	♎ °	♏ ° ′	♐ °	♑ °
22	9.0	9.2	6 7	5.3	5.6
23	1	2	5 52	0	4
24	1	1	5 37	4.8	2
25	2	1	5 21	5	1
26	3	0	5 6	2	4.9
27	9.3	0	4 51	3.9	7
28	4	8.9	4 35	6	6
29	4	9	4 20	3	4
30	5	8	4 4	0	2
31	6	8	3 48	2.7	0
32	9.6	7	3 32	4	3.8
33	7	8.7	3 16	1	6
34	8	6	3 0	1.8	4
35	8	6	2 44	4	2
36	9	5	2 27	1	0
37	10.0	8.4	2 11	0.7	2.8
38	1	4	1 54	4	6
39	1	3	1 37	0	4
40	2	3	1 20	♏ 29.7	1
41	3	8.2	1 2	3	1.9
42	10.4	1	0 45	28.9	6
43	5	1	0 27	5	3
44	5	0	0 8	1	1
45	6	7.9	♎ 29 50	27.6	0.8
46	6	9	29 31	2	5
47	10.7	8	29 12	26.8	1
48	8	7	28 53	4	♐ 29.8
49	8	7.7	28 33	0	5
50	9	6	28 13	25.5	1
51	11.0	5	27 52	0	28.8
52	1	4	27 31	24.5	4
53	2	7.3	27 10	0	0
54	3	3	26 48	23.4	27.5
55	5	2	26 25	22.8	26.9
56	6	1	26 3	2	4

H. M. S. 8 41 41 130° 25′.2 ♌ 8°					
H.	11	12	1	2	3
Lat. °	♍ °	♎ °	♏ ° ′	♐ °	♑ °
22	10.0	10.2	7 2	6.3	6.5
23	1	2	6 47	0	3
24	1	1	6 31	5.7	2
25	2	0	6 15	4	0
26	3	0	6 0	1	5.9
27	10.3	9.9	5 44	4.8	7
28	4	9	5 28	5	5
29	4	8	5 12	2	3
30	5	8	4 56	3.9	1
31	6	9.7	4 40	6	0
32	10.6	6	4 24	3	4.8
33	7	6	4 7	0	6
34	8	5	3 51	2.7	4
35	8	9.5	3 34	3	2
36	9	4	3 17	0	0
37	11.0	3	3 0	1.6	3.8
38	0	3	2 43	3	5
39	1	9.2	2 26	0.9	3
40	2	2	2 8	5	1
41	3	1	1 50	1	2.8
42	11.4	0	1 32	♏ 29.7	5
43	4	8.9	1 13	3	3
44	5	9	0 55	28.9	0
45	6	8	0 36	5	1.7
46	6	7	0 17	1	4
47	11.7	6	♎ 29 57	27.7	1
48	7	8.6	29 37	2	0.8
49	8	5	29 17	26.7	4
50	9	4	28 56	3	0
51	12.0	3	28 35	25.8	♐ 29.7
52	1	8.2	28 14	3	3
53	2	1	27 52	24.8	28.9
54	3	0	27 29	2	4
55	4	0	27 6	23.6	27.9
56	5	7.9	26 43	0	4

H. M. S. 8 45 44 131° 26′.1 ♌ 9°					
H.	11	12	1	2	3
Lat. °	♍ °	♎ °	♏ ° ′	♐ °	♑ °
22	11.1	11.2	7 57	7.2	7.4
23	1	1	7 41	6.9	3
24	2	1	7 25	6	1
25	2	0	7 9	3	0
26	3	10.9	6 53	0	6.8
27	11.3	9	6 37	5.7	6
28	4	8	6 21	4	4
29	5	8	6 4	1	3
30	5	10.7	5 48	4.8	1
31	6	6	5 31	5	5.9
32	11.6	6	5 15	2	7
33	7	5	4 58	3.9	5
34	8	10.4	4 41	5	3
35	8	4	4 24	2	1
36	9	3	4 7	2.8	4.9
37	12.0	2	3 49	5	7
38	0	10.2	3 32	1	5
39	1	1	3 14	1.8	2
40	2	0	2 56	4	0
41	2	0	2 37	0	3.7
42	12.3	9.9	2 19	0.6	5
43	4	8	2 0	2	2
44	4	7	1 41	♏ 29.8	2.9
45	5	6	1 22	3	6
46	5	9.6	1 2	28.9	3
47	12.6	5	0 42	5	0
48	7	4	0 21	0	1.7
49	8	3	0 1	27.6	3
50	8	9.2	♎ 29 40	1	0.9
51	9	1	29 18	26.6	5
52	13.0	1	28 56	1	1
53	1	0	28 34	25.5	♐ 29.7
54	2	8.9	28 11	24.9	3
55	3	8	27 47	3	28.8
56	4	7	27 23	23.7	3

H. M. S. 8 49 48 132° 26′.9 ♌ 10°					
H.	11	12	1	2	3
Lat. °	♍ °	♎ °	♏ ° ′	♐ °	♑ °
22	12.1	12.2	8 51	8.1	8.4
23	1	1	8 35	7.8	2
24	2	0	8 19	5	1
25	2	0	8 3	2	7.9
26	12.3	11.9	7 46	6.9	7
27	3	8	7 30	6	6
28	4	8	7 13	3	4
29	5	7	6 57	0	2
30	12.5	6	6 40	5.7	0
31	6	11.6	6 23	4	6.8
32	6	5	6 6	1	6
33	7	4	5 49	4.8	5
34	12.8	4	5 31	4	3
35	8	3	5 14	1	1
36	9	11.2	4 56	3.7	5.8
37	9	1	4 39	4	6
38	13.0	1	4 21	0	4
39	1	0	4 2	2.6	2
40	1	10.9	3 44	3	4.9
41	2	8	3 25	1.9	7
42	3	7	3 6	5	4
43	13.3	7	2 47	0	2
44	4	10.6	2 27	0.6	3.9
45	4	5	2 7	2	6
46	5	4	1 47	♏ 29.7	3
47	5	3	1 27	3	0
48	13.6	10.2	1 6	28.9	2.6
49	7	2	0 45	4	3
50	7	1	0 23	27.9	1.9
51	8	0	0 1	4	6
52	9	9.9	♎ 29 38	26.9	2
53	14.0	8	29 15	3	0.7
54	1	7	28 51	25.7	3
55	2	6	28 27	1	♐ 29.7
56	3	5	28 3	24.5	2

H. M. S. 8 53 50 133° 27′.5 ♌ 11°					
H.	11	12	1	2	3
Lat. °	♍ °	♎ °	♏ ° ′	♐ °	♑ °
22	13.1	13.1	9 46	9.0	9.3
23	2	1	9 29	8.7	2
24	2	0	9 12	4	0
25	3	12.9	8 56	1	8.8
26	13.3	9	8 39	7.8	7
27	4	8	8 22	5	5
28	4	7	8 5	2	3
29	5	6	7 48	6.9	1
30	13.5	12.6	7 31	6	0
31	6	5	7 14	3	7.8
32	6	4	6 57	5.9	6
33	7	3	6 39	6	4
34	13.7	12.3	6 22	3	2
35	8	2	6 4	4.9	0
36	9	1	5 46	6	6.8
37	9	0	5 28	2	6
38	14.0	11.9	5 9	3.8	4
39	0	9	4 50	5	1
40	1	8	4 31	1	5.9
41	2	7	4 12	2.7	6
42	14.2	11.6	3 53	3	4
43	3	5	3 33	1.9	1
44	3	4	3 13	4	4.8
45	4	3	2 53	0	5
46	14.4	11.2	2 32	0.6	2
47	5	1	2 11	2	3.9
48	5	1	1 50	♏ 29.7	5
49	6	0	1 28	2	1
50	14.6	10.9	1 6	28.7	2.8
51	7	8	0 43	2	4
52	8	7	0 20	27.7	0
53	9	6	♎ 29 57	1	1.6
54	15.0	10.5	29 32	26.5	1
55	1	4	29 8	25.9	0.6
56	2	2	28 42	2	1

H. M. S. 8 57 52 134° 27′.9 ♌ 12°					
H.	11	12	1	2	3
Lat. °	♍ °	♎ °	♏ ° ′	♐ °	♑ °
22	14.1	14.1	10 40	9.9	10.3
23	2	0	10 23	6	1
24	2	0	10 6	3	9.9
25	3	13.9	9 49	0	8
26	3	8	9 32	8.7	6
27	14.4	7	9 15	4	4
28	4	7	8 58	1	3
29	5	13.6	8 40	7.8	1
30	5	5	8 23	5	8.9
31	14.6	4	8 5	2	7
32	6	3	7 48	6.8	5
33	7	13.3	7 30	5	3
34	7	2	7 12	2	1
35	14.8	1	6 53	5.8	7.9
36	8	0	6 35	5	7
37	9	12.9	6 16	1	5
38	9	8	5 57	4.7	3
39	15.0	7	5 38	3	1
40	1	7	5 19	0	6.8
41	1	12.6	4 59	3.5	6
42	2	5	4 39	1	3
43	15.2	4	4 19	2.7	0
44	3	3	3 59	3	5.8
45	3	12.3	3 38	1.8	5
46	4	2	3 17	4	2
47	15.4	1	2 55	0.9	4.8
48	5	0	2 34	5	5
49	5	11.9	2 11	0	2
50	6	7	1 49	♏ 29.5	3.8
51	15.7	6	1 26	0	4
52	8	5	1 2	28.4	0
53	8	11.4	0 38	27.8	2.6
54	9	3	0 13	2	1
55	16.0	1	♎ 29 48	26.6	1.6
56	1	0	29 22	0	0

SID. T. H. M. S. 8 57 52 ARC 134° 27′.9 ♌ 12°					9 1 53 135° 28′.1 ♌ 13°					9 5 53 136° 28′.2 ♌ 14°					9 9 52 137° 28′.0 ♌ 15°					9 13 51 138° 27′.7 ♌ 16°					9 17 49 139° 27′.2 ♌ 17°					
H.	11	12	1	2	3	11	12	1	2	3	11	12	1	2	3	11	12	1	2	3	11	12	1	2	3	11	12	1	2	3
Lat.	♍	♎	♏	♐	♑	♍	♎	♏	♐	♑	♍	♎	♏	♐	♑	♍	♎	♏	♐	♑	♍	♎	♏	♐	♑	♍	♎	♏	♐	♑
°	°	°	° ′	°	°	°	°	° ′	°	°	°	°	° ′	°	°	°	°	° ′	°	°	°	°	° ′	°	°	°	°	° ′	°	°
22	14.1	14.1	10 40	9.9	10.3	15.1	15.1	11 33	10.8	11.2	16.2	16.0	12 27	11.7	12.1	17.2	17.0	13 20	12.6	13. 1	18.2	17.9	14 13	13.5	14.0	19.2	18.9	15 6	14.3	14.9
23	2	0	10 23	6	1	2	0	11 16	5	0	2	15.9	12 9	4	0	2	16.9	13 3	3	12.9	2	9	13 55	2	13.8	2	8	14 48	0	8
24	2	0	10 6	3	9.9	2	14.9	10 59	2	10.9	2	9	11 52	1	11.8	2	8	12 45	0	8	3	8	13 37	12.9	7	3	7	14 30	13.7	6
25	3	13.9	9 49	0	8	3	8	10 42	9.9	7	3	8	11 34	10.8	7	3	8	12 27	11.7	6	3	7	13 19	6	5	3	6	14 11	4	5
26	3	8	9 32	8.7	6	3	7	10 25	6	6	3	7	11 17	5	5	3	7	12 9	4	4	3	17.6	13 1	3	4	3	5	13 52	1	3
27	14.4	7	9 15	4	4	15.4	7	10 7	3	4	16.4	15.6	10 59	2	3	17.4	16.6	11 51	1	3	18.4	5	12 42	0	2	19.3	18.4	13 34	12.8	1
28	4	7	8 58	1	3	4	14.6	9 50	0	2	4	5	10 41	9.9	1	4	5	11 33	10.8	1	4	4	12 24	11.6	0	4	3	13 15	5	13.9
29	5	13.6	8 40	7.8	1	5	5	9 32	8.7	0	5	4	10 23	6	0	4	4	11 14	4	11.9	4	3	12 5	3	12.8	4	2	12 56	2	8
30	5	5	8 23	5	8.9	5	4	9 14	4	9.8	5	3	10 5	2	10.8	5	3	10 56	1	7	5	17.2	11 47	0	7	5	1	12 37	11.9	6
31	14.6	4	8 5	2	7	15.6	3	8 56	0	7	5	15.3	9 47	8.9	6	5	16.2	10 37	9.8	5	5	1	11 28	10.7	5	19.5	0	12 18	6	4
32	6	3	7 48	6.8	5	6	14.3	8 38	7.7	5	16.6	2	9 28	6	4	17.6	1	10 19	5	3	18.6	0	11 8	3	3	5	17.9	11 58	2	2
33	7	13.3	7 30	5	3	7	2	8 20	4	3	6	1	9 10	3	2	6	0	10 0	1	1	6	16.9	10 49	0	1	6	8	11 39	10.9	0
34	7	2	7 12	2	1	7	1	8 1	0	1	7	0	8 51	7.9	0	6	15.9	9 40	8.8	10.9	6	8	10 30	9.7	11.9	6	7	11 19	5	12.8
35	14.8	1	6 53	5.8	7.9	15.8	0	7 43	6.7	8.9	7	14.9	8 32	5	9.8	7	8	9 21	4	7	7	7	10 10	3	7	19.6	6	10 59	1	6
36	8	0	6 35	5	7	8	13.9	7 24	3	7	16.8	8	8 13	2	6	7	7	9 1	0	5	7	6	9 50	8.9	5	7	5	10 38	9.8	4
37	9	12.9	6 16	1	5	9	8	7 5	0	5	8	7	7 53	6.8	4	17.8	6	8 42	7.7	3	18.8	5	9 30	5	2	7	17.3	10 18	4	2
38	9	8	5 57	4.7	3	9	7	6 46	5.7	2	9	6	7 34	4	2	8	5	8 22	3	1	8	16.4	9 9	1	0	8	2	9 57	0	0
39	15.0	7	5 38	3	1	16.0	6	6 26	3	0	9	5	7 14	0	8.9	9	15.4	8 1	6.9	9.9	8	2	8 48	7.7	10.8	19.8	1	9 36	8.6	11.7
40	1	7	5 19	0	6.8	0	5	6 6	4.9	7.8	17.0	14.4	6 53	5.6	7	9	3	7 40	6	6	9	1	8 27	3	5	8	0	9 15	2	5
41	1	12.6	4 59	3.5	6	1	13.4	5 46	5	5	0	3	6 33	2	4	18.0	1	7 20	2	4	9	0	8 6	6.9	3	9	16.9	8 53	7.8	2
42	2	5	4 39	1	3	1	3	5 26	1	2	0	2	6 12	4.8	2	0	0	6 59	5.7	1	19.0	15.9	7 45	5	0	9	7	8 31	4	0
43	15.2	4	4 19	2.7	0	2	2	5 6	3.7	0	1	1	5 51	4	7.9	1	14.9	6 37	3	8.8	0	8	7 23	1	9.8	20.0	6	8 9	6.9	10.7
44	3	3	3 59	3	5.8	16.2	1	4 45	2	6.7	17.1	0	5 30	3.9	6	1	8	6 16	4.8	5	0	7	7 1	5.6	5	0	5	7 46	5	4
45	3	12.3	3 38	1.8	5	3	0	4 23	2.8	4	2	13.9	5 9	5	3	1	7	5 54	3	2	1	6	6 38	1	2	0	16.4	7 23	0	1
46	4	2	3 17	4	2	3	12.9	4 2	3	1	2	8	4 47	0	0	18.2	6	5 31	3.9	7.9	1	15.5	6 15	4.7	8.9	1	3	7 0	5.5	9.8
47	15.4	1	2 55	0.9	4.8	4	9	3 39	1.8	5.8	3	7	4 24	2.5	6.7	2	5	5 8	4	6	19.2	4	5 52	2	6	1	2	6 36	0	5
48	5	0	2 34	5	5	16.4	8	3 18	3	4	17.3	6	4 1	1	4	3	14.4	4 45	0	3	2	2	5 28	3.8	2	20.1	0	6 12	4.6	2
49	5	11.9	2 11	0	2	5	7	2 55	0.8	1	4	5	3 38	1.6	0	3	3	4 21	2.5	6.9	3	1	5 4	3	7.9	2	15.9	5 47	1	8.9
50	6	7	1 49	♏ 29.5	3.8	5	5	2 32	3	4.7	4	13.3	3 14	1	5.6	4	1	3 57	1.9	6	3	14.9	4 39	2.7	5	2	7	5 22	3.5	5
51	15.7	6	1 26	0	4	6	12.4	2 8	♏ 29.8	3	5	2	2 50	0.6	3	18.4	0	3 32	3	2	4	8	4 14	1	1	3	6	4 56	2.9	1
52	8	5	1 2	28.4	0	16.7	3	1 44	2	7.9	17.5	1	2 25	0	4.9	5	13.9	3 7	0.7	5.8	19.4	7	3 48	1.5	6.7	20.3	5	4 30	3	7.6
53	8	11.4	0 38	27.8	2.6	7	2	1 19	28.6	5	6	0	2 0	♏ 29.4	4	5	8	2 41	1	4	5	6	3 22	0.9	3	4	15.4	4 3	1.7	2
54	9	3	0 13	2	1	8	1	0 54	0	0	7	12.9	1 34	28.8	3.9	6	7	2 15	♏ 29.5	4.9	5	14.4	2 55	3	5.8	4	2	3 35	1	6.7
55	16.0	1	♎ 29 48	26.6	1.6	9	11.9	0 28	27.4	2.5	8	7	1 8	1	4	7	5	1 48	28.9	4	6	2	2 27	♏ 29.7	3	5	0	3 7	0.4	2
56	1	0	29 22	0	0	17.0	7	0 2	26.7	0	9	6	0 41	27.4	2.9	7	3	1 20	2	3.8	6	0	1 59	0	4.7	5	14.8	2 38	♏ 29.7	5.6

	SID. T. 9 21 46 (H. M. S.) ARC 140° 26′.6 ♌ 18°					9 25 43 (H. M. S.) 141° 25′.7 ♌ 19°					9 29 39 (H. M. S.) 142° 24′.7 ♌ 20°					9 33 34 (H. M. S.) 143° 23′.5 ♌ 21°					9 37 29 (H. M. S.) 144° 22′.2 ♌ 22°					9 41 23 (H. M. S.) 145° 20′.6 ♌ 23°				
H.	11	12	1	2	3	11	12	1	2	3	11	12	1	2	3	11	12	1	2	3	11	12	1	2	3	11	12	1	2	3
Lat.	♍	♎	♏	♐	♑	♍	♎	♏	♐	♑	♍	♎	♏	♐	♑	♍	♎	♏	♐	♑	♍	♎	♏	♐	♑	♍	♎	♏	♐	♑
°	°	°	° ′	°	°	°	°	° ′	°	°	°	°	° ′	°	°	°	°	° ′	°	°	°	°	° ′	°	°	°	°	° ′	°	°
22	20.2	19.8	15 59	15.2	15.9	21.2	20.8	16 51	16.1	16.8	22.2	21.7	17 43	17.0	17.7	23.2	22.7	18 35	17.9	18.7	24.2	23.6	19 27	18.8	19.6	25.2	24.5	20 19	19.6	20.5
23	2	7	15 40	14.9	7	2	7	16 32	15.8	6	2	6	17 24	16.7	6	2	6	18 16	6	5	2	5	19 7	5	4	2	4	19 59	3	4
24	3	6	15 21	6	5	2	6	16 13	5	5	3	5	17 5	4	4	3	4	17 56	3	3	2	4	18 48	2	3	2	3	19 39	0	2
25	3	5	15 3	3	4	3	5	15 54	2	3	3	4	16 46	1	2	3	3	17 37	0	2	2	2	18 28	17.9	1	2	2	19 18	18.7	0
26	3	4	14 44	0	2	3	20.4	15 35	14.9	1	3	21.3	16 26	15.8	1	3	22.2	17 17	16.7	0	3	1	18 7	5	18.9	3	0	18 58	4	19.9
27	3	19.3	14 25	13.7	0	21.3	2	15 16	6	0	22.3	2	16 6	5	16.9	23.3	1	16 57	4	17.8	24.3	0	17 47	2	8	25.3	23.9	18 37	1	7
28	20.4	2	14 6	4	14.9	4	1	14 56	3	15.8	3	1	15 47	2	7	3	0	16 37	0	7	3	22.9	17 27	16.9	6	3	8	18 17	17.8	5
29	4	1	13 46	1	7	4	0	14 37	0	6	4	20.9	15 27	14.8	6	4	21.8	16 17	15.7	5	3	8	17 6	6	4	3	7	17 56	4	4
30	4	0	13 27	12.8	5	4	19.9	14 17	13.6	4	4	8	15 7	5	4	4	7	15 56	4	3	3	6	16 46	2	2	3	5	17 35	1	2
31	5	18.9	13 7	4	3	4	8	13 57	3	3	4	7	14 46	2	2	4	6	15 36	0	1	4	5	16 25	15.9	1	3	23.4	17 14	16.8	0
32	5	8	12 47	1	1	21.5	7	13 37	0	1	22.4	6	14 26	13.8	0	23.4	5	15 15	14.7	16.9	24.4	22.4	16 4	6	17.9	25.3	3	16 52	4	18.8
33	20.5	7	12 27	11.7	13.9	5	6	13 17	12.6	14.9	5	5	14 5	5	15.8	4	21.3	14 54	3	7	4	2	15 42	2	7	4	1	16 31	1	6
34	6	6	12 7	4	7	5	5	12 56	3	7	5	20.4	13 44	1	6	5	2	14 33	0	5	4	1	15 21	14.8	5	4	0	16 9	15.7	4
35	6	5	11 47	0	5	6	19.3	12 35	11.9	5	5	2	13 23	12.7	4	5	1	14 11	13.6	3	4	0	14 59	4	3	4	22.8	15 47	3	2
36	6	18.3	11 26	10.6	3	6	2	12 14	5	3	5	1	13 2	4	2	5	20.9	13 50	2	1	5	21.8	14 37	1	1	4	7	15 25	14.9	0
37	20.7	2	11 5	3	1	21.6	1	11 53	1	1	22.6	0	12 40	0	0	23.5	8	13 28	12.8	15.9	24.5	7	14 15	13.7	16.9	25.4	5	15 2	5	17.8
38	7	1	10 44	9.9	12.9	7	0	11 31	10.7	13.8	6	19.9	12 19	11.6	14.8	6	7	13 5	4	7	5	6	13 52	3	7	4	4	14 39	1	6
39	7	0	10 23	5	7	7	18.8	11 10	3	6	6	8	11 56	2	5	6	5	12 43	0	5	5	5	13 29	12.8	4	5	2	14 16	13.7	4
40	8	17.8	10 1	1	4	7	7	10 48	9.9	4	7	6	11 34	10.7	3	6	20.4	12 20	11.6	2	5	21.3	13 6	4	2	5	1	13 52	3	1
41	20.8	7	9 39	8.6	2	8	6	10 25	5	1	7	5	11 11	3	0	23.6	2	11 57	1	0	6	2	12 43	0	15.9	5	21.9	13 28	12.8	16.9
42	9	6	9 17	2	11.9	21.8	4	10 2	0	12.8	22.7	19.4	10 48	9.9	13.8	7	1	11 34	10.7	14.7	24.6	0	12 19	11.5	7	25.5	8	13 4	4	6
43	9	5	8 54	7.8	6	8	18.3	9 39	8.6	6	8	2	10 24	4	5	7	19.9	11 10	2	5	6	20.9	11 55	1	4	5	6	12 39	11.9	3
44	9	17.4	8 31	3	3	9	2	9 16	1	3	8	1	10 1	8.9	2	7	8	10 45	9.8	2	6	7	11 30	10.6	1	6	5	12 14	4	0
45	21.0	3	8 8	6.8	0	9	1	8 52	7.6	0	8	18.9	9 36	4	12.9	23.8	7	10 21	3	13.9	7	5	11 5	1	14.8	6	21.4	11 48	10.9	15.7
46	0	1	7 44	3	10.7	9	17.9	8 28	1	11.7	22.9	8	9 12	7.9	6	8	6	9 55	8.8	6	7	4	10 39	9.6	5	6	3	11 22	4	4
47	0	0	7 20	5.8	4	22.0	8	8 3	6.6	4	9	6	8 47	4	3	8	19.4	9 30	2	2	24.7	2	10 13	1	2	25.6	1	10 56	9.9	1
48	1	16.8	6 55	3	1	0	6	7 38	1	0	9	4	8 21	6.9	0	8	2	9 4	7.7	12.9	7	0	9 46	8.5	13.9	7	20.9	10 29	3	14.8
49	21.1	7	6 30	4.8	9.7	1	5	7 12	5.6	10.7	9	3	7 55	4	11.7	23.9	1	8 37	1	6	8	19.8	9 19	0	6	7	7	10 2	8.8	5
50	1	5	6 4	3	4	1	17.3	6 46	1	4	23.0	1	7 28	5.8	3	9	18.9	8 10	6.6	3	8	7	8 52	7.4	2	7	5	9 33	2	2
51	2	4	5 37	3.7	0	1	1	6 19	4.5	0	0	17.9	7 1	2	10.9	9	7	7 42	0	11.9	8	6	8 24	6.8	12.8	7	3	9 5	7.6	13.8
52	2	16.3	5 10	1	8.6	22.2	0	5 52	3.9	9.6	0	8	6 33	4.6	5	9	6	7 14	5.4	5	24.8	4	7 55	2	4	25.8	1	8 35	0	4
53	21.3	2	4 43	2.5	1	2	16.9	5 24	3	1	1	7	6 4	0	1	24.0	4	6 45	4.8	0	9	2	7 25	5.6	0	8	19.9	8 5	6.3	12.9
54	3	0	4 15	1.9	7.7	2	7	4 55	2.6	8.6	23.1	5	5 35	3.4	9.6	0	2	6 15	1	10.5	9	0	6 55	4.9	11.6	8	7	7 34	5.6	4
55	4	15.8	3 47	2	2	3	5	4 26	1.9	1	1	3	5 5	2.7	1	0	0	5 44	3.4	0	9	18.8	6 24	2	0	8	5	7 2	4.9	11.9
56	5	6	3 17	0.5	6.6	3	3	3 56	2	7.6	2	1	4 35	0	8.5	1	17.8	5 13	2.7	9.4	9	6	5 52	3.5	10.5	9	2	6 30	2	3

	SID. T. H. M. S. 9 41 23 ARC 145° 20′.6 ♌ 23°					H. M. S. 9 45 16 146° 19′.0 ♌ 24°					H. M. S. 9 49 8 147° 17′.1 ♌ 25°					H. M. S. 9 53 0 148° 15′.1 ♌ 26°					H. M. S. 9 56 52 149° 12′.9 ♌ 27°					H. M. S. 10 0 42 150° 10′.6 ♌ 28°				
H.	11	12	1	2	3	11	12	1	2	3	11	12	1	2	3	11	12	1	2	3	11	12	1	2	3	11	12	1	2	3
Lat.	♍	♎	♏	♐	♑	♍	♎	♏	♐	♑	♍	♎	♏	♐	♑	♍	♎	♏	♐	♑	♍	♎	♏	♐	♑	♎	♎	♏	♐	♑
°	°	°	° ′	°	°	°	°	° ′	°	°	°	°	° ′	°	°	°	°	° ′	°	°	°	°	° ′	°	°	°	°	° ′	°	°
22	25.2	24.5	20 19	19.6	20.5	26.2	25.5	21 11	20.5	21.4	27.2	26.4	22 2	21.4	22.4	28.2	27.3	22 53	22.3	23.3	29.2	28.2	23 44	23.2	24.3	0.2	29.1	24 35	24.0	25.2
23	2	4	19 59	3	4	2	3	20 50	2	3	2	2	21 41	1	2	2	2	22 32	0	2	2	1	23 23	22.9	2	2	0	24 13	23.7	1
24	2	3	19 39	0	2	2	2	20 30	19.9	1	2	1	21 20	20.8	1	2	0	22 11	21.7	0	2	27.9	23 2	5	0	2	28.8	23 52	4	24.9
25	2	2	19 18	18.7	0	2	1	20 9	6	0	2	0	21 0	5	21.9	2	26.9	21 50	4	22.8	2	8	22 40	2	23.8	2	7	23 30	1	8
26	3	0	18 58	4	19.9	2	24.9	19 48	3	20.8	2	25.9	20 38	2	8	2	8	21 29	0	7	2	7	22 19	21.9	7	2	5	23 9	22.8	6
27	25.3	23.9	18 37	1	7	26.3	8	19 28	0	6	27.2	7	20 17	19.8	6	28.2	6	21 7	20.7	5	29.2	5	21 57	6	5	0.2	4	22 47	4	5
28	3	8	18 17	17.8	5	3	7	19 7	18.6	5	2	6	19 56	5	4	2	5	20 46	4	4	2	27.4	21 35	2	4	2	28.3	22 25	1	3
29	3	7	17 56	4	4	3	5	18 46	3	3	2	4	19 35	2	2	2	26.3	20 24	0	2	2	2	21 13	20.9	2	2	1	22 2	21.8	1
30	3	5	17 35	1	2	3	24.4	18 24	0	1	3	25.3	19 13	18.8	1	2	2	20 2	19.7	0	2	1	20 51	5	0	2	0	21 40	4	23.9
31	3	23.4	17 14	16.8	0	3	3	18 3	17.6	19.9	3	2	18 51	5	20.9	2	1	19 40	3	21.8	2	26.9	20 29	2	22.8	2	27.8	21 17	1	8
32	25.3	3	16 52	4	18.8	26.3	1	17 41	3	8	27.3	0	18 29	1	7	28.2	25.9	19 18	0	6	29.2	8	20 6	19.8	6	0.2	6	20 54	20.7	6
33	4	1	16 31	1	6	3	0	17 19	16.9	6	3	24.9	18 7	17.8	5	2	8	18 55	18.6	5	2	6	19 43	5	4	2	5	20 31	3	4
34	4	0	16 9	15.7	4	3	23.9	16 57	5	4	3	7	17 45	4	3	2	6	18 32	2	3	2	5	19 20	1	2	2	3	20 8	0	2
35	4	22.8	15 47	3	2	4	7	16 35	1	2	3	6	17 22	0	1	3	4	18 9	17.8	1	2	26.3	18 57	18.7	0	2	2	19 44	19.6	0
36	4	7	15 25	14.9	0	4	6	16 12	15.7	0	3	4	16 59	16.6	19.9	3	25.3	17 46	4	20.9	2	1	18 33	3	21.8	2	0	19 20	2	22.8
37	25.4	5	15 2	5	17.8	26.4	4	15 49	3	18.8	27.3	3	16 36	2	7	28.3	1	17 22	0	7	29.2	0	18 9	17.9	6	0.2	26.8	18 56	18.8	6
38	4	4	14 39	1	6	4	23.2	15 26	14.9	5	3	1	16 12	15.8	5	3	0	16 58	16.6	4	2	25.9	17 45	5	4	2	6	18 31	3	4
39	5	2	14 16	13.7	4	4	1	15 2	5	3	3	23.9	15 48	4	3	3	24.8	16 34	2	2	2	7	17 20	1	2	2	5	18 6	17.9	1
40	5	1	13 52	3	1	4	0	14 38	1	1	4	8	15 24	14.9	0	3	6	16 9	15.8	0	2	5	16 55	16.7	0	2	3	17 40	5	21.9
41	5	21.9	13 28	12.8	16.9	4	22.9	14 14	13.7	17.8	4	6	14 59	5	18.8	3	4	15 44	3	19.7	2	3	16 29	3	20.7	2	1	17 14	0	6
42	25.5	8	13 4	4	6	26.5	7	13 49	2	6	27.4	4	14 34	0	5	28.3	2	15 19	14.9	5	29.2	2	16 3	15.8	4	0.2	25.9	16 48	16.5	4
43	5	6	12 39	11.9	3	5	5	13 24	12.7	3	4	23.2	14 8	13.6	2	3	1	14 53	4	2	2	0	15 37	3	1	2	7	16 21	0	1
44	6	5	12 14	4	0	5	3	12 58	3	0	4	1	13 42	1	17.9	3	23.9	14 26	13.9	18.9	2	24.8	15 10	14.8	19.9	2	6	15 54	15.5	20.8
45	6	21.4	11 48	10.9	15.7	5	2	12 32	11.8	16.7	4	0	13 16	12.6	6	3	8	14 0	4	6	2	6	14 43	3	6	2	4	15 27	0	6
46	6	3	11 22	4	4	5	0	12 6	3	4	4	22.8	12 49	1	3	3	6	13 32	12.9	3	2	4	14 15	13.7	3	2	2	14 58	14.5	3
47	25.6	1	10 56	9.9	1	26.5	21.9	11 39	10.7	1	27.4	6	12 22	11.5	0	28.3	4	13 4	3	0	29.3	2	13 47	1	0	0.2	0	14 30	13.9	0
48	7	20.9	10 29	3	14.8	6	7	11 12	2	15.8	4	5	11 54	0	16.7	4	2	12 36	11.8	17.7	3	0	13 18	12.5	18.7	2	24.8	14 0	3	19.7
49	7	7	10 2	8.8	5	6	5	10 44	9.6	5	5	3	11 25	10.4	4	4	0	12 7	2	4	3	23.8	12 49	0	4	2	6	13 30	12.8	4
50	7	5	9 33	2	2	6	3	10 15	0	1	5	1	10 56	9.8	1	4	22.8	11 38	10.6	0	3	6	12 19	11.4	0	2	4	13 0	2	0
51	7	3	9 5	7.6	13.8	6	1	9 46	8.4	14.7	5	21.9	10 27	2	15.7	4	6	11 7	0	16.6	3	4	11 48	10.8	17.6	2	2	12 28	11.5	18.6
52	25.8	1	8 35	0	4	26.6	20.9	9 16	7.7	3	27.5	7	9 56	8.5	3	28.4	4	10 36	9.3	2	29.3	2	11 16	1	2	0.2	0	11 56	10.8	2
53	8	19.9	8 5	6.3	12.9	7	7	8 45	1	13.9	5	5	9 25	7.8	14.8	4	2	10 5	8.6	15.8	3	0	10 44	9.4	16.8	2	23.8	11 23	1	17.7
54	8	7	7 34	5.6	4	7	5	8 13	6.4	4	5	3	8 53	1	3	4	0	9 32	7.9	3	3	22.8	10 11	8.7	3	2	5	10 50	9.4	2
55	8	5	7 2	4.9	11.9	7	3	7 41	5.7	12.9	6	0	8 20	6.4	13.8	4	21.7	8 59	2	14.8	3	5	9 37	7.9	15.8	2	2	10 15	8.7	16.7
56	9	2	6 30	2	3	7	1	7 8	0	3	6	20.8	7 46	5.6	2	4	5	8 24	6.4	2	3	3	9 2	1	2	2	0	9 40	7.9	1

	SID. T. H. M. S. 10 4 33 ARC 151° 8′.1 ♌ 29°					H. M. S. 10 8 22 152° 5′.5 ♍ 0°					H. M. S. 10 12 11 153° 2′.8 ♍ 1°					H. M. S. 10 16 0 153° 59′.9 ♍ 2°					H. M. S. 10 19 47 154° 56′.8 ♍ 3°					H. M. S. 10 23 35 155° 53′.7 ♍ 4°				
H.	11	12	1	2	3	11	12	1	2	3	11	12	1	2	3	11	12	1	2	3	11	12	1	2	3	11	12	1	2	3
Lat.	♎	♏	♏	♐	♑	♎	♏	♏	♐	♑	♎	♏	♏	♐	♑	♎	♏	♏	♐	♑	♎	♏	♏	♐	♑	♎	♏	♏	♐	♒
°	°	°	° ′	°	°	°	°	° ′	°	°	°	°	° ′	°	°	°	°	° ′	°	°	°	°	° ′	°	°	°	°	° ′	°	°
22	1.1	0.0	25 25	24.9	26.2	2.1	1.0	26 16	25.8	27.1	3.1	1.9	27 6	26.6	28.1	4.1	2.8	27 56	27.5	29.0	5.1	3.7	28 46	28.4	29.9	6.0	4.6	29 36	29.2	0.9
23	1	♎ 29.9	25 4	6	0	1	0.8	25 54	5	0	1	7	26 44	3	27.9	1	6	27 34	2	28.8	1	5	28 24	1	8	0	4	29 14	28.9	7
24	1	7	24 42	3	25.9	1	6	25 32	1	26.8	1	5	26 22	0	8	1	5	27 12	26.9	7	0	3	28 1	27.7	6	0	2	28 51	6	6
25	1	6	24 20	0	7	1	5	25 10	24.8	7	1	4	26 0	25.7	6	1	3	26 49	5	5	0	2	27 38	4	5	0	1	28 28	3	4
26	1	4	23 58	23.6	6	1	3	24 48	5	5	3.1	2	25 37	3	4	4.0	1	26 26	2	3	5.0	0	27 15	1	29.3	0	3.9	28 4	27.9	3
27	1.1	29.3	23 36	3	4	2.1	2	24 25	2	4	1	1	25 15	0	27.3	0	1.9	26 4	25.9	2	0	2.8	26 52	26.8	1	0	7	27 41	6	1
28	1	1	23 14	0	2	1	0	24 3	23.8	2	0	0.9	24 52	24.7	1	0	8	25 40	5	0	0	6	26 29	4	0	5.9	5	27 17	3	♑ 29.9
29	1	0	22 51	22.6	1	1	♎ 29.9	23 40	5	0	0	7	24 29	3	0	0	6	25 17	2	27.9	0	5	26 5	1	28.8	9	3	26 53	26.9	8
30	1	28.8	22 28	3	24.9	1	7	23 17	1	25.8	3.0	6	24 5	0	26.8	4.0	4	24 53	24.8	7	4.9	3	25 41	25.7	6	9	2	26 29	6	6
31	1	7	22 5	21.9	7	1	5	22 54	22.8	7	0	4	23 42	23.6	6	0	3	24 29	5	5	9	1	25 17	3	5	9	0	26 5	2	4
32	1.1	5	21 42	6	5	2.1	4	22 30	4	5	0	2	23 18	3	4	0	1	24 5	1	3	9	1.9	24 53	0	3	9	2.8	25 40	25.8	2
33	1	4	21 19	2	3	0	2	22 6	0	3	0	1	22 54	22.9	2	3.9	0.9	23 41	23.8	1	9	8	24 28	24.6	1	5.8	6	25 15	5	0
34	1	2	20 55	20.8	1	0	0	21 42	21.7	1	3.0	♎ 29.9	22 29	5	0	9	7	23 16	4	26.9	9	6	24 3	2	27.9	8	4	24 50	1	28.9
35	1	0	20 31	4	23.9	0	28.9	21 18	3	24.9	0	7	22 5	1	25.8	9	5	22 51	0	7	4.9	4	23 38	23.8	7	8	2	24 24	24.7	7
36	1	27.8	20 6	0	7	0	7	20 53	20.9	7	0	5	21 40	21.7	6	9	3	22 26	22.6	5	8	2	23 12	4	5	8	0	23 58	3	5
37	1.1	7	19 42	19.6	5	2.0	6	20 28	5	5	0	4	21 14	3	4	9	1	22 0	2	3	8	0	22 46	0	3	8	1.8	23 32	23.9	3
38	1	5	19 17	2	3	0	4	20 3	0	3	2.9	2	20 48	20.9	2	3.9	0	21 34	21.7	1	8	0.8	22 20	22.6	1	5.7	6	23 5	4	1
39	1	3	18 51	18.7	1	0	2	19 37	19.6	0	9	0	20 22	4	0	9	♎ 29.8	21 8	3	25.9	8	6	21 53	1	26.9	7	4	22 38	22.9	27.9
40	1	1	18 26	3	22.9	0	0	19 11	1	23.8	9	28.8	19 56	0	24.8	8	6	20 41	20.8	7	4.8	4	21 26	21.6	7	7	2	22 11	5	6
41	1	26.9	17 59	17.8	6	0	27.8	18 44	18.7	6	9	6	19 29	19.6	5	8	4	20 13	3	5	7	2	20 58	2	4	7	0	21 42	0	4
42	1.1	8	17 33	3	3	2.0	6	18 17	2	3	9	4	19 1	1	3	8	2	19 46	19.8	2	7	0	20 30	20.7	2	6	0.8	21 14	21.5	2
43	1	6	17 5	16.8	1	0	4	17 50	17.7	0	2.9	2	18 34	18.6	0	3.8	0	19 17	3	0	7	♎ 29.8	20 1	2	25.9	5.6	6	20 45	0	26.9
44	1	4	16 38	3	21.8	0	2	17 22	1	22.7	9	0	18 5	1	23.7	8	28.8	18 48	18.8	24.7	7	6	19 32	19.6	7	6	4	20 15	20.5	6
45	1	2	16 10	15.8	5	0	0	16 53	16.6	5	9	27.8	17 36	17.5	5	8	6	18 19	3	5	4.7	4	19 2	1	4	6	2	19 45	19.9	3
46	1	0	15 41	3	2	0	26.8	16 24	1	2	9	6	17 7	0	2	8	4	17 49	17.7	2	6	2	18 32	18.5	1	5	♎ 29.9	19 14	3	1
47	1.1	25.7	15 12	14.7	20.9	2.0	6	15 54	15.5	21.9	8	3	16 37	16.4	22.9	7	2	17 19	1	23.9	6	0	18 1	0	24.8	5	7	18 43	18.8	25.8
48	1	5	14 42	1	6	0	4	15 23	14.9	6	2.8	1	16 6	15.8	6	3.7	0	16 48	16.6	6	6	28.7	17 29	17.4	5	5.5	4	18 11	2	5
49	1	3	14 12	13.6	3	0	2	14 52	4	2	8	26.8	15 34	2	3	7	27.7	16 16	0	3	4.6	5	16 57	16.8	2	5	1	17 38	17.6	1
50	1	1	13 41	0	19.9	0	25.9	14 21	13.8	20.9	8	6	15 2	14.6	21.9	7	4	15 43	15.4	22.9	6	2	16 24	2	23.8	5	28.9	17 4	0	24.8
51	0	24.9	13 9	12.3	5	1.9	7	13 49	2	5	8	4	14 29	13.9	5	7	2	15 10	14.7	5	5	27.9	15 50	15.5	4	4	6	16 30	16.3	4
52	1.0	7	12 36	11.6	1	9	5	13 16	12.5	1	2.8	2	13 56	2	1	3.6	0	14 35	0	1	5	7	15 15	14.8	0	5.4	4	15 55	15.6	0
53	0	4	12 3	10.9	18.7	9	3	12 42	11.8	19.7	8	0	13 21	12.5	20.7	6	26.7	14 0	13.3	21.7	4.5	4	14 40	1	22.6	4	1	15 19	14.9	23.6
54	0	2	11 28	2	2	9	0	12 8	0	2	8	25.7	12 46	11.8	2	6	4	13 25	12.5	2	5	1	14 3	13.3	1	3	27.8	14 42	1	1
55	0	23.9	10 54	9.5	17.7	9	24.7	11 32	10.2	18.7	8	4	12 10	0	19.7	6	1	12 48	11.7	20.7	5	26.8	13 26	12.5	21.6	3	5	14 4	13.3	22.6
56	0	6	10 18	8.7	1	8	4	10 55	9.4	1	7	1	11 33	10.2	1	5	25.8	12 10	10.9	1	4	5	12 47	11.6	0	3	2	13 25	12.5	0

SID. T. / ARC	SID. T. H. M. S. 10 23 35, ARC 155° 53′.7, ♍ 4°					H. M. S. 10 27 22, 156° 50′.4, ♍ 5°					H. M. S. 10 31 8, 157° 47′.0, ♍ 6°					H. M. S. 10 34 54, 158° 43′.4, ♍ 7°					H. M. S. 10 38 39, 159° 39′.8, ♍ 8°					H. M. S. 10 42 24, 160° 36′.0, ♍ 9°				
H.	11	12	1	2	3	11	12	1	2	3	11	12	1	2	3	11	12	1	2	3	11	12	1	2	3	11	12	1	2	3
Lat.	♎	♏	♏	♐	♒	♎	♏	♐	♑	♒	♎	♏	♐	♑	♒	♎	♏	♐	♑	♒	♎	♏	♐	♑	♒	♎	♏	♐	♑	♒
°	°	°	° ′	°	°	°	°	° ′	°	°	°	°	° ′	°	°	°	°	° ′	°	°	°	°	° ′	°	°	°	°	° ′	°	°
22	6.0	4.6	29 36	29.2	0.9	7.0	5.5	0 26	0.1	1.8	8.0	6.3	1 15	1.0	2.7	9.0	7.2	2 5	1.8	3.7	9.9	8.1	2 55	2.7	4.6	10.9	9.0	3 44	3.6	5.6
23	0	4	29 14	28.9	7	0	3	0 3	♐ 29.8	7	0	2	0 52	0.6	6	8.9	1	1 42	5	5	9	7.9	2 31	4	5	9	8.8	3 20	2	4
24	0	2	28 51	6	6	0	1	♏ 29 40	5	5	7.9	0	0 29	3	5	9	6.9	1 18	2	4	9	7	2 7	1	3	8	6	2 56	2.9	3
25	0	1	28 28	3	4	6.9	4.9	29 17	1	4	9	5.8	0 6	0	3	9	7	0 54	0.9	2	8	5	1 43	1.7	2	8	4	2 32	6	2
26	0	3.9	28 4	27.9	3	9	7	28 53	28.8	2	9	6	♏ 29 42	♐ 29.7	2	9	5	0 30	5	1	8	3	1 19	4	0	8	2	2 8	3	0
27	0	7	27 41	6	1	9	6	28 29	5	0	9	4	29 18	3	0	8	3	0 6	2	2.9	9.8	2	0 55	1	3.9	10.7	0	1 43	1.9	4.9
28	5.9	5	27 17	3	♑ 29.9	9	4	28 6	1	0.9	9	3	28 54	0	1.8	8.8	1	♏ 29 42	♐ 29.9	8	8	0	0 30	0.7	7	7	7.8	1 18	6	7
29	9	3	26 53	26.9	8	9	2	27 41	27.8	7	7.8	1	28 29	28.6	7	8	5.9	29 17	5	6	7	6.8	0 5	4	6	7	6	0 53	2	5
30	9	2	26 29	6	6	6.8	0	27 17	4	6	8	4.9	28 5	3	5	7	7	28 52	1	5	7	6	♏ 29 40	0	4	6	4	0 28	0.9	4
31	9	0	26 5	2	4	8	3.8	26 52	1	4	8	7	27 40	27.9	3	7	5	28 27	28.8	3	7	4	29 15	♐ 29.6	3	6	2	0 2	5	2
32	9	2.8	25 40	25.8	2	8	6	26 28	26.7	2	8	5	27 15	6	2	7	3	28 2	4	1	9.6	2	28 49	3	1	10.6	0	♏ 29 36	1	0
33	5.8	6	25 15	5	0	8	4	26 2	3	0	7	3	26 49	2	0	8.7	1	27 36	0	1.9	6	0	28 23	28.9	2.9	5	6.8	29 10	♐ 29.8	3.9
34	8	4	24 50	1	28.9	8	3	25 37	25.9	♑ 29.8	7.7	1	26 23	26.8	0.8	6	4.9	27 10	27.6	8	6	5.8	27 56	5	7	5	6	28 43	4	7
35	8	2	24 24	24.7	7	6.7	1	25 11	5	6	7	3.9	25 57	4	6	6	7	26 43	2	6	5	6	27 30	1	5	5	4	28 16	0	5
36	8	0	23 58	3	5	7	2.9	24 44	1	4	7	7	25 30	0	4	6	5	26 17	26.8	4	5	4	27 2	27.6	3	4	2	27 48	28.5	3
37	8	1.8	23 32	23.9	3	7	7	24 18	24.7	2	6	5	25 3	25.6	2	5	4	25 49	4	2	9.5	2	26 35	2	1	10.4	0	27 20	1	1
38	5.7	6	23 5	4	1	7	4	23 51	3	0	6	3	24 36	1	0	8.5	2	25 22	25.9	0	4	0	26 7	26.8	1.9	3	5.8	26 52	27.6	2.9
39	7	4	22 38	22.9	27.9	6	2	23 23	23.8	28.8	7.6	1	24 8	24.6	♑ 29.8	5	0	24 53	5	0.8	4	4.8	25 38	3	7	3	6	26 23	2	7
40	7	2	22 11	5	6	6.6	0	22 55	3	6	5	2.9	23 40	2	6	4	3.7	24 25	0	5	4	5	25 9	25.8	5	3	3	25 54	26.7	5
41	7	0	21 42	0	4	6	1.8	22 27	22.9	4	5	7	23 11	23.7	4	4	5	23 55	24.5	3	3	3	24 40	4	3	2	1	25 24	2	3
42	6	0.8	21 14	21.5	2	6	6	21 58	4	1	5	5	22 42	2	1	8.4	2	23 26	0	1	9.3	0	24 10	24.9	1	10.2	4.8	24 53	25.7	0
43	5.6	6	20 45	0	26.9	5	3	21 28	21.9	27.9	4	2	22 12	22.6	28.9	3	0	22 56	23.5	♑ 29.8	3	3.8	23 39	3	0.8	1	6	24 22	1	1.8
44	6	4	20 15	20.5	6	6.5	1	20 58	3	6	7.4	0	21 42	1	6	3	2.7	22 25	0	6	2	5	23 8	23.8	6	1	3	23 51	24.6	5
45	6	2	19 45	19.9	3	5	0.9	20 28	20.8	3	4	1.7	21 11	21.5	4	3	5	21 54	22.4	4	2	3	22 36	2	4	0	1	23 19	0	3
46	5	♎ 29.9	19 14	3	1	5	7	19 57	2	1	3	5	20 39	0	1	8.2	3	21 22	21.9	1	2	0	22 4	22.7	1	0	3.8	22 46	23.5	1
47	5	7	18 43	18.8	25.8	4	5	19 25	19.6	26.8	3	3	20 7	20.4	27.8	2	1	20 49	3	28.8	9.1	2.7	21 31	1	♑ 29.8	9.9	6	22 12	22.9	0.8
48	5.5	4	18 11	2	5	6.4	3	18 52	0	5	7.3	0	19 34	19.8	5	2	1.8	20 15	20.7	5	1	5	20 57	21.5	5	9	3	21 38	3	5
49	5	1	17 38	17.6	1	4	0	18 19	18.4	1	2	0.7	19 0	2	2	1	5	19 41	0	2	0	2	20 22	20.8	2	9	0	21 3	21.7	2
50	5	28.9	17 4	0	24.8	4	♎ 29.7	17 45	17.8	25.8	2	4	18 25	18.6	26.8	8.1	2	19 6	19.4	27.8	0	1.9	19 46	2	28.8	8	2.7	20 27	0	♑ 29.8
51	4	6	16 30	16.3	4	3	4	17 10	1	4	2	1	17 50	17.9	4	1	0.9	18 30	18.7	4	8.9	6	19 10	19.5	4	8	4	19 50	20.3	4
52	5.4	4	15 55	15.6	0	6.3	1	16 34	16.4	0	7.1	♎ 29.8	17 14	2	0	0	6	17 53	0	0	9	3	18 33	18.8	0	9.7	1	19 12	19.6	0
53	4	1	15 19	14.9	23.6	3	28.8	15 58	15.6	24.6	1	5	16 37	16.4	25.6	0	3	17 16	17.2	26.6	8	0	17 54	0	27.6	7	1.8	18 33	18.8	28.6
54	3	27.8	14 42	1	1	2	5	15 20	14.8	1	0	2	15 59	15.6	1	7.9	0	16 37	16.4	1	7	0.7	17 15	17.2	1	6	5	17 54	0	2
55	3	5	14 4	13.3	22.6	2	2	14 43	0	23.6	0	28.9	15 20	14.8	24.6	9	♎ 29.7	15 57	15.5	25.6	7	4	16 35	16.3	26.6	6	1	17 13	17.1	27.7
56	3	2	13 25	12.5	0	1	27.9	14 2	13.1	1	6.9	6	14 39	13.9	1	8	3	15 17	14.6	1	6	0	15 54	15.4	1	5	0.7	16 31	16.2	2

	H. M. S. SID. T. 10 46 9 ARC 161° 32′.2 ♍ 10°					H. M. S. 10 49 53 162° 28′.2 ♍ 11°					H. M. S. 10 53 37 163° 24′.1 ♍ 12°					H. M. S. 10 57 20 164° 20′.0 ♍ 13°					H. M. S. 11 1 3 165° 15′.7 ♍ 14°					H. M. S. 11 4 46 166° 11′.4 ♍ 15°				
H.	11	12	1	2	3	11	12	1	2	3	11	12	1	2	3	11	12	1	2	3	11	12	1	2	3	11	12	1	2	3
Lat.	♎	♏	♐	♑	♒	♎	♏	♐	♑	♒	♎	♏	♐	♑	♒	♎	♏	♐	♑	♒	♎	♏	♐	♑	♒	♎	♏	♐	♑	♒
°	°	°	° ′	°	°	°	°	° ′	°	°	°	°	° ′	°	°	°	°	° ′	°	°	°	°	° ′	°	°	°	°	° ′	°	°
22	11.9	9.9	4 33	4.4	6.5	12.8	10.7	5 22	5.3	7.5	13.8	11.6	6 11	6.2	8.4	14.7	12.5	7 1	7.0	9.4	15.7	13.3	7 50	7.9	10.3	16.6	14.2	8 38	8.8	11.3
23	8	7	4 9	1	4	8	5	4 58	0	3	7	4	5 47	5.8	3	7	3	6 36	6.7	3	6	1	7 25	6	2	6	0	8 13	4	2
24	8	5	3 45	3.8	3	7	3	4 34	4.6	2	7	2	5 22	5	2	6	1	6 11	4	1	6	12.9	7 0	2	1	5	13.8	7 48	1	0
25	8	3	3 21	5	1	7	1	4 9	3	1	7	0	4 58	2	0	6	11.9	5 46	0	0	5	7	6 35	6.9	0	5	6	7 23	7.8	10.9
26	7	1	2 56	1	0	7	9.9	3 44	0	6.9	6	10.8	4 33	4.8	7.9	6	7	5 21	5.7	8.9	15.5	5	6 9	6	9.8	4	4	6 57	4	8
27	11.7	8.9	2 31	2.8	5.8	12.6	7	3 19	3.6	8	13.6	6	4 7	5	8	14.5	4	4 55	4	7	4	3	5 43	2	7	16.4	1	6 31	1	6
28	7	7	2 6	4	7	6	5	2 54	3	6	5	4	3 42	2	6	5	2	4 30	0	6	4	1	5 17	5.9	5	3	12.9	6 5	6.7	5
29	6	5	1 41	1	5	6	3	2 28	2.9	5	5	2	3 16	3.8	5	4	0	4 4	4.7	4	4	11.9	4 51	5	4	3	7	5 39	4	10.4
30	6	3	1 15	1.7	4	5	1	2 3	6	6.3	4	9.9	2 50	4	7.3	4	10.8	3 37	3	3	15.3	6	4 25	2	2	2	5	5 12	0	2
31	6	1	0 49	4	2	12.5	8.9	1 36	2	2	4	7	2 24	1	1	14.3	6	3 11	3.9	1	3	4	3 58	4.8	1	2	2	4 45	5.7	0
32	11.5	7.9	0 23	0	0	4	7	1 10	1.9	0	13.4	5	1 57	2.7	0	3	4	2 44	6	7.9	2	2	3 30	4	8.9	16.1	0	4 17	3	9.9
33	5	6	♏ 29 56	0.6	4.8	4	5	0 43	5	5.8	3	3	1 30	3	6.8	2	1	2 16	2	8	2	0	3 3	0	7	1	11.8	3 49	4.9	7
34	4	4	29 29	2	6	3	2	0 16	1	7	3	1	1 2	1.9	6	2	9.9	1 48	2.8	6	15.1	10.7	2 35	3.6	6	0	5	3 21	5	5
35	4	2	29 2	♐ 29.8	5	12.3	0	♏ 29 48	0.7	5	2	8.8	0 34	5	4	14.1	6	1 20	4	4	1	5	2 6	2	4	0	3	2 52	1	4
36	4	0	28 34	4	3	3	7.8	29 20	3	3	2	6	0 6	1	2	1	4	0 51	0	2	0	2	1 37	2.8	2	15.9	0	2 23	3.7	2
37	11.3	6.8	28 6	0	1	2	6	28 51	♐ 29.8	1	13.1	4	♏ 29 37	0.7	0	0	2	0 22	1.5	0	0	0	1 7	4	0	9	10.8	1 53	2	0
38	3	6	27 37	28.5	3.9	2	4	28 22	4	4.9	1	2	29 7	2	5.8	0	0	♏ 29 53	1	6.8	14.9	9.8	0 37	1.9	7.8	8	5	1 23	2.8	8.8
39	2	4	27 8	0	7	12.1	2	27 53	28.9	7	0	0	28 38	♐ 29.7	6	13.9	8.8	29 22	0.6	6	8	6	0 7	4	6	7	3	0 52	3	6
40	2	1	26 38	27.5	5	1	6.9	27 23	4	4	0	7.7	28 7	2	4	9	5	28 52	1	4	8	3	♏ 29 36	0.9	4	7	0	0 21	1.8	4
41	11.1	5.9	26 8	0	2	0	7	26 52	27.9	2	12.9	5	27 36	28.7	2	8	3	28 20	♐ 29.6	2	7	0	29 5	4	2	15.6	9.7	♏ 29 49	3	2
42	1	6	25 38	26.5	0	0	4	26 21	4	0	9	2	27 5	2	0	8	0	27 49	1	0	7	8.8	28 32	♐ 29.9	0	6	5	29 16	0.8	7.9
43	0	4	25 6	0	2.8	11.9	1	25 49	26.8	3.8	8	6.9	26 33	27.7	4.7	13.7	7.7	27 16	28.5	5.7	14.6	5	27 59	4	6.7	5	2	28 43	2	7
44	0	1	24 34	25.4	5	9	5.9	25 17	3	5	8	7	26 0	1	5	6	4	26 43	0	5	5	2	27 26	28.8	5	4	8.9	28 9	♐ 29.7	4
45	10.9	4.8	24 2	24.9	3	8	6	24 44	25.7	3	7	4	25 27	26.5	3	6	1	26 9	27.4	3	5	7.9	26 52	2	2	3	6	27 34	1	2
46	9	5	23 28	3	1	8	3	24 10	1	0	12.6	1	24 52	25.9	0	5	6.8	25 34	26.8	0	4	6	26 16	27.6	0	15.3	3	26 59	28.5	0
47	8	3	22 54	23.7	1.8	7	1	23 36	24.5	2.7	6	5.8	24 17	3	3.7	13.4	5	24 59	2	4.7	3	3	25 41	0	5.7	2	0	26 22	27.9	6.7
48	8	0	22 19	1	5	11.7	4.8	23 0	23.9	4	5	5	23 42	24.7	4	4	2	24 23	25.6	4	14.2	0	25 4	26.4	4	1	7.7	25 45	2	4
49	10.7	3.7	21 44	22.4	2	6	5	22 24	3	1	5	2	23 5	1	1	3	5.9	23 46	24.9	1	2	6.7	24 27	25.7	1	1	4	25 7	26.5	1
50	7	4	21 7	21.8	0.8	6	2	21 47	22.6	1.8	4	4.9	22 28	23.4	2.8	3	6	23 8	2	3.8	1	4	23 48	0	4.8	0	1	24 28	25.9	5.8
51	6	1	20 30	1	4	5	3.9	21 9	21.9	4	12.3	6	21 49	22.7	4	13.2	3	22 29	23.5	4	1	1	23 9	24.3	4	14.9	6.8	23 49	2	4
52	6	2.8	19 52	20.4	0	11.5	6	20 31	1	0	3	3	21 10	21.9	0	2	0	21 49	22.7	0	0	5.7	22 28	23.5	0	9	4	23 8	24.4	1
53	10.5	5	19 12	19.6	♑ 29.6	4	2	19 51	20.3	0.6	2	3.9	20 29	1	1.6	1	4.7	21 8	21.9	2.6	13.9	4	21 47	22.7	3.6	8	1	22 26	23.6	4.7
54	5	2	18 32	18.8	2	3	2.9	19 10	19.5	2	2	6	19 48	20.3	2	0	3	20 26	1	2	8	0	21 4	21.9	2	7	5.7	21 42	22.7	3
55	4	1.8	17 50	17.9	28.7	2	5	18 28	18.6	♑ 29.7	1	2	19 5	19.4	0.7	12.9	3.9	19 43	20.2	1.8	8	4.6	20 20	0	2.8	6	3	20 58	21.8	3.9
56	3	4	17 7	0	2	1	1	17 45	17.7	2	1	2.8	18 21	18.5	2	9	5	18 58	19.3	3	7	2	19 35	20.0	3	5	4.9	20 12	20.8	4

	SID. T. H. M. S. 11 4 46 ARC 166° 11′.4 } ♍ 15°					H. M. S. 11 8 28 167° 7′.0 } ♍ 16°				
H.	11	12	1	2	3	11	12	1	2	3
Lat.	♎	♏	♐	♑	♒	♎	♏	♐	♑	♒
°	°	°	° ′	°	°	°	°	° ′	°	°
22	16.6	14.2	8 38	8.8	11.3	17.6	15.0	9 27	9.6	12.3
23	6	0	8 13	4	2	5	14.8	9 2	3	1
24	5	13.8	7 48	1	0	5	6	8 37	0	0
25	5	6	7 23	7.8	10.9	4	4	8 11	8.6	11.9
26	4	4	6 57	4	8	17.4	2	7 45	3	8
27	16.4	1	6 31	1	6	3	0	7 19	0	6
28	3	12.9	6 5	6.7	5	3	13.7	6 53	7.6	5
29	3	7	5 39	4	10.4	2	5	6 26	3	11.3
30	2	5	5 12	0	2	17.1	3	5 59	6.9	2
31	2	2	4 45	5.7	0	1	1	5 32	5	0
32	16.1	0	4 17	3	9.9	0	12.8	5 4	2	10.9
33	1	11.8	3 49	4.9	7	0	6	4 36	5.8	7
34	0	5	3 21	5	5	16.9	3	4 7	4	5
35	0	3	2 52	1	4	9	1	3 38	0	4
36	15.9	0	2 23	3.7	2	8	11.8	3 8	4.5	2
37	9	10.8	1 53	2	0	7	6	2 38	1	0
38	8	5	1 23	2.8	8.8	7	3	2 8	3.6	9.8
39	7	3	0 52	3	6	16.6	1	1 37	1	6
40	7	0	0 21	1.8	4	6	10.8	1 5	2.6	4
41	15.6	9.7	♏ 29 49	3	2	5	5	0 33	1	2
42	6	5	29 16	0.8	7.9	4	2	0 0	1.6	8.9
43	5	2	28 43	2	7	4	0	♏ 29 26	1	7
44	4	8.9	28 9	♐ 29.7	4	16.3	9.7	28 52	0.5	5
45	3	6	27 34	1	2	2	4	28 17	♐ 29.9	3
46	15.3	3	26 59	28.5	0	1	1	27 41	3	1
47	2	0	26 22	27.9	6.7	0	8.8	27 4	28.7	7.8
48	1	7.7	25 45	2	4	0	5	26 26	0	5
49	1	4	25 7	26.5	1	15.9	2	25 48	27.4	2
50	0	1	24 28	25.9	5.8	8	7.8	25 9	26.7	6.9
51	14.9	6.8	23 49	2	4	7	5	24 28	25.9	5
52	9	4	23 8	24.4	1	7	1	23 47	1	1
53	8	1	22 26	23.6	4.7	15.6	6.8	23 4	24.3	5.7
54	7	5.7	21 42	22.7	3	5	4	22 20	23.4	3
55	6	3	20 58	21.8	3.9	4	0	21 35	22.5	4.9
56	5	4.9	20 12	20.8	4	3	5.6	20 49	21.5	4

	H. M. S. 11 12 10 168° 2′.5 } ♍ 17°					H. M. S. 11 15 52 168° 58′.0 } ♍ 18°				
H.	11	12	1	2	3	11	12	1	2	3
Lat.	♎	♏	♐	♑	♒	♎	♏	♐	♑	♒
°	°	°	° ′	°	°	°	°	° ′	°	°
22	18.5	15.9	10 16	10.5	13.2	19.4	16.7	11 5	11.4	14.2
23	4	7	9 51	2	1	4	5	10 39	1	1
24	4	5	9 25	9.8	0	3	3	10 14	10.7	13.9
25	3	2	8 59	5	12.8	3	1	9 48	4	8
26	3	0	8 33	2	7	2	15.8	9 22	1	7
27	18.2	14.8	8 7	8.8	6	19.2	6	8 55	9.7	6
28	2	6	7 40	5	4	1	4	8 28	4	13.4
29	1	3	7 14	1	12.3	0	2	8 1	0	3
30	1	1	6 46	7.8	2	0	14.9	7 34	8.6	1
31	0	13.9	6 19	4	0	18.9	7	7 6	3	0
32	17.9	6	5 51	0	11.9	9	5	6 37	7.9	12.8
33	9	4	5 22	6.7	7	8	2	6 9	5	7
34	8	1	4 53	3	5	7	0	5 39	1	5
35	8	12.9	4 24	5.8	4	7	13.7	5 10	6.7	4
36	17.7	6	3 54	4	2	18.6	4	4 40	3	2
37	6	4	3 24	0	0	5	2	4 9	5.8	0
38	6	1	2 53	4.5	10.8	5	12.9	3 38	4	11.8
39	5	11.8	2 21	0	6	4	6	3 6	4.9	6
40	17.4	6	1 49	3.5	4	3	4	2 34	4	4
41	4	3	1 17	0	2	18.3	1	2 1	3.9	2
42	3	0	0 43	2.5	9.9	2	11.8	1 27	3	0
43	2	10.7	0 9	1.9	7	1	5	0 53	2.8	10.7
44	17.2	4	♏ 29 35	3	5	0	2	0 18	2	5
45	1	2	28 59	0.7	3	17.9	10.9	♏ 29 42	1.6	3
46	0	9.9	28 23	1	1	8	6	29 5	0	1
47	0	6	27 46	♐ 29.5	8.8	8	3	28 28	0.4	9.8
48	16.9	3	27 8	28.9	5	7	0	27 49	♐ 29.7	5
49	8	0	26 29	2	2	17.6	9.7	27 10	1	2
50	7	8.6	25 49	27.5	7.9	5	3	26 29	28.4	8.9
51	6	3	25 8	26.8	6	5	0	25 48	27.6	6
52	16.6	7.9	24 26	0	2	4	8.6	25 5	26.8	2
53	5	5	23 43	25.1	6.8	17.3	2	24 22	25.9	7.8
54	4	1	22 58	24.2	4	2	7.8	23 37	0	4
55	3	6.7	22 13	23.3	0	1	4	22 50	24.1	0
56	2	3	21 26	22.3	5.5	0	0	22 3	23.1	6.5

	H. M. S. 11 19 33 169° 53′.4 } ♍ 19°					H. M. S. 11 23 15 170° 48′.7 } ♍ 20°				
H.	11	12	1	2	3	11	12	1	2	3
Lat.	♎	♏	♐	♑	♒	♎	♏	♐	♑	♒
°	°	°	° ′	°	°	°	°	° ′	°	°
22	20.4	17.6	11 53	12.3	15.2	21.3	18.4	12 42	13.1	16.1
23	3	4	11 28	11.9	0	2	2	12 16	12.8	0
24	2	2	11 2	6	14.9	2	0	11 50	5	15.9
25	2	16.9	10 36	3	8	1	17.8	11 24	2	8
26	20.1	7	10 10	10.9	7	1	6	10 58	11.8	7
27	1	5	9 43	6	5	0	3	10 31	5	5
28	0	2	9 16	2	14.4	20.9	1	10 3	1	15.4
29	19.9	0	8 48	9.9	3	9	16.8	9 36	10.8	3
30	9	15.8	8 21	5	1	8	6	9 8	4	1
31	8	5	7 53	2	0	7	3	8 40	1	0
32	8	3	7 24	8.8	13.8	7	1	8 11	9.7	14.8
33	7	0	6 55	4	7	20.6	15.8	7 42	3	7
34	19.6	14.8	6 26	0	5	5	6	7 12	8.9	5
35	6	5	5 56	7.6	3	5	3	6 42	5	3
36	5	2	5 25	2	2	4	0	6 11	0	2
37	4	0	4 55	6.7	0	3	14.8	5 40	7.6	0
38	4	13.8	4 23	3	12.8	20.2	5	5 8	1	13.8
39	19.3	5	3 51	5.8	6	2	3	4 36	6.6	6
40	2	2	3 18	2	4	1	0	4 3	1	4
41	1	12.9	2 45	4.7	2	0	13.7	3 29	5.6	2
42	1	6	2 11	2	0	19.9	4	2 55	1	0
43	0	3	1 36	3.6	11.7	9	1	2 20	4.5	12.8
44	18.9	0	1 1	1	5	8	12.8	1 44	3.9	5
45	8	11.7	0 24	2.5	3	7	5	1 7	3	3
46	7	4	♏ 29 47	1.9	1	19.6	2	0 30	2.7	1
47	7	0	29 9	2	10.9	5	11.9	♏ 29 51	1	11.8
48	18.6	10.7	28 30	0.6	6	4	5	29 12	1.4	5
49	5	3	27 51	♐ 29.9	3	3	2	28 31	0.8	3
50	4	0	27 10	2	0	19.2	10.8	27 50	1	0
51	3	9.7	26 28	28.5	9.7	1	4	27 8	♐ 29.3	10.7
52	18.2	3	25 45	27.7	3	0	0	26 24	28.5	4
53	1	8.9	25 0	26.8	8.9	18.9	9.6	25 39	27.7	0
54	0	5	24 15	25.9	5	8	2	24 53	26.8	9.6
55	17.9	1	23 28	24.9	1	7	8.8	24 5	25.8	2
56	8	7.7	22 39	23.9	7.6	6	4	23 16	24.8	8.7

SID. T. 11 h 26 m 56 s, ARC 171° 44′.0 — ♍ 21°

H.	11	12	1	2	3
Lat.	♎	♏	♐	♑	♒
°	°	°	° ′	°	°
22	22.2	19.3	13 31	14.0	17.1
23	2	1	13 5	13.7	0
24	1	18.8	12 39	4	16.9
25	0	6	12 13	0	8
26	0	4	11 46	12.7	6
27	21.9	1	11 19	4	5
28	9	17.9	10 51	0	16.4
29	8	7	10 23	11.7	2
30	7	4	9 55	3	1
31	6	2	9 27	10.9	0
32	21.6	16.9	8 57	6	15.8
33	5	6	8 28	2	7
34	4	4	7 58	9.8	5
35	4	1	7 28	4	3
36	3	15.9	6 57	8.9	2
37	21.2	6	6 26	5	0
38	1	4	5 53	0	14.8
39	1	1	5 21	7.5	6
40	0	14.8	4 47	0	4
41	20.9	5	4 13	6.5	2
42	8	2	3 39	5.9	0
43	7	13.9	3 3	4	13.8
44	6	5	2 27	4.8	5
45	20.6	2	1 50	2	3
46	5	12.9	1 12	3.6	1
47	4	6	0 33	2.9	12.9
48	3	3	♏ 29 53	3	6
49	20.2	11.9	29 12	1.6	3
50	1	5	28 30	0.9	0
51	0	1	27 48	1	11.7
52	19.9	10.7	27 3	♐ 29.3	4
53	8	3	26 18	28.5	1
54	7	9.9	25 31	27.6	10.7
55	6	5	24 43	26.6	3
56	5	1	23 53	25.5	9.8

11 h 30 m 37 s, 172° 39′.2 — ♍ 22°

H.	11	12	1	2	3
Lat.	♎	♏	♐	♑	♒
°	°	°	° ′	°	°
22	23.2	20.1	14 20	14.9	18.1
23	1	19.9	13 54	6	0
24	0	7	13 28	2	17.8
25	0	4	13 1	13.9	7
26	22.9	2	12 34	6	6
27	8	0	12 6	2	5
28	8	18.7	11 39	12.9	17.4
29	7	5	11 11	5	2
30	6	2	10 43	2	1
31	22.5	0	10 14	11.8	0
32	5	17.7	9 44	5	16.8
33	4	4	9 15	1	7
34	3	2	8 45	10.7	5
35	22.3	16.9	8 14	2	3
36	2	6	7 43	9.8	2
37	1	3	7 11	3	0
38	0	1	6 39	8.9	15.8
39	21.9	15.8	6 6	4	6
40	9	5	5 32	7.9	4
41	8	2	4 58	4	2
42	7	14.9	4 23	6.8	0
43	21.6	6	3 47	3	14.8
44	5	3	3 10	5.7	6
45	4	0	2 33	1	4
46	3	13.7	1 54	4.5	2
47	21.2	4	1 15	3.8	13.9
48	1	0	0 35	2	6
49	0	12.6	♏ 29 53	2.5	4
50	20.9	2	29 11	1.8	1
51	8	11.8	28 27	0	12.8
52	7	4	27 42	0.2	5
53	6	0	26 56	♐ 29.3	1
54	20.5	10.6	26 9	28.4	11.7
55	4	2	25 20	27.4	3
56	3	9.8	24 30	26.3	10.9

11 h 34 m 18 s, 173° 34′.4 — ♍ 23°

H.	11	12	1	2	3
Lat.	♎	♏	♐	♑	♒
°	°	°	° ′	°	°
22	24.1	21.0	15 9	15.8	19.1
23	0	20.7	14 43	5	18.9
24	0	5	14 16	2	8
25	23.9	3	13 49	14.8	7
26	8	0	13 22	5	6
27	7	19.8	12 55	1	18.5
28	7	5	12 27	13.8	3
29	23.6	3	11 59	4	2
30	5	0	11 30	1	1
31	5	18.8	11 1	12.7	17.9
32	4	5	10 31	3	8
33	23.3	2	10 1	11.9	6
34	2	0	9 31	5	5
35	1	17.7	9 0	1	17.3
36	0	4	8 29	10.7	2
37	22.9	1	7 57	2	0
38	8	16.9	7 24	9.7	16.8
39	7	6	6 51	3	6
40	6	3	6 17	8.8	5
41	22.6	15.9	5 42	2	3
42	5	6	5 7	7.7	0
43	5	3	4 30	1	15.8
44	4	0	3 53	6.5	6
45	22.3	14.7	3 16	5.9	4
46	2	4	2 37	3	2
47	1	0	1 57	4.7	0
48	0	13.6	1 16	0	14.8
49	21.9	3	0 34	3.3	5
50	8	12.9	♏ 29 51	2.6	2
51	7	5	29 7	1.8	13.9
52	6	1	28 22	0	6
53	21.5	11.7	27 35	0.2	2
54	4	3	26 47	♐ 29.2	12.8
55	2	10.9	25 58	28.2	4
56	1	4	25 7	27.1	0

11 h 37 m 58 s, 174° 29′.6 — ♍ 24°

H.	11	12	1	2	3
Lat.	♎	♏	♐	♑	♒
°	°	°	° ′	°	°
22	25.0	21.8	15 58	16.7	20.0
23	24.9	6	15 31	4	19.9
24	9	3	15 5	0	8
25	8	1	14 38	15.7	7
26	7	20.9	14 10	4	6
27	7	6	13 43	0	19.5
28	24.6	4	13 15	14.7	3
29	5	1	12 46	3	2
30	4	19.8	12 17	0	1
31	4	6	11 48	13.6	18.9
32	3	3	11 19	2	8
33	24.2	0	10 48	12.8	7
34	1	18.8	10 18	4	5
35	0	5	9 46	0	18.3
36	0	2	9 15	11.5	2
37	23.9	17.9	8 42	1	0
38	8	6	8 9	10.6	17.8
39	7	4	7 36	1	7
40	6	1	7 2	9.6	5
41	5	16.8	6 27	1	3
42	23.4	5	5 51	8.6	1
43	3	2	5 14	0	16.8
44	2	15.9	4 37	7.4	6
45	1	5	3 58	6.8	4
46	0	2	3 19	2	2
47	22.9	14.9	2 39	5.5	0
48	8	5	1 58	4.9	15.7
49	7	1	1 15	2	5
50	6	13.7	0 32	3.5	2
51	5	3	♏ 29 47	2.7	14.9
52	22.4	12.9	29 2	1.9	6
53	3	5	28 14	0	3
54	2	1	27 26	0.1	13.9
55	0	11.6	26 36	♐ 29.1	5
56	21.9	1	25 44	28.0	1

11 h 41 m 39 s, 175° 24′.7 — ♍ 25°

H.	11	12	1	2	3
Lat.	♎	♏	♐	♑	♒
°	°	°	° ′	°	°
22	25.9	22.7	16 47	17.6	21.0
23	9	4	16 20	3	20.9
24	8	2	15 53	16.9	8
25	7	21.9	15 26	6	7
26	7	7	14 58	3	6
27	25.6	4	14 31	15.9	5
28	5	2	14 3	6	20.3
29	4	20.9	13 34	2	2
30	3	7	13 5	14.9	1
31	25.3	4	12 35	5	0
32	2	1	12 6	1	19.8
33	1	19.9	11 35	13.7	7
34	0	6	11 4	3	5
35	24.9	3	10 33	12.9	4
36	8	0	10 1	4	2
37	8	18.7	9 28	0	0
38	7	4	8 55	11.5	18.9
39	24.6	2	8 21	0	7
40	5	17.9	7 46	10.5	5
41	4	6	7 11	0	3
42	3	3	6 35	9.5	1
43	24.2	16.9	5 58	8.9	17.9
44	1	6	5 20	3	6
45	0	2	4 41	7.7	4
46	23.9	15.9	4 2	1	2
47	8	6	3 21	6.4	0
48	7	2	2 40	5.7	16.8
49	6	14.8	1 57	1	5
50	5	4	1 13	4.4	3
51	23.4	0	0 28	3.6	0
52	3	13.6	♏ 29 41	2.8	15.7
53	2	2	28 53	1.9	4
54	0	12.8	28 4	0.9	0
55	22.8	3	27 13	♐ 29.9	14.6
56	7	11.8	26 21	28.8	2

11 h 45 m 19 s, 176° 19′.8 — ♍ 26°

H.	11	12	1	2	3
Lat.	♎	♏	♐	♑	♒
°	°	°	° ′	°	°
22	26.9	23.5	17 36	18.5	22.0
23	8	3	17 9	2	21.9
24	7	0	16 42	17.8	8
25	6	22.8	16 15	5	7
26	26.6	5	15 47	2	6
27	5	3	15 19	16.8	4
28	4	0	14 50	5	21.3
29	3	21.7	14 22	1	2
30	26.3	5	13 53	15.8	1
31	2	2	13 23	4	0
32	1	20.9	12 53	0	20.8
33	0	7	12 22	14.6	7
34	25.9	4	11 51	2	5
35	8	1	11 19	13.8	4
36	7	19.8	10 47	3	2
37	6	5	10 14	12.9	1
38	25.6	2	9 40	4	19.9
39	5	0	9 6	11.9	7
40	4	18.7	8 31	4	5
41	3	4	7 56	10.9	3
42	25.2	0	7 19	4	1
43	1	17.7	6 42	9.8	18.9
44	0	3	6 4	2	7
45	24.9	0	5 25	8.6	6
46	8	16.6	4 44	0	4
47	7	3	4 3	7.3	2
48	6	15.9	3 21	6.6	0
49	24.4	5	2 38	0	17.7
50	3	1	1 54	5.3	4
51	2	14.7	1 8	4.5	1
52	1	3	0 21	3.7	16.8
53	23.9	13.9	♏ 29 33	2.8	5
54	8	5	28 43	1.8	1
55	6	0	27 51	0.7	15.7
56	5	12.5	26 58	♐ 29.6	3

	SID. T. 11 45 19 ♍ 26° ARC 176° 19′.8					11 48 59 ♍ 27° 177° 14′.8					11 52 40 ♍ 28° 178° 9′.9					11 56 20 ♍ 29° 179° 5′.0					12 0 0 ♎ 0° 180° 0′.0					12 3 40 ♎ 1° 180° 55′.0				
H.	11	12	1	2	3	11	12	1	2	3	11	12	1	2	3	11	12	1	2	3	11	12	1	2	3	11	12	1	2	3
Lat.	♎	♏	♐	♑	♒	♎	♏	♐	♑	♒	♎	♏	♐	♑	♒	♎	♏	♐	♑	♒	♏	♏	♐	♑	♒	♏	♏	♐	♑	♒
°	°	°	° ′	°	°	°	°	° ′	°	°	°	°	° ′	°	°	°	°	° ′	°	°	°	°	° ′	°	°	°	°	° ′	°	°
22	26.9	23.5	17 36	18.5	22.0	27.8	24.3	18 24	19.4	23.0	28.7	25.2	19 14	20.3	24.0	29.7	26.0	20 3	21.2	25.0	0.6	26.8	20 52	22.1	26.0	1.5	27.7	21 41	23.0	27.0
23	8	3	17 9	2	21.9	7	1	17 57	1	22.9	6	24.9	18 47	0	23.9	6	25.8	19 36	20.9	24.9	5	6	20 25	21.8	25.9	4	4	21 14	22.7	26.9
24	7	0	16 42	17.8	8	7	23.8	17 30	18.7	8	6	7	18 19	19.6	8	5	5	19 8	5	8	4	3	19 57	4	8	3	2	20 46	4	8
25	6	22.8	16 15	5	7	6	6	17 3	4	7	5	4	17 52	3	7	4	2	18 40	2	7	3	1	19 29	1	7	2	26.9	20 18	0	7
26	26.6	5	15 47	2	6	27.5	3	16 35	1	6	4	2	17 24	0	6	3	0	18 12	19.9	6	0.2	25.8	19 1	20.8	6	1.1	6	19 50	21.7	6
27	5	3	15 19	16.8	4	4	1	16 7	17.7	5	28.3	23.9	16 55	18.6	5	29.3	24.7	17 44	5	5	2	5	18 33	4	5	0	4	19 21	4	5
28	4	0	14 50	5	21.3	3	22.8	15 38	4	22.3	3	6	16 26	3	23.3	2	4	17 15	2	24.4	1	3	18 4	1	25.4	0	1	18 51	0	26.4
29	3	21.7	14 22	1	2	3	5	15 9	0	2	2	4	15 57	17.9	2	1	2	16 45	18.9	3	0	0	17 34	19.8	3	0.9	25.8	18 22	20.7	3
30	26.3	5	13 53	15.8	1	27.2	3	14 40	16.7	1	1	1	15 28	6	1	0	23.9	16 16	5	2	♎ 29.9	24.7	17 4	4	2	8	5	17 52	3	2
31	2	2	13 23	4	0	1	0	14 10	3	0	0	22.8	14 58	2	0	28.9	6	15 45	1	0	8	4	16 34	0	1	7	2	17 21	0	0
32	1	20.9	12 53	0	20.8	0	21.7	13 39	15.9	21.8	27.9	5	14 27	16.8	22.8	8	3	15 15	17.8	23.9	7	2	16 3	18.7	0	6	0	16 50	19.6	25.9
33	0	7	12 22	14.6	7	26.9	5	13 9	5	7	8	2	13 56	4	7	7	1	14 43	4	8	6	23.9	15 31	3	24.8	5	24.7	16 18	2	8
34	25.9	4	11 51	2	5	8	2	12 38	1	5	7	0	13 24	0	6	6	22.8	14 11	0	6	5	6	14 59	17.9	7	0.4	4	15 45	18.8	6
35	8	1	11 19	13.8	4	7	20.9	12 6	14.7	4	6	21.7	12 52	15.6	4	5	5	13 39	16.6	5	29.4	3	14 26	5	6	3	1	15 13	4	5
36	7	19.8	10 47	3	2	6	6	11 33	2	2	5	4	12 19	1	2	28.4	2	13 6	1	23.3	3	0	13 52	0	4	2	23.8	14 39	17.9	25.3
37	6	5	10 14	12.9	1	5	3	11 0	13.8	1	27.4	1	11 46	14.7	1	3	21.9	12 32	15.7	2	2	22.7	13 18	16.6	3	1	4	14 5	5	2
38	25.6	2	9 40	4	19.9	26.4	0	10 26	3	20.9	3	20.8	11 12	2	21.9	2	6	11 58	2	0	1	3	12 44	1	1	♎ 29.9	1	13 30	0	0
39	5	0	9 6	11.9	7	3	19.7	9 52	12.8	7	2	5	10 37	13.7	8	1	3	11 23	14.7	22.9	0	0	12 8	15.6	23.9	8	22.8	12 54	16.5	24.9
40	4	18.7	8 31	4	5	2	4	9 16	3	6	1	1	10 1	2	6	0	0	10 47	2	7	28.9	21.7	11 32	1	7	7	5	12 17	0	8
41	3	4	7 56	10.9	3	1	0	8 40	11.8	4	0	19.8	9 25	12.7	4	27.9	20.7	10 10	13.7	6	8	3	10 55	14.6	6	6	1	11 40	15.5	6
42	25.2	0	7 19	4	1	0	18.7	8 4	3	2	26.9	5	8 48	2	2	8	3	9 32	1	4	6	0	10 17	1	4	5	21.7	11 2	0	4
43	1	17.7	6 42	9.8	18.9	25.9	4	7 26	10.7	0	8	1	8 10	11.6	1	6	0	8 54	12.6	2	5	20.7	9 38	13.5	2	29.4	4	10 22	14.4	2
44	0	3	6 4	2	7	8	0	6 47	1	19.9	7	18.8	7 31	0	20.9	5	19.6	8 15	0	0	28.4	4	8 59	12.9	0	2	0	9 42	13.8	0
45	24.9	0	5 25	8.6	6	7	17.7	6 8	9.5	7	6	5	6 51	10.4	7	4	2	7 34	11.4	21.8	3	0	8 18	3	22.8	1	20.6	9 1	2	23.8
46	8	16.6	4 44	0	4	6	4	5 27	8.9	5	5	2	6 10	9.7	5	27.3	18.9	6 53	10.7	6	2	19.6	7 36	11.7	5	0	3	8 19	12.6	6
47	7	3	4 3	7.3	2	5	1	4 46	2	3	26.4	17.8	5 28	1	3	2	5	6 10	1	4	1	2	6 53	0	3	28.9	19.9	7 36	11.9	5
48	6	15.9	3 21	6.6	0	25.4	16.7	4 3	7.5	1	3	4	4 45	8.4	1	1	1	5 27	9.4	2	27.9	18.8	6 9	10.3	1	8	5	6 52	2	3
49	24.4	5	2 38	0	17.7	3	3	3 19	6.8	18.8	1	0	4 1	7.7	19.8	0	17.7	4 42	8.7	20.9	8	4	5 24	9.6	21.9	6	1	6 6	10.5	1
50	3	1	1 54	5.3	4	1	15.9	2 34	1	5	0	16.6	3 15	0	5	26.8	3	3 56	7.9	6	7	0	4 38	8.8	7	5	18.7	5 19	9.7	22.9
51	2	14.7	1 8	4.5	1	0	5	1 48	5.3	2	25.8	2	2 29	6.2	2	6	16.9	3 9	1	4	6	17.6	3 50	0	4	28.3	3	4 30	8.9	6
52	1	3	0 21	3.7	16.8	24.9	1	1 1	4.5	17.9	7	15.8	1 40	5.4	18.9	5	5	2 20	6.3	1	27.4	2	3 1	7.1	1	1	17.9	3 40	0	3
53	23.9	13.9	♏ 29 33	2.8	5	8	14.6	0 12	3.6	6	6	3	0 51	4.5	6	4	0	1 30	5.4	19.8	2	16.7	2 10	6.2	20.8	0	4	2 49	7.1	0
54	8	5	28 43	1.8	1	6	1	♏ 29 21	2.6	2	5	14.8	0 0	3.5	3	3	15.5	0 38	4.4	4	0	2	1 17	5.2	5	27.9	16.9	1 56	6.1	21.7
55	6	0	27 51	0.7	15.7	4	13.6	28 29	1.6	16.8	3	3	♏ 29 7	2.5	0	1	0	♏ 29 45	3.3	1	26.9	15.7	0 23	4.2	2	7	4	1 1	5.1	4
56	5	12.5	26 58	♐ 29.6	3	3	1	27 35	0.5	4	2	13.8	28 13	1.4	17.6	25.9	14.5	28 50	2.2	18.7	7	2	♏ 29 28	3.0	19.9	5	15.9	0 5	4.0	1

	SID. T. 12 7 20 (H. M. S.) ARC 181° 50′.1 ♎ 2°					12 11 1 (H. M. S.) 182° 45′.2 ♎ 3°					12 14 41 (H. M. S.) 183° 40′.2 ♎ 4°					12 18 21 (H. M. S.) 184° 35′.3 ♎ 5°					12 22 2 (H. M. S.) 185° 30′.4 ♎ 6°					12 25 42 (H. M. S.) 186° 25′.6 ♎ 7°				
H.	11	12	1	2	3	11	12	1	2	3	11	12	1	2	3	11	12	1	2	3	11	12	1	2	3	11	12	1	2	3
Lat.	♏	♏	♐	♑	♒	♏	♏	♐	♑	♒	♏	♐	♐	♑	♓	♏	♐	♐	♑	♓	♏	♐	♐	♑	♓	♏	♐	♐	♑	♓
°	°	°	° ′	°	°	°	°	° ′	°	°	°	°	° ′	°	°	°	°	° ′	°	°	°	°	° ′	°	°	°	°	° ′	°	°
22	2.4	28.5	22 31	23.9	28.0	3.3	29.3	23 20	24.8	29.0	4.2	0.2	24 10	25.7	0.0	5.1	1.0	24 59	26.6	1.1	6.0	1.8	25 49	27.6	2.1	6.9	2.6	26 40	28.5	3.1
23	3	2	22 3	6	27.9	2	1	22 53	5	28.9	1	♏ 29.9	23 42	4	♒ 29.9	0	0.7	24 31	3	0	5.9	5	25 21	3	0	8	4	26 11	2	0
24	2	0	21 35	3	8	1	28.8	22 25	2	8	0	6	23 14	1	9	4.9	5	24 3	0	0.9	8	3	24 53	0	1.9	7	1	25 43	27.9	2.9
25	1	27.7	21 7	22.9	7	0	6	21 56	23.9	7	3.9	4	22 45	24.8	8	8	2	23 35	25.7	8	7	0	24 24	26.6	8	6	1.8	25 14	6	8
26	0	5	20 38	6	6	2.9	3	21 27	5	6	8	1	22 17	4	7	7	♏ 29.9	23 6	4	7	6	0.7	23 55	3	7	5	5	24 45	3	7
27	1.9	2	20 9	3	5	8	0	20 58	2	5	7	28.8	21 47	1	6	6	6	22 36	0	6	5	4	23 26	0	6	6.4	3	24 15	26.9	7
28	8	26.9	19 40	21.9	27.4	7	27.7	20 29	22.9	28.4	6	5	21 18	23.8	29.5	5	4	22 6	24.7	5	5.4	2	22 56	25.7	5	3	0	23 45	6	2.6
29	7	6	19 10	6	3	6	4	19 59	5	3	5	3	20 47	4	3	4.4	1	21 36	4	0.4	3	♏ 29.9	22 25	3	1.4	2	0.7	23 14	3	5
30	7	3	18 40	3	2	5	2	19 28	2	2	3.4	0	20 17	1	2	3	28.8	21 5	0	3	2	6	21 54	0	3	1	4	22 43	25.9	4
31	6	1	18 9	20.9	1	2.4	26.9	18 57	21.8	1	3	27.7	19 45	22.8	1	2	5	20 34	23.7	2	1	3	21 22	24.6	2	0	1	22 11	6	3
32	1.5	25.8	17 37	5	26.9	3	6	18 26	4	0	2	4	19 14	4	0	1	2	20 1	3	1	0	0	20 50	3	1	5.8	♏ 29.8	21 38	2	2.2
33	4	5	17 5	1	8	2	3	17 53	0	27.8	1	1	18 41	0	28.9	0	27.9	19 29	22.9	0	4.9	28.7	20 17	23.9	0	7	5	21 5	24.8	1
34	3	2	16 33	19.7	7	1	0	17 20	20.6	7	0	26.8	18 8	21.6	8	3.9	6	18 56	5	♒ 29.8	7	4	19 44	5	0.9	6	2	20 32	4	0
35	1	24.9	15 59	3	5	0	25.7	16 47	2	6	2.9	5	17 34	2	6	8	2	18 22	1	7	6	0	19 9	0	8	5	28.8	19 57	0	1.9
36	0	5	15 26	18.9	26.4	1.9	3	16 13	19.8	5	8	1	17 0	20.7	5	6	26.9	17 47	21.7	6	5	27.7	18 35	22.6	7	5.4	5	19 22	23.5	7
37	0.9	2	14 51	4	2	8	0	15 38	3	27.3	6	25.8	16 25	3	28.4	5	6	17 12	2	5	4.4	4	17 59	1	5	3	2	18 47	1	6
38	8	23.9	14 16	17.9	1	7	24.7	15 2	18.9	2	5	5	15 49	19.8	2	3.4	3	16 36	20.7	29.3	3	0	17 23	21.7	0.4	1	27.8	18 10	22.6	5
39	7	6	13 40	5	0	6	4	14 26	4	0	2.4	1	15 12	3	1	3	25.9	15 59	2	2	2	26.7	16 46	2	3	0	5	17 32	1	1.4
40	6	3	13 3	0	25.9	1.4	1	13 49	17.9	26.9	3	24.8	14 35	18.8	0	2	6	15 21	19.7	1	0	4	16 7	20.7	2	4.9	2	16 54	21.6	2
41	5	0	12 25	16.4	7	3	23.8	13 11	4	7	2	4	13 57	3	27.9	0	2	14 42	2	28.9	3.9	0	15 28	2	0	8	26.9	16 15	1	1
42	0.3	22.6	11 47	15.9	5	2	4	12 32	16.8	5	0	1	13 17	17.8	7	2.9	24.8	14 3	18.7	8	8	25.6	14 48	19.6	♒ 29.9	6	5	15 34	20.6	0.9
43	2	3	11 7	3	3	1	0	11 52	3	4	1.9	23.7	12 37	2	5	8	5	13 22	1	6	6	3	14 7	1	7	5	1	14 53	0	8
44	1	21.9	10 27	14.7	1	0.9	22.7	11 11	15.7	2	8	3	11 56	16.6	4	6	1	12 40	17.5	4	5	24.9	13 25	18.5	6	4.3	25.7	14 10	19.4	6
45	0	5	9 45	1	24.9	8	3	10 29	1	0	6	22.9	11 13	0	2	5	23.7	11 58	16.9	3	3.3	5	12 42	17.8	4	2	3	13 27	18.8	5
46	♎ 29.9	1	9 3	13.5	8	7	21.9	9 46	14.4	25.8	5	5	10 30	15.3	0	2.3	3	11 14	3	1	2	1	11 58	2	2	0	24.9	12 42	1	0.3
47	8	20.7	8 19	12.8	6	6	5	9 2	13.7	7	1.3	1	9 45	14.6	26.8	2	22.9	10 29	15.6	27.9	1	23.7	11 12	16.5	0	3.9	5	11 56	17.5	1
48	6	3	7 34	1	4	0.4	1	8 16	0	5	2	21.7	8 59	13.9	6	1	5	9 42	14.9	7	2.9	3	10 25	15.8	28.8	8	1	11 9	16.8	0
49	5	19.9	6 48	11.4	2	3	20.7	7 30	12.3	3	1	3	8 12	2	4	1.9	1	8 54	2	5	8	22.9	9 37	1	6	6	23.6	10 20	0	♒ 29.8
50	3	5	6 0	10.6	0	2	2	6 41	11.5	1	0	20.9	7 23	12.5	2	8	21.6	8 5	13.4	3	6	4	8 47	14.4	4	4	1	9 29	15.3	6
51	1	1	5 11	9.8	23.7	0	19.8	5 52	10.7	24.9	0.9	5	6 33	11.7	25.9	6	2	7 15	12.6	1	4	21.9	7 56	13.6	2	2	22.6	8 38	14.5	3
52	28.9	18.6	4 21	8.9	4	♎ 29.9	3	5 1	9.8	6	7	0	5 41	10.8	6	4	20.7	6 22	11.7	26.8	2	4	7 3	12.7	0	0	1	7 44	13.6	1
53	8	1	3 29	0	1	7	18.8	4 8	8.9	3	5	19.5	4 48	9.9	3	2	2	5 29	10.8	6	0	20.9	6 8	11.7	27.8	2.9	21.6	6 49	12.7	28.8
54	6	17.6	2 35	7.0	22.8	5	3	3 14	7.9	0	3	0	3 53	8.9	1	1	19.7	4 33	9.8	3	1.9	4	5 12	10.7	5	7	1	5 52	11.7	6
55	5	1	1 40	6.0	5	3	17.8	2 18	6.9	23.7	1	18.5	2 56	7.8	24.8	0.9	2	3 35	8.7	0	7	19.9	4 14	9.6	2	5	20.5	4 53	10.6	3
56	3	16.6	0 42	4.9	2	1	3	1 20	5.7	4	♎ 29.9	17.9	1 58	6.6	5	6	18.6	2 36	7.5	25.7	5	3	3 14	8.4	26.8	3	19.9	3 52	9.4	0

SID. T. 12 H. 25 M. 42 S. — ARC 186° 25′.6 — ♎ 7°

Lat. °	11 ♏ °	12 ♐ °	1 ♐ ° ′	2 ♑ °	3 ♓ °
22	6.9	2.6	26 40	28.5	3.1
23	8	4	26 11	2	0
24	7	1	25 43	27.9	2.9
25	6	1.8	25 14	6	8
26	5	5	24 45	3	7
27	6.4	3	24 15	26.9	7
28	3	0	23 45	6	2.6
29	2	0.7	23 14	3	5
30	1	4	22 43	25.9	4
31	0	1	22 11	6	3
32	5.8	♏29.8	21 38	2	2.2
33	7	5	21 5	24.8	1
34	6	2	20 32	4	0
35	5	28.8	19 57	0	1.9
36	5.4	5	19 22	23.5	7
37	3	2	18 47	1	6
38	1	27.8	18 10	22.6	5
39	0	5	17 32	1	1.4
40	4.9	2	16 54	21.6	2
41	8	26.9	16 15	1	1
42	6	5	15 34	20.6	0.9
43	5	1	14 53	0	8
44	4.3	25.7	14 10	19.4	6
45	2	3	13 27	18.8	5
46	0	24.9	12 42	1	0.3
47	3.9	5	11 56	17.5	1
48	8	1	11 9	16.8	0
49	6	23.6	10 20	0	♒29.8
50	4	1	9 29	15.3	6
51	2	22.6	8 38	14.5	3
52	0	1	7 44	13.6	1
53	2.9	21.6	6 49	12.7	28.8
54	7	1	5 52	11.7	6
55	5	20.5	4 53	10.6	3
56	3	19.9	3 52	9.4	0

12 H. 29 M. 23 S. — 187° 20′.8 — ♎ 8°

Lat. °	11 ♏ °	12 ♐ °	1 ♐ ° ′	2 ♑ °	3 ♓ °
22	7.8	3.5	27 29	29.4	4.1
23	7	2	27 1	1	0
24	6	2.9	26 33	28.8	0
25	5	6	26 4	5	3.9
26	7.4	4	25 34	2	8
27	3	1	25 4	27.9	7
28	2	1.8	24 34	5	6
29	1	5	24 3	2	5
30	6.9	2	23 32	26.9	3.4
31	8	0.9	23 0	5	3
32	7	6	22 27	1	2
33	6	3	21 54	25.8	1
34	5	0	21 20	4	0
35	6.4	♏29.6	20 45	24.9	2.9
36	3	3	20 10	5	8
37	1	0	19 34	1	7
38	0	28.6	18 57	23.6	6
39	5.9	3	18 19	1	2.4
40	7	27.9	17 41	22.6	3
41	6	5	17 1	1	2
42	5	2	16 21	21.5	0
43	5.3	26.8	15 39	0	1.9
44	2	4	14 56	20.4	7
45	0	0	14 12	19.8	6
46	4.9	25.5	13 27	1	5
47	8	1	12 40	18.4	3
48	7	24.7	11 52	17.7	1
49	5	3	11 3	0	0.9
50	3	23.8	10 12	16.3	7
51	1	3	9 20	15.5	5
52	3.9	22.8	8 26	14.6	2
53	7	3	7 30	13.6	0
54	5	21.8	6 32	12.6	♒29.8
55	3	2	5 32	11.5	5
56	1	20.6	4 31	10.3	3

12 H. 33 M. 4 S. — 188° 16′.0 — ♎ 9°

Lat. °	11 ♏ °	12 ♐ °	1 ♐ ° ′	2 ♒ °	3 ♓ °
22	8.7	4.3	28 20	0.4	5.1
23	6	0	27 52	1	1
24	5	3.7	27 23	♑29.8	0
25	4	5	26 54	5	4.9
26	8.3	2	26 24	1	8
27	2	2.9	25 54	28.8	7
28	0	6	25 24	5	7
29	7.9	3	24 53	2	4.6
30	8	0	24 21	27.8	5
31	7	1.7	23 49	5	4
32	6	4	23 16	1	3
33	5	1	22 43	26.7	4.2
34	7.4	0.8	22 9	3	1
35	2	4	21 34	25.9	0
36	1	1	20 58	5	3.9
37	0	♏29.8	20 21	0	8
38	6.9	4	19 45	24.6	6
39	7	1	19 7	1	5
40	6	28.7	18 28	23.6	3.4
41	5	3	17 48	1	3
42	6.3	27.9	17 7	22.5	1
43	2	5	16 25	21.9	0
44	0	1	15 41	3	2.9
45	5.9	26.7	14 57	20.7	8
46	7	3	14 12	1	6
47	6	25.9	13 25	19.4	4
48	5	5	12 37	18.7	2
49	3	0	11 47	0	1
50	1	24.5	10 55	17.3	1.9
51	4.9	0	10 2	16.5	6
52	7	23.5	9 7	15.6	4
53	5	0	8 10	14.6	2
54	3	22.5	7 12	13.6	0.9
55	1	21.9	6 12	12.5	7
56	3.8	3	5 10	11.3	5

12 H. 36 M. 45 S. — 189° 11′.3 — ♎ 10°

Lat. °	11 ♏ °	12 ♐ °	1 ♐ ° ′	2 ♒ °	3 ♓ °
22	9.6	5.1	29 10	1.3	6.2
23	5	4.8	28 42	0	1
24	4	6	28 13	0.7	0
25	3	3	27 44	4	0
26	1	0	27 14	1	5.9
27	0	3.7	26 44	♑29.8	8
28	8.9	4	26 14	5	7
29	8	1	25 42	1	6
30	7	2.8	25 11	28.8	5
31	6	5	24 38	4	5.4
32	5	2	24 5	1	3
33	8.4	1.9	23 32	27.7	2
34	2	6	22 57	3	1
35	1	2	22 22	26.9	0
36	0	0.9	21 47	5	4.9
37	7.9	6	21 10	0	8
38	7	2	20 32	25.6	7
39	6	♏29.8	19 54	1	6
40	5	5	19 15	24.6	5
41	7.3	1	18 34	1	4.4
42	2	28.7	17 53	23.6	3
43	0	3	17 11	0	2
44	6.9	27.9	16 27	22.4	1
45	7	5	15 42	21.8	3.9
46	5	0	14 56	2	7
47	4	26.6	14 9	20.5	5
48	2	2	13 20	19.8	3
49	1	25.8	12 30	1	2
50	5.9	3	11 38	18.3	0
51	7	24.8	10 44	17.5	2.8
52	6	3	9 49	16.6	6
53	4	23.8	8 52	15.6	3
54	2	2	7 53	14.5	1
55	0	22.6	6 51	13.4	1.9
56	4.7	0	5 48	12.2	7

12 H. 40 M. 27 S. — 190° 6′.6 — ♎ 11°

Lat. °	11 ♏ °	12 ♐ °	1 ♑ ° ′	2 ♒ °	3 ♓ °
22	10.5	5.9	0 1	2.3	7.2
23	4	7	♐29 32	0	1
24	3	4	29 4	1.7	1
25	1	1	28 34	4	0
26	0	4.8	28 5	1	6.9
27	9.9	5	27 34	0.7	8
28	8	2	27 4	4	8
29	7	3.9	26 32	1	7
30	6	6	26 0	♑29.8	6.6
31	5	3	25 28	4	5
32	9.4	0	24 54	1	4
33	2	2.7	24 21	28.7	3
34	1	4	23 46	3	6.2
35	0	0	23 11	27.9	1
36	8.9	1.7	22 35	4	0
37	7	3	21 58	0	5.9
38	6	0	21 20	26.6	8
39	5	0.6	20 42	1	7
40	8.3	3	20 2	25.6	6
41	2	♏29.9	19 22	0	5
42	0	5	18 40	24.5	5.3
43	7.9	1	17 57	0	2
44	7	28.7	17 13	23.4	1
45	5	2	16 28	22.8	0
46	4	27.8	15 41	1	4.8
47	3	4	14 53	21.4	7
48	1	0	14 4	20.7	5
49	6.9	26.5	13 13	0	4
50	7	0	12 21	19.3	2
51	5	25.5	11 27	18.5	0
52	3	0	10 31	17.6	3.7
53	2	24.5	9 33	16.6	5
54	0	23.9	8 33	15.5	3
55	5.8	3	7 31	14.4	1
56	5	22.7	6 27	13.2	2.9

12 H. 44 M. 8 S. — 191° 2′.0 — ♎ 12°

Lat. °	11 ♏ °	12 ♐ °	1 ♑ ° ′	2 ♒ °	3 ♓ °
22	11.4	6.8	0 52	3.2	8.2
23	3	5	0 23	2.9	2
24	1	2	♐29 54	6	1
25	0	5.9	29 25	3	0
26	10.9	6	28 55	0	0
27	8	3	28 25	1.7	7.9
28	7	0	27 54	4	8
29	6	4.7	27 22	1	7
30	5	4	26 50	0.7	7
31	10.3	1	26 17	4	7.6
32	2	3.8	25 44	0	5
33	1	5	25 10	♑29.6	4
34	0	2	24 35	2	3
35	9.9	2.8	24 0	28.8	7.2
36	7	5	23 24	4	1
37	6	1	22 47	0	0
38	5	1.8	22 9	27.6	6.9
39	9.3	4	21 30	1	8
40	2	0	20 50	26.6	7
41	0	0.6	20 9	0	6
42	8.9	2	19 27	25.5	4
43	7	♏29.8	18 43	0	6.3
44	6	4	17 59	24.4	2
45	4	0	17 14	23.8	1
46	8.2	28.5	16 27	1	0
47	1	1	15 38	22.5	5.8
48	0	27.7	14 48	21.8	6
49	7.8	2	13 57	0	5
50	6	26.7	13 4	20.3	4
51	4	2	12 9	19.5	2
52	2	25.7	11 13	18.6	4.9
53	0	2	10 14	17.6	7
54	6.8	24.6	9 14	16.5	5
55	6	0	8 11	15.4	3
56	3	23.4	7 6	14.1	0

SID. T. H. M. S. 12 47 50 ARC 191° 57′.5 ♎ 13°					H. M. S. 12 51 32 192° 53′.0 ♎ 14°					H. M. S. 12 55 14 193° 48′.6 ♎ 15°					H. M. S. 12 58 57 194° 44′.3 ♎ 16°					H. M. S. 13 2 40 195° 40′.0 ♎ 17°					H. M. S. 13 6 23 196° 35′.9 ♎ 18°					
H.	11	12	1	2	3	11	12	1	2	3	11	12	1	2	3	11	12	1	2	3	11	12	1	2	3	11	12	1	2	3
Lat.	♏	♐	♑	♒	♓	♏	♐	♑	♒	♓	♏	♐	♑	♒	♓	♏	♐	♑	♒	♓	♏	♐	♑	♒	♓	♏	♐	♑	♒	♓
°	°	°	° ′	°	°	°	°	° ′	°	°	°	°	° ′	°	°	°	°	° ′	°	°	°	°	° ′	°	°	°	°	° ′	°	°
22	12.3	7.6	1 43	4.2	9.3	13.1	8.4	2 34	5.2	10.3	14.0	9.3	3 26	6.1	11.4	14.9	10.1	4 18	7.1	12.4	15.8	11.0	5 10	8.1	13.5	16.7	11.8	6 1	9.1	14.6
23	1	3	1 14	3.9	2	0	2	2 5	4.9	3	13.9	0	2 57	5.9	3	8	9.8	3 49	6.8	4	7	10.7	4 41	7.8	4	6	5	5 33	8.8	5
24	0	0	0 45	6	2	12.9	7.9	1 36	6	2	8	8.7	2 28	6	3	7	6	3 19	6	3	6	4	4 11	5	4	5	2	5 3	6	5
25	11.9	6.8	0 16	3	1	8	6	1 7	3	1	7	4	1 58	3	2	6	3	2 50	3	3	5	1	3 41	2	3	4	10.9	4 33	3	4
26	8	5	♐ 29 46	0	0	7	3	0 36	0	1	6	1	1 28	0	11.1	5	0	2 19	0	2	15.4	9.8	3 11	6.9	3	16.3	6	4 3	0	14.4
27	7	2	29 15	2.7	0	6	0	0 6	3.7	0	5	7.8	0 57	4.7	1	14.4	8.7	1 49	5.7	12.2	2	5	2 40	6	13.2	1	3	3 32	7.7	3
28	6	5.9	28 44	4	8.9	5	6.7	♐ 29 35	3	9.9	13.4	5	0 26	3	0	2	3	1 17	3	1	1	2	2 9	3	2	0	0	3 0	4	3
29	5	6	28 12	0	8	12.4	4	29 3	0	9	2	2	♐ 29 54	0	10.9	1	0	0 45	0	0	0	8.8	1 37	0	1	15.9	9.7	2 28	1	2
30	11.4	2	27 40	1.7	7	2	1	28 31	2.7	8	1	6.9	29 22	3.7	9	0	7.7	0 13	4.7	0	14.9	5	1 4	5.7	0	8	3	1 55	6.7	14.1
31	2	4.9	27 8	4	6	1	5.7	27 58	4	7	0	6	28 49	4	8	13.9	4	♐ 29 40	4	11.9	7	2	0 31	4	0	6	0	1 22	4	1
32	1	6	26 34	0	8.6	0	4	27 24	0	6	12.9	2	28 15	0	7	7	1	29 6	0	8	6	7.9	♐ 29 57	0	12.9	5	8.7	0 48	1	0
33	0	3	26 0	0.6	5	11.9	1	26 50	1.6	9.6	7	5.9	27 40	2.6	7	6	6.7	28 31	3.7	7	5	5	29 22	4.7	8	15.4	3	0 13	5.7	13.9
34	10.9	0	25 25	2	4	7	4.8	26 15	2	5	6	6	27 5	2	10.6	5	4	27 55	3	7	14.4	2	28 46	3	8	2	0	♐ 29 37	3	9
35	7	3.6	24 49	♑ 29.8	3	6	4	25 39	0.8	4	5	2	26 28	1.8	5	13.3	0	27 19	2.9	11.6	2	6.8	28 9	3.9	7	1	7.6	29 0	4.9	8
36	6	3	24 13	4	8.2	5	1	25 2	4	3	12.3	4.9	25 51	4	4	2	5.7	26 41	5	5	1	5	27 32	5	12.6	14.9	3	28 22	5	7
37	5	2.9	23 35	0	1	11.3	3.7	24 24	0	9.2	2	5	25 14	0	3	1	3	26 3	0	4	13.9	1	26 54	1	5	8	6.9	27 44	1	7
38	10.3	6	22 57	28.6	1	2	4	23 46	♑ 29.5	1	1	2	24 35	0.5	10.3	12.9	0	25 24	1.6	3	8	5.7	26 15	2.6	5	6	5	27 4	3.7	13.6
39	2	2	22 18	1	0	0	0	23 6	1	0	11.9	3.8	23 55	1	2	8	4.6	24 44	1	11.2	6	4	25 34	2	4	5	2	26 24	2	6
40	0	1.8	21 38	27.6	7.9	10.9	2.6	22 26	28.6	0	7	4	23 15	♑ 29.6	1	6	2	24 4	0.6	2	5	0	24 53	1.7	12.3	14.3	5.8	25 42	2.7	5
41	9.9	4	20 57	0	8	7	2	21 44	0	8.9	6	0	22 33	1	0	4	3.8	23 22	1	1	13.3	4.6	24 11	1	2	2	4	25 0	2	4
42	7	0	20 14	26.5	7	6	1.8	21 2	27.5	8	4	2.6	21 50	28.5	9.9	3	4	22 38	♑ 29.6	0	1	2	23 27	0.6	1	0	4.9	24 16	1.7	13.3
43	6	0.6	19 31	0	5	4	4	20 18	0	7	3	2	21 6	0	8	1	0	21 54	0	10.9	0	3.7	22 42	0	0	13.8	5	23 31	1	2
44	4	2	18 46	25.4	7.4	10.3	0	19 33	26.4	5	1	1.7	20 20	27.4	7	11.9	2.5	21 8	28.4	8	12.8	3	21 55	♑ 29.4	11.9	6	1	22 44	0.5	1
45	2	♏ 29.7	18 0	24.8	3	1	0.5	18 46	25.8	8.4	10.9	3	19 33	26.8	6	8	1	20 20	27.8	7	6	2.8	21 7	28.8	8	4	3.6	21 56	♑ 29.9	0
46	0	3	17 13	1	1	0	1	17 58	2	3	7	0.9	18 44	2	9.4	7	1.6	19 31	2	6	4	4	20 18	2	7	3	2	21 6	3	12.9
47	8.9	28.8	16 24	23.4	0	9.8	♏ 29.6	17 9	24.5	1	6	5	17 55	25.6	3	5	2	18 41	26.6	10.5	3	1.9	19 27	27.6	6	1	2.7	20 14	28.7	8
48	8	4	15 34	22.8	6.9	6	2	16 18	23.8	0	4	0	17 3	24.9	2	3	0.7	17 49	25.9	3	1	4	18 35	26.9	5	12.9	2	19 21	1	7
49	6	0	14 42	1	7	4	28.7	15 25	1	7.9	2	♏ 29.5	16 11	2	0	1	2	16 55	1	2	11.9	0.9	17 41	2	11.4	7	1.7	18 27	27.4	6
50	4	27.5	13 48	21.3	5	2	2	14 31	22.3	7	1	0	15 16	23.4	8.9	10.9	♏ 29.7	16 0	24.4	1	7	4	16 45	25.5	3	5	2	17 31	26.6	12.5
51	2	0	12 52	20.5	3	0	27.7	13 36	21.5	5	9.9	28.5	14 19	22.6	7	7	2	15 3	23.6	9.9	5	♏ 29.9	15 48	24.7	1	3	0.6	16 32	25.8	4
52	0	26.5	11 55	19.6	1	8.8	2	12 38	20.6	3	7	27.9	13 20	21.7	6	5	28.6	14 4	22.7	8	3	3	14 48	23.8	0	0	0	15 32	24.9	2
53	7.8	25.9	10 55	18.6	5.9	6	26.6	11 38	19.6	1	4	3	12 20	20.7	4	2	0	13 3	21.7	6	1	28.7	13 46	22.7	10.8	11.8	♏ 29.4	14 29	23.9	0
54	6	3	9 54	17.5	8	4	0	10 36	18.6	0	2	26.7	11 17	19.6	2	0	27.4	11 59	20.7	4	10.9	1	12 42	21.7	7	6	28.8	13 24	22.8	11.9
55	4	24.7	8 51	16.4	6	2	25.4	9 32	17.5	6.8	0	1	10 13	18.5	0	9.8	26.8	10 54	19.6	2	6	27.5	11 35	20.6	5	4	2	12 16	21.7	7
56	1	1	7 46	15.1	4	7.9	24.8	8 25	16.3	5	8.7	25.5	9 5	17.2	7.8	5	2	9 45	18.3	0	3	26.9	10 26	19.3	3	1	27.5	11 6	20.4	6

SID. T. 13 h 6 m 23 s — ARC 196° 35′.9 — ♎ 18°

H.	11	12	1	2	3
Lat.	♏	♐	♑	♒	♓
°	°	°	° ′	°	°
22	16.7	11.8	6 1	9.1	14.6
23	6	5	5 33	8.8	5
24	5	2	5 3	6	5
25	4	10.9	4 33	3	4
26	16.3	6	4 3	0	14.4
27	1	3	3 32	7.7	3
28	0	0	3 0	4	3
29	15.9	9.7	2 28	1	2
30	8	3	1 55	6.7	14.1
31	6	0	1 22	4	1
32	5	8.7	0 48	1	0
33	15.4	3	0 13	5.7	13.9
34	2	0	♐ 29 37	3	9
35	1	7.6	29 0	4.9	8
36	14.9	3	28 22	5	7
37	8	6.9	27 44	1	7
38	6	5	27 4	3.7	13.6
39	5	2	26 24	2	6
40	14.3	5.8	25 42	2.7	5
41	2	4	25 0	2	4
42	0	4.9	24 16	1.7	13.3
43	13.8	5	23 31	1	2
44	6	1	22 44	0.5	1
45	4	3.6	21 56	♑ 29.9	0
46	3	2	21 6	3	12.9
47	1	2.7	20 14	28.7	8
48	12.9	2	19 21	1	7
49	7	1.7	18 27	27.4	6
50	5	2	17 31	26.6	12.5
51	3	0.6	16 32	25.8	4
52	0	0	15 32	24.9	2
53	11.8	♏ 29.4	14 29	23.9	0
54	6	28.8	13 24	22.8	11.9
55	4	2	12 16	21.7	7
56	1	27.5	11 6	20.4	6

SID. T. 13 h 10 m 7 s — ARC 197° 31′.8 — ♎ 19°

H.	11	12	1	2	3
Lat.	♏	♐	♑	♒	♓
°	°	°	° ′	°	°
22	17.6	12.6	6 54	10.1	15.6
23	5	3	6 26	9.8	6
24	4	0	5 56	6	5
25	3	11.7	5 26	3	5
26	1	4	4 56	0	4
27	0	1	4 25	8.7	15.4
28	16.9	10.8	3 53	4	3
29	8	5	3 21	1	3
30	6	2	2 48	7.8	2
31	5	9.8	2 14	4	15.2
32	16.4	5	1 40	1	1
33	2	2	1 4	6.7	0
34	1	8.8	0 28	4	0
35	0	5	♐ 29 51	0	14.9
36	15.8	1	29 13	5.6	9
37	7	7.7	28 35	2	8
38	5	3	27 55	4.7	7
39	3	0	27 14	3	6
40	2	6.6	26 33	3.8	14.6
41	0	2	25 50	3	5
42	14.8	5.7	25 5	2.7	4
43	7	3	24 20	2	4
44	5	4.8	23 32	1.6	14.3
45	3	4	22 44	0	2
46	2	3.9	21 54	0.4	1
47	0	4	21 2	♑ 29.7	0
48	13.8	2.9	20 8	1	13.9
49	6	4	19 13	28.4	8
50	4	1.9	18 16	27.7	7
51	2	3	17 17	26.9	6
52	12.9	0.7	16 16	0	13.4
53	7	1	15 12	25.0	3
54	5	♏ 29.5	14 6	23.9	1
55	2	28.9	12 58	22.8	0
56	11.9	2	11 47	21.5	12.9

SID. T. 13 h 13 m 51 s — ARC 198° 27′.8 — ♎ 20°

H.	11	12	1	2	3
Lat.	♏	♐	♑	♒	♓
°	°	°	° ′	°	°
22	18.5	13.5	7 47	11.1	16.7
23	4	2	7 18	10.8	6
24	3	12.9	6 49	6	6
25	1	6	6 19	3	6
26	0	3	5 48	0	5
27	17.9	0	5 17	9.7	16.5
28	8	11.6	4 45	4	4
29	6	3	4 13	1	4
30	5	0	3 40	8.8	3
31	17.4	10.7	3 6	5	3
32	3	3	2 31	1	16.2
33	1	0	1 56	7.8	2
34	0	9.6	1 20	4	1
35	16.8	3	0 43	0	0
36	7	8.9	0 5	6.6	0
37	5	5	♐ 29 26	2	15.9
38	4	2	28 46	5.8	8
39	2	7.8	28 5	3	8
40	0	4	27 23	4.9	7
41	15.9	6.9	26 39	4	6
42	7	5	25 55	3.9	15.5
43	5	1	25 9	4	5
44	3	5.6	24 21	2.8	4
45	2	2	23 32	2	4
46	0	4.7	22 42	1.6	15.3
47	14.8	2	21 49	0	2
48	6	3.7	20 55	0.3	1
49	4	2	20 0	♑ 29.6	0
50	2	2.7	19 2	28.8	14.9
51	13.9	1	18 2	0	8
52	7	1.5	17 0	27.1	7
53	5	0.9	15 56	26.1	5
54	3	3	14 49	25.1	14.4
55	0	♏ 29.7	13 40	24.0	2
56	12.7	0	12 28	22.7	1

SID. T. 13 h 17 m 36 s — ARC 199° 24′.0 — ♎ 21°

H.	11	12	1	2	3
Lat.	♏	♐	♑	♒	♓
°	°	°	° ′	°	°
22	19.4	14.3	8 41	12.1	17.8
23	3	0	8 12	11.9	7
24	1	13.7	7 42	6	7
25	0	4	7 12	3	7
26	18.9	1	6 41	0	6
27	8	12.8	6 10	10.7	17.6
28	6	5	5 38	4	5
29	5	2	5 6	1	5
30	18.4	11.8	4 33	9.8	4
31	3	5	3 59	5	4
32	1	2	3 24	2	17.3
33	0	10.8	2 48	8.8	3
34	17.8	5	2 12	5	2
35	7	1	1 35	1	2
36	5	9.7	0 56	7.7	17.1
37	4	3	0 17	3	1
38	2	8.9	♐ 29 37	6.8	0
39	1	5	28 56	4	0
40	16.9	1	28 13	5.9	16.9
41	7	7.7	27 30	4	9
42	5	3	26 45	4.9	8
43	4	6.9	25 58	4	7
44	2	4	25 10	3.9	16.6
45	0	5.9	24 21	3	6
46	15.8	4	23 30	2.7	5
47	6	4.9	22 37	1	4
48	4	4	21 43	1.4	16.3
49	2	3.9	20 47	0.7	2
50	0	4	19 48	♑ 29.9	1
51	14.8	2.8	18 48	1	0
52	5	2	17 45	28.2	15.8
53	3	1.6	16 40	27.2	7
54	0	0	15 33	26.2	6
55	13.8	0.4	14 23	25.1	5
56	5	♏ 29.7	13 10	23.8	3

SID. T. 13 h 21 m 21 s — ARC 200° 20′.2 — ♎ 22°

H.	11	12	1	2	3
Lat.	♏	♐	♑	♒	♓
°	°	°	° ′	°	°
22	20.3	15.1	9 34	13.2	18.8
23	2	14.8	9 5	12.9	8
24	0	5	8 35	6	8
25	19.9	2	8 5	3	7
26	8	13.9	7 35	1	7
27	7	6	7 3	11.8	18.7
28	5	3	6 31	5	6
29	19.4	0	5 59	2	6
30	3	12.7	5 25	10.9	5
31	1	3	4 51	6	5
32	0	0	4 16	2	18.4
33	18.9	11.6	3 41	9.9	4
34	7	3	3 4	5	3
35	6	10.9	2 27	1	3
36	4	5	1 48	8.7	2
37	3	1	1 9	3	18.2
38	1	9.7	0 29	7.9	1
39	17.9	3	♐ 29 47	5	1
40	8	8.9	29 4	0	0
41	6	5	28 20	6.5	17.9
42	4	1	27 35	0	9
43	2	7.6	26 48	5.5	8
44	0	2	26 0	0	8
45	16.8	6.7	25 10	4.4	7
46	7	2	24 19	3.8	17.7
47	5	5.8	23 26	2	6
48	3	3	22 31	2.5	5
49	1	4.7	21 34	1.8	4
50	15.9	2	20 35	0	17.3
51	7	3.6	19 34	0.2	2
52	4	0	18 30	♑ 29.3	1
53	2	2.4	17 25	28.3	0
54	14.9	1.8	16 16	27.3	16.9
55	6	1	15 6	26.2	8
56	3	0.4	13 52	25.0	7

SID. T. 13 h 25 m 6 s — ARC 201° 16′.6 — ♎ 23°

H.	11	12	1	2	3
Lat.	♏	♐	♑	♒	♓
°	°	°	° ′	°	°
22	21.2	16.0	10 28	14.2	19.9
23	1	15.7	9 59	13.9	9
24	20.9	4	9 29	7	9
25	8	1	8 59	4	8
26	7	14.8	8 28	1	8
27	5	5	7 57	12.8	19.8
28	20.4	1	7 25	5	7
29	3	13.8	6 52	2	7
30	1	5	6 19	11.9	6
31	0	1	5 44	6	6
32	19.9	12.8	5 10	3	19.6
33	7	4	4 34	10.9	5
34	6	1	3 57	6	5
35	4	11.7	3 20	2	4
36	19.3	3	2 41	9.8	19.4
37	1	0	2 1	4	3
38	0	10.6	1 21	0	3
39	18.8	2	0 39	8.5	2
40	6	9.7	♐ 29 56	1	19.2
41	4	3	29 12	7.6	1
42	3	8.9	28 26	1	0
43	1	4	27 39	6.6	0
44	17.9	7.9	26 50	0	18.9
45	7	5	26 0	5.5	8
46	5	0	25 8	4.9	8
47	3	6.5	24 15	3	7
48	1	0	23 19	3.6	18.7
49	16.9	5.5	22 22	2.9	6
50	7	4.9	21 22	2	5
51	4	3	20 20	1.4	4
52	1	3.7	19 16	0.5	18.3
53	15.9	1	18 10	♑ 29.5	2
54	7	2.5	17 1	28.5	2
55	4	1.8	15 49	27.4	1
56	1	1	14 34	26.2	0

Lat.	SID. T. 13 28 52 ARC 202° 13′.0 ♎ 24°					13 32 38 203° 9′.6 ♎ 25°				
H.	11	12	1	2	3	11	12	1	2	3
°	♏ °	♐ °	♑ ° ′	♒ °	♓ °	♏ °	♐ °	♑ ° ′	♒ °	♓ °
22	22.1	16.8	11 22	15.2	21.0	23.0	17.7	12 16	16.3	22.1
23	21.9	5	10 53	0	0	22.8	4	11 47	0	1
24	8	2	10 23	14.7	20.9	7	1	11 18	15.8	1
25	7	15.9	9 53	4	9	6	16.8	10 47	5	0
26	6	6	9 22	2	9	4	5	10 17	2	0
27	21.4	3	8 51	13.9	9	22.3	1	9 45	0	0
28	3	0	8 19	6	8	2	15.8	9 13	14.7	21.9
29	2	14.6	7 46	3	20.8	0	5	8 40	4	9
30	0	3	7 12	0	8	21.9	2	8 7	1	9
31	20.9	0	6 38	12.7	7	8	14.8	7 32	13.8	8
32	7	13.6	6 3	3	7	6	5	6 57	4	8
33	6	3	5 27	0	6	5	1	6 21	1	21.8
34	4	12.9	4 50	11.7	20.6	21.3	13.8	5 44	12.8	7
35	20.3	6	4 13	3	6	2	4	5 6	4	7
36	1	2	3 34	10.9	5	0	0	4 27	0	7
37	0	11.8	2 54	5	5	20.9	12.6	3 47	11.6	6
38	19.8	4	2 13	1	4	7	2	3 6	2	21.6
39	7	0	1 31	9.6	20.4	5	11.8	2 24	10.8	5
40	5	10.6	0 48	2	4	4	4	1 40	4	5
41	3	1	0 3	8.7	4	3	10.9	0 55	9.9	4
42	1	9.7	♐29 17	2	3	1	5	0 9	4	4
43	18.9	2	28 30	7.7	3	19.9	0	♐29 21	8.9	21.3
44	7	8.7	27 41	1	20.2	7	9.5	28 32	4	3
45	5	3	26 50	6.5	1	5	1	27 41	7.8	2
46	3	7.8	25 58	0	1	3	8.6	26 48	2	2
47	1	3	25 4	5.4	0	1	0	25 54	6.6	21.1
48	17.9	6.8	24 8	4.7	19.9	18.9	7.5	24 57	5.9	1
49	7	3	23 10	0	9	7	6.9	23 58	2	0
50	5	5.7	22 10	3.3	8	4	4	22 58	4.5	0
51	2	1	21 7	2.5	7	2	5.8	21 55	3.7	20.9
52	0	4.5	20 2	1.6	19.6	17.9	2	20 49	2.8	9
53	16.8	3.9	18 55	0.7	5	6	4.6	19 41	1.9	8
54	5	2	17 45	♑29.7	4	3	3.9	18 30	0.9	7
55	2	2.5	16 32	28.6	3	0	2	17 17	♑29.8	6
56	15.9	1.8	15 17	27.4	2	16.7	2.5	16 0	28.6	4

Lat.	13 36 25 204° 6′.3 ♎ 26°					13 40 13 205° 3′.2 ♎ 27°				
H.	11	12	1	2	3	11	12	1	2	3
°	♏ °	♐ °	♑ ° ′	♒ °	♓ °	♏ °	♐ °	♑ ° ′	♒ °	♓ °
22	23.9	18.5	13 11	17.3	23.2	24.7	19.4	14 6	18.4	24.3
23	7	2	12 42	1	2	6	1	13 37	1	3
24	6	17.9	12 12	16.8	1	5	18.8	13 7	17.9	2
25	5	6	11 42	6	1	4	5	12 37	6	2
26	23.3	3	11 11	3	1	2	2	12 6	4	2
27	2	0	10 40	0	23.1	1	17.8	11 35	1	24.2
28	1	16.7	10 8	15.7	1	23.9	5	11 3	16.8	2
29	22.9	3	9 35	4	0	8	2	10 30	5	1
30	8	0	9 1	1	0	7	16.8	9 56	2	1
31	6	15.7	8 27	14.8	0	5	5	9 22	15.9	24.1
32	5	3	7 51	5	22.9	23.4	1	8 46	6	1
33	22.4	14.9	7 15	2	9	2	15.8	8 10	3	1
34	2	6	6 38	13.9	9	1	4	7 33	0	0
35	.1	2	6 0	5	8	22.9	0	6 55	14.6	24.0
36	21.9	13.8	5 21	1	8	8	14.6	6 16	2	0
37	7	4	4 41	12.7	22.8	6	2	5 35	13.8	0
38	6	0	4 0	3	7	4	13.8	4 54	4	0
39	4	12.6	3 17	11.9	7	2	4	4 11	0	23.9
40	2	2	2 33	5	7	1	0	3 27	12.6	9
41	0	11.7	1 48	0	6	21.9	12.5	2 41	1	9
42	20.8	3	1 1	10.5	22.6	7	1	1 54	11.6	9
43	6	10.8	0 13	0	5	5	11.6	1 5	1	8
44	4	3	♐29 23	9.5	5	3	1	0 15	10.6	23.8
45	2	9.8	28 32	8.9	5	1	10.6	♐29 24	1	8
46	0	3	27 39	3	4	20.8	1	28 30	9.5	7
47	19.8	8.8	26 44	7.7	22.4	6	9.6	27 34	8.9	7
48	6	3	25 47	1	4	4	1	26 37	3	23.6
49	4	7.8	24 48	6.4	3	2	8.6	25 37	7.6	6
50	2	2	23 46	5.7	3	0	0	24 35	6.9	5
51	18.9	6.6	22 42	4.9	22.2	19.7	7.4	23 31	1	5
52	7	0	21 36	1	1	4	6.8	22 24	5.3	23.4
53	5	5.4	20 27	3.2	1	2	1	21 14	4.4	3
54	2	4.7	19 16	2.2	0	0	5.4	20 1	3.4	3
55	17.9	0	18 1	1.1	21.9	18.7	4.7	18 46	2.3	2
56	5	3.3	16 43	♑29.9	8	3	0	17 27	1.1	1

Lat.	13 44 0 206° 0′.1 ♎ 28°					13 47 49 206° 57′.2 ♎ 29°				
H.	11	12	1	2	3	11	12	1	2	3
°	♏ °	♐ °	♑ ° ′	♒ °	♓ °	♏ °	♐ °	♑ ° ′	♒ °	♓ °
22	25.6	20.3	15 2	19.4	25.4	26.5	21.1	15 58	20.5	26.5
23	5	0	14 33	2	4	4	20.8	15 29	3	5
24	4	19.6	14 3	18.9	4	3	5	14 59	0	5
25	2	3	13 33	7	4	1	2	14 29	19.8	4
26	1	0	13 2	4	3	0	19.9	13 58	5	4
27	0	18.7	12 31	2	25.3	25.9	5	13 26	3	26.4
28	24.8	4	11 58	17.9	3	7	2	12 54	0	4
29	7	0	11 25	6	3	6	18.9	12 21	18.7	4
30	5	17.7	10 51	3	3	4	5	11 47	4	4
31	4	3	10 17	0	25.2	25.3	2	11 13	1	4
32	24.3	0	9 41	16.7	2	1	17.8	10 37	17.8	26.4
33	1	16.6	9 5	4	2	0	4	10 1	5	3
34	0	2	8 28	1	2	24.8	1	9 23	2	3
35	23.8	15.9	7 49	15.7	25.2	7	16.7	8 45	16.8	3
36	6	5	7 10	3	1	5	3	8 5	5	3
37	5	1	6 30	0	1	3	15.9	7 25	1	26.3
38	3	14.7	5 48	14.6	1	2	5	6 43	15.7	3
39	1	2	5 5	2	25.1	0	1	5 59	4	2
40	22.9	13.8	4 20	13.8	0	23.8	14.6	5 15	0	2
41	7	4	3 35	4	0	6	2	4 29	14.6	2
42	5	12.9	2 48	12.9	0	4	13.7	3 41	1	26.2
43	3	4	1 59	4	24.9	2	3	2 52	13.6	2
44	1	11.9	1 8	11.9	9	0	12.8	2 1	1	1
45	21.9	4	0 16	4	9	22.8	3	1 9	12.6	1
46	7	10.9	♐29 22	10.8	8	6	11.8	0 14	0	1
47	6	4	28 26	2	8	4	2	♐29 18	11.4	26.1
48	4	9.9	27 28	9.6	24.8	2	10.7	28 19	10.8	0
49	2	3	26 27	8.9	7	21.9	1	27 18	1	0
50	20.9	8.7	25 25	2	7	7	9.5	26 14	9.4	0
51	6	1	24 20	7.4	6	4	8.9	25 9	8.7	25.9
52	3	7.5	23 12	6.6	24.6	1	3	24 0	7.9	9
53	1	6.8	22 1	5.7	5	20.9	7.6	22 49	0	9
54	19.8	1	20 48	4.7	5	6	6.9	21 35	6.0	8
55	5	5.4	19 31	3.6	5	3	2	20 17	4.9	8
56	1	4.7	18 12	2.4	4	0	5.4	18 56	3.7	8

	SID. T. H. M. S. 13 47 49 ARC 206° 57′.2 ♎ 29°					13 51 38 207° 54′.5 ♏ 0°				
H.	11	12	1	2	3	11	12	1	2	3
Lat.	♏	♐	♑	♒	♓	♏	♐	♑	♒	♓
°	°	°	° ′	°	°	°	°	° ′	°	°
22	26.5	21.1	15 58	20.5	26.5	27.4	22.0	16 54	21.6	27.6
23	4	20.8	15 29	3	5	3	21.7	16 25	3	6
24	3	5	14 59	0	5	2	4	15 56	1	6
25	1	2	14 29	19.8	4	0	0	15 25	20.9	6
26	0	19.9	13 58	5	4	26.9	20.7	14 54	6	6
27	25.9	5	13 26	3	26.4	7	4	14 23	4	27.5
28	7	2	12 54	0	4	6	1	13 51	1	5
29	6	18.9	12 21	18.7	4	5	19.7	13 17	19.8	5
30	4	5	11 47	4	4	26.3	4	12 44	6	5
31	25.3	2	11 13	1	4	2	0	12 9	3	5
32	1	17.8	10 37	17.8	26.4	0	18.7	11 33	18.9	27.5
33	0	4	10 1	5	3	25.9	3	10 57	6	5
34	24.8	1	9 23	2	3	7	17.9	10 19	3	5
35	7	16.7	8 45	16.8	3	5	5	9 41	0	5
36	5	3	8 5	5	3	4	1	9 1	17.6	5
37	3	15.9	7 25	1	26.3	3	16.7	8 20	2	27.4
38	2	5	6 43	15.7	3	1	3	7 38	16.9	4
39	0	1	5 59	4	2	24.9	15.9	6 54	5	4
40	23.8	14.6	5 15	0	2	7	5	6 10	1	4
41	6	2	4 29	14.6	2	5	0	5 23	15.7	4
42	4	13.7	3 41	1	26.2	3	14.6	4 36	2	27.4
43	2	3	2 52	13.6	2	1	1	3 46	14.7	4
44	0	12.8	2 1	1	1	23.9	13.6	2 55	2	4
45	22.8	3	1 9	12.6	1	7	1	2 2	13.7	3
46	6	11.8	0 14	0	1	5	12.6	1 7	2	3
47	4	2	♐ 29 18	11.4	26.1	3	0	0 10	12.6	27.3
48	2	10.7	28 19	10.8	0	0	11.5	♐ 29 11	0	3
49	21.9	1	27 18	1	0	22.8	10.9	28 9	11.4	3
50	7	9.5	26 14	9.4	0	5	3	27 5	10.7	2
51	4	8.9	25 9	8.7	25.9	2	9.6	25 59	0	2
52	1	3	24 0	7.9	9	21.9	0	24 49	9.2	27.2
53	20.9	7.6	22 49	0	9	6	8.3	23 37	8.3	2
54	6	6.9	21 35	6.0	8	4	7.6	22 22	7.3	1
55	3	2	20 17	4.9	8	1	6.9	21 3	6.2	1
56	0	5.4	18 56	3.7	8	20.8	1	19 42	5.0	1

	13 55 27 208° 51′.9 ♏ 1°					13 59 18 209° 49′.4 ♏ 2°				
H.	11	12	1	2	3	11	12	1	2	3
Lat.	♏	♐	♑	♒	♓	♏	♐	♑	♒	♓
°	°	°	° ′	°	°	°	°	° ′	°	°
22	28.3	22.8	17 51	22.7	28.7	29.2	23.7	18 48	23.8	29.8
23	2	5	17 22	4	7	1	4	18 19	5	8
24	1	2	16 52	2	7	0	1	17 50	3	8
25	27.9	21.9	16 22	0	7	28.8	22.8	17 20	1	8
26	8	6	15 51	21.7	7	7	4	16 49	22.9	8
27	6	3	15 20	5	28.7	5	1	16 17	6	29.8
28	5	20.9	14 47	2	7	4	21.8	15 45	3	8
29	27.3	6	14 14	0	7	2	4	15 12	1	8
30	2	2	13 40	20.7	7	1	1	14 38	21.8	8
31	0	19.9	13 6	4	6	27.9	20.7	14 3	5	8
32	26.9	5	12 30	1	28.6	8	4	13 27	2	29.8
33	7	1	11 53	19.8	6	6	0	12 50	20.9	8
34	6	18.8	11 16	5	6	5	19.6	12 13	6	8
35	4	4	10 37	1	6	3	2	11 34	3	8
36	2	0	9 57	18.8	6	1	18.8	10 54	0	8
37	1	17.6	9 16	4	28.6	26.9	4	10 13	19.6	29.8
38	25.9	2	8 34	1	6	8	0	9 31	2	8
39	7	16.7	7 50	17.7	6	6	17.6	8 47	18.9	8
40	5	3	7 5	3	6	4	1	8 1	5	8
41	3	15.8	6 19	16.9	6	2	16.7	7 15	1	8
42	1	4	5 31	4	28.6	0	2	6 26	17.7	29.8
43	24.9	14.9	4 41	15.9	6	25.8	15.7	5 36	2	8
44	7	4	3 49	4	6	6	2	4 44	16.7	8
45	5	13.9	2 56	14.9	5	3	14.7	3 50	2	8
46	3	4	2 0	4	5	1	2	2 55	15.7	8
47	1	12.8	1 3	13.8	28.5	24.9	13.6	1 56	1	29.8
48	23.9	3	0 3	2	5	7	1	0 56	14.5	8
49	7	11.7	♐ 29 1	12.6	5	5	12.5	♐ 29 53	13.9	8
50	4	1	27 56	11.9	5	2	11.9	28 48	2	8
51	1	10.5	26 49	2	5	23.9	3	27 40	12.5	8
52	22.8	9.9	25 39	10.4	28.5	6	10.6	26 29	11.7	29.8
53	5	2	24 26	9.5	4	3	9.9	25 16	10.8	8
54	2	8.5	23 10	8.5	4	0	2	23 58	9.9	8
55	21.9	7.7	21 50	7.5	4	22.7	8.4	22 38	8.9	8
56	5	6.9	20 27	6.4	4	3	7.6	21 14	7.8	8

	14 3 8 210° 47′.1 ♏ 3°					14 7 0 211° 44′.9 ♏ 4°				
H.	11	12	1	2	3	11	12	1	2	3
Lat.	♐	♐	♑	♒	♈	♐	♐	♑	♒	♈
°	°	°	° ′	°	°	°	°	° ′	°	°
22	0.1	24.6	19 46	24.9	0.9	1.0	25.4	20 44	25.9	2.0
23	0	3	19 17	7	9	0.9	1	20 15	7	0
24	♏ 29.8	0	18 48	4	9	7	24.8	19 46	5	0
25	7	23.6	18 17	2	9	6	5	19 16	3	0.
26	6	3	17 47	0	9	5	2	18 45	1	0
27	4	0	17 15	23.7	0.9	0.3	23.8	18 13	24.9	2.1
28	29.3	22.6	16 43	5	9	2	5	17 41	6	1
29	1	3	16 9	2	9	0	2	17 8	4	1
30	0	21.9	15 35	0	9	♏ 29.9	22.8	16 34	1	1
31	28.8	6	15 1	22.7	0.9	7	5	15 59	23.8	1
32	7	2	14 25	4	9	5	1	15 23	6	2.1
33	5	20.8	13 48	1	9	4	21.7	14 46	3	1
34	3	5	13 10	21.8	9	2	3	14 9	0	1
35	2	1	12 32	5	1.0	0	20.9	13 30	22.7	1
36	1	19.7	11 52	2	0	28.9	5	12 50	3	1
37	27.9	3	11 10	20.8	0	7	1	12 8	0	2.2
38	7	18.8	10 28	4	0	5	19.7	11 25	21.7	2
39	5	4	9 44	1	0	3	3	10 41	4	2
40	3	0	8 58	19.7	1.0	1	18.8	9 55	0	2
41	1	17.5	8 11	3	0	27.9	4	9 8	20.6	2
42	26.9	0	7 22	18.9	0	7	17.9	8 19	2	2.2
43	7	16.5	6 32	5	0	5	4	7 29	19.8	2
44	5	0	5 40	0	1.0	3	16.9	6 36	3	2
45	3	15.5	4 46	17.5	0	1	3	5 42	18.8	2
46	1	0	3 50	0	0	26.9	15.8	4 45	3	3
47	25.8	14.4	2 51	16.4	0	7	2	3 46	17.8	2.3
48	6	13.9	1 50	15.8	1.0	4	14.7	2 45	2	3
49	3	3	0 47	2	0	1	1	1 41	16.6	3
50	0	12.7	♐ 29 41	14.5	0	25.9	13.5	0 34	15.9	3
51	24.7	1	28 32	13.8	1	6	12.9	♐ 29 24	2	3
52	4	11.4	27 20	0	1.1	3	2	28 12	14.4	2.3
53	2	10.7	26 6	12.2	1	0	11.5	26 56	13.6	4
54	23.9	0	24 48	11.3	1	24.7	10.7	25 37	12.7	4
55	6	9.2	23 26	10.3	1	4	9.9	24 15	11.7	4
56	2	8.4	22 1	9.2	1	0	1	22 48	10.6	4

SID. T.	H. M. S. 14 10 52					H. M. S. 14 14 44					H. M. S. 14 18 37					H. M. S. 14 22 31					H. M. S. 14 26 26					H. M. S. 14 30 21				
ARC	212° 42′.9 ♏ 5°					213° 41′.0 ♏ 6°					214° 39′.4 ♏ 7°					215° 37′.8 ♏ 8°					216° 36′.5 ♏ 9°					217° 35′.3 ♏ 10°				
H.	11	12	1	2	3	11	12	1	2	3	11	12	1	2	3	11	12	1	2	3	11	12	1	2	3	11	12	1	2	3
° Lat.	♐	♐	♑	♒	♈	♐	♐	♑	♒	♈	♐	♐	♑	♒	♈	♐	♐	♑	♓	♈	♐	♐	♑	♓	♈	♐	♑	♑	♓	♈
	°	°	° ′	°	°	°	°	° ′	°	°	°	°	° ′	°	°	°	°	° ′	°	°	°	°	° ′	°	°	°	°	° ′	°	°
22	1.9	26.3	21 43	27.1	3.1	2.8	27.2	22 42	28.2	4.3	3.7	28.1	23 41	29.3	5.4	4.6	29.0	24 41	0.5	6.5	5.5	29.9	25 42	1.6	7.6	6.4	0.8	26 43	2.8	8.8
23	8	0	21 14	26.9	2	7	26.9	22 13	0	3	6	27.8	23 13	2	4	5	28.7	24 13	3	5	4	6	25 13	4	7	3	5	26 14	6	8
24	6	25.7	20 45	7	2	5	6	21 44	27.8	3	4	5	22 43	0	4	3	3	23 43	1	6	2	2	24 44	2	7	1	1	25 45	4	8
25	5	4	20 14	5	2	4	3	21 14	6	3	3	1	22 13	28.8	4	2	0	23 14	♒ 29.9	6	1	28.9	24 14	0	7	0	♐ 29.8	25 16	2	9
26	1.4	0	19 43	2	2	2	25.9	20 43	4	3	1	26.8	21 43	6	5	0	27.7	22 43	7	6	4.9	6	23 44	0.8	7.7	5.8	5	24 46	0	9
27	2	24.7	19 12	0	3.2	1	6	20 11	2	4.3	0	5	21 11	3	5.5	3.9	4	22 12	5	6.6	8	3	23 13	6	8	7	1	24 15	1.8	9
28	1	4	18 40	25.8	2	1.9	3	19 39	26.9	3	2.8	1	20 39	1	5	7	0	21 39	3	7	6	27.9	22 41	4	8	5	28.8	23 43	6	9.0
29	0.9	0	18 7	5	2	8	24.9	19 6	7	4	7	25.8	20 6	27.9	5	6	26.7	21 7	0	7	5	6	22 8	2	8	4	5	23 10	4	0
30	7	23.7	17 33	3	2	6	6	18 32	4	4	5	4	19 32	6	5	4	3	20 33	28.8	7	4.3	2	21 34	0	7.9	2	1	22 36	2	0
31	6	3	16 58	0	2	5	2	17 57	2	4	4	1	18 57	4	6	3	0	19 58	6	6.7	1	26.9	20 59	♒ 29.8	9	0	27.7	22 1	0	1
32	4	0	16 22	24.7	3.3	1.3	23.8	17 22	25.9	4.4	2	24.7	18 22	1	5.6	1	25.6	19 22	3	8	0	5	20 23	5	9	4.9	4	21 25	0.7	1
33	3	22.6	15 45	4	3	1	5	16 45	6	4	0	3	17 45	26.8	6	2.9	2	18 45	0	8	3.8	1	19 46	3	8.0	7	0	20 48	5	9.1
34	1	2	15 7	1	3	0	1	16 7	3	5	1.9	23.9	17 7	5	6	8	24.8	18 7	27.8	8	6	25.7	19 8	0	0	5	26.6	20 10	2	2
35	♏ 29.9	21.8	14 28	23.8	3	0.8	22.7	15 28	0	5	7	5	16 27	3	7	6	4	17 28	5	6.8	5	3	18 29	28.7	0	4	2	19 31	0	2
36	8	4	13 48	5	3	6	3	14 47	24.7	5	6	1	15 47	0	7	4	0	16 47	2	9	3	24.9	17 49	4	1	2	25.8	18 50	♒ 29.7	2
37	6	0	13 6	2	3.3	4	21.8	14 6	4	4.5	4	22.7	15 5	25.7	5.7	2	23.6	16 5	0	9	1	5	17 7	2	1	0	4	18 9	5	3
38	4	20.6	12 23	22.9	4	3	4	13 22	1	5	2	3	14 22	4	7	0	2	15 22	26.7	9	2.9	0	16 23	27.9	8.1	3.8	24.9	17 25	2	9.3
39	2	1	11 39	6	4	1	0	12 38	23.7	6	0	21.8	13 37	1	8	1.8	22.7	14 37	3	7.0	7	23.6	15 38	6	2	6	5	16 40	28.9	4
40	0	19.7	10 53	2	4	♏ 29.9	20.5	11 52	4	6	0.8	4	12 51	24.7	8	6	3	13 51	0	0	5	1	14 52	3	2	4	0	15 53	6	4
41	28.8	2	10 6	21.8	4	7	1	11 4	0	6	6	20.9	12 3	3	8	4	21.8	13 3	25.6	0	3	22.6	14 4	0	3	2	23.5	15 5	3	5
42	6	18.7	9 17	4	3.4	5	19.6	10 15	22.6	4.6	4	4	11 14	23.9	5.9	2	3	12 14	2	1	1	1	13 13	26.6	8.3	2.9	0	14 15	27.9	9.5
43	4	2	8 26	0	4	3	1	9 24	2	6	2	19.9	10 23	5	9	0	20.8	11 22	24.8	1	1.8	21.6	12 22	2	4	7	22.5	13 22	5	6
44	2	17.7	7 33	20.6	5	0	18.5	8 31	21.8	7	0	4	9 29	1	9	0.7	2	10 28	4	7.2	6	1	11 28	25.8	4	5	21.9	12 28	1	6
45	0	2	6 38	1	5	28.8	0	7 35	4	7	♏ 29.8	18.8	8 33	22.7	9	5	19.7	9 32	0	2	4	20.5	10 31	4	5	2	4	11 31	26.7	7
46	27.8	16.6	5 41	19.6	5	6	17.4	6 38	20.9	4.7	5	3	7 35	2	6.0	3	1	8 33	23.5	3	2	0	9 32	0	8.5	0	20.8	10 32	3	9.7
47	5	1	4 41	1	3.5	4	16.9	5 38	4	7	3	17.7	6 35	21.7	0	0	18.5	7 32	0	3	0	19.4	8 31	24.5	5	1.8	2	9 31	25.8	8
48	3	15.5	3 39	18.5	6	1	3	4 36	19.8	7	0	1	5 32	2	0	♏ 29.8	17.9	6 29	22.5	7.3	0.7	18.8	7 27	0	6	6	19.6	8 26	3	8
49	0	14.9	2 35	17.9	6	27.9	15.7	3 30	2	8	28.7	16.5	4 26	20.6	1	6	3	5 23	0	4	4	2	6 20	23.4	6	3	0	7 19	24.8	9
50	26.7	3	1 28	2	6	6	1	2 22	18.6	4.8	4	15.9	3 18	0	1	3	16.7	4 14	21.4	4	1	17.5	5 11	22.8	8.7	0	18.4	6 8	2	10.0
51	4	13.6	0 18	16.5	6	3	14.4	1 11	17.9	8	1	2	2 6	19.4	6.1	0	0	3 1	20.8	4	♏ 29.8	16.9	3 58	2	7	0.7	17.7	4 55	23.6	0
52	1	12.9	♐ 29 4	15.8	3.6	26.9	13.7	♐ 29 57	2	9	27.8	14.5	0 51	18.7	2	28.6	15.3	1 46	1	7.5	5	2	2 41	21.5	8	3	0	3 37	22.9	1
53	25.8	2	27 48	0	7	6	0	28 40	16.4	9	6	13.8	♐ 29 33	17.9	2	3	14.6	0 26	19.3	6	2	15.4	1 21	20.7	9	0	16.2	2 16	2	2
54	5	11.5	26 28	14.1	7	3	12.3	27 19	15.5	5.0	3	0	28 11	0	3	0	13.8	♐ 29 3	18.4	7	28.9	14.6	♐ 29 57	19.9	9.0	♏ 29.7	15.4	0 51	21.4	10.3
55	2	10.7	25 4	13.1	7	0	11.5	25 54	14.5	1	26.9	12.3	26 45	16.0	4	27.7	0	27 36	17.5	7	5	13.8	28 28	0	0	3	14.6	♐ 29 21	20.5	4
56	24.8	9.9	23 36	12.0	7	25.6	10.7	24 25	13.4	1	5	11.5	25 15	14.9	5	3	12.2	26 5	16.5	8	1	0	26 56	18.0	1	28.9	13.8	27 48	19.5	5

	SID. T. 14 30 21 (H. M. S.) ARC 217° 35′.3	♏ 10°				14 34 17 (H. M. S.) 218° 34′.3	♏ 11°				14 38 14 (H. M. S.) 219° 33′.4	♏ 12°				14 42 11 (H. M. S.) 220° 32′.8	♏ 13°				14 46 9 (H. M. S.) 221° 32′.3	♏ 14°				14 50 8 (H. M. S.) 222° 32′.0	♏ 15°			
H.	11	12	1	2	3	11	12	1	2	3	11	12	1	2	3	11	12	1	2	3	11	12	1	2	3	11	12	1	2	3
Lat.	♐	♑	♑	♓	♈	♐	♑	♑	♓	♈	♐	♑	♑	♓	♈	♐	♑	♑	♓	♈	♐	♑	♒	♓	♈	♐	♑	♒	♓	♈
°	°	°	° ′	°	°	°	°	° ′	°	°	°	°	° ′	°	°	°	°	° ′	°	°	°	°	° ′	°	°	°	°	° ′	°	°
22	6.4	0.8	26 43	2.8	8.8	7.3	1.7	27 44	3.9	9.9	8.2	2.6	28 46	5.1	11.0	9.1	3.5	29 49	6.3	12.2	10.1	4.4	0 52	7.4	13.3	11.0	5.3	1 56	8.6	14.5
23	3	5	26 14	6	8	2	4	27 16	7	9	1	3	28 18	4.9	1	0	2	29 21	1	2	9.9	1	0 25	3	4	10.8	0	1 29	5	5
24	1	1	25 45	4	8	0	0	26 47	6	10.0	0	1.9	27 50	8	1	8.9	2.9	28 53	5.9	3	8	3.8	♑ 29 56	1	4	7	4.7	1 1	4	6
25	0	♐ 29.8	25 16	2	9	6.9	0.7	26 18	4	0	7.8	6	27 20	6	1	7	5	28 24	8	3	6	4	29 27	0	4	5	4	0 32	2	6
26	5.8	5	24 46	0	9	7	4	25 48	2	0	7	3	26 50	4	2	6	2	27 54	6	3	5	1	28 57	6.8	5	4	0	0 2	1	7
27	7	1	24 15	1.8	9	6	0	25 17	0	1	5	0.9	26 19	2	11.2	4	1.9	27 23	5	12.4	9.3	2.8	28 27	7	13.5	2	3.7	♑ 29 32	7.9	14.7
28	5	28.8	23 43	6	9.0	4	♐ 29.7	24 45	2.8	1	3	6	25 48	0	3	2	5	26 51	3	4	1	4	27 55	5	6	0	3	29 0	7	8
29	4	5	23 10	4	0	3	4	24 12	6	10.1	2	3	25 15	3.8	3	1	2	26 18	1	5	0	1	27 23	3	6	9.9	0	28 28	6	8
30	2	1	22 36	2	0	1	0	23 38	4	2	0	♐ 29.9	24 41	6	4	7.9	0.8	25 45	4.9	5	8.8	1.7	26 49	1	7	7	2.6	27 55	4	9
31	0	27.7	22 1	0	1	5.9	28.6	23 3	2	2	6.8	5	24 6	4	4	7	5	25 10	7	12.6	6	4	26 15	5.9	13.7	5	3	27 20	2	9
32	4.9	4	21 25	0.7	1	8	3	22 27	0	3	7	2	23 31	2	11.4	6	1	24 35	5	6	5	0	25 39	7	8	4	1.9	26 45	0	15.0
33	7	0	20 48	5	9.1	6	27.9	21 51	1.7	3	5	28.8	22 54	0	5	4	♐ 29.7	23 58	3	7	3	0.6	25 3	5	8	2	5	26 9	6.8	0
34	5	26.6	20 10	2	2	4	5	21 13	5	10.3	3	4	22 16	2.8	5	2	3	23 20	0	7	1	2	24 25	3	9	0	1	25 31	6	1
35	4	2	19 31	0	2	2	1	20 34	2	4	1	0	21 37	5	6	0	28.9	22 41	3.8	12.8	7.9	♐ 29.8	23 46	1	14.0	8.8	0.7	24 52	4	1
36	2	25.8	18 50	♒ 29.7	2	1	26.7	19 53	0	4	5.9	27.6	20 56	3	11.6	6.8	5	22 1	6	8	7	4	23 5	4.9	0	6	3	24 11	2	2
37	0	4	18 9	5	3	4.9	3	19 11	0.7	5	7	2	20 15	0	6	6	1	21 19	3	9	5	0	22 23	5	1	4	♐ 29.8	23 29	0	15.3
38	3.8	24.9	17 25	2	9.3	7	25.8	18 28	4	5	5	26.7	19 31	1.8	7	4	27.6	20 35	0	9	3	28.5	21 40	4	1	2	4	22 46	5.7	3
39	6	5	16 40	28.9	4	5	4	17 43	2	10.6	3	3	18 46	5	7	2	2	19 50	2.8	13.0	1	1	20 55	1	2	0	28.9	22 0	5	4
40	4	0	15 53	6	4	3	24.9	16 56	♒ 29.9	6	1	25.8	17 59	2	11.8	0	26.7	19 3	5	0	6.9	27.6	20 8	3.9	14.3	7.8	4	21 13	2	5
41	2	23.5	15 5	3	5	0	4	16 7	6	7	4.9	3	17 10	0.9	8	5.8	2	18 14	2	1	7	1	19 19	6	4	6	27.9	20 24	4.9	6
42	2.9	0	14 15	27.9	9.5	3.8	23.9	15 17	3	7	7	24.8	16 20	6	9	6	25.6	17 23	1.9	2	5	26.5	18 28	3	4	4	4	19 34	6	15.6
43	7	22.5	13 22	5	6	6	4	14 24	28.9	10.8	5	2	15 27	3	9	4	1	16 30	6	13.3	3	0	17 35	0	5	1	26.9	18 40	3	7
44	5	21.9	12 28	1	6	4	22.8	13 29	5	8	2	23.7	14 32	0	12.0	1	24.6	15 35	3	4	0	25.5	16 39	2.7	5	6.9	4	17 45	0	8
45	2	4	11 31	26.7	7	1	3	12 32	1	9	0	1	13 35	♒ 29.6	1	4.9	0	14 38	0	4	5.8	24.9	15 42	4	14.6	6	25.8	16 47	3.7	9
46	0	20.8	10 32	3	9.7	2.9	21.7	11 33	27.7	9	3.8	22.6	12 35	2	2	7	23.4	13 37	0.6	5	6	3	14 41	0	7	4	2	15 46	4	16.0
47	1.8	2	9 31	25.8	8	7	1	10 31	3	11.0	6	0	11 32	28.8	3	4	22.8	12 34	2	13.5	3	23.7	13 38	1.6	8	2	24.6	14 42	0	1
48	6	19.6	8 26	3	8	4	20.5	9 26	26.8	1	3	21.4	10 27	3	12.4	2	2	11 29	♒ 29.7	6	0	1	12 32	2	9	5.9	0	13 35	2.6	2
49	3	0	7 19	24.8	9	1	19.9	8 18	3	2	0	20.7	9 19	27.8	5	3.9	21.6	10 20	2	7	4.7	22.5	11 22	0.7	15.0	6	23.3	12 25	2	3
50	0	18.4	6 8	2	10.0	1.8	2	7 7	25.7	3	2.7	0	8 7	2	5	6	20.9	9 7	28.7	8	4	21.8	10 9	2	1	3	22.6	11 12	1.7	16.4
51	0.7	17.7	4 55	23.6	0	5	18.5	5 52	1	4	4	19.4	6 51	26.6	6	2	2	7 51	1	14.0	1	1	8 52	♒ 29.6	3	0	21.9	9 54	2	5
52	3	0	3 37	22.9	1	2	17.8	4 34	24.5	11.5	1	18.7	5 32	0	12.7	2.9	19.5	6 31	27.5	1	3.8	20.4	7 32	0	4	4.6	2	8 33	0.6	7
53	0	16.2	2 16	2	2	0.8	0	3 12	23.8	5	1.8	17.9	4 9	25.3	8	6	18.7	5 7	26.8	2	4	19.6	6 7	28.4	15.5	3	20.4	7 7	0	8
54	♏ 29.7	15.4	0 51	21.4	10.3	5	16.2	1 46	0	6	4	0	2 42	24.5	9	3	17.9	3 39	0	3	1	18.8	4 37	27.7	6	0	19.5	5 36	♒ 29.3	17.0
55	3	14.6	♐ 29 21	20.5	4	2	15.4	0 15	22.1	7	0	16.2	1 10	23.6	13.1	1.9	0	2 6	25.2	4	2.7	17.9	3 3	26.9	7	3.6	18.7	4 1	28.5	1
56	28.9	13.8	27 48	19.5	5	♏ 29.8	14.5	♐ 28 40	21.1	9	0.6	15.3	♐ 29 34	22.6	3	5	16.1	0 28	24.2	5	3	0	1 24	25.9	9	1	17.8	2 20	27.6	3

	H. M. S. SID. T. 14 54 7 ARC 223° 31′.8 ♏ 16°					H. M. S. 14 58 7 224° 31′.9 ♏ 17°					H. M. S. 15 2 8 225° 32′.1 ♏ 18°					H. M. S. 15 6 10 226° 32′.5 ♏ 19°					H. M. S. 15 10 12 227° 33′.1 ♏ 20°					H. M. S. 15 14 16 228° 33′.9 ♏ 21°				
H.	11	12	1	2	3	11	12	1	2	3	11	12	1	2	3	11	12	1	2	3	11	12	1	2	3	11	12	1	2	3
Lat.	♐	♑	♒	♓	♈	♐	♑	♒	♓	♈	♐	♑	♒	♓	♈	♐	♑	♒	♓	♈	♐	♑	♒	♓	♈	♐	♑	♒	♓	♈
°	°	°	° ′	°	°	°	°	° ′	°	°	°	°	° ′	°	°	°	°	° ′	°	°	°	°	° ′	°	°	°	°	° ′	°	°
22	11.9	6.3	3 1	9.8	15.6	12.8	7.2	4 6	11.0	16.7	13.7	8.1	5 11	12.3	17.9	14.6	9.1	6 17	13.5	19.0	15.5	10.0	7 24	14.7	20.2	16.5	11.0	8 32	16.0	21.3
23	7	0	2 33	7	7	6	6.9	3 39	10.9	8	6	7.8	4 45	1	9	5	8.8	5 51	4	1	4	9.7	6 58	6	2	3	10.7	8 6	15.9	4
24	6	5.6	2 5	6	7	5	6	3 11	8	8	4	5	4 17	0	18.0	3	5	5 24	3	1	2	4	6 31	5	3	2	4	7 39	8	4
25	4	3	1 37	4	8	3	2	2 42	7	9	3	2	3 49	11.9	1	2	1	4 56	1	2	1	1	6 3	4	3	0	0	7 12	7	5
26	11.3	0	1 7	9.3	15.8	2	5.9	2 13	5	9	1	6.8	3 20	8	1	0	7.8	4 27	0	3	14.9	8.7	5 35	14.3	20.4	15.9	9.7	6 43	6	6
27	1	4.6	0 37	1	9	0	6	1 43	10.4	17.0	12.9	5	2 50	6	2	13.9	4	3 57	12.9	19.3	8	4	5 5	2	5	7	4	6 14	5	21.6
28	0	3	0 6	0	9	11.9	2	1 12	2	1	8	1	2 19	5	2	7	1	3 27	8	4	6	0	4 35	1	6	5	0	5 44	15.4	7
29	10.8	3.9	♑ 29 34	8.8	16.0	7	4.9	0 40	1	1	6	5.8	1 47	11.4	18.3	5	6.7	2 55	7	5	4	7.7	4 4	13.9	6	4	8.7	5 13	3	8
30	6	6	29 0	7	0	5	5	0 7	0	2	4	4	1 14	2	4	4	4	2 23	5	5	3	3	3 31	8	20.7	2	3	4 41	1	9
31	5	2	28 26	5	1	4	1	♑ 29 33	9.8	2	3	1	0 41	1	4	2	0	1 49	12.4	6	1	0	2 58	7	8	0	7.9	4 8	0	9
32	3	2.8	27 51	3	1	2	3.8	28 58	6	17.3	1	4.7	0 6	10.9	5	0	5.6	1 14	2	19.7	13.9	6.6	2 23	6	9	14.8	5	3 34	14.9	22.0
33	1	4	27 15	1	2	0	4	28 22	4	4	11.9	3	♑ 29 30	8	6	12.8	2	0 39	1	7	7	2	1 48	13.4	9	7	1	2 58	8	1
34	9.9	0	26 37	7.9	16.3	10.8	0	27 44	3	5	7	3.9	28 52	6	18.6	6	4.8	0 1	11.9	8	6	5.8	1 11	3	21.0	5	6.7	2 21	6	2
35	7	1.6	25 58	7	3	6	2.6	27 5	1	5	5	5	28 14	4	7	4	4	♑ 29 23	8	9	4	4	0 33	1	1	3	3	1 43	5	3
36	5	2	25 18	5	4	4	1	26 25	8.9	6	3	1	27 34	2	7	2	0	28 42	6	20.0	2	4.9	♑ 29 53	12.9	2	1	5.9	1 4	14.3	4
37	3	0.8	24 36	3	5	2	1.7	25 44	7	17.7	1	2.6	26 52	0	8	0	3.6	28 1	4	1	0	5	29 11	8	3	13.9	4	0 23	2	22.5
38	1	3	23 52	1	6	0	2	25 0	4	8	10.9	2	26 8	9.8	9	11.8	1	27 17	2	2	12.8	0	28 28	6	4	7	0	♑ 29 40	0	6
39	8.9	♐ 29.8	23 7	6.8	16.6	9.8	0.8	24 15	2	8	7	1.7	25 23	6	19.0	6	2.6	26 32	0	3	5	3.6	27 43	4	21.5	5	4.5	28 55	13.8	7
40	7	4	22 20	6	7	6	3	23 28	0	9	5	2	24 36	4	1	4	1	25 46	10.8	4	3	1	26 56	2	6	2	0	28 8	6	8
41	5	28.9	21 31	3	8	4	♐ 29.8	22 39	7.7	18.0	3	0.7	23 47	1	2	2	1.6	24 57	5	20.5	1	2.6	26 7	0	7	0	3.5	27 19	4	9
42	3	4	20 40	0	9	2	3	21 47	5	1	1	2	22 56	8.9	3	0	1	24 6	3	6	11.9	0	25 16	11.8	8	12.8	0	26 28	2	23.0
43	0	27.8	19 47	5.7	17.0	8.9	28.7	20 54	2	2	9.8	♐ 29.7	22 2	7	4	10.7	0.6	23 12	1	7	6	1.5	24 22	6	9	5	2.4	25 34	0	2
44	7.8	3	18 51	4	1	7	2	19 58	6.9	3	6	1	21 6	4	19.5	5	0	22 16	9.9	8	4	0.9	23 26	3	22.1	3	1.8	24 38	12.8	3
45	5	26.7	17 53	2	1	4	27.6	19 0	7	4	3	28.5	20 8	1	6	2	♐ 29.4	21 17	6	21.0	1	3	22 27	1	2	0	3	23 39	5	5
46	2	1	16 51	4.9	2	1	0	17 58	4	18.5	0	27.9	19 6	7.8	7	9.9	28.8	20 15	3	1	10.9	♐ 29.7	21 25	10.8	4	11.7	0.7	22 36	3	23.6
47	0	25.5	15 47	5	3	7.9	26.4	16 54	1	6	8.8	3	18 1	5	9	7	2	19 10	0	2	6	1	20 20	5	5	4	0	21 31	0	7
48	6.8	24.9	14 40	1	17.5	6	25.8	15 46	5.7	7	5	26.7	16 53	1	20.0	4	27.6	18 1	8.7	3	3	28.5	19 11	2	22.6	1	♐ 29.4	20 22	11.7	8
49	5	2	13 30	3.7	6	3	1	14 35	3	9	2	0	15 42	6.7	2	1	26.9	16 50	3	21.5	0	27.8	17 59	9.9	7	10.8	28.7	19 9	4	24.0
50	2	23.5	12 16	2	7	0	24.4	13 20	4.8	19.0	7.9	25.3	14 26	3	3	8.8	2	15 34	7.9	6	9.7	1	16 42	5	9	5	0	17 52	1	2
51	5.8	22.8	10 57	2.7	8	6.6	23.7	12 2	3	2	6	24.6	13 7	5.9	5	5	25.5	14 14	5	8	4	26.4	15 22	1	23.1	2	27.3	16 31	10.7	4
52	5	0	9 35	2	18.0	3	22.9	10 39	3.8	4	3	23.8	11 43	4	7	1	24.7	12 49	0	22.0	0	25.6	13 56	8.7	3	9.9	26.5	15 5	3	6
53	2	21.2	8 8	1.6	1	0	1	9 11	2	5	6.9	0	10 15	4.9	9	7.8	23.9	11 19	6.5	1	8.6	24.7	12 26	2	4	5	25.6	13 33	9.9	8
54	4.8	20.4	6 37	0.9	3	5.7	21.3	7 38	2.6	7	5	22.1	8 41	3	21.0	4	0	9 44	5.9	3	2	23.8	10 50	7.7	6	1	24.7	11 56	4	25.0
55	4	19.5	5 0	2	4	3	20.4	6 0	1.9	8	1	21.2	7 1	3.6	1	0	22.1	8 4	3	5	7.8	22.9	9 8	1	8	8.7	23.8	10 13	8.9	2
56	0	18.6	3 18	♒ 29.3	6	4.9	19.4	4 17	1	20.0	5.6	20.2	5 16	2.8	3	6.6	21.1	6 17	4.6	7	4	21.9	7 20	6.4	24.0	2	22.8	8 24	3	4

SID. T. 15 H. 14 M. 16 S. — ARC 228° 33′.9 — ♏ 21°

H.	11	12	1	2	3
Lat.	♐	♑	♒	♓	♈
°	°	°	° ′	°	°
22	16.5	11.0	8 32	16.0	21.3
23	3	10.7	8 6	15.9	4
24	2	4	7 39	8	4
25	0	0	7 12	7	5
26	15.9	9.7	6 43	6	6
27	7	4	6 14	5	21.6
28	5	0	5 44	15.4	7
29	4	8.7	5 13	3	8
30	2	3	4 41	1	9
31	0	7.9	4 8	0	9
32	14.8	5	3 34	14.9	22.0
33	7	1	2 58	8	1
34	5	6.7	2 21	6	2
35	3	3	1 43	5	3
36	1	5.9	1 4	14.3	4
37	13.9	4	0 23	2	22.5
38	7	0	♑ 29 40	0	6
39	5	4.5	28 55	13.8	7
40	2	0	28 8	6	8
41	0	3.5	27 19	4	9
42	12.8	0	26 28	2	23.0
43	5	2.4	25 34	0	2
44	3	1.8	24 38	12.8	3
45	0	3	23 39	5	5
46	11.7	0.7	22 36	3	23.6
47	4	0	21 31	0	7
48	1	♐ 29.4	20 22	11.7	8
49	10.8	28.7	19 9	4	24.0
50	5	0	17 52	1	2
51	2	27.3	16 31	10.7	4
52	9.9	26.5	15 5	3	6
53	5	25.6	13 33	9.9	8
54	1	24.7	11 56	4	25.0
55	8.7	23.8	10 13	8.9	2
56	2	22.8	8 24	3	4

SID. T. 15 H. 18 M. 19 S. — ARC 229° 34′.8 — ♏ 22°

H.	11	12	1	2	3
Lat.	♐	♑	♒	♓	♈
°	°	°	° ′	°	°
22	17.4	12.0	9 40	17.2	22.5
23	3	11.6	9 15	1	5
24	1	3	8 48	0	6
25	16.9	0	8 21	16.9	7
26	8	10.7	7 53	8	22.7
27	6	3	7 24	7	8
28	5	0	6 54	6	9
29	3	9.6	6 23	5	23.0
30	1	2	5 51	16.4	0
31	15.9	8.9	5 19	3	1
32	8	5	4 45	2	2
33	6	1	4 9	1	23.3
34	4	7.7	3 33	0	4
35	2	3	2 55	15.8	5
36	0	6.8	2 16	7	6
37	14.8	4	1 35	6	23.7
38	6	5.9	0 52	4	8
39	4	4	0 7	2	9
40	1	0	♑ 29 20	1	24.0
41	13.9	4.5	28 31	14.9	1
42	7	3.9	27 40	7	3
43	4	4	26 47	5	4
44	2	2.8	25 51	3	24.6
45	12.9	2	24 52	0	7
46	6	1.6	23 49	13.8	8
47	3	0	22 44	6	9
48	0	0.3	21 35	3	25.1
49	11.7	♐ 29.6	20 21	1	2
50	4	28.9	19 4	12.8	4
51	0	2	17 42	5	6
52	10.7	27.4	16 15	1	8
53	4	26.5	14 43	11.7	26.1
54	0	25.6	13 4	2	3
55	9.6	24.6	11 20	10.7	5
56	1	23.6	9 29	1	7

SID. T. 15 H. 22 M. 24 S. — ARC 230° 36′.0 — ♏ 23°

H.	11	12	1	2	3
Lat.	♐	♑	♒	♓	♈
°	°	°	° ′	°	°
22	18.3	12.9	10 49	18.4	23.6
23	2	6	10 24	4	7
24	0	3	9 58	3	7
25	17.9	0	9 31	2	8
26	7	11.6	9 3	1	9
27	5	3	8 34	0	24.0
28	4	10.9	8 5	17.9	0
29	2	6	7 34	9	1
30	0	2	7 3	8	2
31	16.9	9.8	6 30	7	24.3
32	7	5	5 56	6	4
33	5	1	5 21	17.5	5
34	3	8.7	4 45	3	6
35	1	2	4 8	2	24.7
36	15.9	7.8	3 29	1	8
37	7	4	2 48	0	9
38	5	6.9	2 5	16.8	25.0
39	3	4	1 21	7	1
40	0	5.9	0 34	5	2
41	14.8	4	♑ 29 45	3	4
42	6	4.9	28 54	2	25.5
43	3	3	28 1	0	7
44	1	3.8	27 5	15.8	8
45	13.8	2	26 6	6	9
46	5	2.6	25 3	3	26.0
47	2	1.9	23 58	1	2
48	12.9	3	22 48	14.8	4
49	6	0.6	21 35	6	6
50	3	♐ 29.8	20 17	4	7
51	11.9	1	18 54	1	9
52	6	28.3	17 27	13.8	27.1
53	2	27.4	15 53	4	3
54	10.8	26.5	14 14	0	6
55	4	25.5	12 29	12.5	8
56	0	24.4	10 36	0	28.1

SID. T. 15 H. 26 M. 29 S. — ARC 231° 37′.3 — ♏ 24°

H.	11	12	1	2	3
Lat.	♐	♑	♒	♓	♈
°	°	°	° ′	°	°
22	19.3	13.9	11 59	19.7	24.7
23	1	6	11 33	6	8
24	0	3	11 8	6	9
25	18.8	12.9	10 41	5	25.0
26	6	6	10 13	4	0
27	5	3	9 45	19.3	1
28	3	11.9	9 16	2	2
29	1	6	8 46	2	25.3
30	0	2	8 15	1	4
31	17.8	10.8	7 42	0	5
32	6	4	7 9	18.9	6
33	4	0	6 35	8	25.7
34	2	9.6	5 59	7	8
35	0	2	5 21	6	9
36	16.8	8.8	4 43	5	26.0
37	6	3	4 2	18.4	1
38	4	7.8	3 20	2	2
39	2	4	2 35	1	3
40	0	6.9	1 49	0	26.5
41	15.7	4	1 0	17.8	6
42	5	5.9	0 10	7	7
43	3	3	♑ 29 16	5	9
44	0	4.7	28 20	3	27.0
45	14.7	1	27 21	1	2
46	4	3.5	26 19	16.9	3
47	1	2.9	25 13	7	4
48	13.8	2	24 3	5	5
49	5	1.5	22 50	3	7
50	2	0.8	21 31	1	28.0
51	12.8	0	20 8	15.8	2
52	5	♐ 29.2	18 40	5	4
53	1	28.4	17 6	2	7
54	11.7	27.5	15 26	14.8	9
55	3	26.4	13 39	4	29.2
56	10.8	25.3	11 45	13.9	4

SID. T. 15 H. 30 M. 35 S. — ARC 232° 38′.8 — ♏ 25°

H.	11	12	1	2	3
Lat.	♐	♑	♒	♓	♈
°	°	°	° ′	°	°
22	20.2	14.9	13 9	20.9	25.9
23	0	6	12 44	9	26.0
24	19.9	3	12 18	8	0
25	7	13.9	11 52	8	1
26	6	6	11 25	7	2
27	4	2	10 57	20.6	26.3
28	2	12.9	10 28	6	4
29	1	5	9 58	5	5
30	18.9	2	9 28	4	6
31	7	11.8	8 56	3	26.7
32	5	4	8 23	20.3	8
33	3	0	7 49	2	9
34	2	10.6	7 13	1	27.0
35	0	2	6 36	0	1
36	17.8	9.8	5 57	19.9	2
37	6	3	5 17	8	3
38	3	8.8	4 35	7	27.4
39	1	4	3 51	6	5
40	16.9	7.9	3 5	19.4	7
41	6	4	2 17	3	8
42	4	6.8	1 26	1	28.0
43	1	3	0 33	0	1
44	15.9	5.7	♑ 29 37	18.8	3
45	6	1	28 38	6	4
46	3	4.5	27 35	5	28.5
47	0	3.8	26 30	3	7
48	14.7	2	25 20	1	9
49	4	2.5	24 6	17.9	29.1
50	1	1.7	22 47	8	3
51	13.8	0	21 24	6	5
52	4	0.2	19 55	3	7
53	0	♐ 29.3	18 20	0	9
54	12.6	28.4	16 39	16.7	♉ 0.2
55	2	27.3	14 51	3	5
56	11.7	26.3	12 55	15.9	8

SID. T. 15 H. 34 M. 42 S. — ARC 233° 40′.5 — ♏ 26°

H.	11	12	1	2	3
Lat.	♐	♑	♒	♓	♈
°	°	°	° ′	°	°
22	21.1	15.9	14 19	22.2	27.0
23	0	6	13 55	2	1
24	20.8	2	13 30	1	2
25	7	14.9	13 4	1	3
26	5	6	12 37	0	27.4
27	3	2	12 10	21.9	5
28	2	13.9	11 41	9	5
29	0	5	11 12	8	6
30	19.8	2	10 41	8	27.7
31	6	12.8	10 10	7	8
32	5	4	9 37	21.6	9
33	3	0	9 3	5	28.0
34	1	11.6	8 28	5	2
35	18.9	2	7 52	4	3
36	7	10.8	7 14	21.3	4
37	5	3	6 34	2	28.5
38	3	9.8	5 52	1	6
39	0	4	5 8	0	8
40	17.8	8.9	4 22	20.9	9
41	6	3	3 34	8	29.0
42	3	7.8	2 43	6	2
43	0	3	1 51	5	3
44	16.8	6.7	0 55	20.4	5
45	5	1	♑ 29 56	2	6
46	2	5.5	28 54	1	8
47	15.9	4.8	27 48	19.9	♉
48	6	1	26 38	7	0.2
49	3	3.4	25 24	6	3
50	0	2.7	24 5	5	5
51	14.7	1.9	22 41	3	8
52	3	1	21 11	1	1.0
53	13.9	0.2	19 36	18.8	2
54	5	♐ 29.3	17 54	5	5
55	1	28.3	16 4	2	8
56	12.6	27.2	14 7	17.9	2.1

	SID. T. 15 38 49 ARC 234° 42′.3 ♏ 27°					15 42 57 235° 44′.4 ♏ 28°					15 47 6 236° 46′.6 ♏ 29°					15 51 16 237° 48′.9 ♐ 0°					15 55 26 238° 51′.5 ♐ 1°					15 59 37 239° 54′.2 ♐ 2°				
H.	11	12	1	2	3	11	12	1	2	3	11	12	1	2	3	11	12	1	2	3	11	12	1	2	3	11	12	1	2	3
Lat.	♐	♑	♒	♓	♈	♐	♑	♒	♓	♈	♐	♑	♒	♓	♉	♐	♑	♒	♓	♉	♐	♑	♒	♓	♉	♐	♑	♒	♓	♉
°	°	°	° ′	°	°	°	°	° ′	°	°	°	°	° ′	°	°	°	°	° ′	°	°	°	°	° ′	°	°	°	°	° ′	°	°
22	22.1	16.9	15 30	23.5	28.2	23.0	17.9	16 42	24.8	29.3	24.0	18.9	17 55	26.0	0.5	24.9	19.9	19 8	27.3	1.6	25.9	20.9	20 22	28.6	2.8	26.8	22.0	21 36	29.9	3.9
23	21.9	6	15 6	4	3	22.9	6	16 19	7	4	23.8	6	17 32	0	6	8	6	18 45	3	7	7	6	19 59	6	9	7	21.7	21 15	9	4.0
24	8	2	14 42	4	3	7	2	15 54	7	5	6	3	17 8	0	7	6	3	18 22	3	8	6	3	19 37	6	3.0	5	4	20 52	9	1
25	6	15.9	14 16	3	4	5	16.9	15 29	7	6	5	17.9	16 43	25.9	8	5	18.9	17 58	3	9	4	0	19 13	6	1	3	1	20 29	9	2
26	4	6	13 50	23.3	5	4	6	15 4	6	29.7	3	6	16 18	9	9	24.3	6	17 33	2	2.0	2	19.7	18 49	6	2	2	20.8	20 5	9	3
27	3	2	13 23	2	28.6	2	2	14 37	24.6	8	2	3	15 52	9	1.0	1	3	17 7	27.2	1	1	4	18 24	28.5	3	0	5	19 41	29.9	4
28	1	14.9	12 55	2	7	0	15.9	14 9	5	9	0	16.9	15 25	8	1	0	17.9	16 41	2	2	24.9	0	17 58	5	4	25.8	1	19 15	9	4.5
29	20.9	5	12 26	1	8	21.9	5	13 41	5	♉	22.8	6	14 57	8	2	23.8	6	16 13	2	3	7	18.6	17 31	5	3.5	7	19.7	18 49	9	7
30	8	2	11 56	23.1	9	7	2	13 11	4	0.1	6	2	14 28	25.8	3	6	2	15 45	1	4	5	2	17 3	5	6	5	3	18 21	9	8
31	6	13.8	11 25	0	29.0	5	14.8	12 41	24.4	2	5	15.8	13 57	7	4	4	16.8	15 15	1	2.5	4	17.8	16 34	5	7	3	18.9	17 53	9	9
32	4	4	10 52	0	1	3	4	12 9	3	3	3	4	13 26	7	1.5	2	5	14 44	27.1	6	2	4	16 3	28.5	8	1	5	17 23	29.9	5.0
33	2	0	10 19	22.9	2	1	0	11 36	3	4	1	0	12 54	7	6	0	1	14 12	1	8	0	0	15 32	5	4.0	24.9	1	16 52	9	2
34	0	12.6	9 44	9	3	0	13.6	11 1	2	0.5	21.9	14.6	12 20	25.6	7	22.8	15.6	13 39	0	9	23.8	16.6	14 59	5	1	7	17.7	16 20	9	3
35	19.8	2	9 8	8	29.5	20.8	2	10 26	24.2	6	7	2	11 44	6	8	6	2	13 4	0	3.0	6	2	14 24	4	2	5	3	15 46	9	4
36	6	11.8	8 30	7	6	6	12.8	9 48	1	8	5	13.8	11 7	5	9	4	14.8	12 27	0	1	4	15.8	13 48	4	3	3	16.9	15 11	9	5.5
37	4	3	7 51	22.6	7	3	3	9 9	1	9	3	3	10 28	5	2.0	2	3	11 49	26.9	3	2	4	13 11	28.4	4.4	1	4	14 33	29.9	6
38	2	10.8	7 10	6	8	1	11.8	8 28	0	1.0	1	12.8	9 48	25.4	1	0	13.9	11 9	9	4	0	14.9	12 31	4	6	23.9	15.9	13 55	9	8
39	0	4	6 26	5	♉	19.9	4	7 45	23.9	2	20.8	4	9 5	4	3	21.8	4	10 27	9	3.6	22.7	4	11 50	4	7	7	5	13 14	9	9
40	18.7	9.9	5 41	4	0.1	7	10.9	7 0	9	3	6	11.9	8 21	3	5	5	12.9	9 43	8	7	5	13.9	11 6	3	9	4	0	12 31	9	6.1
41	5	3	4 53	22.3	3	4	3	6 13	8	5	4	4	7 34	3	6	3	4	8 57	8	9	2	4	10 20	28.3	5.1	2	14.4	11 45	9	3
42	2	8.8	4 3	2	4	2	9.8	5 23	7	1.7	1	10.8	6 45	25.2	8	1	11.8	8 8	26.8	4.0	0	12.8	9 32	3	2	22.9	13.9	10 58	29.9	4
43	0	3	3 10	1	6	18.9	3	4 31	23.6	8	19.8	2	5 53	2	3.0	20.8	3	7 16	7	2	21.7	2	8 41	3	4	6	3	10 6	8	6
44	17.7	7.7	2 14	21.9	7	6	8.7	3 35	5	9	6	9.7	4 58	1	2	5	10.7	6 21	7	4	4	11.6	7 47	2	6	4	12.7	9 14	8	8
45	4	1	1 16	8	8	4	1	2 37	4	2.1	3	1	3 59	0	4	3	1	5 23	6	6	1	0	6 49	28.2	8	1	1	8 17	8	7.0
46	1	6.5	0 13	7	1.0	1	7.4	1 35	3	3	0	8.4	2 57	24.9	6	0	9.4	4 22	6	8	20.9	10.4	5 48	2	6.0	21.8	11.5	7 16	8	2
47	16.8	5.8	♑ 29 7	6	2	17.8	6.8	0 29	23.2	5	18.7	7.8	1 52	9	7	19.7	8.8	3 17	26.5	5.0	6	9.7	4 43	2	2	5	10.8	6 12	29.8	4
48	5	1	27 58	21.4	4	5	1	♑ 29 19	1	7	4	1	0 42	8	9	3	1	2 7	5	2	3	0	3 34	1	4	2	1	5 3	8	6
49	2	4.4	26 43	3	6	2	5.4	28 5	0	9	1	6.4	♑ 29 28	7	4.1	0	7.4	0 53	4	4	19.9	8.3	2 20	28.1	6	20.9	9.4	3 49	8	8
50	15.9	3.7	25 24	2	8	16.8	4.7	26 46	22.9	3.1	17.7	5.6	28 9	6	4	18.7	6.6	♑ 29 34	4	6	6	7.6	1 0	1	9	5	8.7	2 29	8	8.1
51	5	2.9	24 0	0	2.1	5	3.9	25 21	8	3	4	4.8	26 44	24.5	6	3	5.8	28 8	26.3	9	2	6.8	♑ 29 35	0	7.2	2	7.9	1 4	8	4
52	2	1	22 30	20.8	3	1	1	23 50	7	6	0	0	25 13	4	8	17.9	0	26 37	2	6.1	18.8	0	28 4	0	5	19.8	0	♑ 29 33	29.8	7
53	14.8	1.2	20 53	6	5	15.7	2.2	22 13	5	8	16.6	3.1	23 35	3	5.1	5	4.1	24 59	1	4	4	5.1	26 25	27.9	8	4	6.1	27 54	8	9.0
54	4	0.2	19 10	4	8	3	1.2	20 29	3	4.1	2	2.2	21 51	2	4	1	3.1	23 14	0	7	0	4.1	24 39	9	8.1	18.9	5.1	26 7	8	3
55	0	♐ 29.2	17 20	1	3.1	14.9	0.1	18 38	1	4	15.8	1.1	19 58	0	7	16.7	2.1	21 20	25.9	7.0	17.6	3.1	22 44	9	3	5	4.1	24 11	8	6
56	13.5	28.2	15 22	19.8	4	4	♐ 29.0	16 38	21.9	7	3	0.0	17 56	23.8	6.0	2	1.0	19 17	8	4	1	2.0	20 40	8	7	0	3.0	22 6	8	9

	SID. T. 15 h. 59 m. 37 s. ARC 239° 54′.2 ♐ 2°					16 h. 3 m. 48 s. 240° 57′.1 ♐ 3°					16 h. 8 m. 0 s. 242° 0′.1 ♐ 4°					16 h. 12 m. 13 s. 243° 3′.3 ♐ 5°					16 h. 16 m. 27 s. 244° 6′.7 ♐ 6°					16 h. 20 m. 41 s. 245° 10′.2 ♐ 7°				
H.	11	12	1	2	3	11	12	1	2	3	11	12	1	2	3	11	12	1	2	3	11	12	1	2	3	11	12	1	2	3
Lat.	♐	♑	♒	♓	♉	♐	♑	♒	♈	♉	♐	♑	♒	♈	♉	♐	♑	♒	♈	♉	♑	♑	♒	♈	♉	♑	♑	♒	♈	♉
°	°	°	° ′	°	°	°	°	° ′	°	°	°	°	°	°	°	°	°	° ′	°	°	°	°	° ′	°	°	°	°	° ′	°	°
22	26.8	22.0	21 36	29.9	3.9	27.8	23.0	22 51	1.2	5.1	28.8	24.0	24 7	2.5	6.2	29.7	25.1	25 24	3.7	7.3	0.7	26.2	26 41	5.0	8.5	1.7	27.2	27 59	6.3	9.6
23	7	21.7	21 15	9	4.0	6	22.7	22 30	2	2	6	23.7	23 47	5	3	6	24.8	25 4	8	4	5	25.8	26 22	1	6	5	26.9	27 40	4	7
24	5	4	20 52	9	1	5	4	22 8	2	3	4	4	23 25	5	4	4	5	24 43	8	5	4	5	26 2	1	7	3	6	27 21	4	8
25	3	1	20 29	9	2	3	1	21 46	2	4	3	1	23 3	5	5	2	1	24 22	8	6	2	2	25 41	1	8	2	3	27 0	5	9
26	2	20.8	20 5	9	3	1	21.8	21 23	2	5	1	22.8	22 41	5	6.6	1	23.8	24 0	3.8	8	0	24.9	25 19	2	9	0	0	26 40	6.5	10.1
27	0	5	19 41	29.9	4	0	5	20 59	1.2	5.6	27.9	4	22 17	2.5	7	28.9	5	23 37	9	9	♐ 29.9	6	24 57	5.2	9.0	0.8	25.6	26 18	6	2
28	25.8	1	19 15	9	4.5	26.8	1	20 34	2	7	8	1	21 53	6	9	7	1	23 13	9	8.0	7	2	24 34	2	2	7	3	25 56	6	3
29	7	19.7	18 49	9	7	6	20.7	20 8	2	8	6	21.7	21 28	6	7.0	6	22.8	22 48	9	1	5	23.9	24 10	3	3	5	0	25 32	7	4
30	5	3	18 21	9	8	4	3	19 41	2	9	4	4	21 2	6	1	4	4	22 23	4.0	3	3	5	23 45	3	4	3	24.6	25 8	6.7	10.6
31	3	18.9	17 53	9	9	3	19.9	19 13	2	6.1	2	0	20 34	6	2	2	1	21 56	0	4	2	2	23 19	4	9.6	1	2	24 43	8	7
32	1	5	17 23	29.9	5.0	1	5	18 44	1.3	2	0	20.6	20 6	2.7	4	0	21.7	21 29	0	8.5	0	22.8	22 52	5.4	7	♐ 29.9	23.9	24 17	8	9
33	24.9	1	16 52	9	2	25.9	1	18 14	3	3	26.8	2	19 36	7	7.5	27.8	3	20 59	1	6	28.8	4	22 24	5	8	7	5	23 49	9	11.0
34	7	17.7	16 20	9	3	7	18.7	17 42	3	5	6	19.8	19 5	7	6	6	20.9	20 29	1	8	6	0	21 54	5	10.0	5	1	23 20	7.0	2
35	5	3	15 46	9	4	5	3	17 9	3	6.6	4	4	18 32	7	7	4	5	19 57	4.2	9	4	21.6	21 23	6	1	3	22.7	22 50	0	3
36	3	16.9	15 11	9	5.5	3	17.9	16 34	3	7	2	0	17 58	2.7	8	2	1	19 24	2	9.1	2	1	20 50	6	3	1	2	22 18	1	5
37	1	4	14 33	29.9	6	1	5	15 57	1.3	8	0	18.5	17 22	8	8.0	0	19.6	18 49	2	2	27.9	20.7	20 16	5.7	4	28.9	21.8	21 45	2	6
38	23.9	15.9	13 55	9	8	24.9	0	15 19	3	7.0	25.8	1	16 45	8	1	26.8	1	18 12	3	4	7	2	19 40	8	10.6	7	3	21 10	7.3	8
39	7	5	13 14	9	9	6	16.5	14 39	3	1	6	17.6	16 5	8	3	5	18.7	17 33	3	5	5	19.7	19 2	8	8	5	20.8	20 33	3	12.0
40	4	0	12 31	9	6.1	4	0	13 57	4	3	3	1	15 24	2.9	5	3	2	16 53	4.4	7	3	2	18 22	9	9	2	3	19 54	4	1
41	2	14.4	11 45	9	3	1	15.5	13 12	4	5	1	16.6	14 40	9	7	1	17.6	16 9	4	9	0	18.7	17 40	6.0	11.0	0	19.8	19 12	5	3
42	22.9	13.9	10 58	29.9	4	23.9	14.9	12 25	1.4	6	24.9	0	13 54	9	9	25.8	1	15 24	5	10.1	26.7	2	16 56	0	2	27.7	3	18 28	7.6	5
43	6	3	10 6	8	6	6	3	11 35	4	8	6	15.4	13 4	3.0	9.1	5	16.5	14 35	5	3	5	17.6	16 8	1	4	4	18.7	17 42	7	6
44	4	12.7	9 14	8	8	3	13.7	10 42	4	8.0	3	14.8	12 12	0	2	2	15.9	13 44	6	5	2	0	15 17	2	6	2	1	16 52	8	8
45	1	1	8 17	8	7.0	0	1	9 46	4	2	0	2	11 17	1	4	24.9	3	12 49	4.7	7	25.9	16.4	14 23	6.3	9	26.9	17.5	15 59	9	13.0
46	21.8	11.5	7 16	8	2	22.7	12.5	8 46	5	5	23.7	13.6	10 17	1	6	6	14.7	11 50	8	9	6	15.8	13 25	4	12.1	6	16.8	15 2	8.1	2
47	5	10.8	6 12	29.8	4	4	11.8	7 42	1.5	7	4	12.9	9 14	2	8	3	0	10 48	8	11.1	3	1	12 23	5	3	3	2	14 1	2	4
48	2	1	5 3	8	6	1	1	6 33	5	9	1	2	8 6	3.2	10.0	0	13.3	9 40	9	4	0	14.4	11 17	6	5	25.9	15.5	12 56	3	7
49	20.9	9.4	3 49	8	8	21.8	10.4	5 20	5	9.1	22.8	11.5	6 53	3	3	23.7	12.6	8 28	5.0	6	24.6	13.7	10 5	6.7	8	6	14.7	11 45	5	14.0
50	5	8.7	2 29	8	8.1	5	9.7	4 1	6	4	4	10.7	5 34	3	6	4	11.8	7 10	1	9	3	12.9	8 48	8	13.1	3	0	10 28	8.6	3
51	2	7.9	1 4	8	4	1	8.9	2 36	6	7	1	9.9	4 9	4	9	0	0	5 45	2	12.2	23.9	1	7 24	9	4	24.9	13.2	9 5	7	6
52	19.8	0	♑ 29 33	29.8	7	20.7	1	1 4	1.7	10.0	21.7	1	2 38	3.5	11.2	22.6	10.1	4 14	3	5	5	11.2	5 53	7.1	7	5	12.3	7 35	9	9
53	4	6.1	27 54	8	9.0	3	7.2	♑ 29 25	7	3	2	8.2	0 59	6	5	2	9.2	2 35	5.4	8	1	10.3	4 14	3	14.1	1	11.3	5 57	9.1	15.2
54	18.9	5.1	26 7	8	3	19.9	6.2	27 38	8	6	20.8	7.2	♑ 29 11	7	8	21.7	8.2	0 47	6	13.1	22.7	9.3	2 27	5	4	23.6	10.3	4 9	3	6
55	5	4.1	24 11	8	6	4	5.1	25 41	8	9	3	6.1	27 14	7	12.2	3	7.1	♑ 28 50	7	5	2	8.2	0 28	7	8	1	9.3	2 10	6	16.1
56	0	3.0	22 6	8	9	18.9	3.9	23 35	8	11.3	19.8	5.0	25 6	8	5	20.8	6.0	26 41	9	9	21.7	7.0	♑ 28 19	9	15.2	22.6	8.1	0 0	9	5

SID. T. 16 h 24 m 55 s, **ARC** 246° 13′.8 — ♐ 8°

H. / Lat.	11 ♑	12 ♑	1 ♒	2 ♈	3 ♉
°	°	°	° ′	°	°
22	2.6	28.3	29 18	7.6	10.7
23	5	0	28 59	7	8
24	3	27.7	28 40	7	11.0
25	2	4	28 21	8	1
26	0	1	28 1	8	2
27	1.8	26.7	27 40	9	3
28	6	4	27 18	8.0	11.5
29	5	0	26 56	0	6
30	3	25.7	26 32	1	7
31	1	3	26 8	2	9
32	0.9	0	25 42	2	12.0
33	7	24.6	25 15	8.3	2
34	5	2	24 47	4	3
35	3	23.8	24 18	5	5
36	1	3	23 47	6	6
37	♐ 29.9	22.9	23 15	8.6	8
38	7	4	22 40	7	13.0
39	4	21.9	22 4	8	1
40	2	4	21 26	9	3
41	28.9	20.9	20 46	9.0	5
42	7	4	20 3	2	7
43	4	19.8	19 17	3	9
44	1	2	18 29	4	14.1
45	27.8	18.6	17 36	9.6	3
46	5	17.9	16 41	7	6
47	2	3	15 41	8	8
48	26.9	16.6	14 36	9	15.0
49	6	15.8	13 27	10.1	3
50	2	1	12 11	3	6
51	25.8	14.3	10 49	5	9
52	4	13.4	9 19	7	16.2
53	0	12.4	7 42	9	6
54	24.6	11.4	5 54	11.2	9
55	1	10.3	3 56	5	17.3
56	23.6	9.1	1 45	8	7

SID. T. 16 h 29 m 11 s, **ARC** 247° 17′.6 — ♐ 9°

H. / Lat.	11 ♑	12 ♑	1 ♓	2 ♈	3 ♉
°	°	°	° ′	°	°
22	3.6	29.4	0 37	8.9	11.9
23	5	1	0 19	9.0	12.0
24	3	28.8	0 1	1	1
25	1	5	♒ 29 42	1	2
26	0	2	29 23	2	3
27	2.8	27.8	29 2	3	12.5
28	6	5	28 41	9.3	6
29	4	1	28 20	4	7
30	3	26.8	27 57	5	9
31	1	4	27 33	6	13.0
32	1.9	1	27 8	9.6	2
33	7	25.7	26 42	7	3
34	5	3	26 15	8	5
35	3	24.9	25 47	9	13.6
36	1	4	25 17	10.0	8
37	0.8	0	24 45	1	9
38	6	23.5	24 12	2	14.0
39	4	0	23 37	3	2
40	2	22.5	23 0	4	4
41	♐ 29.9	0	22 21	10.5	6
42	7	21.5	21 39	6	8
43	4	20.9	20 55	7	15.0
44	1	3	20 7	9	2
45	28.8	19.7	19 16	11.1	4
46	5	0	18 22	3	7
47	2	18.4	17 23	5	9
48	27.9	17.7	16 19	7	16.2
49	5	16.9	15 11	9	5
50	2	2	13 56	12.1	8
51	26.8	15.4	12 35	3	17.2
52	4	14.5	11 7	6	5
53	0	13.5	9 30	9	8
54	25.5	12.5	7 43	13.2	18.2
55	0	11.4	5 45	5	6
56	24.5	10.2	3 34	9	19.0

SID. T. 16 h 33 m 26 s, **ARC** 248° 21′.6 — ♐ 10°

H. / Lat.	11 ♑	12 ♒	1 ♓	2 ♈	3 ♉
°	°	°	° ′	°	°
22	4.6	0.5	1 57	10.3	13.0
23	4	2	1 40	3	1
24	3	♑ 29.9	1 22	4	2
25	1	6	1 4	5	4
26	3.9	3	0 45	5	13.5
27	8	28.9	0 26	10.6	6
28	6	6	0 5	7	7
29	4	3	♒ 29 44	8	9
30	2	27.9	29 22	9	14.0
31	1	5	29 0	11.0	2
32	2.9	2	28 36	1	3
33	7	26.8	28 11	2	5
34	5	4	27 44	3	6
35	3	0	27 17	4	8
36	1	25.6	26 48	11.5	15.0
37	1.8	1	26 17	6	1
38	6	24.7	25 45	7	2
39	4	2	25 11	8	4
40	1	23.7	24 35	12.0	6
41	0.9	2	23 57	1	8
42	6	22.6	23 17	3	16.0
43	4	0	22 33	5	2
44	1	21.4	21 47	12.6	5
45	♐ 29.8	20.8	20 57	7	7
46	5	2	20 4	9	9
47	2	19.5	19 7	13.1	17.1
48	28.9	18.8	18 5	3	4
49	5	1	16 58	5	7
50	1	17.3	15 44	8	18.0
51	27.8	16.5	14 24	14.1	3
52	4	15.6	12 57	4	6
53	0	14.7	11 21	7	19.0
54	26.5	13.6	9 35	15.0	4
55	0	12.5	7 38	4	8
56	25.5	11.3	5 27	8	20.2

SID. T. 16 h 37 m 42 s, **ARC** 249° 25′.6 — ♐ 11°

H. / Lat.	11 ♑	12 ♒	1 ♓	2 ♈	3 ♉
°	°	°	° ′	°	°
22	5.6	1.6	3 17	11.6	14.1
23	4	3	3 1	6	2
24	3	0	2 44	7	4
25	1	0.7	2 26	8	5
26	4.9	4	2 8	9	14.6
27	8	0	1 50	12.0	7
28	6	♑ 29.7	1 30	1	9
29	4	4	1 10	2	15.0
30	2	0	0 49	3	2
31	0	28.7	0 27	4	3
32	3.8	3	0 4	12.5	5
33	6	27.9	♒ 29 40	6	15.6
34	4	5	29 14	7	8
35	2	1	28 48	8	9
36	0	26.7	28 20	9	16.0
37	2.8	3	27 51	13.1	2
38	6	25.8	27 20	2	4
39	4	3	26 47	4	6
40	1	24.8	26 12	5	8
41	1.9	3	25 35	7	17.0
42	6	23.8	24 56	9	2
43	3	2	24 14	14.1	4
44	1	22.6	23 29	3	7
45	0.8	0	22 40	5	9
46	5	21.3	21 48	7	18.1
47	2	20.6	20 52	9	3
48	♐ 29.8	19.9	19 52	15.1	6
49	5	2	18 46	3	9
50	1	18.4	17 35	6	19.2
51	28.7	17.6	16 16	9	5
52	3	16.7	14 50	16.2	9
53	27.9	15.8	13 15	5	20.3
54	4	14.8	11 31	9	7
55	26.9	13.7	9 35	17.3	21.1
56	4	12.5	7 25	8	5

SID. T. 16 h 41 m 59 s, **ARC** 250° 29′.8 — ♐ 12°

H. / Lat.	11 ♑	12 ♒	1 ♓	2 ♈	3 ♉
°	°	°	° ′	°	°
22	6.6	2.7	4 38	12.9	15.2
23	4	4	4 22	13.0	4
24	3	1	4 6	1	5
25	1	1.8	3 49	1	6
26	5.9	5	3 32	2	7
27	7	1	3 14	3	9
28	6	0.8	2 56	13.4	16.0
29	4	5	2 36	5	2
30	2	2	2 16	7	3
31	0	♑ 29.8	1 55	8	5
32	4.8	5	1 33	9	16.6
33	6	1	1 10	14.0	8
34	4	28.7	0 45	1	9
35	2	3	0 20	3	17.1
36	0	27.8	♒ 29 53	4	3
37	3.8	4	29 25	14.6	5
38	6	26.9	28 55	7	6
39	3	5	28 23	9	8
40	1	0	27 50	15.0	18.0
41	2.9	25.5	27 14	2	2
42	6	24.9	26 36	4	4
43	3	3	25 55	6	6
44	0	23.7	25 12	8	9
45	1.7	1	24 25	16.0	19.1
46	4	22.5	23 35	2	3
47	1	21.8	22 41	4	6
48	0.8	1	21 42	7	9
49	5	20.4	20 38	17.0	20.2
50	1	19.6	19 28	3	5
51	♐ 29.7	18.8	18 11	6	8
52	3	17.9	16 47	18.0	21.1
53	28.9	16.9	15 14	4	5
54	4	15.9	13 31	8	9
55	27.9	14.8	11 36	19.3	22.3
56	4	13.6	9 27	8	7

SID. T. 16 h 46 m 16 s, **ARC** 251° 34′.1 — ♐ 13°

H. / Lat.	11 ♑	12 ♒	1 ♓	2 ♈	3 ♉
°	°	°	° ′	°	°
22	7.6	3.8	5 59	14.2	16.4
23	4	5	5 44	3	5
24	2	2	5 29	4	6
25	1	2.9	5 13	5	8
26	6.9	6	4 56	14.6	9
27	7	3	4 39	7	17.0
28	6	0	4 22	8	2
29	4	1.6	4 3	9	3
30	2	3	3 44	15.1	5
31	0	0.9	3 24	2	17.6
32	5.8	6	3 3	3	8
33	6	2	2 40	4	9
34	4	♑ 29.8	2 17	15.6	18.0
35	2	4	1 53	7	1
36	0	0	1 27	9	3
37	4.8	28.5	1 0	16.0	5
38	6	1	0 32	2	7
39	3	27.6	0 1	4	9
40	1	1	♒ 29 29	5	19.1
41	3.8	26.6	28 54	7	3
42	6	1	28 18	9	5
43	3	25.5	27 39	17.1	8
44	0	24.9	26 57	3	20.0
45	2.7	3	26 12	6	3
46	4	23.6	25 23	8	6
47	1	0	24 31	18.1	8
48	1.8	22.3	23 34	4	21.1
49	5	21.5	22 32	7	4
50	1	20.8	21 24	19.0	7
51	0.7	19.9	20 9	4	22.0
52	3	0	18 46	8	4
53	♐ 29.9	18.1	17 15	20.2	7
54	4	17.1	15 34	7	23.1
55	28.9	16.0	13 41	21.2	6
56	3	14.8	11 33	8	24.0

	SID. T. 16h 46m 16s — ARC 251° 34′.1 — ♐ 13°					16h 50m 34s — 252° 38′.5 — ♐ 14°				
H.	11	12	1	2	3	11	12	1	2	3
Lat.	♑	♒	♓	♈	♉	♑	♒	♓	♈	♉
°	°	°	° ′	°	°	°	°	° ′	°	°
22	7.6	3.8	5 59	14.2	16.4	8.6	4.9	7 21	15.5	17.5
23	4	5	5 44	3	5	4	6	7 7	6	6
24	2	2	5 29	4	6	2	3	6 52	7	8
25	1	2.9	5 13	5	8	1	0	6 37	8	9
26	6.9	6	4 56	14.6	9	7.9	3.7	6 21	9	18.0
27	7	3	4 39	7	17.0	7	4	6 5	16.0	2
28	6	0	4 22	8	2	6	1	5 48	2	3
29	4	1.6	4 3	9	3	4	2.8	5 31	3	4
30	2	3	3 44	15.1	5	2	4	5 12	4	18.6
31	0	0.9	3 24	2	17.6	0	1	4 53	16.6	7
32	5.8	6	3 3	3	8	6.8	1.7	4 33	7	9
33	6	2	2 40	4	9	6	4	4 12	9	19.0
34	4	♑ 29.8	2 17	15.6	18.0	4	0	3 50	17.0	2
35	2	4	1 53	7	1	2	0.6	3 27	2	4
36	0	0	1 27	9	3	0	1	3 2	4	6
37	4.8	28.5	1 0	16.0	5	5.8	♑ 29.7	2 37	5	7
38	6	1	0 32	2	7	6	3	2 9	7	9
39	3	27.6	0 1	4	9	3	28.8	1 40	9	20.1
40	1	1	♒ 29 29	5	19.1	1	3	1 9	18.0	3
41	3.8	26.6	28 54	7	3	4.8	27.8	0 36	2	5
42	6	1	28 18	9	5	6	3	0 1	5	7
43	3	25.5	27 39	17.1	8	3	26.7	♒ 29 24	7	9
44	0	24.9	26 57	3	20.0	0	1	28 44	9	21.2
45	2.7	3	26 12	6	3	3.7	25.5	28 0	19.2	5
46	4	23.6	25 23	8	6	4	24.8	27 14	4	7
47	1	0	24 31	18.1	8	1	1	26 23	7	22.0
48	1.8	22.3	23 34	4	21.1	2.8	23.4	25 28	20.0	3
49	5	21.5	22 32	7	4	4	22.7	24 28	3	6
50	1	20.8	21 24	19.0	7	1	21.9	23 22	7	9
51	0.7	19.9	20 9	4	22.0	1.7	1	22 10	21.1	23.2
52	3	0	18 46	8	4	3	20.2	20 50	5	6
53	♐ 29.9	18.1	17 15	20.2	7	0.9	19.2	19 21	22.0	24.0
54	4	17.1	15 34	7	23.1	4	18.2	17 41	5	4
55	28.9	16.0	13 41	21.2	6	♐ 29.9	17.1	15 50	23.1	8
56	3	14.8	11 33	8	24.0	3	15.9	13 45	7	25.2

	16h 54m 52s — 253° 43′.1 — ♐ 15°					16h 59m 11s — 254° 47′.7 — ♐ 16°				
H.	11	12	1	2	3	11	12	1	2	3
Lat.	♑	♒	♓	♈	♉	♑	♒	♓	♈	♉
°	°	°	° ′	°	°	°	°	° ′	°	°
22	9.6	6.1	8 43	16.8	18.6	10.6	7.2	10 6	18.1	19.7
23	4	5.8	8 30	9	7	4	6.9	9 53	2	9
24	2	5	8 16	17.0	9	3	6	9 40	4	20.0
25	1	2	8 2	2	19.0	1	3	9 27	5	1
26	8.9	4.9	7 47	3	1	9.9	0	9 13	18.6	3
27	7	6	7 31	4	3	8	5.7	8 59	8	4
28	6	2	7 15	17.5	4	6	4	8 44	9	20.5
29	4	3.9	6 59	7	19.6	4	1	8 28	19.0	7
30	2	6	6 42	8	7	2	4.7	8 11	2	9
31	0	3	6 23	18.0	9	0	4	7 54	4	21.0
32	7.8	2.9	6 4	1	20.0	8.8	1	7 36	5	2
33	6	5	5 45	3	2	6	3.7	7 18	7	3
34	4	1	5 24	4	4	4	3	6 58	9	5
35	2	1.7	5 2	6	5	2	2.9	6 37	20.0	7
36	0	3	4 38	8	7	0	5	6 15	2	9
37	6.8	0.9	4 14	19.0	9	7.8	1	5 52	4	22.1
38	6	4	3 48	2	21.1	6	1.6	5 27	6	2
39	3	0	3 20	4	3	3	2	5 1	8	4
40	1	♑ 29.5	2 51	5	5	1	0.7	4 34	21.0	6
41	5.8	0	2 19	7	7	6.9	2	4 4	2	8
42	6	28.4	1 46	9	9	6	♑ 29.6	3 32	5	23.0
43	3	27.9	1 10	20.2	22.1	3	1	2 58	8	3
44	0	3	0 32	5	4	0	28.5	2 22	22.1	5
45	4.7	26.7	♒ 29 50	8	6	5.7	27.9	1 42	4	8
46	4	0	29 6	21.1	9	4	2	1 0	7	24.1
47	1	25.3	28 17	4	23.2	1	26.6	0 13	23.0	4
48	3.8	24.6	27 25	7	5	4.8	25.9	♒ 29 23	3	7
49	4	23.9	26 27	22.0	8	4	2	28 28	7	25.0
50	1	1	25 23	4	24.1	1	24.4	27 27	24.1	3
51	2.7	22.3	24 13	8	4	3.7	23.5	26 20	5	7
52	3	21.4	22 56	23.2	8	3	22.6	25 5	25.0	26.0
53	1.9	20.4	21 30	7	25.2	2.9	21.7	23 42	5	3
54	4	19.4	19 53	24.3	6	4	20.6	22 9	26.1	7
55	0.9	18.3	18 4	9	26.0	1.9	19.5	20 23	8	27.2
56	3	17.0	16 1	25.6	5	3	18.2	18 22	27.6	8

	17h 3m 30s — 255° 52′.5 — ♐ 17°					17h 7m 49s — 256° 57′.3 — ♐ 18°				
H.	11	12	1	2	3	11	12	1	2	3
Lat.	♑	♒	♓	♈	♉	♑	♒	♓	♈	♉
°	°	°	° ′	°	°	°	°	° ′	°	°
22	11.6	8.3	11 29	19.4	20.8	12.6	9.5	12 53	20.7	21.9
23	4	1	11 17	5	21.0	4	2	12 42	9	22.1
24	3	7.8	11 5	7	1	3	8.9	12 31	21.0	2
25	1	5	10 53	8	2	1	6	12 19	1	4
26	10.9	2	10 40	20.0	4	0	3	12 7	3	5
27	8	6.9	10 26	1	21.5	11.8	0	11 54	4	22.6
28	6	6	10 12	3	7	6	7.7	11 41	6	8
29	4	3	9 57	4	8	4	4	11 27	8	9
30	2	5.9	9 42	20.6	22.0	3	1	11 13	22.0	23.1
31	0	6	9 26	8	1	1	6.8	10 58	1	3
32	9.8	2	9 9	9	3	10.9	4	10 43	3	4
33	6	4.9	8 52	21.1	5	7	1	10 26	5	6
34	4	5	8 33	3	6	5	5.7	10 9	7	7
35	2	1	8 13	5	8	3	3	9 51	9	9
36	0	3.7	7 53	7	23.0	1	4.9	9 32	23.1	24.1
37	8.8	2	7 31	9	2	9.8	5	9 11	3	3
38	6	2.8	7 8	22.1	4	6	0	8 50	6	5
39	4	3	6 44	3	6	4	3.6	8 27	8	7
40	1	1.9	6 18	5	8	2	1	8 3	24.0	9
41	7.9	4	5 50	8	24.0	8.9	2.6	7 36	3	25.1
42	6	0.9	5 20	23.1	2	6	1	7 8	6	3
43	3	3	4 48	4	4	4	1.5	6 38	9	6
44	1	♑ 29.7	4 13	7	7	1	0.9	6 6	25.2	8
45	6.8	1	3 36	24.0	25.0	7.8	3	5 31	5	26.1
46	5	28.5	2 55	3	2	5	♑ 29.7	4 53	8	4
47	1	27.8	2 12	6	5	1	0	4 12	26.2	7
48	5.8	1	1 24	25.0	8	6.8	28.3	3 27	6	27.0
49	4	26.4	0 32	4	26.1	5	27.6	2 37	27.0	3
50	1	25.6	♒ 29 34	8	4	1	26.8	1 42	5	6
51	4.7	24.8	28 29	26.3	8	5.7	0	0 42	28.0	9
52	3	23.9	27 18	8	27.2	3	25.1	♒ 29 34	5	28.3
53	3.9	22.9	25 58	27.4	6	4.9	24.2	28 18	29.1	7
54	4	21.8	24 28	28.0	28.0	4	23.2	26 52	8	29.1
55	2.9	20.8	22 46	7	4	3.9	22.0	25 14	♉ 0.5	6
56	3	19.6	20 50	29.5	9	3	20.8	23 22	1.3	♊ 0.2

	H. M. S. SID. T. 17 12 9 ARC 258° 2′.2 ♐ 19°					H. M. S. 17 16 29 259° 7′.2 ♐ 20°					H. M. S. 17 20 49 260° 12′.3 ♐ 21°					H. M. S. 17 25 10 261° 17′.4 ♐ 22°					H. M. S. 17 29 30 262° 22′.6 ♐ 23°					H. M. S. 17 33 51 263° 27′.8 ♐ 24°				
H.	11	12	1	2	3	11	12	1	2	3	11	12	1	2	3	11	12	1	2	3	11	12	1	2	3	11	12	1	2	3
Lat.	♑	♒	♓	♈	♉	♑	♒	♓	♈	♉	♑	♒	♓	♈	♉	♑	♒	♓	♈	♉	♑	♒	♓	♈	♉	♑	♒	♓	♈	♉
°	°	°	° ′	°	°	°	°	° ′	°	°	°	°	° ′	°	°	°	°	° ′	°	°	°	°	° ′	°	°	°	°	° ′	°	°
22	13.6	10.7	14 17	22.0	23.0	14.6	11.8	15 42	23.3	24.1	15.6	13.0	17 6	24.6	25.2	16.7	14.2	18 32	25.9	26.3	17.7	15.4	19 57	27.2	27.4	18.8	16.6	21 23	28.5	28.5
23	5	4	14 7	2	2	5	6	15 32	5	3	5	12.7	16 58	8	4	5	13.9	18 24	26.1	5	5	1	19 51	4	6	6	3	21 17	7	6
24	3	1	13 57	3	3	3	3	15 23	6	4	3	5	16 50	9	5	4	7	18 17	2	6	4	14.9	19 44	6	7	4	1	21 11	9	8
25	1	9.8	13 46	5	5	2	0	15 13	8	6	2	2	16 41	25.1	7	2	4	18 9	4	8	2	6	19 37	7	9	3	15.8	21 5	29.1	9
26	0	5	13 35	6	23.6	0	10.7	15 3	24.0	7	0	11.9	16 31	3	8	0	1	18 0	6	9	1	3	19 30	9	28.0	1	5	20 59	3	29.1
27	12.8	2	13 23	8	8	13.8	4	14 52	1	9	14.8	6	16 22	5	26.0	15.9	12.8	17 52	8	27.1	16.9	0	19 22	28.1	2	17.9	3	20 53	5	3
28	6	8.9	13 11	23.0	9	6	1	14 41	3	25.0	7	3	16 12	6	1	7	5	17 43	27.0	2	7	13.7	19 14	3	3	8	0	20 46	7	4
29	4	6	12 58	1	24.0	5	9.8	14 30	5	2	5	0	16 1	8	3	5	2	17 33	2	4	6	5	19 6	5	5	6	14.7	20 39	9	6
30	3	3	12 45	3	2	3	5	14 17	7	3	3	10.7	15 50	26.0	4	3	11.9	17 24	4	5	4	2	18 57	8	6	4	4	20 31	♉ 0.1	7
31	1	0	12 31	5	4	1	2	14 5	9	5	1	4	15 39	2	6	2	6	17 13	6	7	2	12.9	18 48	29.0	8	2	1	20 24	3	9
32	11.9	7.6	12 17	7	5	12.9	8.9	13 51	25.1	7	13.9	1	15 27	4	8	0	3	17 3	8	9	0	5	18 39	2	29.0	1	13.8	20 16	5	♊ 0.1
33	7	3	12 2	9	7	7	5	13 37	3	8	7	9.7	15 14	7	27.0	14.8	0	16 51	28.0	28.1	15.8	2	18 29	4	2	16.9	4	20 7	8	3
34	5	6.9	11 46	24.1	9	5	1	13 23	5	26.0	5	3	15 1	9	1	6	10.6	16 39	3	3	6	11.8	18 18	6	4	7	1	19 58	1.0	5
35	3	5	11 29	3	25.1	3	7.7	13 7	7	2	3	0	14 47	27.1	3	4	2	16 27	5	4	4	4	18 7	9	6	5	12.7	19 48	3	7
36	1	1	11 11	5	3	1	3	12 51	26.0	4	1	8.6	14 32	4	5	2	9.8	16 14	8	6	2	1	17 56	♉ 0.2	8	3	3	19 38	6	9
37	10.8	5.7	10 52	8	5	11.9	6.9	12 34	2	6	12.9	2	14 16	6	7	13.9	4	15 59	29.1	8	0	10.7	17 43	5	♊	0	11.9	19 27	9	1.1
38	6	2	10 32	25.0	7	7	5	12 15	5	8	7	7.7	14 0	9	9	7	0	15 44	4	29.0	14.8	3	17 30	8	0.2	15.8	5	19 16	2.2	3
39	4	4.8	10 11	3	9	4	0	11 56	8	27.0	5	3	13 42	28.2	28.1	5	8.6	15 28	7	3	5	9.8	17 16	1.1	4	6	1	19 4	5	5
40	2	3	9 48	5	26.1	2	5.6	11 35	27.0	2	2	6.8	13 23	5	3	2	1	15 11	♉	5	3	4	17 1	4	6	3	10.7	18 51	8	7
41	9.9	3.8	9 24	8	3	10.9	1	11 13	3	4	0	3	13 3	9	5	0	7.6	14 53	0.3	7	0	8.9	16 45	8	8	1	2	18 37	3.2	2.0
42	6	3	8 58	26.1	5	7	4.6	10 49	6	6	11.7	5.8	12 41	29.2	7	12.7	1	14 34	7	♊	13.8	4	16 28	2.2	1.1	14.8	9.7	18 22	6	2
43	4	2.8	8 30	4	7	4	0	10 23	9	9	4	3	12 18	6	29.0	5	6.6	14 13	1.1	0.2	5	7.9	16 9	6	4	6	2	18 6	4.0	5
44	1	2	8 0	7	27.0	1	3.5	9 55	28.3	28.1	1	4.7	11 52	♉	3	2	0	13 50	5	4	2	3	15 49	3.0	6	3	8.6	17 49	5	7
45	8.8	1.6	7 27	27.1	2	9.8	2.9	9 26	7	4	10.8	1	11 25	0.4	6	11.9	5.4	13 26	9	7	12.9	6.7	15 27	4	9	0	0	17 30	9	3.0
46	5	0	6 52	5	5	5	2	8 53	29.1	7	5	3.5	10 55	7	9	6	4.8	12 59	2.3	1.0	6	1	15 4	8	2.2	13.7	7.4	17 9	5.3	3
47	2	0.3	6 14	9	8	2	1.6	8 17	5	29.0	2	2.8	10 23	1.1	♊ 0.2	3	1	12 29	7	3	3	5.5	14 38	4.2	4	3	6.8	16 47	7	6
48	7.8	♑ 29.6	5 32	28.3	28.2	8.9	0.9	7 38	9	3	9.9	1	9 47	5	5	10.9	3.4	11 57	3.1	6	0	4.8	14 9	7	7	0	1	16 22	6.2	9
49	5	28.9	4 45	7	5	5	1	6 55	♉ 0.3	6	5	1.4	9 8	2.0	8	6	2.7	11 22	6	2.0	11.6	1	13 37	5.2	3.1	12.7	5.4	15 55	7	4.3
50	1	1	3 54	29.2	8	1	♑ 29.4	6 8	8	♊	2	0.7	8 24	5	1.2	2	0	10 42	4.1	3	2	3.4	13 2	7	4	3	4.7	15 24	7.3	6
51	6.7	27.3	2 57	7	29.2	7.8	28.6	5 15	1.3	0.4	8.8	♑ 29.9	7 35	3.1	5	9.8	1.2	9 58	7	7	10.9	2.6	12 23	6.3	8	11.9	3.9	14 50	9	5.0
52	3	26.4	1 53	♉ 0.3	5	4	27.7	4 15	9	8	4	0	6 41	7	9	4	0.3	9 9	5.3	3.1	5	1.7	11 39	7.0	4.2	5	0	14 12	8.6	4
53	5.9	25.4	0 42	9	9	6.9	26.8	3 8	2.6	1.2	7.9	28.1	5 39	4.4	2.3	0	♑ 29.4	8 13	6.0	5	0	0.7	10 48	7	6	1	2.1	13 28	9.4	8
54	4	24.4	♒ 29 20	1.6	♊ 0.3	4	25.8	1 52	3.3	6	4	27.1	4 28	5.1	8	8.5	28.3	7 8	8	9	9.5	♑ 29.7	9 51	8.5	5.1	10.6	1.1	12 37	10.2	6.2
55	4.9	23.3	27 47	2.3	8	5.9	24.6	0 25	4.1	2.0	6.9	25.9	3 7	9	3.3	0	27.2	5 54	7.6	4.4	0	28.6	8 44	9.4	6	0	0.0	11 38	11.1	7
56	3	22.0	26 0	3.1	1.3	3	23.3	♒ 28 44	5.0	5	4	24.6	1 33	6.8	9	7.4	26.0	4 27	8.5	9	8.4	27.4	7 26	10.4	6.2	9.5	♑ 28.8	10 30	12.1	7.2

	SID. T. H. M. S. 17 33 51 ARC 263° 27′.8 ♐ 24°					17 38 13 264° 33′.1 ♐ 25°					17 42 34 265° 38′.5 ♐ 26°					17 46 55 266° 43′.8 ♐ 27°					17 51 17 267° 49′.2 ♐ 28°					17 55 38 268° 54′.6 ♐ 29°				
H.	11	12	1	2	3	11	12	1	2	3	11	12	1	2	3	11	12	1	2	3	11	12	1	2	3	11	12	1	2	3
Lat.	♑	♒	♓	♈	♉	♑	♒	♓	♈	♉	♑	♒	♓	♉	♊	♑	♒	♓	♉	♊	♑	♒	♓	♉	♊	♑	♒	♓	♉	♊
°	°	°	° ′	°	°	°	°	° ′	°	°	°	°	° ′	°	°	°	°	° ′	°	°	°	°	° ′	°	°	°	°	° ′	°	°
22	18.8	16.6	21 23	28.5	28.5	19.8	17.8	22 49	29.8	29.6	20.8	19.0	24 15	1.0	0.7	21.9	20.2	25 41	2.3	1.7	22.9	21.5	27 7	3.6	2.8	24.0	22.7	28 33	4.8	3.9
23	6	3	21 17	7	6	6	5	22 44	9	7	7	18.8	24 11	2	8	7	0	25 38	5	9	8	2	27 5	8	3.0	23.8	5	28 33	5.0	4.0
24	4	1	21 11	9	8	5	3	22 39	♉ 0.1	9	5	5	24 7	4	1.0	6	19.8	25 35	7	2.0	6	0	27 3	4.0	1	7	2	28 32	2	2
25	3	15.8	21 5	29.1	9	3	0	22 34	3	♊	4	3	24 3	6	1	4	5	25 32	9	2	5	20.7	27 1	2	3	5	0	28 31	5	3
26	1	5	20 59	3	29.1	2	16.8	22 29	5	0.2	2	0	23 59	8	3	3	3	25 29	3.1	3	22.3	5	26 59	4	4	4	21.8	28 29	7	5
27	17.9	3	20 53	5	3	0	5	22 24	7	3	0	17.8	23 55	2.1	4	1	0	25 26	4	5	2	2	26 57	6	3.6	2	5	28 28	9	7
28	8	0	20 46	7	4	18.8	2	22 18	1.0	5	19.9	5	23 50	3	1.6	20.9	18.7	25 22	6	7	0	0	26 55	9	7	0	3	28 27	6.2	8
29	6	14.7	20 39	9	6	7	15.9	22 12	2	7	7	2	23 45	5	7	8	5	25 19	8	8	21.8	19.7	26 52	5.1	9	22.9	0	28 26	4	5.0
30	4	4	20 31	♉ 0.1	7	5	6	22 6	4	8	5	16.9	23 40	7	9	6	2	25 15	4.1	3.0	6	4	26 50	4	4.1	7	20.7	28 25	7	1
31	2	1	20 24	3	9	3	3	21 59	6	1.0	3	6	23 35	3.0	2.1	4	17.9	25 11	3	2	5	2	26 47	6	3	5	5	28 23	9	3
32	1	13.8	20 16	5	♊ 0.1	1	0	21 52	9	2	2	3	23 29	2	3	2	6	25 7	5	3	3	18.9	26 44	9	4	4	2	28 22	7.2	5
33	16.9	4	20 7	8	3	17.9	14.7	21 45	2.1	4	0	0	23 23	5	4	0	3	25 2	8	5	1	6	26 41	6.1	6	2	19.9	28 21	5	7
34	7	1	19 58	1.0	5	7	4	21 38	4	5	18.8	15.6	23 17	7	6	19.8	16.9	24 58	5.1	7	20.9	2	26 38	4	8	0	6	28 19	8	9
35	5	12.7	19 48	3	7	5	0	21 30	7	7	6	3	23 11	4.0	8	6	6	24 53	4	9	7	17.9	26 35	7	5.0	21.8	2	28 18	8.1	6.1
36	3	3	19 38	6	9	3	13.6	21 21	3.0	9	4	14.9	23 4	3	3.0	4	2	24 48	7	4.1	5	5	26 32	7.1	2	6	18.9	28 16	4	3
37	0	11.9	19 27	9	1.1	1	2	21 12	3	2.1	1	5	22 57	7	2	2	15.9	24 43	6.0	3	3	2	26 28	4	4	3	5	28 14	8	5
38	15.8	5	19 16	2.2	3	16.9	12.8	21 2	6	4	17.9	1	22 49	5.0	5	0	5	24 37	4	5	1	16.8	26 24	8	6	1	1	28 12	9.1	7
39	6	1	19 4	5	5	6	4	20 52	9	6	7	13.7	22 41	4	7	18.8	1	24 31	7	8	19.8	4	26 20	8.1	9	20.9	17.7	28 10	5	9
40	3	10.7	18 51	8	7	4	0	20 41	4.3	8	4	3	22 33	7	9	5	14.6	24 24	7.1	5.0	6	0	26 16	5	6.1	6	3	28 8	9	7.2
41	1	2	18 37	3.2	2.0	1	11.5	20 30	7	3.1	2	12.8	22 23	6.1	4.2	3	2	24 17	5	2	3	15.5	26 11	9	3	4	16.9	28 6	10.3	4
42	14.8	9.7	18 22	6	2	15.9	0	20 17	5.1	3	16.9	4	22 13	5	4	0	13.7	24 10	8.0	5	1	1	26 6	9.4	6	2	4	28 3	8	7
43	6	2	18 6	4.0	5	6	10.5	20 4	5	6	7	11.9	22 2	7.0	7	17.7	2	24 1	4	8	18.8	14.6	26 1	8	9	19.9	0	28 0	11.2	8.0
44	3	8.6	17 49	5	7	3	9.9	19 49	6.0	8	4	3	21 51	4	9	5	12.7	23 52	9	6.0	5	1	25 55	10.3	7.1	6	15.5	27 57	7	2
45	0	0	17 30	9	3.0	0	4	19 33	4	4.1	1	10.8	21 38	9	5.2	2	1	23 43	9.4	3	2	13.5	25 48	8	4	3	14.9	27 54	12.2	5
46	13.7	7.4	17 9	5.3	3	14.7	8.8	19 16	8	4	15.8	2	21 24	8.3	5	16.9	11.6	23 32	9	6	17.9	12.9	25 41	11.3	7	0	4	27 51	7	8
47	3	6.8	16 47	7	6	4	2	18 57	7.3	7	5	9.6	21 9	8	8	5	0	23 21	10.4	9	6	3	25 34	8	8.0	18.7	13.9	27 47	13.2	9.1
48	0	1	16 22	6.2	9	1	7.5	18 37	8	5.0	1	8.9	20 52	9.3	6.1	2	10.4	23 8	9	7.2	3	11.7	25 25	12.4	3	3	3	27 42	8	4
49	12.7	5.4	15 55	7	4.3	13.7	6.8	18 13	8.3	3	14.8	2	20 33	9	4	15.8	9.7	22 54	11.5	5	16.9	1	25 16	13.0	6	0	12.6	27 38	14.4	7
50	3	4.7	15 24	7.3	6	3	1	17 48	9	7	4	7.5	20 12	10.5	8	5	0	22 38	12.1	9	6	10.4	25 5	6	9.0	17.6	11.9	27 33	15.1	10.1
51	11.9	3.9	14 50	9	5.0	0	5.3	17 19	9.5	6.1	0	6.7	19 49	11.2	7.2	1	8.2	22 21	8	8.3	2	9.6	24 53	14.3	4	2	2	27 27	8	5
52	5	0	14 12	8.6	4	12.6	4.4	16 46	10.2	5	13.6	5.9	19 23	9	6	14.7	7.4	22 1	13.5	7	15.8	8.8	24 40	15.1	8	16.8	10.4	27 20	16.6	9
53	1	2.1	13 28	9.4	8	1	3.5	16 9	11.0	9	2	0	18 52	12.7	8.0	2	6.5	21 38	14.3	9.1	3	7.9	24 25	9	10.2	4	9.5	27 12	17.5	11.3
54	10.6	1.1	12 37	10.2	6.2	11.6	2.5	15 26	9	7.4	12.7	4.0	18 18	13.6	5	13.7	5.5	21 12	15.2	6	14.8	6.9	24 7	16.8	7	15.9	8.5	27 3	18.4	8
55	0	0.0	11 38	11.1	7	1	1.4	14 36	12.8	9	2	2.9	17 37	14.5	9.0	2	4.4	20 41	16.1	10.1	3	5.9	23 46	17.8	11.2	4	7.4	26 53	19.4	12.3
56	9.5	♑ 28.8	10 30	12.1	7.2	10.5	0.2	13 38	13.8	8.5	11.6	1.7	16 49	15.5	6	12.7	3.2	20 4	17.1	7	13.7	4.7	23 21	18.9	8	14.8	6.2	26 40	20.5	9

	SID. T. 18 0 0 (H. M. S.) ARC 270° 0′.0 ♑ 0°					18 4 22 (H. M. S.) 271° 5′.4 ♑ 1°					18 8 43 (H. M. S.) 272° 10′.8 ♑ 2°					18 13 5 (H. M. S.) 273° 16′.2 ♑ 3°					18 17 26 (H. M. S.) 274° 21′.5 ♑ 4°					18 21 47 (H. M. S.) 275° 26′.9 ♑ 5°				
H.	11	12	1	2	3	11	12	1	2	3	11	12	1	2	3	11	12	1	2	3	11	12	1	2	3	11	12	1	2	3
Lat.	♑	♒	♈	♉	♊	♑	♒	♈	♉	♊	♑	♒	♈	♉	♊	♑	♒	♈	♉	♊	♑	♒	♈	♉	♊	♒	♓	♈	♉	♊
°	°	°	° ′	°	°	°	°	° ′	°	°	°	°	° ′	°	°	°	°	° ′	°	°	°	°	° ′	°	°	°	°	° ′	°	°
22	25.0	23.9	0 0	6.1	5.0	26.1	25.2	1 27	7.3	6.0	27.2	26.4	2 53	8.5	7.1	28.3	27.7	4 19	9.8	8.1	29.3	29.0	5 45	11.0	9.2	0.4	0.2	7 11	12.2	10.2
23	24.9	7	0 0	3	1	0	0	1 27	5	2	0	2	2 55	8	2	1	5	4 22	10.0	3	2	28.8	5 49	2	3	3	1	7 16	5	4
24	7	5	0 0	5	3	25.8	24.8	1 28	8	3	26.9	0	2 57	9.0	4	0	3	4 25	2	4	0	6	5 53	5	5	1	♒ 29.9	7 21	7	5
25	6	3	0 0	7	4	7	5	1 29	8.0	5	7	25.8	2 59	3	5	27.8	1	4 28	5	6	28.9	4	5 57	7	6	0	7	7 26	13.0	7
26	4	0	0 0	7.0	5.6	5	3	1 31	2	6	6	6	3 1	5	7	7	26.9	4 31	7	7	7	2	6 1	12.0	8	♑ 29.8	5	7 31	2	8
27	3	22.8	0 0	2	7	3	1	1 32	5	8	4	4	3 3	8	8	5	6	4 34	11.0	9	6	27.9	6 5	2	10.0	7	3	7 36	5	11.0
28	1	5	0 0	5	9	2	23.8	1 33	7	7.0	3	1	3 5	10.0	8.0	3	4	4 38	3	9.1	4	7	6 10	5	1	5	0	7 42	8	2
29	23.9	3	0 0	7	6.1	0	6	1 34	9.0	1	1	24.9	3 8	3	2	2	2	4 41	5	2	3	5	6 15	8	3	3	28.8	7 48	14.1	3
30	8	0	0 0	8.0	2	24.9	3	1 35	3	3	25.9	6	3 10	6	4	0	25.9	4 45	8	4	1	3	6 20	13.1	5	2	6	7 54	4	5
31	6	21.8	0 0	2	4	7	1	1 37	5	5	7	4	3 13	8	5	26.8	7	4 49	12.1	6	27.9	0	6 25	4	7	0	4	8 1	7	7
32	4	5	0 0	5	6	5	22.8	1 38	8	6	6	1	3 16	11.1	7	7	5	4 53	4	8	7	26.8	6 31	7	8	28.8	1	8 8	15.0	9
33	2	2	0 0	8	8	3	5	1 39	10.1	8	4	23.9	3 19	4	9	5	2	4 58	7	10.0	6	5	6 37	14.0	11.0	6	27.9	8 15	3	12.1
34	0	20.9	0 0	9.1	7.0	1	2	1 41	4	8.0	2	6	3 22	8	9.1	3	24.9	5 2	13.1	2	4	3	6 43	4	2	5	6	8 22	6	3
35	22.8	6	0 0	4	2	23.9	21.9	1 42	8	2	0	3	3 25	12.1	3	1	6	5 7	4	4	2	0	6 49	7	4	3	3	8 30	16.0	5
36	6	2	0 0	8	4	7	6	1 44	11.1	4	24.8	22.9	3 28	5	5	25.9	3	5 12	8	6	0	25.7	6 56	15.1	6	1	0	8 39	4	7
37	4	19.9	0 0	10.1	6	5	2	1 46	5	7	6	6	3 32	8	7	7	0	5 17	14.1	8	26.8	3	7 3	5	9	27.9	26.7	8 48	8	9
38	2	5	0 0	5	8	3	20.9	1 48	9	9	4	2	3 36	13.2	9	5	23.6	5 23	5	11.0	5	0	7 11	9	12.1	6	4	8 58	17.2	13.1
39	0	1	0 0	9	8.0	1	5	1 50	12.3	9.1	1	21.9	3 40	6	10.2	2	3	5 29	9	2	3	24.6	7 19	16.3	3	4	1	9 8	6	4
40	21.7	18.7	0 0	11.3	3	22.8	1	1 52	7	4	23.9	5	3 44	14.0	4	0	22.9	5 36	15.4	5	1	3	7 27	7	6	2	25.7	9 19	18.0	6
41	5	3	0 0	7	5	6	19.7	1 54	13.1	6	7	1	3 49	5	7	24.8	5	5 43	8	7	25.8	23.9	7 37	17.2	8	26.9	3	9 30	5	9
42	2	17.8	0 0	12.2	8	3	2	1 57	6	8	4	20.6	3 54	9	9	5	0	5 50	16.3	12.0	6	5	7 47	6	13.1	7	24.9	9 43	19.0	14.1
43	0	4	0 0	6	9.0	0	18.8	2 0	14.0	10.1	1	2	3 59	15.4	11.2	2	21.6	5 59	8	3	3	0	7 58	18.1	3	4	5	9 56	5	4
44	20.7	16.9	0 0	13.1	3	21.8	3	2 3	5	4	22.9	19.7	4 5	9	5	0	1	6 8	17.3	5	1	22.6	8 9	7	6	2	0	10 11	20.1	7
45	4	3	0 0	7	6	5	17.8	2 6	15.1	7	6	2	4 12	16.5	8	23.7	20.6	6 17	9	8	24.8	1	8 22	19.2	9	25.9	23.6	10 27	6	15.0
46	1	15.8	0 0	14.2	9	2	3	2 9	6	11.0	3	18.7	4 19	17.1	12.1	4	1	6 28	18.4	13.1	5	21.7	8 36	8	14.2	6	2	10 44	21.2	3
47	19.8	3	0 0	7	10.2	20.9	16.8	2 13	16.1	3	0	2	4 26	7	4	1	19.6	6 39	19.0	5	2	2	8 51	20.4	5	3	22.7	11 3	8	6
48	4	14.7	0 0	15.3	6	6	2	2 18	7	7	21.7	17.6	4 35	18.3	7	22.8	1	6 52	6	8	23.9	20.7	9 8	21.1	9	0	2	11 23	22.5	9
49	1	0	0 0	16.0	9	3	15.6	2 22	17.4	12.0	4	0	4 44	9	13.1	5	18.5	7 6	20.3	14.2	6	1	9 27	8	15.2	24.7	21.7	11 47	23.2	16.3
50	18.7	13.4	0 0	6	11.3	19.9	14.9	2 27	18.1	4	0	16.4	4 55	19.6	4	1	17.9	7 22	21.0	5	2	19.5	9 48	22.5	6	3	1	12 12	9	7
51	3	12.7	0 0	17.3	7	5	2	2 33	8	8	20.6	15.7	5 7	20.4	8	21.7	2	7 39	8	9	22.8	18.8	10 11	23.3	16.0	23.9	20.5	12 41	24.7	17.0
52	17.9	11.9	0 0	18.1	12.1	1	13.4	2 40	19.6	13.2	2	14.9	5 20	21.2	14.2	3	16.5	7 59	22.6	15.3	4	1	10 37	24.1	4	5	19.8	13 14	25.6	4
53	5	0	0 0	19.0	5	18.7	12.5	2 48	20.5	6	19.8	1	5 35	22.1	7	20.9	15.7	8 22	23.5	8	0	17.3	11 8	25.0	8	1	0	13 51	26.5	9
54	0	10.0	0 0	20.0	13.0	2	11.6	2 57	21.5	14.1	3	13.2	5 53	23.1	15.2	4	14.8	8 48	24.5	16.3	21.5	16.4	11 42	26.0	17.3	22.6	18.1	14 34	27.5	18.4
55	16.5	9.0	0 0	21.0	5	17.7	10.6	3 7	22.6	6	18.8	12.2	6 14	24.1	7	19.9	13.9	9 19	25.6	8	0	15.5	12 23	27.1	8	1	17.2	15 24	28.6	9
56	15.9	7.9	0 0	22.1	14.1	1	9.5	3 20	23.8	15.2	2	11.1	6 39	25.3	16.3	3	12.9	9 56	26.8	17.3	20.4	14.5	13 11	28.3	18.4	21.5	16.2	16 22	29.8	19.5

H.	11	12	1	2	3	11	12	1	2	3
	SID. T. H. M. S. 18 21 47 ARC 275° 26′.9		♑ 5°			H. M. S. 18 26 9 276° 32′.2		♑ 6°		
Lat.	♒	♓	♈	♉	♊	♒	♓	♈	♉	♊
°	°	°	° ′	°	°	°	°	° ′	°	°
22	0.4	0.2	7 11	12.2	10.2	1.5	1.5	8 37	13.4	11.2
23	3	1	7 16	5	4	4	3	8 43	7	4
24	1	♒ 29.9	7 21	7	5	2	1	8 49	9	6
25	0	7	7 26	13.0	7	1	0.9	8 55	14.2	7
26	♑ 29.8	5	7 31	2	8	0.9	7	9 1	5	9
27	7	3	7 36	5	11.0	7	5	9 7	7	12.1
28	5	0	7 42	8	2	6	3	9 14	15.0	2
29	3	28.8	7 48	14.1	3	4	1	9 21	3	4
30	2	6	7 54	4	5	3	♒ 29.9	9 29	6	6
31	0	4	8 1	7	7	1	7	9 36	9	8
32	28.8	1	8 8	15.0	9	♑ 29.9	5	9 44	16.2	9
33	6	27.9	8 15	3	12.1	7	2	9 53	6	13.1
34	5	6	8 22	6	3	5	0	10 2	9	3
35	3	3	8 30	16.0	5	3	28.7	10 12	17.3	5
36	1	0	8 39	4	7	1	4	10 22	7	7
37	27.9	26.7	8 48	8	9	28.9	1	10 33	18.1	14.0
38	6	4	8 58	17.2	13.1	7	27.8	10 44	5	2
39	4	1	9 8	6	4	5	5	10 56	9	4
40	2	25.7	9 19	18.0	6	3	2	11 9	19.3	7
41	26.9	3	9 30	5	9	0	26.8	11 23	8	9
42	7	24.9	9 43	19.0	14.1	27.8	4	11 38	20.3	15.2
43	4	5	9 56	5	4	5	0	11 54	8	4
44	2	0	10 11	20.1	7	3	25.5	12 11	21.4	7
45	25.9	23.6	10 27	6	15.0	0	1	12 30	22.0	16.0
46	6	2	10 44	21.2	3	26.7	24.7	12 51	6	3
47	3	22.7	11 3	8	6	4	3	13 13	23.2	7
48	0	2	11 23	22.5	9	1	23.8	13 38	9	17.0
49	24.7	21.7	11 47	23.2	16.3	25.7	3	14 5	24.6	3
50	3	1	12 12	9	7	4	22.7	14 36	25.3	7
51	23.9	20.5	12 41	24.7	17.0	0	1	15 10	26.1	18.1
52	5	19.8	13 14	25.6	4	24.6	21.4	15 48	27.0	5
53	1	0	13 51	26.5	9	2	20.6	16 32	9	9
54	22.6	18.1	14 34	27.5	18.4	23.8	19.8	17 23	28.9	19.4
55	1	17.2	15 24	28.6	9	3	18.9	18 22	♊	20.0
56	21.5	16.2	16 22	29.8	19.5	22.8	17.9	19 30	1.2	5

H.	11	12	1	2	3	11	12	1	2	3
	H. M. S. 18 30 30 277° 37′.4		♑ 7°			H. M. S. 18 34 50 278° 42′.6		♑ 8°		
Lat.	♒	♓	♈	♉	♊	♒	♓	♈	♉	♊
°	°	°	° ′	°	°	°	°	° ′	°	°
22	2.6	2.8	10 3	14.6	12.3	3.7	4.1	11 28	15.8	13.3
23	4	6	10 9	9	5	5	3.9	11 36	16.1	5
24	3	4	10 16	15.1	6	4	8	11 43	3	6
25	1	3	10 23	4	8	2	6	11 51	6	8
26	0	1	10 30	7	9	1	4	12 0	9	14.0
27	1.8	1.9	10 38	16.0	13.1	2.9	2	12 8	17.2	1
28	7	7	10 45	3	3	8	0	12 17	5	3
29	5	5	10 54	5	4	6	2.8	12 27	8	5
30	4	2	11 3	8	6	5	6	12 36	18.1	7
31	2	0	11 12	17.1	8	3	4	12 47	4	8
32	0	0.8	11 21	5	14.0	1	2	12 57	7	15.0
33	0.8	6	11 31	8	2	1.9	0	13 9	19.0	2
34	6	4	11 42	18.2	4	7	1.7	13 21	4	4
35	4	1	11 53	6	6	6	5	13 33	8	6
36	2	♒ 29.8	12 4	9	8	4	2	13 46	20.2	8
37	0	5	12 17	19.3	15.0	2	0.9	14 1	6	16.1
38	♑ 29.8	2	12 30	7	2	0	6	14 16	21.0	3
39	6	28.9	12 44	20.2	5	0.7	3	14 32	4	5
40	4	6	12 59	6	7	5	0	14 49	9	7
41	2	2	13 15	21.1	16.0	3	♒ 29.7	15 7	22.4	17.0
42	28.9	27.8	13 32	6	2	0	3	15 26	9	3
43	6	4	13 51	22.1	5	♑ 29.8	28.9	15 47	23.4	5
44	4	0	14 11	7	8	6	5	16 10	24.0	8
45	1	26.6	14 33	23.3	17.1	3	1	16 34	6	18.1
46	27.8	2	14 56	9	4	0	27.7	17 1	25.2	4
47	6	25.8	15 22	24.5	7	28.7	3	17 31	9	7
48	3	3	15 51	25.2	18.0	4	26.9	18 3	26.6	19.1
49	26.9	24.8	16 23	9	4	0	4	18 38	27.3	4
50	6	3	16 58	26.6	8	27.7	25.9	19 18	28.0	8
51	2	23.7	17 37	27.4	19.1	3	3	20 2	8	20.2
52	25.8	0	18 21	28.3	5	26.9	24.7	20 51	29.7	6
53	4	22.3	19 12	29.3	20.0	5	0	21 47	♊ 0.6	21.0
54	24.9	21.5	20 9	♊ 0.3	5	1	23.2	22 52	1.7	5
55	4	20.6	21 16	1.4	21.0	25.6	22.4	24 6	2.8	22.0
56	23.8	19.6	22 34	2.6	6	1	21.5	25 33	4.0	6

H.	11	12	1	2	3	11	12	1	2	3
	H. M. S. 18 39 11 279° 47′.7		♑ 9°			H. M. S. 18 43 31 280° 52′.8		♑ 10°		
Lat.	♒	♓	♈	♉	♊	♒	♓	♈	♉	♊
°	°	°	° ′	°	°	°	°	° ′	°	°
22	4.8	5.4	12 54	17.0	14.4	5.9	6.7	14 18	18.2	15.4
23	6	2	13 2	3	5	7	5	14 28	4	5
24	5	1	13 10	5	7	6	4	14 37	7	7
25	3	4.9	13 19	8	8	4	2	14 47	19.0	8
26	2	7	13 29	18.1	15.0	5.3	0	14 57	3	16.0
27	0	5	13 38	4	2	1	5.9	15 8	6	2
28	3.9	4	13 48	7	3	0	7	15 19	9	4
29	7	2	13 59	19.0	5	4.8	5	15 30	20.2	5
30	6	0	14 10	3	7	7	3	15 43	5	7
31	4	3.8	14 21	6	9	5	1	15 55	8	9
32	2	6	14 33	9	16.1	3	4.9	16 9	21.1	17.1
33	0	3	14 46	20.3	3	2	7	16 23	5	3
34	2.9	1	14 59	7	5	0	5	16 37	9	5
35	7	2.9	15 13	21.0	7	3.8	3	16 53	22.3	7
36	5	6	15 28	4	9	6	0	17 9	7	9
37	3	4	15 44	8	17.1	4	3.8	17 26	23.1	18.1
38	1	1	16 0	22.3	3	2	5	17 45	5	3
39	1.9	1.8	16 18	7	5	0	2	18 4	24.0	6
40	7	5	16 37	23.2	8	2.8	0	18 25	4	8
41	5	1	16 57	7	18.0	6	2.7	18 47	9	19.1
42	3	0.8	17 19	24.2	3	4	4	19 11	25.4	3
43	0	4	17 42	7	6	1	1	19 37	26.0	6
44	0.7	0	18 8	25.3	9	1.9	1.7	20 5	5	9
45	4	♒ 29.6	18 35	9	19.2	6	3	20 34	27.1	20.2
46	1	3	19 5	26.5	5	3	0.9	21 7	8	5
47	♑ 29.8	28.9	19 37	27.2	8	0	5	21 43	28.4	8
48	5	5	20 13	9	20.1	0.7	1	22 22	29.1	21.1
49	2	0	20 52	28.6	5	4	♒ 29.7	23 5	9	5
50	28.8	27.5	21 36	29.3	8	0	2	23 52	♊ 0.6	9
51	5	26.9	22 25	♊ 0.1	21.2	♑ 29.6	28.7	24 45	1.4	22.2
52	1	3	23 19	1.0	6	2	1	25 45	2.3	6
53	27.7	25.6	24 21	9	22.1	28.8	27.4	26 52	3.2	23.1
54	2	24.9	25 32	2.9	6	4	26.7	28 8	4.2	6
55	26.7	1	26 53	4.1	23.1	0	25.9	29 35	5.4	24.1
56	1	23.2	28 27	5.4	6	27.5	0	♉ 1 16	6.7	7

SID. T. H. M. S. / ARC	18 47 51 / 281° 57′.8	♑ 11°				18 52 11 / 283° 2′.7	♑ 12°				18 56 30 / 284° 7′.5	♑ 13°				19 0 49 / 285° 12′.3	♑ 14°				19 5 8 / 286° 16′.9	♑ 15°				19 9 26 / 287° 21′.5	♑ 16°			
H.	11	12	1	2	3	11	12	1	2	3	11	12	1	2	3	11	12	1	2	3	11	12	1	2	3	11	12	1	2	3
Lat.	♒	♓	♈	♉	♊	♒	♓	♈	♉	♊	♒	♓	♈	♉	♊	♒	♓	♈	♉	♊	♒	♓	♈	♉	♊	♒	♓	♈	♉	♊
°	°	°	° ′	°	°	°	°	° ′	°	°	°	°	° ′	°	°	°	°	° ′	°	°	°	°	° ′	°	°	°	°	° ′	°	°
22	7.0	8.0	15 43	19.3	16.4	8.1	9.3	17 7	20.5	17.4	9.2	10.6	18 31	21.7	18.4	10.3	11.9	19 54	22.8	19.4	11.4	13.2	21 17	23.9	20.4	12.5	14.5	22 39	25.1	21.4
23	6.8	7.8	15 53	6	5	7.9	1	17 18	8	6	0	5	18 43	9	6	1	8	20 7	23.1	6	3	1	21 30	24.2	6	4	4	22 53	4	6
24	7	7	16 3	9	7	8	0	17 29	21.1	7	8.9	3	18 55	22.2	7	0	6	20 20	4	7	1	0	21 44	5	8	2	3	23 8	7	8
25	5	5	16 14	20.2	9	6	8.9	17 41	4	9	8	2	19 7	5	9	9.9	5	20 33	7	9	0	12.8	21 58	8	9	1	2	23 23	26.0	9
26	4	4	16 25	5	17.0	5	7	17 53	7	18.0	6	0	19 20	8	19.1	7	11.4	20 47	24.0	20.1	10.9	7	22 13	25.1	21.1	0	1	23 39	3	22.1
27	6.2	2	16 37	8	2	7.4	6	18 6	22.0	2	5	9.9	19 34	23.1	2	6	2	21 1	3	2	7	6	22 29	4	3	11.8	0	23 55	6	3
28	1	0	16 49	21.1	4	2	4	18 19	3	4	8.3	7	19 48	4	4	5	1	21 16	6	4	6	5	22 45	8	4	7	13.8	24 12	9	4
29	0	6.9	17 2	4	6	1	2	18 33	6	6	2	6	20 3	7	6	9.3	0	21 32	9	6	4	12.3	23 1	26.1	6	6	7	24 29	27.2	6
30	5.8	7	17 15	7	7	6.9	0	18 47	9	7	0	4	20 18	24.1	8	1	10.8	21 49	25.3	8	10.3	2	23 18	4	8	4	6	24 48	6	8
31	6	5	17 29	22.0	9	7	7.9	19 2	23.2	9	7.9	2	20 34	4	20.0	0	6	22 6	6	21.0	1	0	23 37	7	22.0	11.3	4	25 7	9	23.0
32	5	3	17 43	4	18.1	6	7	19 17	6	19.1	7	1	20 51	8	2	8.8	5	22 24	9	2	0	11.9	23 56	27.1	2	1	13.3	25 27	28.3	2
33	3	1	17 58	7	3	4	5	19 34	9	3	5	8.9	21 8	25.1	4	7	3	22 42	26.3	4	9.8	7	24 15	5	4	0	1	25 48	6	4
34	1	5.9	18 14	23.1	5	3	3	19 51	24.3	5	4	7	21 27	5	6	5	1	23 2	7	6	6	6	24 36	9	6	10.8	0	26 10	29.0	6
35	4.9	7	18 31	5	7	1	1	20 9	7	7	2	5	21 47	9	8	3	0	23 23	27.1	8	5	4	24 58	28.3	8	6	12.8	26 33	4	8
36	7	5	18 49	9	9	5.9	6.9	20 28	25.1	9	0	3	22 7	26.3	21.0	1	9.8	23 45	5	22.0	3	2	25 22	7	23.0	4	6	26 58	9	24.0
37	5	2	19 8	24.3	19.2	7	7	20 49	5	20.2	6.8	1	22 29	8	2	7.9	6	24 8	9	2	1	0	25 46	29.1	2	3	5	27 23	♊ 0.3	2
38	3	0	19 28	8	4	5	4	21 10	26.0	4	6	7.9	22 52	27.2	4	8	4	24 33	28.4	4	8.9	10.8	26 12	6	4	1	3	27 51	7	4
39	1	4.7	19 49	25.2	6	3	2	21 33	4	6	4	7	23 16	7	6	6	2	24 59	8	7	7	6	26 40	♊	7	9.9	1	28 20	1.2	7
40	3.9	5	20 12	7	8	1	0	21 57	9	9	2	5	23 42	28.1	9	4	0	25 26	29.3	9	5	5	27 9	0.5	9	7	0	28 51	7	9
41	7	2	20 36	26.2	20.1	4.9	5.7	22 24	27.4	21.1	0	2	24 10	6	22.1	2	8.8	25 56	8	23.1	3	3	27 41	1.0	24.2	5	11.8	29 24	2.2	25.2
42	5	3.9	21 2	7	4	7	4	22 52	9	4	5.8	6.9	24 40	29.1	4	0	5	26 28	♊ 0.4	4	1	1	28 14	6	4	3	5	29 59	7	4
43	3	6	21 30	27.2	6	4	1	23 22	28.5	6	6	6	25 12	7	7	6.7	2	27 2	9	7	7.9	9.8	28 50	2.1	7	1	3	♉ 0 36	3.3	7
44	0	3	22 0	8	9	2	4.8	23 54	29.1	9	3	3	25 47	♊ 0.3	9	.5	7.9	27 38	1.5	24.0	6	5	29 28	7	25.0	8.8	1	1 16	9	26.0
45	2.8	2.9	22 33	28.4	21.2	3.9	5	24 29	7	22.2	0	0	26 24	9	23.2	2	6	28 18	2.1	3	4	2	♉ 0 10	3.3	3	5	10.8	2 0	4.5	3
46	5	5	23 8	29.0	5	6	2	25 7	♊ 0.3	5	4.8	5.7	27 5	1.5	5	5.9	3	29 0	8	6	1	8.9	0 54	4.0	6	3	6	2 46	5.2	6
47	2	1	23 46	7	8	3	3.8	25 48	1.0	9	5	4	27 48	2.2	9	6	0	29 47	3.4	9	6.8	6	1 43	7	9	0	3	3 37	9	9
48	1.8	1.7	24 28	♊ 0.4	22.2	0	4	26 33	7	23.2	2	0	28 36	9	24.2	3	6.7	♉ 0 37	4.1	25.2	5	3	2 35	5.4	26.2	7.7	0	4 32	6.6	27.2
49	5	3	25 15	1.1	5	2.7	0	27 23	2.4	5	3.9	4.6	29 28	3.6	6	0	3	1 32	8	6	2	0	3 33	6.1	6	4	9.7	5 32	7.3	6
50	2	0.8	26 6	9	9	4	2.5	28 18	3.2	9	6	2	♉ 0 26	4.4	9	4.7	5.9	2 33	5.6	9	5.9	7.6	4 37	9	9	1	3	6 38	8.1	9
51	0.8	3	27 3	2.7	23.3	1	0	29 18	4.0	24.3	2	3.7	1 31	5.2	25.3	3	5	3 40	6.5	26.3	6	2	5 47	7.7	27.3	6.8	8.9	7 50	9	28.3
52	5	♒ 29.7	28 7	3.6	7	1.7	1.5	♉ 0 26	9	7	2.8	2	2 42	6.1	7	0	0	4 55	7.4	7	2	6.8	7 4	8.6	7	4	5	9 10	9.8	7
53	1	1	29 18	4.6	24.1	3	0.9	1 42	5.8	25.1	4	2.6	4 2	7.1	26.1	3.7	4.5	6 18	8.3	27.1	4.8	3	8 30	9.6	28.1	0	0	10 39	10.8	29.1
54	♑ 29.7	28.4	♉ 0 40	5.6	6	0.9	2	3 8	6.8	6	0	0	5 32	8.2	6	3	3.9	7 51	9.4	6	4	5.7	10 7	10.6	6	5.6	7.5	12 19	11.8	6
55	2	27.7	2 13	6.7	25.1	4	♒ 29.5	4 46	8.0	26.1	1.6	1.3	7 14	9.2	27.1	2.8	2	9 37	10.5	28.1	0	1	11 56	11.7	29.1	2	6.9	14 10	12.9	♋ 0.1
56	28.7	26.9	4 0	8.0	7	♑ 29.8	28.7	6 38	9.2	7	1	0.5	9 10	10.4	7	2	2.4	11 38	11.8	7	3.5	4.4	13 59	13.0	7	4.8	3	16 15	14.1	7

SID. T. 19 H. 9 M. 26 S. — ARC 287° 21′.5 — ♑ 16°

Lat.	11 ♒	12 ♓	1 ♈	2 ♉	3 ♊
°	°	°	° ′	°	°
22	12.5	14.5	22 39	25.1	21.4
23	4	4	22 53	4	6
24	2	3	23 8	7	8
25	1	2	23 23	26.0	9
26	0	1	23 39	3	22.1
27	11.8	0	23 55	6	3
28	7	13.8	24 12	9	4
29	6	7	24 29	27.2	6
30	4	6	24 48	6	8
31	11.3	4	25 7	9	23.0
32	1	13.3	25 27	28.3	2
33	0	1	25 48	6	4
34	10.8	0	26 10	29.0	6
35	6	12.8	26 33	4	8
36	4	6	26 58	9	24.0
37	3	5	27 23	♊ 0.3	2
38	1	3	27 51	7	4
39	9.9	1	28 20	1.2	7
40	7	0	28 51	7	9
41	5	11.8	29 24	2.2	25.2
42	3	5	29 59	7	4
43	1	3	♉ 0 36	3.3	7
44	8.8	1	1 16	9	26.0
45	5	10.8	2 0	4.5	3
46	3	6	2 46	5.2	6
47	0	3	3 37	9	9
48	7.7	0	4 32	6.6	27.2
49	4	9.7	5 32	7.3	6
50	1	3	6 38	8.1	9
51	6.8	8.9	7 50	9	28.3
52	4	5	9 10	9.8	7
53	0	0	10 39	10.8	29.1
54	5.6	7.5	12 19	11.8	6
55	2	6.9	14 10	12.9	♋ 0.1
56	4.8	3	16 15	14.1	7

SID. T. 19 H. 13 M. 44 S. — ARC 288° 25′.9 — ♑ 17°

Lat.	11 ♒	12 ♓	1 ♈	2 ♉	3 ♊
°	°	°	° ′	°	°
22	13.6	15.8	24 1	26.2	22.4
23	5	7	24 16	5	6
24	4	6	24 31	8	8
25	2	5	24 47	27.1	9
26	1	15.4	25 4	4	23.1
27	0	3	25 21	7	3
28	12.8	2	25 38	28.0	4
29	7	1	25 57	4	6
30	5	14.9	26 16	7	8
31	4	8	26 36	29.1	24.0
32	12.2	7	26 57	4	2
33	1	6	27 20	8	4
34	0	14.4	27 43	♊ 0.2	6
35	11.9	3	28 7	6	8
36	7	1	28 33	1.0	25.0
37	5	0	29 0	5	2
38	3	13.8	29 28	9	4
39	1	6	29 59	2.4	7
40	10.9	5	♉ 0 31	9	9
41	7	3	1 6	3.4	26.2
42	5	1	1 42	9	4
43	2	12.9	2 21	4.5	7
44	0	7	3 3	5.1	27.0
45	9.7	4	3 48	7	3
46	4	2	4 37	6.4	6
47	2	11.9	5 29	7.0	9
48	8.9	6	6 26	7	28.2
49	6	3	7 28	8.5	5
50	3	0	8 36	9.2	9
51	0	10.6	9 51	10.1	29.3
52	7.6	2	11 14	11.0	7
53	3	9.8	12 45	9	♋ 0.1
54	6.9	3	14 26	12.9	6
55	4	8.8	16 19	14.0	1.1
56	0	2	18 27	15.2	7

SID. T. 19 H. 18 M. 1 S. — ARC 289° 30′.2 — ♑ 18°

Lat.	11 ♒	12 ♓	1 ♈	2 ♉	3 ♊
°	°	°	° ′	°	°
22	14.8	17.1	25 22	27.3	23.4
23	6	0	25 38	6	6
24	5	16.9	25 54	9	7
25	4	9	26 11	28.2	9
26	14.3	8	26 28	5	24.1
27	1	7	26 46	9	3
28	0	6	27 4	29.2	4
29	13.8	16.5	27 24	5	6
30	7	3	27 44	8	8
31	5	2	28 5	♊ 0.2	25.0
32	4	1	28 27	5	2
33	2	0	28 50	9	4
34	1	15.9	29 15	1.3	6
35	12.9	7	29 40	7	8
36	7	6	♉ 0 7	2.2	26.0
37	5	4	0 35	6	2
38	4	15.3	1 5	3.1	4
39	2	1	1 37	5	7
40	0	0	2 10	4.0	9
41	11.8	14.8	2 46	5	27.1
42	6	6	3 24	5.1	4
43	4	4	4 5	7	7
44	1	2	4 48	6.3	28.0
45	10.9	0	5 35	9	3
46	7	13.8	6 25	7.5	6
47	4	6	7 19	8.2	9
48	1	3	8 18	9	29.2
49	9.8	0	9 22	9.6	5
50	5	12.7	10 32	10.4	9
51	2	4	11 49	11.2	♋ 0.3
52	8.9	0	13 13	12.1	7
53	5	11.6	14 46	13.1	1.1
54	1	2	16 29	14.1	6
55	7.7	10.7	18 24	15.2	2.1
56	3	2	20 33	16.4	6

SID. T. 19 H. 22 M. 18 S. — ARC 290° 34′.4 — ♑ 19°

Lat.	11 ♒	12 ♓	1 ♈	2 ♉	3 ♊
°	°	°	° ′	°	°
22	15.9	18.4	26 43	28.4	24.4
23	8	4	26 59	7	6
24	6	3	27 16	29.0	7
25	5	2	27 34	3	9
26	15.4	1	27 52	6	25.1
27	3	0	28 10	♊	2
28	1	17.9	28 30	0.3	4
29	0	8	28 50	6	6
30	14.8	7	29 11	1.0	8
31	7	6	29 33	3	26.0
32	5	5	29 56	7	2
33	4	17.4	♉ 0 20	2.1	4
34	14.2	3	0 46	5	6
35	1	2	1 12	9	8
36	0	1	1 40	3.3	27.0
37	13.8	16.9	2 9	7	2
38	6	8	2 40	4.2	4
39	4	6	3 13	7	6
40	2	5	3 48	5.2	9
41	0	3	4 25	7	28.1
42	12.8	1	5 4	6.2	4
43	6	15.9	5 46	8	7
44	3	7	6 31	7.4	9
45	1	5	7 20	8.0	29.2
46	11.9	3	8 12	7	5
47	7	1	9 8	9.4	8
48	4	14.9	10 8	10.1	♋ 0.2
49	1	7	11 14	8	5
50	10.8	4	12 25	11.6	9
51	5	1	13 44	12.4	1.3
52	1	13.8	15 10	13.3	7
53	9.7	5	16 45	14.2	2.1
54	3	1	18 29	15.2	6
55	8.9	12.7	20 25	16.3	3.1
56	5	2	22 35	17.5	6

SID. T. 19 H. 26 M. 34 S. — ARC 291° 38′.4 — ♑ 20°

Lat.	11 ♒	12 ♓	1 ♈	2 ♉	3 ♊
°	°	°	° ′	°	°
22	17.0	19.7	28 3	29.5	25.4
23	16.9	7	28 20	8	6
24	8	6	28 38	♊ 0.1	7
25	6	5	28 56	4	9
26	5	5	29 15	7	26.1
27	16.4	19.4	29 34	1.1	2
28	3	3	29 55	4	4
29	1	2	♉ 0 16	7	6
30	0	1	0 38	2.1	8
31	15.8	0	1 0	5	9
32	7	18.9	1 24	8	27.1
33	5	8	1 49	3.2	3
34	4	7	2 16	6	5
35	2	6	2 43	4.0	7
36	0	5	3 12	4	9
37	14.9	18.4	3 43	9	28.2
38	8	3	4 15	5.3	4
39	6	2	4 49	8	6
40	4	0	5 25	6.3	9
41	2	17.9	6 3	8	29.1
42	0	7	6 43	7.4	4
43	13.8	5	7 27	8.0	6
44	5	4	8 13	6	9
45	3	3	9 3	9.2	♋ 0.2
46	1	1	9 56	8	5
47	12.9	16.9	10 53	10.5	8
48	6	7	11 55	11.2	1.1
49	3	5	13 2	9	5
50	0	2	14 16	12.7	9
51	11.7	15.9	15 36	13.5	2.2
52	4	6	17 3	14.4	6
53	0	3	18 39	15.3	3.0
54	10.6	0	20 25	16.4	5
55	2	14.6	22 22	17.5	4.0
56	9.8	2	24 33	18.7	5

SID. T. 19 H. 30 M. 49 S. — ARC 292° 42′.4 — ♑ 21°

Lat.	11 ♒	12 ♓	1 ♈	2 ♊	3 ♊
°	°	°	° ′	°	°
22	18.1	21.1	29 23	0.6	26.4
23	0	0	29 41	9	5
24	17.9	20.9	29 59	1.2	7
25	8	9	♉ 0 18	5	9
26	7	8	0 37	8	27.0
27	5	7	0 58	2.2	2
28	17.4	7	1 19	5	4
29	3	20.6	1 40	9	6
30	1	5	2 3	3.2	7
31	0	4	2 27	6	9
32	16.8	4	2 52	9	28.1
33	7	20.3	3 18	4.3	3
34	5	2	3 45	7	5
35	4	1	4 13	5.1	7
36	16.2	0	4 43	6	9
37	1	19.9	5 15	6.0	29.2
38	0	8	5 48	5	4
39	15.8	7	6 23	7.0	6
40	6	6	7 0	5	8
41	4	19.5	7 39	8.0	♋ 0.1
42	2	4	8 21	5	3
43	0	3	9 5	9.1	6
44	14.8	1	9 53	7	9
45	6	18.9	10 44	10.3	1.2
46	3	7	11 38	11.0	5
47	1	5	12 37	6	8
48	13.8	3	13 41	12.3	2.1
49	5	1	14 49	13.1	5
50	2	17.9	16 4	8	8
51	12.8	7	17 25	14.6	3.2
52	5	4	18 53	15.5	6
53	2	1	20 30	16.5	4.0
54	11.8	16.8	22 17	17.5	5
55	4	5	24 15	18.6	5.0
56	0	1	26 26	19.8	5

SID. T. 19 h 35 m 5 s — ARC 293° 46′.2 — ♑ 22°

H.	11	12	1	2	3
° Lat.	♒	♓	♉	♊	♊
	°	°	° ′	°	°
22	19.3	22.4	0 42	1.7	27.4
23	2	3	1 1	2.0	5
24	0	3	1 20	3	7
25	18.9	2	1 39	6	8
26	8	22.2	1 59	9	28.0
27	7	1	2 20	3.3	2
28	5	0	2 42	6	4
29	18.4	0	3 4	4.0	5
30	3	21.9	3 28	3	7
31	1	8	3 52	7	9
32	0	8	4 18	5.0	29.1
33	17.8	7	4 45	4	3
34	7	21.6	5 13	8	5
35	5	5	5 42	6.2	7
36	4	4	6 13	7	9
37	2	4	6 45	7.1	♋ 0.1
38	0	21.3	7 20	6	3
39	16.9	2	7 56	8.1	6
40	7	1	8 34	6	8
41	5	0	9 14	9.1	1.1
42	3	20.8	9 57	6	3
43	1	7	10 43	10.2	6
44	15.9	6	11 31	8	9
45	7	4	12 24	11.4	2.2
46	4	20.3	13 19	12.1	5
47	2	2	14 19	7	8
48	0	1	15 24	13.4	3.1
49	14.7	19.9	16 33	14.2	4
50	4	7	17 49	9	8
51	1	5	19 11	15.7	4.2
52	13.8	3	20 41	16.6	6
53	4	1	22 18	17.6	5.0
54	1	18.8	24 6	18.6	4
55	12.7	5	26 4	19.7	9
56	3	2	28 15	20.9	6.4

SID. T. 19 h 39 m 19 s — ARC 294° 49′.8 — ♑ 23°

H.	11	12	1	2	3
° Lat.	♒	♓	♉	♊	♊
	°	°	° ′	°	°
22	20.4	23.7	2 1	2.8	28.3
23	3	6	2 20	3.1	5
24	2	6	2 39	4	7
25	1	5	3 0	7	8
26	19.9	5	3 20	4.0	29.0
27	8	23.4	3 42	4	2
28	7	4	4 4	7	3
29	6	3	4 28	5.0	5
30	19.4	3	4 52	4	7
31	3	2	5 17	8	9
32	1	23.2	5 43	6.1	♋ 0.1
33	0	1	6 11	5	3
34	18.8	0	6 40	9	5
35	7	0	7 10	7.3	7
36	5	22.9	7 42	8	9
37	4	8	8 15	8.2	1.1
38	2	7	8 50	7	3
39	0	7	9 27	9.2	5
40	17.9	6	10 6	7	8
41	7	22.5	10 48	10.2	2.0
42	5	4	11 32	7	3
43	4	3	12 18	11.3	6
44	2	2	13 8	9	8
45	0	1	14 1	12.5	3.1
46	16.8	21.9	14 58	13.2	4
47	6	8	15 59	8	7
48	3	7	17 4	14.5	4.1
49	0	5	18 15	15.3	4
50	15.7	21.4	19 32	16.0	7
51	4	3	20 55	8	5.1
52	1	1	22 25	17.7	5
53	14.8	20.9	24 3	18.7	9
54	4	7	25 51	19.7	6.4
55	13.9	4	27 50	20.7	9
56	5	1	♊ 0 0	21.9	7.4

SID. T. 19 h 43 m 33 s — ARC 295° 53′.3 — ♑ 24°

H.	11	12	1	2	3
° Lat.	♒	♓	♉	♊	♊
	°	°	° ′	°	°
22	21.5	25.0	3 19	3.8	29.3
23	4	24.9	3 38	4.2	5
24	3	9	3 58	5	6
25	2	9	4 19	8	8
26	1	8	4 41	5.1	♋
27	0	8	5 3	4	0.1
28	20.8	24.8	5 26	8	3
29	7	7	5 50	6.1	5
30	6	7	6 15	5	7
31	4	6	6 41	8	8
32	20.3	6	7 8	7.2	1.0
33	2	24.5	7 36	6	2
34	0	5	8 6	8.0	4
35	19.9	4	8 37	4	6
36	7	4	9 10	9	8
37	6	3	9 44	9.3	2.1
38	4	24.2	10 20	8	3
39	19.2	2	10 58	10.3	5
40	1	1	11 38	8	7
41	0	0	12 20	11.3	3.0
42	18.8	0	13 4	8	3
43	6	23.9	13 52	12.4	5
44	4	8	14 43	13.0	8
45	1	7	15 37	6	4.1
46	17.9	6	16 35	14.2	4
47	7	5	17 37	9	7
48	5	23.4	18 43	15.6	5.0
49	2	3	19 55	16.3	4
50	16.9	2	21 12	17.1	7
51	6	1	22 36	9	6.1
52	3	22.9	24 7	18.8	5
53	15.9	7	25 46	19.7	9
54	6	5	27 33	20.7	7.3
55	2	3	29 32	21.8	8
56	14.8	1	♊ 1 41	23.0	8.3

SID. T. 19 h 47 m 47 s — ARC 296° 56′.7 — ♑ 25°

H.	11	12	1	2	3
° Lat.	♒	♓	♉	♊	♋
	°	°	° ′	°	°
22	22.7	26.3	4 36	4.9	0.3
23	6	2	4 56	5.2	4
24	5	2	5 17	5	6
25	4	2	5 38	9	8
26	22.2	26.2	6 0	6.2	9
27	1	1	6 23	5	1.1
28	0	1	6 47	9	3
29	21.9	1	7 12	7.2	4
30	7	26.0	7 37	6	6
31	6	0	8 4	9	8
32	5	0	8 31	8.3	2.0
33	21.4	25.9	9 1	7	2
34	2	9	9 31	9.1	4
35	1	8	10 3	5	6
36	20.9	8	10 36	9	8
37	8	8	11 11	10.4	3.0
38	6	25.7	11 48	9	2
39	5	7	12 27	11.3	5
40	3	6	13 7	8	7
41	1	6	13 51	12.4	9
42	19.9	25.5	14 36	9	4.2
43	7	5	15 25	13.5	5
44	5	4	16 16	14.1	8
45	3	3	17 11	7	5.1
46	1	25.2	18 10	15.3	4
47	18.9	2	19 12	16.0	7
48	6	1	20 20	7	6.0
49	4	0	21 32	17.4	3
50	1	24.9	22 50	18.2	6
51	17.8	8	24 15	19.0	7.0
52	5	7	25 46	9	4
53	2	6	27 25	20.8	8
54	16.9	24.4	29 13	21.8	8.3
55	5	3	♊ 1 10	22.9	7
56	1	1	3 19	24.0	9.2

SID. T. 19 h 51 m 59 s — ARC 297° 59′.9 — ♑ 26°

H.	11	12	1	2	3
° Lat.	♒	♓	♉	♊	♋
	°	°	° ′	°	°
22	23.8	27.5	5 53	6.0	1.2
23	7	5	6 13	3	4
24	6	5	6 35	6	6
25	5	5	6 57	9	7
26	23.4	5	7 19	7.2	9
27	3	27.5	7 43	6	2.1
28	1	4	8 7	9	2
29	0	4	8 32	8.3	4
30	22.9	4	8 58	6	6
31	8	4	9 26	9.0	8
32	6	27.3	9 54	4	3.0
33	5	3	10 24	8	2
34	22.4	3	10 55	10.2	4
35	3	3	11 28	6	6
36	2	3	12 2	11.0	8
37	0	27.2	12 38	5	4.0
38	21.9	2	13 15	9	2
39	7	2	13 55	12.4	4
40	5	1	14 36	9	7
41	3	27.1	15 20	13.4	9
42	1	1	16 6	14.0	5.1
43	20.9	0	16 56	6	4
44	8	0	17 48	15.2	7
45	6	26.9	18 43	8	6.0
46	4	9	19 43	16.4	3
47	2	8	20 46	17.1	6
48	0	8	21 54	8	9
49	19.7	26.7	23 7	18.5	7.2
50	4	7	24 26	19.3	6
51	1	6	25 51	20.1	9
52	18.8	5	27 22	9	8.3
53	5	26.4	29 1	21.8	8
54	2	3	♊ 0 49	22.8	9.2
55	17.8	3	2 46	23.9	7
56	5	2	4 54	25.0	10.2

SID. T. 19 h 56 m 12 s — ARC 299° 2′.9 — ♑ 27°

H.	11	12	1	2	3
° Lat.	♒	♓	♉	♊	♋
	°	°	° ′	°	°
22	24.9	28.8	7 9	7.0	2.2
23	8	8	7 30	3	4
24	7	8	7 52	6	5
25	6	8	8 14	9	7
26	5	8	8 37	8.2	9
27	24.4	28.8	9 1	5	3.0
28	3	8	9 26	9	2
29	2	8	9 52	9.3	4
30	1	8	10 19	7	6
31	23.9	8	10 47	10.1	7
32	8	28.7	11 16	5	9
33	7	7	11 46	9	4.1
34	5	7	12 18	11.3	3
35	23.4	7	12 51	7	5
36	3	7	13 26	12.1	7
37	2	28.7	14 3	5	9
38	0	7	14 41	13.0	5.1
39	22.9	7	15 21	5	4
40	7	6	16 3	14.0	6
41	5	6	16 48	5	9
42	4	28.6	17 35	15.1	6.1
43	2	6	18 25	7	4
44	0	6	19 18	16.3	7
45	21.8	6	20 14	9	7.0
46	5	5	21 14	17.5	3
47	3	28.5	22 18	18.2	6
48	1	5	23 27	9	9
49	20.9	5	24 40	19.6	8.2
50	6	4	25 59	20.3	5
51	3	4	27 24	21.1	9
52	0	28.3	28 56	9	9.3
53	19.7	3	♊ 0 35	22.8	7
54	4	2	2 22	23.8	10.1
55	1	2	4 19	24.9	6
56	18.7	2	6 25	26.1	11.1

	SID. T. 19 h 56 m 12 s, ARC 299° 2′.9, ♑ 27°					20 h 0 m 23 s, 300° 5′.8, ♑ 28°					20 h 4 m 34 s, 301° 8′.5, ♑ 29°					20 h 8 m 44 s, 302° 11′.1, ♒ 0°					20 h 12 m 54 s, 303° 13′.4, ♒ 1°					20 h 17 m 3 s, 304° 15′.6, ♒ 2°				
H.	11	12	1	2	3	11	12	1	2	3	11	12	1	2	3	11	12	1	2	3	11	12	1	2	3	11	12	1	2	3
Lat.	♒	♓	♉	♊	♋	♒	♈	♉	♊	♋	♒	♈	♉	♊	♋	♒	♈	♉	♊	♋	♒	♈	♉	♊	♋	♓	♈	♉	♊	♋
°	°	°	° ′	°	°	°	°	° ′	°	°	°	°	° ′	°	°	°	°	° ′	°	°	°	°	° ′	°	°	°	°	° ′	°	°
22	24.9	28.8	7 9	7.0	2.2	26.1	0.1	8 24	8.0	3.2	27.2	1.4	9 38	9.1	4.1	28.4	2.7	10 52	10.1	5.1	29.5	4.0	12 5	11.1	6.0	0.7	5.2	13 18	12.1	7.0
23	8	8	7 30	3	4	0	1	8 45	3	3	1	4	10 1	4	3	3	7	11 15	4	2	4	0	12 28	4	2	6	3	13 41	4	1
24	7	8	7 52	6	5	25.9	1	9 8	6	5	0	4	10 23	7	4	2	7	11 38	7	4	3	0	12 52	7	4	5	3	14 6	8	3
25	6	8	8 14	9	7	8	1	9 31	9	7	26.9	4	10 47	10.0	6	1	7	12 2	11.1	5	2	1	13 17	12.1	5	4	3	14 31	13.1	5
26	5	8	8 37	8.2	9	7	1	9 55	9.2	8	8	4	11 11	3	8	0	2.8	12 27	4	7	1	1	13 42	4	7	0.3	5.4	14 56	4	6
27	24.4	28.8	9 1	5	3.0	6	0.1	10 19	5	4.0	7	1.5	11 36	6	9	27.9	8	12 53	7	9	0	4.1	14 8	7	8	2	4	15 23	8	8
28	3	8	9 26	9	2	5	1	10 45	9	2	6	5	12 2	11.0	5.1	8	8	13 19	12.1	6.0	28.9	2	14 35	13.1	7.0	1	5	15 51	14.1	8.0
29	2	8	9 52	9.3	4	25.3	1	11 11	10.3	3	5	5	12 29	4	3	7	8	13 47	4	2	8	2	15 3	4	2	0	5	16 19	5	1
30	1	8	10 19	7	6	2	1	11 39	7	5	26.4	5	12 57	8	5	6	2.9	14 15	8	4	7	2	15 32	8	4	♒ 29.9	5.6	16 49	8	3
31	23.9	8	10 47	10.1	7	1	1	12 7	11.1	7	3	5	13 26	12.2	6	5	9	14 45	13.2	6	6	3	16 3	14.2	5	8	6	17 19	15.2	5
32	8	28.7	11 16	5	9	0	0.1	12 37	5	9	2	1.5	13 57	6	8	27.4	9	15 16	5	8	5	4.3	16 34	6	7	7	7	17 51	6	7
33	7	7	11 46	9	4.1	24.8	1	13 8	9	5.1	0	5	14 28	13.0	6.0	2	9	15 48	9	7.0	28.4	3	17 6	15.0	9	6	7	18 24	16.0	9
34	5	7	12 18	11.3	3	7	1	13 40	12.3	3	25.9	5	15 1	4	2	1	3.0	16 21	14.4	2	3	4	17 40	4	8.1	5	5.8	18 59	4	9.0
35	23.4	7	12 51	7	5	6	1	14 14	7	5	8	6	15 36	8	4	0	0	16 56	8	4	2	4	18 16	8	3	29.4	8	19 34	8	2
36	3	7	13 26	12.1	7	5	1	14 49	13.1	7	7	6	16 12	14.2	6	26.9	0	17 33	15.2	6	1	5	18 53	16.2	5	2	9	20 12	17.2	4
37	2	28.7	14 3	5	9	24.4	0.1	15 27	6	9	6	1.6	16 49	6	8	7	1	18 11	7	8	0	4.5	19 32	7	7	1	9	20 51	7	7
38	0	7	14 41	13.0	5.1	2	1	16 5	14.1	6.1	25.4	6	17 29	15.1	7.0	6	1	18 51	16.1	8.0	27.9	6	20 12	17.2	9	0	6.0	21 32	18.2	9
39	22.9	7	15 21	5	4	1	1	16 46	5	3	3	6	18 10	6	3	4	3.1	19 33	6	2	7	6	20 55	6	9.2	28.8	1	22 15	6	10.1
40	7	6	16 3	14.0	6	23.9	1	17 29	15.0	6	1	7	18 54	16.1	5	26.3	2	20 17	17.1	5	5	7	21 39	18.1	4	7	1	23 0	19.1	3
41	5	6	16 48	5	9	7	1	18 15	6	8	24.9	7	19 40	6	8	1	2	21 3	6	7	4	4.7	22 26	6	6	5	2	23 47	7	6
42	4	28.6	17 35	15.1	6.1	6	0.1	19 2	16.1	7.1	8	1.7	20 28	17.2	8.0	0	2	21 52	18.2	9	2	8	23 15	19.2	9	3	6.3	24 37	20.2	8
43	2	6	18 25	7	4	4	2	19 54	7	4	6	7	21 19	8	3	25.8	3	22 44	7	9.2	0	8	24 7	8	10.2	2	4	25 29	7	11.1
44	0	6	19 18	16.3	7	2	2	20 46	17.3	6	4	8	22 13	18.4	6	6	3.3	23 39	19.3	5	26.8	9	25 2	20.3	4	1	5	26 25	21.3	4
45	21.8	6	20 14	9	7.0	0	2	21 43	9	9	2	8	23 11	19.0	9	4	4	24 37	9	7	6	5.0	26 1	9	7	27.9	6	27 23	9	6
46	5	5	21 14	17.5	3	22.8	2	22 44	18.5	8.2	0	8	24 12	6	9.1	2	4	25 38	20.6	10.0	4	1	27 3	21.6	11.0	7	6.7	28 25	22.6	9
47	3	28.5	22 18	18.2	6	6	0.2	23 48	19.2	5	23.8	1.8	25 17	20.3	4	0	5	26 43	21.2	3	3	1	28 8	22.2	3	5	8	29 31	23.2	12.2
48	1	5	23 27	9	9	4	2	24 57	9	8	6	9	26 26	21.0	7	24.8	5	27 53	9	7	1	2	29 18	9	6	3	9	♊ 0 41	9	5
49	20.9	5	24 40	19.6	8.2	2	2	26 11	20.6	9.1	4	9	27 40	7	10.1	6	3.6	29 7	22.6	11.0	25.9	3	♊ 0 32	23.6	9	1	7.0	1 55	24.6	8
50	6	4	25 59	20.3	5	21.9	2	27 31	21.3	5	1	9	29 0	22.4	4	4	6	♊ 0 26	23.4	3	6	5.4	1 51	24.4	12.3	26.9	1	3 14	25.3	13.2
51	3	4	27 24	21.1	9	6	2	28 56	22.1	8	22.8	2.0	♊ 0 25	23.2	8	1	7	1 52	24.2	7	4	5	3 16	25.2	6	7	2	4 39	26.1	5
52	0	28.3	28 56	9	9.3	3	0.2	♊ 0 27	23.0	10.2	5	0	1 56	24.0	11.2	23.9	8	3 23	25.0	12.1	2	6	4 47	26.0	13.0	4	3	6 10	9	9
53	19.7	3	♊ 0 35	22.8	7	0	2	2 6	9	6	2	1	3 35	9	6	6	9	5 1	9	5	24.9	7	6 25	9	4	2	7.5	7 47	27.8	14.3
54	4	2	2 22	23.8	10.1	20.7	2	3 53	24.9	11.1	21.9	1	5 21	25.9	12.0	3	4.0	6 46	26.9	9	6	8	8 9	27.8	8	25.9	7	9 31	28.8	7
55	1	2	4 19	24.9	6	4	2	5 49	25.9	5	7	2	7 16	26.9	4	0	1	8 40	27.9	13.3	3	6.0	10 2	28.9	14.2	6	9	11 22	29.9	15.1
56	18.7	2	6 25	26.1	11.1	1	2	7 54	27.0	12.0	3	2	9 20	28.0	9	22.6	2	10 43	29.0	8	0	2	12 4	♋	7	3	8.1	13 22	♋ 1.0	6

SID. T. H. M. S. / ARC	20 21 11 / 305° 17′.7 } ♒ 3°					20 25 18 / 306° 19′.5 } ♒ 4°					20 29 25 / 307° 21′.2 } ♒ 5°					20 33 31 / 308° 22′.7 } ♒ 6°					20 37 36 / 309° 24′.0 } ♒ 7°					20 41 41 / 310° 25′.2 } ♒ 8°				
H.	11	12	1	2	3	11	12	1	2	3	11	12	1	2	3	11	12	1	2	3	11	12	1	2	3	11	12	1	2	3
Lat. °	♓ °	♈ °	♉ ° ′	♊ °	♋ °	♓ °	♈ °	♉ ° ′	♊ °	♋ °	♓ °	♈ °	♉ ° ′	♊ °	♋ °	♓ °	♈ °	♉ ° ′	♊ °	♋ °	♓ °	♈ °	♉ ° ′	♊ °	♋ °	♓ °	♈ °	♉ ° ′	♊ °	♋ °
22	1.8	6.5	14 30	13.1	7.9	3.0	7.8	15 41	14.1	8.9	4.1	9.1	16 51	15.1	9.8	5.3	10.3	18 1	16.1	10.7	6.4	11.6	19 11	17.1	11.7	7.5	12.8	20 20	18.0	12.6
23	7	6	14 54	4	8.1	2.9	8	16 5	4	9.0	0	1	17 16	4	10.0	2	4	18 27	4	9	3	6	19 36	4	8	5	9	20 45	4	7
24	7	6	15 18	8	2	8	9	16 30	8	2	0	2	17 42	7	1	1	4	18 52	7	11.0	3	7	20 2	7	12.0	4	13.0	21 12	7	9
25	6	7	15 44	14.1	4	7	9	16 56	15.1	3	3.9	2	18 8	16.1	3	0	5	19 19	17.1	2	2	8	20 29	18.0	1	3	1	21 39	19.0	13.1
26	5	7	16 10	4	6	6	8.0	17 23	4	5	8	3	18 35	4	4	0	6	19 47	4	4	6.1	9	20 57	4	3	3	2	22 7	3	2
27	1.4	6.8	16 37	8	7	2.5	1	17 50	8	7	7	9.4	19 3	8	10.6	4.9	10.7	20 15	7	5	0	12.0	21 26	7	5	7.2	3	22 36	7	4
28	3	8	17 5	15.1	9	5	1	18 19	16.1	8	6	4	19 32	17.1	8	8	8	20 44	18.1	7	0	1	21 55	19.1	6	1	4	23 6	20.0	5
29	2	9	17 34	5	9.1	4	2	18 48	5	10.0	5	5	20 2	5	9	7	8	21 14	4	9	5.9	1	22 26	4	8	0	13.5	23 37	4	7
30	1	9	18 4	8	2	3	2	19 19	8	2	3.4	6	20 32	8	11.1	6	9	21 45	8	12.0	8	2	22 57	8	13.0	0	6	24 9	8	9
31	0	7.0	18 35	16.2	4	2.2	8.3	19 50	17.2	4	3	9.7	21 4	18.2	3	5	11.0	22 18	19.2	2	7	3	23 30	20.2	1	6.9	7	24 41	21.1	14.1
32	0.9	0	19 8	6	6	1	4	20 23	6	5	2	7	21 37	6	5	4.4	1	22 51	6	4	6	12.4	24 4	5	3	8	8	25 15	5	2
33	8	1	19 41	17.0	8	0	5	20 57	18.0	7	1	8	22 11	19.0	7	3	2	23 25	20.0	6	5	5	24 39	9	5	7	9	25 51	9	4
34	7	1	20 16	4	10.0	1.8	5	21 32	4	9	0	9	22 47	4	8	2	3	24 1	4	8	5.4	7	25 15	21.3	7	6	14.0	26 27	22.3	6
35	5	2	20 52	8	2	7	8.6	22 8	8	11.1	2.9	10.0	23 24	8	12.0	1	4	24 39	8	13.0	3	8	25 52	8	9	5	2	27 5	7	8
36	0.4	7.3	21 30	18.2	4	6	7	22 46	19.2	3	8	1	24 3	20.2	2	0	11.5	25 17	21.2	2	2	9	26 31	22.2	14.1	6.4	3	27 44	23.2	15.0
37	3	4	22 9	7	6	5	8	23 26	7	5	7	2	24 43	7	4	3.9	6	25 58	7	4	1	13.0	27 12	6	3	3	4	28 25	6	2
38	2	4	22 50	19.2	8	1.4	9	24 8	20.2	7	6	3	25 25	21.2	7	8	8	26 40	22.2	6	0	2	27 55	23.1	5	2	14.6	29 8	24.1	4
39	0	5	23 34	6	11.0	2	9.0	24 52	6	12.0	2.5	10.4	26 9	6	9	7	9	27 25	6	8	4.9	3	28 39	6	7	1	8	29 53	6	6
40	♒ 29.9	7.6	24 19	20.1	3	1	1	25 38	21.1	2	3	6	26 55	22.1	13.1	5	12.0	28 11	23.1	14.0	8	5	29 26	24.1	15.0	0	9	♊ 0 40	25.0	9
41	7	7	25 7	7	5	0	2	26 26	7	4	2	7	27 43	6	4	3.4	2	29 0	6	3	6	7	♊ 0 15	6	2	5.9	15.1	1 29	5	16.1
42	6	8	25 57	21.2	8	0.8	4	27 17	22.2	7	0	9	28 34	23.2	6	3	3	29 50	24.1	5	5	8	1 6	25.1	4	7	3	2 20	26.1	3
43	4	9	26 50	7	12.0	7	9.5	28 9	7	13.0	1.9	11.0	29 27	7	9	1	5	♊ 0 44	7	7	4.3	14.0	1 59	7	7	6	5	3 13	6	6
44	29.3	8.1	27 46	22.3	3	5	6	29 5	23.3	2	7	2	♊ 0 23	24.3	14.1	0	7	1 40	25.3	15.0	2	2	2 55	26.2	9	4	7	4 9	27.2	8
45	2	2	28 44	9	6	4	8	♊ 0 4	9	5	6	4	1 22	9	4	2.8	9	2 39	9	3	1	4	3 54	8	16.2	5.3	16.0	5 8	8	17.1
46	0	3	29 47	23.5	9	2	9	1 6	24.5	8	5	5	2 25	25.5	7	7	13.1	3 41	26.5	6	0	7	4 57	27.4	5	2	2	6 11	28.4	4
47	28.8	4	♊ 0 53	24.2	13.2	0	10.1	2 12	25.2	14.1	3	7	3 30	26.2	15.0	6	3	4 47	27.1	9	3.8	9	6 2	28.1	8	1	4	7 16	29.0	7
48	6	8.6	2 2	9	5	♒ 29.8	3	3 22	9	4	1	9	4 40	8	3	5	5	5 57	8	16.2	6	15.2	7 12	7	17.1	4.9	7	8 25	7	18.0
49	4	7	3 17	25.6	8	7	4	4 36	26.6	7	0.9	12.1	5 54	27.5	6	3	7	7 10	28.5	5	4	4	8 25	29.4	4	8	9	9 39	♋ 0.4	3
50	2	8	4 36	26.3	14.1	5	5	5 55	27.3	15.0	7	2	7 13	28.3	9	0	9	8 29	29.2	8	3	6	9 43	♋ 0.2	7	6	17.2	10 56	1.1	6
51	27.9	9.0	6 0	27.1	5	2	7	7 19	28.1	3	5	4	8 36	29.0	16.2	1.8	14.2	9 52	♋	17.2	1	9	11 6	9	18.1	4	5	12 18	8	19.0
52	7	2	7 30	9	8	0	9	8 49	9	7	3	7	10 5	8	6	6	5	11 20	0.8	5	2.9	16.2	12 33	1.7	4	2	9	13 45	2.6	3
53	5	4	9 7	28.8	15.2	28.8	11.2	10 24	29.8	16.1	1	13.0	11 40	♋ 0.7	17.0	3	8	12 54	1.6	9	7	6	14 7	2.6	8	3.9	18.3	15 17	3.5	6
54	2	6	10 50	29.8	6	5	5	12 6	♋ 0.7	5	♒ 29.8	3	13 21	1.6	4	1	15.2	14 34	2.5	18.3	4	17.0	15 46	3.5	19.2	7	8	16 56	4.4	20.0
55	26.9	9	12 40	♋ 0.8	16.0	2	8	13 56	1.7	9	5	7	15 9	2.6	8	0.8	6	16 21	3.6	7	2	5	17 31	4.5	6	5	19.3	18 40	5.3	4
56	6	10.2	14 38	1.8	5	27.9	12.1	15 53	2.8	17.4	2	14.1	17 5	3.7	18.3	6	16.1	18 15	4.7	19.2	1.9	18.0	19 24	5.6	20.0	3	9	20 31	6.4	9

UPPER MERIDIAN, CUSP OF 10th H.

	SID. T. (H. M. S.) 20 41 41 · ARC 310° 25′.2 · ♒ 8°					20 45 44 · 311° 26′.1 · ♒ 9°					20 49 48 · 312° 26′.9 · ♒ 10°				
H.	11	12	1	2	3	11	12	1	2	3	11	12	1	2	3
Lat.	♓	♈	♉	♊	♋	♓	♈	♉	♊	♋	♓	♈	♉	♊	♋
°	°	°	° ′	°	°	°	°	° ′	°	°	°	°	° ′	°	°
22	7.5	12.8	20 20	18.0	12.6	8.7	14.0	21 28	19.0	13.5	9.8	15.3	22 36	20.0	14.5
23	5	9	20 45	4	7	6	1	21 54	3	7	8	4	23 2	3	6
24	4	13.0	21 12	7	9	6	2	22 21	6	8	7	5	23 29	6	8
25	3	1	21 39	19.0	13.1	5	3	22 48	20.0	14.0	7	6	23 57	9	9
26	3	2	22 7	3	2	8.4	4	23 17	3	1	6	15.7	24 25	21.3	15.1
27	7.2	3	22 36	7	4	4	14.5	23 46	6	3	9.5	8	24 55	6	2
28	1	4	23 6	20.0	5	3	6	24 16	21.0	5	4	9	25 25	22.0	4
29	0	13.5	23 37	4	7	2	7	24 47	3	6	4	16.1	25 56	3	6
30	0	6	24 9	8	9	8.1	9	25 19	7	8	3	2	26 29	7	7
31	6.9	7	24 41	21.1	14.1	1	15.0	25 52	22.1	15.0	9.2	3	27 2	23.0	9
32	8	8	25 15	5	2	0	1	26 26	5	2	1	4	27 37	4	16.1
33	7	9	25 51	9	4	7.9	2	27 2	9	3	1	16.6	28 12	8	3
34	6	14.0	26 27	22.3	6	8	4	27 39	23.3	5	0	7	28 49	24.2	4
35	5	2	27 5	7	8	7	15.5	28 17	7	7	8.9	9	29 27	6	6
36	6.4	3	27 44	23.2	15.0	6	7	28 56	24.1	9	8	17.1	♊ 0 7	25.1	8
37	3	4	28 25	6	2	5	8	29 37	6	16.1	7	2	0 49	5	17.0
38	2	14.6	29 8	24.1	4	7.4	16.0	♊ 0 20	25.0	3	6	4	1 32	26.0	2
39	1	8	29 53	6	6	3	2	1 5	5	5	5	6	2 17	4	5
40	0	9	♊ 0 40	25.0	9	2	4	1 52	26.0	8	8.4	8	3 4	9	7
41	5.9	15.1	1 29	5	16.1	1	6	2 41	5	17.0	3	18.0	3 53	27.4	9
42	7	3	2 20	26.1	3	0	8	3 32	27.0	2	2	2	4 44	28.0	18.1
43	6	5	3 13	6	6	6.8	17.0	4 26	6	5	1	4	5 38	5	4
44	4	7	4 9	27.2	8	7	2	5 22	28.2	7	7.9	7	6 34	29.1	6
45	5.3	16.0	5 8	8	17.1	5	5	6 21	7	18.0	8	9	7 33	7	9
46	2	2	6 11	28.4	4	4	7	7 24	29.3	3	6	19.2	8 35	♋ 0.3	19.1
47	1	4	7 16	29.0	7	6.3	18.0	8 29	♋	6	5	5	9 40	9	4
48	4.9	7	8 25	7	18.0	2	3	9 38	0.6	9	7.4	8	10 49	1.5	7
49	8	9	9 39	♋ 0.4	3	0	6	10 51	1.3	19.2	3	20.1	12 1	2.2	20.0
50	6	17.2	10 56	1.1	6	5.8	9	12 8	2.0	5	1	5	13 18	9	3
51	4	5	12 18	8	19.0	6	19.3	13 29	7	8	6.9	9	14 38	3.6	6
52	2	9	13 45	2.6	3	4	7	14 55	3.5	20.1	7	21.3	16 4	4.4	21.0
53	3.9	18.3	15 17	3.5	6	2	20.1	16 27	4.4	5	6	8	17 34	5.3	4
54	7	8	16 56	4.4	20.0	0	6	18 4	5.3	9	4	22.3	19 10	6.2	8
55	5	19.3	18 40	5.3	4	4.8	21.1	19 47	6.2	21.3	2	9	20 52	7.1	22.2
56	3	9	20 31	6.4	9	6	7	21 36	7.2	8	0	23.6	22 40	8.1	6

	20 53 50 · 313° 27′.5 · ♒ 11°					20 57 52 · 314° 27′.9 · ♒ 12°					21 1 53 · 315° 28′.1 · ♒ 13°				
H.	11	12	1	2	3	11	12	1	2	3	11	12	1	2	3
Lat.	♓	♈	♉	♊	♋	♓	♈	♉	♊	♋	♓	♈	♉	♊	♋
°	°	°	° ′	°	°	°	°	° ′	°	°	°	°	° ′	°	°
22	11.0	16.5	23 43	20.9	15.4	12.1	17.7	24 49	21.9	16.3	13.3	19.0	25 54	22.8	17.2
23	10.9	6	24 9	21.2	5	1	9	25 15	22.2	4	2	1	26 21	23.1	4
24	9	7	24 36	5	7	0	18.0	25 43	5	6	2	2	26 49	4	5
25	8	9	25 4	9	8	11.9	1	26 11	8	7	1	3	27 18	8	7
26	7	17.0	25 33	22.2	16.0	9	2	26 40	23.2	9	1	19.5	27 47	24.1	8
27	7	1	26 3	6	1	8	4	27 10	5	17.1	0	6	28 17	4	18.0
28	10.6	2	26 33	9	3	8	18.5	27 41	9	2	12.9	8	28 48	8	1
29	5	3	27 5	23.3	5	7	6	28 13	24.2	4	9	9	29 20	25.1	3
30	5	17.5	27 37	6	6	11.6	8	28 46	6	6	8	20.0	29 53	5	5
31	4	6	28 11	24.0	8	6	9	29 19	9	7	8	2	♊ 0 27	9	6
32	3	8	28 46	4	17.0	5	19.1	29 54	25.3	9	7	4	1 2	26.2	8
33	10.3	9	29 21	8	2	4	2	♊ 0 30	7	18.1	12.6	6	1 38	6	19.0
34	2	18.1	29 59	25.2	4	4	4	1 8	26.1	3	5	7	2 16	27.0	2
35	1	2	♊ 0 37	6	6	11.3	6	1 46	5	5	5	9	2 55	4	4
36	0	4	1 18	26.0	8	3	8	2 26	9	7	4	21.1	3 35	9	6
37	9.9	6	1 59	4	18.0	2	20.0	3 8	27.4	9	3	3	4 16	28.3	8
38	8	8	2 43	9	2	1	2	3 52	8	19.1	12.2	6	5 0	8	20.0
39	7	19.0	3 28	27.4	4	0	4	4 37	28.3	3	2	8	5 45	29.2	2
40	6	2	4 14	9	6	10.9	6	5 24	8	5	1	22.0	6 32	7	4
41	5	5	5 3	28.4	8	8	9	6 13	29.3	7	0	3	7 21	♋ 0.2	6
42	9.4	7	5 54	9	19.0	7	21.1	7 4	8	9	11.9	5	8 13	7	8
43	3	9	6 48	29.4	3	6	3	7 58	♋ 0.3	20.2	8	8	9 6	1.3	21.1
44	2	20.1	7 44	♋	5	5	6	8 54	9	4	7	23.1	10 2	8	3
45	0	4	8 43	0.6	8	10.4	9	9 52	1.5	7	6	3	11 0	2.4	6
46	8.9	7	9 45	1.2	20.1	3	22.2	10 54	2.1	21.0	5	6	12 2	3.0	9
47	8	21.0	10 50	8	3	1	5	11 59	7	2	11.4	9	13 6	6	22.1
48	7	3	11 59	2.4	6	0	9	13 7	3.3	5	3	24.3	14 14	4.2	4
49	5	7	13 10	3.1	9	9.8	23.3	14 18	4.0	8	1	7	15 25	9	7
50	8.4	22.1	14 26	8	21.2	7	7	15 34	7	22.1	0	25.2	16 40	5.6	23.0
51	2	5	15 46	4.5	5	5	24.1	16 53	5.4	4	10.8	7	17 58	6.3	4
52	0	23.0	17 11	5.3	9	3	6	18 17	6.2	7	6	26.2	19 21	7.1	7
53	7.9	5	18 41	6.1	22.2	1	25.1	19 45	7.0	23.1	5	8	20 49	9	24.0
54	7	24.1	20 16	7.0	6	0	7	21 19	9	5	3	27.4	22 22	8.7	3
55	5	7	21 56	9	23.0	8.9	26.4	22 59	8.8	9	2	28.1	24 0	9.6	7
56	3	25.4	23 43	8.9	4	7	27.2	24 44	9.8	24.4	0	9	25 43	10.6	25.1

	SID. T. 21 5 53 (H. M. S.) ARC 316° 28′.2 ♒ 14°					21 9 52 (H. M. S.) 317° 28′.0 ♒ 15°					21 13 51 (H. M. S.) 318° 27′.7 ♒ 16°					21 17 49 (H. M. S.) 319° 27′.2 ♒ 17°					21 21 46 (H. M. S.) 320° 26′.6 ♒ 18°					21 25 43 (H. M. S.) 321° 25′.7 ♒ 19°				
H.	11	12	1	2	3	11	12	1	2	3	11	12	1	2	3	11	12	1	2	3	11	12	1	2	3	11	12	1	2	3
Lat.	♓	♈	♉	♊	♋	♓	♈	♉	♊	♋	♓	♈	♉	♊	♋	♓	♈	♊	♊	♋	♓	♈	♊	♊	♋	♓	♈	♊	♊	♋
°	°	°	° ′	°	°	°	°	° ′	°	°	°	°	° ′	°	°	°	°	° ′	°	°	°	°	° ′	°	°	°	°	° ′	°	°
22	14.4	20.2	26 59	23.7	18.1	15.5	21.4	28 4	24.7	19.0	16.7	22.6	29 8	25.6	19.9	17.8	23.7	0 11	26.5	20.9	19.0	24.9	1 14	27.4	21.8	20.1	26.1	2 16	28.3	22.7
23	3	3	27 27	24.0	3	5	5	28 31	25.0	2	6	7	29 35	9	20.1	8	9	0 39	8	21.0	18.9	25.1	1 42	7	9	1	3	2 44	6	8
24	3	4	27 55	4	4	4	6	28 59	3	3	6	9	♊ 0 4	26.2	2	7	24.1	1 7	27.1	1	9	2	2 10	28.1	22.0	0	4	3 13	29.0	23.0
25	2	6	28 23	7	6	4	8	29 28	6	5	6	23.0	0 33	6	4	7	2	1 36	5	3	9	4	2 40	4	2	0	6	3 42	3	1
26	2	7	28 53	25.0	7	15.3	9	29 58	26.0	6	5	2	1 3	9	5	7	4	2 6	8	4	8	6	3 10	7	3	0	8	4 12	6	3
27	14.1	9	29 23	4	9	3	22.1	♊ 0 28	3	8	16.5	3	1 33	27.2	7	17.6	5	2 37	28.1	21.6	8	8	3 41	29.1	5	19.9	27.0	4 43	♋	4
28	1	21.0	29 54	7	19.0	2	3	1 0	7	20.0	4	5	2 5	6	9	6	7	3 9	5	8	18.7	26.0	4 12	4	7	9	2	5 15	0.3	23.6
29	0	2	♊ 0 26	26.1	2	2	4	1 32	27.0	1	4	7	2 37	9	21.0	5	9	3 42	8	9	7	2	4 45	7	8	9	4	5 48	6	7
30	0	3	1 0	4	4	15.1	6	2 5	4	3	3	9	3 11	28.3	2	5	25.1	4 15	29.2	22.1	6	4	5 19	♋ 0.1	23.0	8	6	6 22	1.0	9
31	13.9	5	1 34	8	5	1	8	2 40	7	5	3	24.1	3 45	6	4	4	3	4 50	5	3	6	6	5 54	5	2	8	8	6 57	4	24.1
32	9	7	2 9	27.2	7	0	23.0	3 15	28.1	6	16.2	3	4 21	29.0	5	17.4	5	5 25	9	4	6	8	6 29	8	3	19.7	28.0	7 33	7	2
33	8	9	2 45	6	9	0	2	3 51	5	8	2	5	4 57	4	7	3	7	6 2	♋ 0.3	6	18.5	27.0	7 6	1.2	5	7	3	8 9	2.1	4
34	7	22.1	3 23	28.0	20.1	14.9	4	4 29	9	21.0	1	7	5 35	8	9	3	26.0	6 40	7	8	5	2	7 44	6	7	7	5	8 47	5	6
35	7	3	4 2	4	3	9	6	5 8	29.3	2	0	9	6 14	♋ 0.2	22.1	2	2	7 19	1.1	23.0	4	5	8 23	2.0	9	6	8	9 26	9	8
36	13.6	5	4 42	8	5	8	8	5 49	7	4	0	25.1	6 55	6	3	2	4	7 59	5	2	4	7	9 4	4	24.1	19.6	29.0	10 7	3.3	9
37	5	7	5 24	29.2	7	7	24.0	6 31	♋ 0.2	6	15.9	4	7 37	1.0	5	17.1	7	8 41	9	4	18.4	28.0	9 45	8	3	5	3	10 49	7	25.1
38	4	9	6 8	7	9	7	3	7 14	6	8	9	6	8 20	5	7	1	27.0	9 25	2.4	6	3	2	10 29	3.3	5	5	6	11 32	4.2	3
39	4	23.2	6 53	♋ 0.2	21.1	14.6	5	8 0	1.1	22.0	8	9	9 5	9	9	0	2	10 10	8	8	3	5	11 14	7	7	4	8	12 17	6	5
40	13.3	4	7 40	6	3	5	8	8 47	6	2	7	26.1	9 52	2.4	23.1	0	5	10 57	3.3	24.0	2	8	12 1	4.2	9	19.4	♉ 0.1	13 4	5.1	7
41	2	7	8 29	1.1	5	4	25.1	9 36	2.1	4	6	4	10 41	9	3	16.9	8	11 46	8	2	18.2	29.1	12 50	7	25.1	3	4	13 53	6	26.0
42	1	24.0	9 20	6	7	4	4	10 26	6	6	15.6	7	11 32	3.5	5	8	28.1	12 37	4.4	4	1	4	13 40	5.2	3	3	7	14 43	6.1	2
43	0	3	10 13	2.2	22.0	14.3	7	11 20	3.1	9	5	27.0	12 25	4.0	7	7	4	13 30	9	6	1	7	14 33	8	5	2	1.1	15 36	6	4
44	12.9	6	11 9	7	2	2	26.0	12 15	6	23.1	5	3	13 21	5	24.0	6	7	14 25	5.4	9	0	♉	15 28	6.3	8	19.2	5	16 31	7.2	6
45	9	8	12 7	3.3	5	1	3	13 13	4.2	4	4	6	14 18	5.1	2	16.6	29.0	15 22	6.0	25.1	17.9	0.4	16 25	9	26.0	1	9	17 28	7	9
46	8	25.1	13 9	9	8	0	6	14 14	8	6	15.3	28.0	15 19	7	4	5	4	16 23	6	3	8	8	17 25	7.4	2	1	2.3	18 27	8.3	27.1
47	7	5	14 13	4.5	23.0	13.9	27.0	15 18	5.4	8	2	4	16 22	6.3	7	5	8	17 26	7.2	6	7	1.2	18 28	8.0	4	0	7	19 29	9	3
48	5	9	15 20	5.1	2	8	4	16 25	6.0	24.1	1	8	17 28	9	25.0	4	♉ 0.3	18 31	8	8	6	7	19 33	6	7	18.9	3.2	20 34	9.5	6
49	12.4	26.3	16 30	8	5	7	8	17 35	7	4	0	29.3	18 38	7.5	3	16.3	8	19 40	8.4	26.1	5	2.2	20 41	9.3	27.0	8	7	21 42	10.1	9
50	3	8	17 44	6.5	8	6	28.3	18 48	7.4	7	14.9	8	19 51	8.2	6	2	1.3	20 53	9.1	4	17.5	8	21 53	10.0	3	7	4.3	22 53	8	28.2
51	2	27.3	19 3	7.2	24.2	13.5	8	20 6	8.1	25.0	7	♉ 0.4	21 8	9	9	0	9	22 9	8	8	4	3.4	23 9	6	6	6	9	24 8	11.5	5
52	0	8	20 25	8.0	5	3	29.4	21 27	8	4	6	1.0	22 28	9.6	26.2	15.9	2.5	23 29	10.5	27.1	3	4.0	24 28	11.3	9	18.5	5.5	25 26	12.2	8
53	11.9	28.4	21 52	8	8	2	♉	22 53	9.6	7	5	6	23 53	10.4	6	8	3.2	24 53	11.3	4	2	7	25 51	12.1	28.2	5	6.2	26 48	13.0	29.2
54	7	29.1	23 23	9.6	25.2	0	0.7	24 24	10.5	26.0	14.4	2.3	25 23	11.2	9	7	4.0	26 21	12.1	7	1	5.5	27 18	13.0	6	4	7.0	28 14	8	5
55	6	8	25 0	10.5	6	12.9	1.5	25 59	11.3	4	3	3.1	26 57	12.1	27.3	6	8	27 54	13.0	28.1	16.9	6.4	28 50	8	29.0	3	9	29 45	14.6	8
56	4	♉ 0.7	26 42	11.4	26.0	7	2.4	27 40	12.2	9	1	4.1	28 36	13.0	7	5	5.8	29 32	9	5	7	7.4	♋ 0 26	14.7	4	1	8.9	♋ 1 20	15.5	♌ 0.2

	SID. T. H. M. S. 21 25 43 ARC 321° 25′.7 ♒ 19°					H. M. S. 21 29 39 322° 24′.7 ♒ 20°					H. M. S. 21 33 34 323° 23′.5 ♒ 21°					H. M. S. 21 37 29 324° 22′.2 ♒ 22°					H. M. S. 21 41 23 325° 20′.6 ♒ 23°					H. M. S. 21 45 16 326° 19′.0 ♒ 24°				
H.	11	12	1	2	3	11	12	1	2	3	11	12	1	2	3	11	12	1	2	3	11	12	1	2	3	11	12	1	2	3
Lat.	♓	♈	♊	♊	♋	♓	♈	♊	♊	♋	♓	♈	♊	♋	♋	♓	♈	♊	♋	♋	♓	♉	♊	♋	♋	♓	♉	♊	♋	♋
°	°	°	° ′	°	°	°	°	° ′	°	°	°	°	° ′	°	°	°	°	° ′	°	°	°	°	° ′	°	°	°	°	° ′	°	°
22	20.1	26.1	2 16	28.3	22.7	21.2	27.2	3 17	29.2	23.6	22.4	28.4	4 18	0.1	24.5	23.5	29.5	5 19	1.0	25.4	24.6	0.7	6 19	1.9	26.3	25.7	1.8	7 18	2.8	27.2
23	1	3	2 44	6	8	2	4	3 46	5	7	3	6	4 47	4	6	5	7	5 47	3	5	6	8	6 47	2.2	4	7	2.0	7 47	3.1	3
24	0	4	3 13	29.0	23.0	2	6	4 15	9	9	3	8	5 16	8	8	4	9	6 17	7	7	6	1.0	7 17	5	6	7	2	8 16	4	5
25	0	6	3 42	3	1	1	8	4 44	♋ 0.2	24.0	3	29.0	5 46	1.1	9	4	♉ 0.1	6 46	2.0	8	6	2	7 47	9	7	7	4	8 46	7	6
26	0	8	4 12	6	3	1	28.0	5 14	5	2	3	2	6 16	4	25.1	4	3	7 17	3	26.0	5	4	8 17	3.2	9	7	6	9 17	4.1	8
27	19.9	27.0	4 43	♋	4	21.1	2	5 45	9	3	22.2	4	6 47	7	2	23.4	5	7 48	6	1	24.5	7	8 49	5	27.0	25.7	8	9 49	4	9
28	9	2	5 15	0.3	23.6	0	4	6 17	1.2	5	2	6	7 19	2.1	4	3	7	8 21	3.0	3	5	9	9 21	9	2	7	3.1	10 21	7	28.1
29	9	4	5 48	6	7	0	6	6 50	5	6	2	8	7 52	4	5	3	1.0	8 53	3	4	5	2.1	9 54	4.2	3	6	3	10 54	5.1	2
30	8	6	6 22	1.0	9	0	8	7 24	9	8	1	♉	8 26	8	7	3	2	9 27	7	26.6	5	4	10 28	6	5	6	6	11 28	4	4
31	8	8	6 57	4	24.1	20.9	29.0	7 59	2.3	25.0	1	0.2	9 1	3.1	9	3	4	10 2	4.0	7	4	6	11 3	9	6	6	8	12 3	8	5
32	19.7	28.0	7 33	7	2	9	3	8 35	6	1	22.1	5	9 37	5	26.0	23.2	7	10 38	4	9	24.4	9	11 38	5.3	8	25.6	4.1	12 38	6.2	7
33	7	3	8 9	2.1	4	9	5	9 12	3.0	3	0	7	10 14	9	2	2	2.0	11 15	8	27.1	4	3.2	12 15	7	28.0	6	4	13 15	5	9
34	7	5	8 47	5	6	8	8	9 50	4	5	0	1.0	10 52	4.3	4	2	2	11 53	5.2	2	4	5	12 53	6.1	1	5	7	13 53	9	29.0
35	6	8	9 26	9	8	8	♉	10 29	8	6	0	3	11 31	7	5	2	5	12 32	6	4	3	7	13 33	5	3	5	5.0	14 32	7.3	2
36	19.6	29.0	10 7	3.3	9	20.8	0.3	11 10	4.2	8	21.9	6	12 11	5.1	7	1	8	13 13	6.0	6	3	4.0	14 14	9	4	5	3	15 13	7	4
37	5	3	10 49	7	25.1	7	5	11 51	6	26.0	9	8	12 53	5	9	23.1	3.0	13 55	4	8	24.3	3	14 55	7.3	6	25.5	6	15 54	8.2	6
38	5	6	11 32	4.2	3	7	8	12 35	5.1	2	9	2.1	13 37	6.0	27.1	1	3	14 38	8	28.0	3	6	15 38	7	8	5	9	16 38	6	7
39	4	8	12 17	6	5	6	1.1	13 20	5	4	8	4	14 22	4	3	0	7	15 23	7.3	2	2	9	16 23	8.2	29.0	4	6.3	17 22	9.0	9
40	19.4	♉ 0.1	13 4	5.1	7	20.6	4	14 7	6.0	6	8	7	15 8	9	5	0	4.0	16 9	7	4	2	5.3	17 9	6	2	4	6	18 8	5	♌ 0.1
41	3	4	13 53	6	26.0	5	7	14 55	5	8	21.7	3.0	15 56	7.4	7	0	4	16 57	8.2	6	24.2	7	17 57	9.1	4	4	7.0	18 56	9	3
42	3	7	14 43	6.1	2	5	2.1	15 45	7.0	27.1	7	4	16 47	9	9	22.9	8	17 46	7	8	1	6.1	18 46	6	6	25.4	4	19 45	10.4	5
43	2	1.1	15 36	6	4	4	5	16 38	5	3	6	8	17 38	8.4	28.2	9	5.2	18 38	9.2	29.0	1	5	19 37	10.1	8	4	8	20 36	9	7
44	19.2	5	16 31	7.2	6	20.4	9	17 32	8.1	5	6	4.2	18 32	9	4	8	6	19 32	8	3	1	9	20 31	6	♌	3	8.2	21 29	11.5	1.0
45	1	9	17 28	7	9	3	3.3	18 29	6	8	5	6	19 29	9.5	6	8	6.0	20 28	10.3	5	24.1	7.3	21 27	11.2	0.2	3	6	22 25	12.0	2
46	1	2.3	18 27	8.3	27.1	3	7	19 28	9.2	28.0	21.5	5.0	20 28	10.0	8	7	5	21 27	9	7	0	8	22 25	7	5	3	9.1	23 22	6	4
47	0	7	19 29	9	3	2	4.2	20 29	8	2	5	5	21 29	6	29.0	22.7	7.0	22 28	11.5	♌	0	8.3	23 25	12.3	7	25.3	6	24 22	13.1	6
48	18.9	3.2	20 34	9.5	6	20.2	7	21 34	10.4	4	4	6.0	22 33	11.2	3	7	5	23 31	12.1	0.2	0	8	24 28	9	1.0	3	10.2	25 24	7	9
49	8	7	21 42	10.1	9	1	5.2	22 41	11.0	7	4	6	23 40	8	6	6	8.0	24 37	7	4	23.9	9.4	25 34	13.5	3	2	8	26 30	14.3	2.1
50	7	4.3	22 53	8	28.2	0	8	23 52	6	29.0	3	7.2	24 49	12.5	9	6	6	25 46	13.3	7	9	10.0	26 42	14.1	6	2	11.4	27 38	9	4
51	6	9	24 8	11.5	5	0	6.4	25 5	12.3	3	21.3	8	26 2	13.1	♌ 0.2	6	9.2	26 59	14.0	1.0	9	6	27 54	8	9	25.2	12.1	28 49	15.6	7
52	18.5	5.5	25 26	12.2	8	19.9	7.1	26 23	13.0	7	2	8.5	27 19	8	5	22.5	9	28 14	7	4	8	11.3	29 9	15.5	2.2	1	8	♋ 0 3	16.3	3.1
53	5	6.2	26 48	13.0	29.2	8	8	27 44	8	♌	1	9.3	28 39	14.6	8	4	10.7	29 34	15.4	7	23.8	12.1	♋ 0 27	16.2	4	1	13.6	1 20	17.0	4
54	4	7.0	28 14	8	5	7	8.6	29 9	14.6	0.3	0	10.1	♋ 0 3	15.4	1.1	3	11.6	♋ 0 57	16.2	2.0	7	13.0	1 49	17.0	7	0	14.5	2 41	7	7
55	3	9	29 45	14.6	8	6	9.5	♋ 0 39	15.4	7	20.9	11.0	1 32	16.2	5	3	12.5	2 24	17.0	3	6	14.0	3 15	7	3.1	24.9	15.5	4 6	18.5	4.0
56	1	8.9	♋ 1 20	15.5	♌ 0.2	5	10.5	2 12	16.2	1.1	9	12.0	3 4	17.0	9	2	13.5	3 55	8	7	5	15.1	4 45	18.5	5	9	16.6	5 35	19.3	4

	SID. T. H. M. S. 21 49 8 ARC 327° 17′.1 ♒ 25°					H. M. S. 21 53 0 328° 15′.1 ♒ 26°					H. M. S. 21 56 52 329° 12′.9 ♒ 27°					H. M. S. 22 0 42 330° 10′.6 ♒ 28°					H. M. S. 22 4 33 331° 8′.1 ♒ 29°					H. M. S. 22 8 22 332° 5′.5 ♓ 0°				
H.	11	12	1	2	3	11	12	1	2	3	11	12	1	2	3	11	12	1	2	3	11	12	1	2	3	11	12	1	2	3
Lat.	♓	♉	♊	♋	♋	♓	♉	♊	♋	♋	♓	♉	♊	♋	♋	♈	♉	♊	♋	♌	♈	♉	♊	♋	♌	♈	♉	♊	♋	♌
°	°	°	° ′	°	°	°	°	° ′	°	°	°	°	° ′	°	°	°	°	° ′	°	°	°	°	° ′	°	°	°	°	° ′	°	°
22	26.9	2.9	8 17	3.7	28.1	28.0	4.1	9 16	4.6	29.0	29.1	5.1	10 14	5.4	29.9	0.2	6.2	11 12	6.3	0.8	1.3	7.3	12 9	7.2	1.7	2.4	8.4	13 6	8.0	2.6
23	8	3.1	8 46	4.0	2	0	3	9 45	9	1	1	3	10 43	7	♌	2	5	11 41	6	9	3	6	12 38	5	8	4	7	13 35	3	7
24	8	3	9 15	3	4	0	5	10 14	5.2	3	1	6	11 12	6.0	0.2	2	7	12 10	9	1.0	3	8	13 8	8	9	4	9	14 4	6	8
25	8	5	9 46	6	5	0	7	10 44	5	4	1	8	11 43	4	3	2	9	12 40	7.2	2	3	8.0	13 38	8.1	2.1	4	9.1	14 35	9.0	3.0
26	8	8	10 17	5.0	28.6	0	9	11 15	8	29.5	1	6.0	12 13	7	4	2	7.1	13 11	6	3	3	3	14 9	4	2	4	4	15 6	3	1
27	26.8	4.0	10 48	3	8	27.9	5.1	11 47	6.2	7	29.1	3	12 45	7.0	6	0.2	4	13 43	9	5	1.3	5	14 40	7	4	2.5	6	15 37	6	3
28	8	2	11 20	6	9	9	4	12 19	5	8	1	5	13 17	4	7	2	7	14 15	8.2	1.6	3	8	15 13	9.1	5	5	9	16 9	9	4
29	8	5	11 53	6.0	29.1	9	6	12 52	8	♌	1	8	13 51	7	9	2	9	14 48	6	8	3	9.0	15 46	4	7	5	10.2	16 43	10.3	3.5
30	8	7	12 27	3	3	9	9	13 26	7.2	0.1	1	7.0	14 25	8.1	1.0	2	8.2	15 22	9	9	3	3	16 20	8	8	5	4	17 16	6	7
31	8	5.0	13 2	7	4	9	6.2	14 1	5	3	1	3	14 59	4	2	2	5	15 57	9.3	2.1	4	6	16 54	10.1	3.0	5	7	17 51	11.0	8
32	26.7	3	13 38	7.0	6	27.9	4	14 37	9	5	29.1	6	15 35	8	3	0.2	8	16 33	6	2	1.4	9	17 30	5	1	2.5	11.1	18 27	3	4.0
33	7	6	14 15	4	7	9	7	15 14	8.3	6	1	9	16 12	9.2	5	2	9.1	17 10	10.0	4	4	10.2	18 7	9	3	5	4	19 3	7	1
34	7	9	14 53	8	9	9	7.0	15 51	7	8	1	8.2	16 50	5	1.7	2	4	17 47	4	5	4	5	18 44	11.2	4	5	7	19 41	12.1	3
35	7	6.2	15 32	8.2	♌ 0.1	9	3	16 30	9.1	1.0	0	5	17 28	9	8	2	7	18 26	8	7	4	9	19 23	6	3.6	5	12.0	20 19	5	5
36	7	5	16 12	6	2	9	7	17 10	5	1	0	8	18 8	10.3	9	2	10.0	19 6	11.2	9	4	11.2	20 3	12.0	8	5	4	20 59	9	4.6
37	26.7	8	16 54	9.0	4	27.8	8.0	17 52	9	3	29.0	9.2	18 50	7	2.1	0.2	4	19 47	6	3.1	1.4	6	20 44	4	9	2.6	8	21 40	13.3	7
38	6	7.1	17 37	4	6	8	3	18 35	10.3	5	0	6	19 32	11.2	3	2	8	20 29	12.0	2	4	9	21 26	8	4.1	6	13.1	22 22	7	9
39	6	4	18 21	9	8	8	6	19 19	7	7	0	9	20 16	6	5	2	11.1	21 13	4	4	4	12.3	22 10	13.3	3	6	5	23 6	14.1	5.1
40	6	8	19 7	10.3	1.0	8	9.0	20 5	11.2	9	0	10.3	21 2	12.0	7	2	5	21 59	9	6	4	7	22 55	7	5	6	9	23 50	5	3
41	6	8.2	19 54	8	2	8	4	20 52	6	2.1	0	7	21 49	5	9	2	9	22 45	13.3	8	4	13.1	23 41	14.2	7	6	14.3	24 37	15.0	5
42	26.6	6	20 43	11.3	4	27.8	8	21 41	12.1	3	29.0	11.1	22 38	13.0	3.1	0.2	12.3	23 34	8	4.0	1.4	6	24 29	6	9	2.6	8	25 24	4	7
43	6	9.0	21 34	8	6	8	10.2	22 31	6	5	0	5	23 28	5	3	2	8	24 24	14.3	2	4	14.1	25 19	15.1	5.1	6	15.3	26 14	9	9
44	5	4	22 27	12.3	8	8	7	23 24	13.1	7	0	12.0	24 20	14.0	5	2	13.3	25 16	8	4	4	6	26 11	6	3	6	8	27 5	16.4	6.1
45	5	9	23 22	8	2.0	8	11.2	24 18	7	9	0	5	25 14	5	7	2	8	26 10	15.3	7	5	15.1	27 4	16.1	5	7	16.3	27 58	9	3
46	5	10.4	24 19	13.4	2	7	7	25 15	14.2	3.1	0	13.0	26 10	15.0	9	2	14.3	27 5	8	9	5	6	28 0	6	7	7	8	28 53	17.4	5
47	26.5	9	25 19	9	5	27.7	12.2	26 14	8	3	29.0	6	27 9	6	4.2	0.2	9	28 4	16.4	5.1	1.5	16.2	28 57	17.2	9	2.7	17.4	29 50	18.0	7
48	4	11.5	26 21	14.5	7	7	8	27 15	15.3	6	0	14.2	28 10	16.1	4	2	15.5	29 4	9	3	5	8	29 57	7	6.1	7	18.0	♋ 0 49	5	7.0
49	4	12.1	27 25	15.1	3.0	7	13.4	28 19	9	9	0	8	29 13	7	7	2	16.1	♋ 0 7	17.5	5	5	17.4	♋ 0 59	18.3	3	7	6	1 51	19.1	2
50	4	8	28 32	7	3	7	14.1	29 26	16.5	4.1	0	15.5	♋ 0 19	17.3	5.0	2	8	1 12	18.1	8	5	18.1	2 4	9	6	8	19.3	2 55	7	5
51	4	13.5	29 42	16.4	6	7	8	♋ 0 36	17.1	4	28.9	16.2	1 28	9	3	2	17.5	2 20	7	6.1	5	8	3 11	19.5	9	8	20.0	4 1	20.4	8
52	26.4	14.2	♋ 0 56	17.1	9	27.7	15.6	1 48	8	7	9	17.0	2 40	18.6	6	0.2	18.3	3 31	19.4	4	1.5	19.6	4 21	20.1	7.2	2.8	8	5 11	21.0	8.1
53	3	15.0	2 12	8	4.2	6	16.4	3 4	18.5	5.0	9	8	3 54	19.3	8	2	19.2	4 44	20.1	7	5	20.5	5 34	8	5	8	21.7	6 23	7	4
54	3	9	3 32	18.5	5	6	17.3	4 23	19.3	3	9	18.7	5 12	20.0	6.1	2	20.1	6 2	8	7.0	6	21.5	6 50	21.5	8	9	22.7	7 38	22.4	6
55	3	16.9	4 56	19.3	8	6	18.3	5 45	20.1	6	9	19.7	6 34	8	4	2	21.1	7 22	21.6	3	6	22.5	8 10	22.3	8.1	9	23.8	8 57	23.1	9
56	3	18.0	6 24	20.1	5.2	6	19.4	7 12	9	6.0	9	20.8	7 59	21.6	8	2	22.2	8 46	22.4	7	6	23.6	9 33	23.1	5	9	25.0	10 18	9	9.2

UPPER MERIDIAN, CUSP OF 10th H.

	SID. T. H. M. S. 22 8 22 ARC 332° 5′.5 ♓ 0°					H. M. S. 22 12 11 333° 2′.8 ♓ 1°					H. M. S. 22 16 0 333° 59′.9 ♓ 2°					H. M. S. 22 19 47 334° 56′.8 ♓ 3°					H. M. S. 22 23 35 335° 53′.7 ♓ 4°					H. M. S. 22 27 22 336° 50′.4 ♓ 5°				
H.	11	12	1	2	3	11	12	1	2	3	11	12	1	2	3	11	12	1	2	3	11	12	1	2	3	11	12	1	2	3
Lat.	♈	♉	♊	♋	♌	♈	♉	♊	♋	♌	♈	♉	♊	♋	♌	♈	♉	♊	♋	♌	♈	♉	♊	♋	♌	♈	♉	♊	♋	♌
°	°	°	° ′	°	°	°	°	° ′	°	°	°	°	° ′	°	°	°	°	° ′	°	°	°	°	° ′	°	°	°	°	° ′	°	°
22	2.4	8.4	13 6	8.0	2.6	3.5	9.5	14 2	8.9	3.5	4.6	10.6	14 58	9.7	4.4	5.7	11.6	15 54	10.6	5.3	6.8	12.7	16 49	11.5	6.1	7.9	13.7	17 44	12.3	7.0
23	4	7	13 35	3	7	5	7	14 31	9.2	6	6	8	15 27	10.0	5	7	9	16 23	9	4	8	9	17 18	8	3	9	14.0	18 13	6	2
24	4	9	14 4	6	8	5	10.0	15 1	5	7	6	11.1	15 57	4	6	8	12.1	16 53	11.2	5	9	13.2	17 48	12.1	4	9	2	18 42	9	3
25	4	9.1	14 35	9.0	3.0	6	2	15 31	8	9	6	3	16 27	7	8	8	4	17 23	5	6	9	4	18 18	4	5	8.0	5	19 13	13.2	4
26	4	4	15 6	3	1	6	5	16 2	10.1	4.0	7	6	16 58	11.0	9	5.8	6	17 54	8	8	6.9	7	18 49	7	6.7	0	8	19 43	5	7.6
27	2.5	6	15 37	6	3	3.6	7	16 34	5	1	4.7	8	17 29	3	5.0	8	9	18 25	12.2	9	9	14.0	19 20	13.0	8	0	15.0	20 15	9	7
28	5	9	16 9	9	4	6	11.0	17 6	8	3	7	12.1	18 2	6	2	8	13.2	18 57	5	6.1	9	3	19 52	3	9	1	3	20 47	14.2	8
29	5	10.2	16 43	10.3	3.5	6	3	17 39	11.1	4	7	4	18 35	12.0	3	9	5	19 30	8	2	7.0	6	20 25	7	7.1	1	6	21 20	5	8.0
30	5	4	17 16	6	7	6	6	18 13	5	4.6	7	7	19 9	3	5	5.9	8	20 4	13.2	3	0	9	20 59	14.0	2	8.1	9	21 53	8	1
31	5	7	17 51	11.0	8	6	9	18 47	8	7	8	13.0	19 43	7	5.6	9	14.1	20 38	5	5	0	15.2	21 33	3	4	2	16.2	22 28	15.2	2
32	2.5	11.1	18 27	3	4.0	3.6	12.2	19 23	12.2	9	4.8	3	20 19	13.0	7	9	4	21 14	9	6.6	1	5	22 9	7	5	2	6	23 3	5	4
33	5	4	19 3	7	1	7	5	19 59	6	5.0	8	6	20 55	4	9	9	7	21 50	14.2	8	1	8	22 45	15.1	7.6	2	9	23 39	9	8.5
34	5	7	19 41	12.1	3	7	8	20 37	9	2	8	9	21 32	8	6.0	6.0	15.0	22 27	6	9	7.1	16.1	23 22	4	8	3	17.2	24 16	16.2	7
35	5	12.0	20 19	5	5	7	13.2	21 15	13.3	3	8	14.3	22 11	14.1	2	0	4	23 5	15.0	7.1	2	5	24 0	8	9	8.3	6	24 54	6	8
36	5	4	20 59	9	4.6	3.7	5	21 55	7	5	4.9	7	22 50	5	4	0	8	23 44	4	2	2	9	24 39	16.2	8.1	3	18.0	25 33	17.0	9.0
37	2.6	8	21 40	13.3	7	7	9	22 35	14.1	7	9	15.0	23 30	9	5	0	16.2	24 25	8	4	2	17.3	25 19	6	3	4	4	26 13	4	1
38	6	13.1	22 22	7	9	7	14.3	23 17	5	8	9	4	24 12	15.3	7	0	6	25 6	16.2	6	3	7	26 0	17.0	4	4	8	26 54	8	3
39	6	5	23 6	14.1	5.1	8	6	24 1	9	6.0	9	8	24 55	8	9	6.1	17.0	25 49	6	8	7.3	18.1	26 43	4	6	5	19.2	27 36	18.2	5
40	6	9	23 50	5	3	3.8	15.0	24 45	15.4	2	5.0	16.2	25 40	16.2	7.1	1	4	26 33	17.0	9	3	5	27 27	8	8	8.5	6	28 20	6	9.6
41	6	14.3	24 37	15.0	5	8	4	25 31	8	4	0	6	26 25	6	3	1	9	27 19	5	8.1	4	19.0	28 12	18.3	9.0	6	20.1	29 5	19.1	7
42	2.6	8	25 24	4	7	8	9	26 19	16.3	6	0	17.1	27 12	17.1	5	1	18.4	28 6	9	3	4	5	28 59	7	2	6	6	29 51	5	9
43	6	15.3	26 14	9	9	8	16.4	27 8	7	8	1	6	28 1	6	7	2	9	28 55	18.4	5	5	20.0	29 47	19.2	4	7	21.1	♋ 0 39	20.0	10.1
44	6	8	27 5	16.4	6.1	3.9	9	27 59	17.2	7.0	5.1	18.1	28 52	18.1	9	6.2	19.4	29 45	9	7	7.5	5	♋ 0 37	7	6	7	6	1 28	5	3
45	7	16.3	27 58	9	3	9	17.4	28 51	7	2	1	6	29 44	6	8.1	2	9	♋ 0 36	19.4	9	5	21.1	1 28	20.2	8	8.8	22.2	2 19	9	5
46	7	8	28 53	17.4	5	9	18.0	29 46	18.2	4	2	19.2	♋ 0 38	19.1	3	3	20.5	1 30	9	9.2	6	7	2 21	7	10.0	8	8	3 12	21.4	7
47	2.7	17.4	29 50	18.0	7	9	6	♋ 0 42	8	6	2	8	1 34	6	4	3	21.1	2 26	20.4	4	6	22.3	3 16	21.2	2	9	23.4	4 6	22.0	9
48	7	18.0	♋ 0 49	5	7.0	4.0	19.2	1 41	19.3	8	5.2	20.4	2 32	20.1	6	6.4	7	3 23	9	6	6	9	4 13	7	4	9	24.1	5 3	5	11.1
49	7	6	1 51	19.1	2	0	9	2 42	9	8.1	3	21.1	3 33	7	8	4	22.4	4 23	21.4	8	7.7	23.6	5 12	22.2	6	9.0	8	6 2	23.1	3
50	8	19.3	2 55	7	5	0	20.6	3 46	20.5	3	3	8	4 35	21.3	9.1	5	23.1	5 25	22.0	10.0	7	24.3	6 14	8	8	0	25.5	7 2	6	6
51	8	20.0	4 1	20.4	8	1	21.3	4 51	21.1	6	4	22.6	5 40	9	4	5	9	6 29	6	3	8	25.1	7 18	23.4	11.1	1	26.3	8 5	24.2	8
52	2.8	8	5 11	21.0	8.1	4.1	22.1	6 0	7	9	5.4	23.4	6 48	22.5	7	6.6	24.7	7 36	23.2	6	9	9	8 24	24.0	3	1	27.2	9 11	8	12.1
53	8	21.7	6 23	7	4	1	23.0	7 11	22.4	9.1	5	24.3	7 59	23.2	9	7	25.6	8 46	9	8	9	26.8	9 33	6	5	9.2	28.1	10 19	25.4	4
54	9	22.7	7 38	22.4	6	2	24.0	8 25	23.1	4	5	25.3	9 12	9	10.2	7	26.6	9 59	24.6	11.0	8.0	27.8	10 44	25.3	8	3	29.1	11 30	26.1	7
55	9	23.8	8 57	23.1	9	2	25.1	9 43	8	7	5	26.4	10 29	24.6	5	8	27.7	11 14	25.3	3	1	28.9	11 59	26.0	12.1	4	♊ 0.2	12 43	8	13.0
56	9	25.0	10 18	9	9.2	2	26.3	11 4	24.6	10.0	6	27.6	11 48	25.3	9	9	28.9	12 33	26.0	7	2	♊ 0.1	13 17	7	5	6	1.4	14 0	27.5	3

SID. T. 22 h 31 m 8 s, ARC 337° 47′.0 — ♓ 6°

Lat.	H. 11 ♈	12 ♉	1 ♊	2 ♋	3 ♌
°	°	°	° ′	°	°
22	9.0	14.8	18 38	13.2	7.9
23	0	15.0	19 7	5	8.1
24	1	3	19 37	8	2
25	1	6	20 7	14.1	3
26	1	8	20 38	4	4
27	9.1	16.1	21 9	7	8.6
28	2	4	21 41	15.0	7
29	2	7	22 14	4	8
30	2	17.0	22 48	7	9.0
31	3	3	23 22	16.0	1
32	9.3	7	23 57	4	3
33	4	18.0	24 33	7	4
34	4	3	25 10	17.1	9.6
35	4	7	25 47	4	7
36	5	19.1	26 26	8	9
37	9.5	5	27 6	18.2	10.0
38	6	9	27 47	6	2
39	6	20.4	28 29	19.0	3
40	6	8	29 12	4	5
41	6	21.3	29 57	9	7
42	9.7	8	♋ 0 43	20.3	9
43	7	22.3	1 30	8	11.1
44	8	9	2 19	21.3	3
45	9	23.4	3 10	7	5
46	9	24.0	4 2	22.2	7
47	10.0	6	4 56	7	9
48	1	25.3	5 52	23.2	12.1
49	1	26.0	6 50	7	3
50	2	7	7 50	24.3	5
51	3	27.5	8 53	9	8
52	10.4	28.4	9 58	25.5	13.0
53	5	29.3	11 5	26.1	2
54	6	♊ 0.3	12 15	8	5
55	7	1.4	13 28	27.5	8
56	8	2.6	14 43	28.2	14.1

SID. T. 22 h 34 m 54 s, ARC 338° 43′.4 — ♓ 7°

Lat.	H. 11 ♈	12 ♉	1 ♊	2 ♋	3 ♌
°	°	°	° ′	°	°
22	10.1	15.8	19 32	14.0	8.8
23	1	16.1	20 1	3	9
24	1	3	20 31	6	9.1
25	2	6	21 1	9	2
26	2	9	21 32	15.2	3
27	10.2	17.2	22 3	5	5
28	3	5	22 35	9	9.6
29	3	8	23 8	16.2	7
30	4	18.1	23 41	5	9
31	4	4	24 16	9	10.0
32	10.4	7	24 50	17.2	1
33	5	19.1	25 26	6	3
34	5	4	26 3	9	4
35	6	8	26 40	18.3	10.6
36	6	20.2	27 19	7	7
37	10.7	6	27 59	19.0	9
38	7	21.0	28 39	4	11.0
39	8	5	29 21	8	2
40	8	9	♋ 0 4	20.3	4
41	9	22.4	0 48	7	6
42	11.0	9	1 34	21.1	7
43	0	23.4	2 21	6	9
44	1	24.0	3 10	22.1	12.1
45	2	5	4 0	5	3
46	2	25.1	4 52	23.0	5
47	11.3	7	5 45	5	7
48	3	26.4	6 41	24.0	9
49	4	27.1	7 38	5	13.1
50	5	8	8 38	25.1	3
51	6	28.6	9 40	7	6
52	11.7	29.5	10 44	26.3	9
53	8	♊ 0.5	11 50	9	14.1
54	8	1.5	12 59	27.5	3
55	9	2.6	14 11	28.2	6
56	12.0	3.8	15 26	9	9

SID. T. 22 h 38 m 39 s, ARC 339° 39′.8 — ♓ 8°

Lat.	H. 11 ♈	12 ♉	1 ♊	2 ♋	3 ♌
°	°	°	° ′	°	°
22	11.2	16.8	20 26	14.9	9.7
23	2	17.1	20 55	15.2	8
24	2	4	21 25	5	10.0
25	3	7	21 55	8	1
26	3	9	22 25	16.1	2
27	11.3	18.2	22 57	4	3
28	4	5	23 29	7	10.5
29	4	8	24 1	17.0	6
30	5	19.1	24 35	3	7
31	5	4	25 9	7	9
32	11.6	8	25 44	18.0	11.0
33	6	20.1	26 19	4	1
34	7	5	26 56	7	3
35	7	9	27 33	19.1	4
36	11.8	21.3	28 12	5	11.6
37	8	7	28 51	9	7
38	9	22.1	29 31	20.3	9
39	9	5	♋ 0 13	7	12.1
40	12.0	23.0	0 56	21.1	2
41	1	5	1 40	5	4
42	1	24.0	2 25	9	6
43	2	5	3 12	22.4	8
44	2	25.0	4 0	8	13.0
45	12.3	6	4 50	23.3	2
46	3	26.2	5 41	8	3
47	4	8	6 34	24.2	5
48	5	27.5	7 29	7	7
49	12.6	28.2	8 26	25.3	9
50	7	29.0	9 25	8	14.1
51	8	8	10 26	26.4	3
52	9	♊ 0.7	11 30	27.0	6
53	13.0	1.7	12 35	6	8
54	1	2.7	13 44	28.2	15.1
55	2	3.8	14 54	9	4
56	3	5.0	16 8	29.6	7

SID. T. 22 h 42 m 24 s, ARC 340° 36′.0 — ♓ 9°

Lat.	H. 11 ♈	12 ♉	1 ♊	2 ♋	3 ♌
°	°	°	° ′	°	°
22	12.2	17.9	21 19	15.7	10.6
23	3	18.1	21 48	16.0	7
24	3	4	22 18	3	9
25	3	7	22 48	6	11.0
26	12.4	19.0	23 19	9	1
27	4	3	23 50	17.2	2
28	5	6	24 22	5	4
29	5	9	24 54	8	11.5
30	12.6	20.2	25 27	18.2	6
31	6	5	26 1	5	7
32	7	8	26 36	8	9
33	7	21.2	27 12	19.2	12.0
34	12.8	5	27 48	5	2
35	8	9	28 25	9	3
36	9	22.3	29 4	20.3	5
37	9	7	29 43	7	12.6
38	13.0	23.2	♋ 0 23	21.1	8
39	0	6	1 4	5	9
40	1	24.1	1 47	9	13.1
41	1	6	2 30	22.3	3
42	2	25.1	3 15	7	5
43	13.3	6	4 2	23.1	6
44	4	26.1	4 50	6	8
45	4	7	5 39	24.1	14.0
46	5	27.3	6 30	6	2
47	13.6	9	7 23	25.1	4
48	7	28.6	8 17	6	6
49	8	29.3	9 13	26.1	8
50	9	♊ 0.1	10 12	6	15.0
51	14.0	9	11 12	27.2	2
52	2	1.8	12 15	8	5
53	3	2.8	13 20	28.4	7
54	4	3.8	14 27	29.0	16.0
55	5	4.9	15 37	6	2
56	7	6.2	16 50	♌ 0.3	5

SID. T. 22 h 46 m 9 s, ARC 341° 32′.2 — ♓ 10°

Lat.	H. 11 ♈	12 ♉	1 ♊	2 ♋	3 ♌
°	°	°	° ′	°	°
22	13.3	18.9	22 13	16.5	11.5
23	4	19.2	22 42	8	6
24	4	4	23 11	17.1	7
25	4	7	23 41	4	9
26	5	20.0	24 12	7	12.0
27	13.5	3	24 43	18.0	1
28	6	6	25 15	4	2
29	6	9	25 47	7	4
30	7	21.2	26 20	19.0	12.5
31	13.7	5	26 54	3	6
32	8	9	27 29	7	7
33	8	22.2	28 4	20.0	9
34	9	6	28 40	4	13.0
35	14.0	23.0	29 17	7	2
36	0	4	29 55	21.1	3
37	1	8	♋ 0 34	5	5
38	2	24.2	1 14	8	6
39	2	7	1 55	22.2	8
40	14.3	25.1	2 37	6	14.0
41	4	6	3 21	23.1	1
42	5	26.1	4 5	5	3
43	5	6	4 51	9	5
44	6	27.2	5 39	24.4	7
45	14.6	8	6 28	8	8
46	7	28.4	7 18	25.3	15.0
47	8	29.0	8 11	8	2
48	9	7	9 5	26.3	4
49	15.0	♊ 0.4	10 0	8	6
50	1	1.2	10 58	27.3	8
51	2	2.0	11 58	9	16.1
52	3	9	13 0	28.5	3
53	15.5	3.9	14 4	29.1	5
54	6	4.9	15 11	7	7
55	8	6.0	16 20	♌ 0.3	17.0
56	9	7.3	17 32	1.0	3

SID. T. 22 h 49 m 53 s, ARC 342° 28′.2 — ♓ 11°

Lat.	H. 11 ♈	12 ♉	1 ♊	2 ♋	3 ♌
°	°	°	° ′	°	°
22	14.4	19.9	23 6	17.4	12.4
23	4	20.2	23 34	7	5
24	5	4	24 4	18.0	6
25	5	7	24 34	3	7
26	14.6	21.0	25 4	6	9
27	6	3	25 35	9	13.0
28	7	6	26 7	19.2	1
29	7	9	26 39	5	2
30	14.8	22.2	27 12	8	4
31	8	6	27 46	20.2	13.5
32	9	9	28 20	5	6
33	15.0	23.3	28 56	8	8
34	0	6	29 32	21.2	9
35	1	24.0	♋ 0 9	5	14.0
36	1	4	0 47	9	2
37	2	8	1 25	22.3	3
38	15.3	25.3	2 5	7	5
39	4	7	2 46	23.0	7
40	4	26.2	3 27	4	8
41	5	7	4 10	8	15.0
42	6	27.3	4 55	24.3	2
43	15.6	8	5 40	7	3
44	7	28.4	6 28	25.2	5
45	8	29.0	7 16	6	7
46	9	6	8 6	26.1	8
47	16.0	♊ 0.3	8 58	6	16.0
48	1	9	9 52	27.1	2
49	2	1.6	10 47	6	4
50	3	2.3	11 44	28.1	6
51	16.4	3.1	12 43	7	8
52	6	4.0	13 44	29.3	17.1
53	7	5.0	14 48	9	3
54	9	6.1	15 54	♌ 0.5	5
55	17.0	7.2	17 2	1.1	8
56	1	8.5	18 13	8	18.1

SID. T. / ARC	H. M. S. 22 49 53, 342° 28′.2 ♓ 11°					H. M. S. 22 53 37, 343° 24′.1 ♓ 12°					H. M. S. 22 57 20, 344° 20′.0 ♓ 13°				
H.	11	12	1	2	3	11	12	1	2	3	11	12	1	2	3
Lat.	♈	♉	♊	♋	♌	♈	♉	♊	♋	♌	♈	♉	♊	♋	♌
°	°	°	° ′	°	°	°	°	° ′	°	°	°	°	° ′	°	°
22	14.4	19.9	23 6	17.4	12.4	15.4	20.9	23 59	18.2	13.3	16.5	21.9	24 50	19.0	14.2
23	4	20.2	23 34	7	5	5	21.2	24 27	5	4	6	22.2	25 19	3	3
24	5	4	24 4	18.0	6	5	4	24 57	8	5	6	5	25 49	6	4
25	5	7	24 34	3	7	6	7	25 27	19.1	6	7	8	26 19	9	5
26	14.6	21.0	25 4	6	9	6	22.0	25 57	4	7	16.7	23.1	26 49	20.2	14.6
27	6	3	25 35	9	13.0	15.7	3	26 28	7	9	8	4	27 20	5	8
28	7	6	26 7	19.2	1	7	6	27 0	20.0	14.0	8	7	27 51	8	9
29	7	9	26 39	5	2	8	9	27 32	3	1	9	24.0	28 23	21.2	15.0
30	14.8	22.2	27 12	8	4	9	23.3	28 5	7	2	17.0	3	28 56	5	1
31	8	6	27 46	20.2	13.5	9	6	28 38	21.0	4	0	6	29 29	8	3
32	9	9	28 20	5	6	16.0	9	29 12	3	14.5	1	25.0	♋ 0 3	22.1	4
33	15.0	23.3	28 56	8	8	1	24.3	29 47	7	6	2	3	0 38	5	15.5
34	0	6	29 32	21.2	9	1	7	♋ 0 23	22.0	8	2	7	1 14	8	6
35	1	24.0	♋ 0 9	5	14.0	2	25.1	1 0	4	9	17.3	26.1	1 51	23.2	8
36	1	4	0 47	9	2	3	5	1 38	7	15.1	4	5	2 28	5	9
37	2	8	1 25	22.3	3	16.3	9	2 16	23.1	2	5	9	3 6	9	16.1
38	15.3	25.3	2 5	7	5	4	26.3	2 56	5	4	5	27.4	3 45	24.3	2
39	4	7	2 46	23.0	7	4	8	3 36	8	5	17.6	8	4 26	6	4
40	4	26.2	3 27	4	8	5	27.3	4 18	24.2	7	7	28.3	5 7	25.0	5
41	5	7	4 10	8	15.0	16.6	8	5 0	6	8	8	9	5 49	4	7
42	6	27.3	4 55	24.3	2	7	28.3	5 44	25.1	16.0	9	29.4	6 33	8	9
43	15.6	8	5 40	7	3	8	9	6 29	5	2	18.0	♊	7 18	26.3	17.0
44	7	28.4	6 28	25.2	5	9	29.5	7 16	9	4	1	0.6	8 5	7	2
45	8	29.0	7 16	6	7	17.0	♊ 0.1	8 4	26.4	6	2	1.2	8 53	27.2	4
46	9	6	8 6	26.1	8	1	7	8 54	8	7	3	8	9 42	6	6
47	16.0	♊ 0.3	8 58	6	16.0	2	1.3	9 46	27.3	9	4	2.4	10 33	28.1	7
48	1	9	9 52	27.1	2	3	9	10 39	8	17.1	18.5	3.1	11 25	6	9
49	2	1.6	10 47	6	4	17.4	2.6	11 33	28.3	3	6	8	12 19	29.1	18.1
50	3	2.3	11 44	28.1	6	5	3.4	12 29	8	5	7	4.5	13 15	6	3
51	16.4	3.1	12 43	7	8	6	4.2	13 28	29.4	7	9	5.3	14 12	♌ 0.1	5
52	6	4.0	13 44	29.3	17.1	8	5.1	14 28	♌	18.0	19.0	6.2	15 12	7	7
53	7	5.0	14 48	9	3	18.0	6.1	15 31	0.6	2	2	7.2	16 14	1.3	9
54	9	6.1	15 54	♌ 0.5	5	1	7.2	16 36	1.2	4	3	8.3	17 18	9	19.1
55	17.0	7.2	17 2	1.1	8	3	8.3	17 44	8	6	5	9.4	18 25	2.5	4
56	1	8.5	18 13	8	18.1	4	9.6	18 54	2.5	9	7	10.7	19 34	3.1	7

SID. T. / ARC	H. M. S. 23 1 3, 345° 15′.7 ♓ 14°					H. M. S. 23 4 46, 346° 11′.4 ♓ 15°					H. M. S. 23 8 28, 347° 7′.0 ♓ 16°				
H.	11	12	1	2	3	11	12	1	2	3	11	12	1	2	3
Lat.	♈	♉	♊	♋	♌	♈	♉	♊	♋	♌	♈	♉	♊	♋	♌
°	°	°	° ′	°	°	°	°	° ′	°	°	°	°	° ′	°	°
22	17.6	22.9	25 42	19.9	15.1	18.6	23.9	26 34	20.7	16.0	19.7	24.8	27 26	21.6	16.9
23	6	23.2	26 11	20.2	2	7	24.1	27 3	21.0	1	7	25.1	27 55	8	17.0
24	7	4	26 41	4	3	7	4	27 32	3	2	8	4	28 24	22.1	1
25	7	7	27 10	7	4	8	7	28 2	6	3	9	7	28 53	4	2
26	17.8	24.0	27 41	21.0	15.5	9	25.0	28 32	9	4	9	26.0	29 24	7	3
27	8	3	28 11	3	6	9	3	29 3	22.2	16.5	20.0	3	29 54	23.0	4
28	9	7	28 43	7	8	19.0	7	29 34	5	6	1	7	♋ 0 25	3	17.5
29	18.0	25.0	29 15	22.0	9	1	26.0	♋ 0 6	8	8	1	27.0	0 57	6	6
30	0	3	29 47	3	16.0	1	3	0 38	23.1	9	2	3	1 29	9	8
31	1	6	♋ 0 20	6	1	2	6	1 11	4	17.0	20.3	6	2 2	24.3	9
32	2	26.0	0 54	9	3	3	27.0	1 45	8	1	4	28.0	2 36	6	18.0
33	3	3	1 29	23.3	4	19.3	4	2 20	24.1	3	4	4	3 10	9	1
34	18.3	7	2 5	6	16.5	4	8	2 55	4	4	5	8	3 45	25.2	3
35	4	27.1	2 41	24.0	7	5	28.2	3 32	8	17.5	20.6	29.2	4 21	6	4
36	5	5	3 19	3	8	6	6	4 9	25.1	7	7	6	4 58	9	18.5
37	6	28.0	3 57	7	9	19.7	29.0	4 46	5	8	8	♊	5 36	26.3	7
38	18.7	4	4 36	25.0	17.1	7	5	5 25	8	9	9	0.5	6 14	6	8
39	8	9	5 16	4	2	8	9	6 5	26.2	18.1	21.0	9	6 54	27.0	19.0
40	8	29.4	5 56	8	4	9	♊ 0.4	6 45	6	3	0	1.4	7 34	4	1
41	9	9	6 38	26.2	6	20.0	9	7 27	27.0	4	1	2.0	8 16	8	3
42	19.0	♊ 0.4	7 22	6	7	1	1.5	8 10	4	6	2	5	8 58	28.2	4
43	1	1.0	8 6	27.0	9	2	2.0	8 54	8	7	3	3.0	9 42	6	19.6
44	2	6	8 52	5	18.1	3	6	9 40	28.3	9	21.5	6	10 27	29.0	7
45	3	2.2	9 40	9	2	20.4	3.2	10 27	7	19.1	6	4.2	11 14	5	9
46	4	8	10 29	28.4	3	6	8	11 16	29.1	3	7	8	12 2	9	20.0
47	19.5	3.4	11 19	8	5	7	4.4	12 5	5	4	9	5.5	12 51	♌ 0.4	2
48	7	4.1	12 11	29.3	7	8	5.1	12 57	♌	6	22.0	6.2	13 42	8	4
49	8	9	13 5	8	9	21.0	8	13 49	0.5	8	1	9	14 35	1.3	6
50	9	5.6	14 0	♌ 0.3	19.1	1	6.6	14 44	1.0	9	3	7.7	15 29	8	8
51	20.1	6.4	14 57	8	3	3	7.4	15 41	5	20.1	5	8.5	16 24	2.3	21.0
52	2	7.3	15 56	1.4	5	4	8.3	16 40	2.1	3	7	9.4	17 22	8	2
53	4	8.3	16 57	2.0	8	6	9.3	17 40	7	6	9	10.4	18 22	3.4	4
54	6	9.3	18 1	6	20.0	8	10.4	18 43	3.3	8	23.0	11.4	19 24	4.0	6
55	8	10.4	19 6	3.2	2	22.0	11.5	19 47	9	21.0	2	12.5	20 28	6	8
56	21.0	11.7	20 15	8	5	2	12.8	20 55	4.5	3	5	13.7	21 35	5.2	22.1

	SID. T. H. M. S. 23 12 10 ARC 348° 2′.5 ♓ 17°					23 15 52 348° 58′.0 ♓ 18°					23 19 33 349° 53′.4 ♓ 19°					23 23 15 350° 48′.7 ♓ 20°					23 26 56 351° 44′.0 ♓ 21°					23 30 37 352° 39′.2 ♓ 22°				
H.	11	12	1	2	3	11	12	1	2	3	11	12	1	2	3	11	12	1	2	3	11	12	1	2	3	11	12	1	2	3
Lat.	♈	♉	♊	♋	♌	♈	♉	♊	♋	♌	♈	♉	♊	♋	♌	♈	♉	♋	♋	♌	♈	♉	♋	♋	♌	♈	♊	♋	♋	♌
°	°	°	° ′	°	°	°	°	° ′	°	°	°	°	° ′	°	°	°	°	° ′	°	°	°	°	° ′	°	°	°	°	° ′	°	°
22	20.7	25.8	28 17	22.4	17.7	21.8	26.8	29 8	23.2	18.6	22.8	27.7	29 59	24.1	19.5	23.8	28.7	0 50	24.9	20.4	24.9	29.6	1 40	25.7	21.3	25.9	0.6	2 31	26.5	22.2
23	8	26.1	28 46	7	9	8	27.1	29 37	5	7	9	28.0	♋ 0 28	3	6	9	29.0	1 18	25.2	5	9	9	2 8	26.0	4	26.0	9	2 59	8	3
24	8	4	29 15	23.0	18.0	9	4	♋ 0 6	8	9	9	3	0 56	6	7	24.0	3	1 47	4	6	25.0	♊ 0.2	2 37	3	5	0	1.2	3 27	27.1	4
25	9	7	29 44	2	1	22.0	7	0 35	24.1	19.0	23.0	6	1 26	9	9	0	6	2 16	7	7	1	5	3 6	5	6	1	5	3 56	4	5
26	21.0	27.0	♋ 0 14	5	2	0	28.0	1 5	4	1	1	9	1 55	25.2	20.0	1	9	2 46	26.0	9	2	9	3 36	8	7	2	8	4 26	6	22.6
27	0	3	0 45	8	3	1	3	1 35	7	2	2	29.3	2 26	5	1	2	♊ 0.2	3 16	3	21.0	3	1.2	4 6	27.1	8	26.3	2.1	4 56	9	7
28	1	6	1 16	24.1	4	2	6	2 6	25.0	3	2	6	2 56	8	2	24.3	5	3 46	6	1	25.3	5	4 36	4	22.0	4	5	5 26	28.2	8
29	2	28.0	1 48	4	18.5	22.3	9	2 38	3	4	23.3	9	3 28	26.1	3	4	9	4 18	9	2	4	8	5 7	7	1	5	8	5 57	5	9
30	3	3	2 20	8	6	3	29.3	3 10	6	19.5	4	♊ 0.2	4 0	4	4	5	1.2	4 49	27.2	3	5	2.2	5 39	28.0	2	6	3.1	6 28	8	23.1
31	21.4	6	2 52	25.1	8	4	6	3 43	9	7	5	6	4 32	7	20.5	6	6	5 22	5	4	6	5	6 11	3	3	26.7	5	7 0	29.1	2
32	4	29.0	3 26	4	9	5	♊	4 16	26.2	8	6	9	5 6	27.0	6	24.7	9	5 55	8	21.5	25.7	9	6 44	6	4	8	9	7 33	4	3
33	5	4	4 0	7	19.0	22.6	0.4	4 50	5	9	23.7	1.3	5 39	3	8	8	2.3	6 28	28.1	6	8	3.3	7 17	9	22.5	9	4.2	8 6	7	4
34	6	8	4 35	26.0	1	7	8	5 25	8	20.0	8	7	6 14	6	9	9	7	7 3	4	8	9	7	7 51	29.2	6	27.0	6	8 40	♌	23.5
35	21.7	♊ 0.2	5 11	4	3	8	1.2	6 0	27.2	1	9	2.1	6 49	28.0	21.0	25.0	3.1	7 38	8	9	26.0	4.1	8 26	6	8	1	5.1	9 15	0.4	6
36	8	6	5 47	7	4	9	6	6 36	5	3	24.0	6	7 25	3	1	1	5	8 13	29.1	22.0	1	5	9 2	9	9	2	5	9 50	7	7
37	9	1.0	6 25	27.1	19.5	23.0	2.0	7 13	9	4	1	3.0	8 2	7	3	2	4.0	8 50	4	1	2	5.0	9 39	♌ 0.2	23.0	3	9	10 26	1.0	9
38	9	4	7 3	4	7	1	4	7 51	28.2	20.5	2	4	8 40	29.0	4	3	4	9 28	8	3	4	4	10 15	6	1	27.4	6.4	11 3	4	24.0
39	22.0	9	7 42	8	8	2	9	8 30	6	7	3	9	9 18	4	21.5	4	9	10 6	♌ 0.2	4	26.5	9	10 53	9	3	6	9	11 41	7	1
40	1	2.4	8 22	28.2	20.0	3	3.4	9 10	29.0	8	4	4.4	9 58	7	7	25.5	5.4	10 45	5	22.5	6	6.4	11 32	1.3	4	7	7.4	12 19	2.1	3
41	2	3.0	9 3	6	1	4	4.0	9 51	4	21.0	24.5	5.0	10 38	♌ 0.1	8	6	9	11 26	9	7	7	9	12 12	7	23.5	8	9	12 59	5	4
42	3	5	9 46	29.0	3	23.6	5	10 33	8	1	7	5	11 20	5	22.0	7	6.4	12 7	1.3	8	9	7.5	12 53	2.1	7	28.0	8.5	13 39	8	24.5
43	22.5	4.0	10 29	4	4	7	5.0	11 17	♌ 0.2	3	8	6.0	12 3	9	1	8	7.0	12 49	7	23.0	27.0	8.1	13 35	5	8	1	9.0	14 21	3.2	7
44	6	6	11 14	8	6	8	6	12 1	6	4	9	6	12 47	1.3	3	9	6	13 33	2.1	1	1	7	14 19	9	24.0	3	6	15 4	6	8
45	7	5.2	12 0	♌ 0.3	8	9	6.2	12 46	1.0	21.6	25.0	7.2	13 32	8	5	26.1	8.2	14 18	5	3	2	9.3	15 3	3.3	1	4	10.2	15 48	4.0	25.0
46	9	9	12 47	7	21.0	24.0	9	13 33	5	8	2	9	14 19	2.2	22.6	3	8	15 4	3.0	5	4	9	15 48	7	3	28.5	9	16 33	5	1
47	23.0	6.6	13 36	1.2	1	2	7.5	14 22	9	9	3	8.6	15 7	6	7	5	9.5	15 51	4	23.6	27.6	10.6	16 35	4.1	4	7	11.6	17 20	9	2
48	1	7.2	14 26	6	2	4	8.2	15 12	2.3	22.0	5	9.3	15 56	3.0	9	7	10.2	16 40	8	8	8	11.3	17 23	5	24.5	9	12.3	18 8	5.3	3
49	3	9	15 18	2.0	4	5	9.0	16 3	8	2	6	10.0	16 47	5	23.1	8	9	17 30	4.2	9	9	12.0	18 13	5.0	7	29.1	13.0	18 57	7	25.5
50	5	8.7	16 12	5	6	6	7	16 56	3.3	4	8	7	17 39	4.0	3	27.0	11.7	18 22	7	24.1	28.1	7	19 5	5	9	3	7	19 48	6.2	7
51	7	9.5	17 8	3.0	8	8	10.5	17 51	8	6	26.0	11.5	18 33	5	5	2	12.5	19 16	5.2	3	4	13.5	19 58	6.0	25.1	5	14.5	20 40	7	9
52	9	10.4	18 5	5	22.0	25.1	11.4	18 47	4.3	8	3	12.4	19 29	5.0	7	4	13.4	20 11	7	4	6	14.4	20 53	5	3	8	15.4	21 34	7.2	26.1
53	24.1	11.4	19 5	4.1	2	3	12.4	19 46	8	23.0	5	13.4	20 27	5	8	7	14.4	21 8	6.2	6	8	15.4	21 50	7.0	5	♉	16.4	22 30	7	3
54	2	12.5	20 6	7	4	5	13.5	20 46	5.4	2	7	14.5	21 27	6.1	24.0	9	15.5	22 7	8	8	29.1	16.4	22 48	5	7	0.2	17.4	23 28	8.2	5
55	4	13.6	21 9	5.3	6	7	14.6	21 49	6.0	4	9	15.6	22 29	7	2	28.1	16.6	23 9	7.4	25.0	3	17.5	23 48	8.1	9	5	18.5	24 28	8	7
56	6	14.9	22 14	9	9	26.0	15.9	22 54	6	7	27.1	16.8	23 33	7.3	5	3	17.8	24 12	8.0	3	5	18.7	24 50	7	26.2	7	19.7	25 29	9.4	9

SID. T. 23 H. 30 M. 37 S. — ARC 352° 39′.2 — ♓ 22°

H.	11	12	1	2	3
Lat.	♈	♊	♋	♋	♌
°	°	°	° ′	°	°
22	25.9	0.6	2 31	26.5	22.2
23	26.0	9	2 59	8	3
24	0	1.2	3 27	27.1	4
25	1	5	3 56	4	5
26	2	8	4 26	6	22.6
27	26.3	2.1	4 56	9	7
28	4	5	5 26	28.2	8
29	5	8	5 57	5	9
30	6	3.1	6 28	8	23.1
31	26.7	5	7 0	29.1	2
32	8	9	7 33	4	3
33	9	4.2	8 6	7	4
34	27.0	6	8 40	♌	23.5
35	1	5.1	9 15	0.4	6
36	2	5	9 50	7	7
37	3	9	10 26	1.0	9
38	27.4	6.4	11 3	4	24.0
39	6	9	11 41	7	1
40	7	7.4	12 19	2.1	3
41	8	9	12 59	5	4
42	28.0	8.5	13 39	8	24.5
43	1	9.0	14 21	3.2	7
44	3	6	15 4	6	8
45	4	10.2	15 48	4.0	25.0
46	28.5	9	16 33	5	1
47	7	11.6	17 20	9	2
48	9	12.3	18 8	5.3	3
49	29.1	13.0	18 57	7	25.5
50	3	7	19 48	6.2	7
51	5	14.5	20 40	7	9
52	8	15.4	21 34	7.2	26.1
53	♉	16.4	22 30	7	3
54	0.2	17.4	23 28	8.2	5
55	5	18.5	24 28	8	7
56	7	19.7	25 29	9.4	9

23 H. 34 M. 18 S. — 353° 34′.4 — ♓ 23°

H.	11	12	1	2	3
Lat.	♈	♊	♋	♋	♌
°	°	°	° ′	°	°
22	26.9	1.5	3 20	27.4	23.1
23	27.0	8	3 49	6	2
24	1	2.1	4 17	9	3
25	2	4	4 46	28.2	4
26	3	7	5 15	5	5
27	27.3	3.1	5 45	7	23.6
28	4	4	6 15	29.0	7
29	5	7	6 46	3	8
30	6	4.1	7 17	6	9
31	27.7	4	7 49	9	24.0
32	8	8	8 22	♌ 0.2	2
33	9	5.2	8 55	5	3
34	28.0	6	9 28	8	4
35	1	6.0	10 3	1.2	24.5
36	3	5	10 38	5	6
37	4	9	11 13	8	7
38	28.5	7.4	11 50	2.2	9
39	6	9	12 28	5	25.0
40	8	8.4	13 6	8	1
41	9	9	13 45	3.1	2
42	29.1	9.4	14 26	5	4
43	2	10.0	15 7	9	25.5
44	4	6	15 50	4.3	7
45	5	11.2	16 33	7	8
46	7	9	17 18	5.1	26.0
47	9	12.5	18 4	5	1
48	♉	13.2	18 51	9	2
49	0.2	14.0	19 40	6.4	4
50	4	7	20 31	9	6
51	7	15.5	21 22	7.4	8
52	9	16.4	22 16	9	27.0
53	1.2	17.3	23 11	8.4	1
54	4	18.3	24 8	9	3
55	7	19.4	25 7	9.5	5
56	2.0	20.6	26 8	10.1	7

23 H. 37 M. 58 S. — 354° 29′.6 — ♓ 24°

H.	11	12	1	2	3
Lat.	♈	♊	♋	♋	♌
°	°	°	° ′	°	°
22	27.9	2.4	4 11	28.2	24.0
23	28.0	7	4 39	5	1
24	1	3.0	5 7	7	2
25	2	4	5 36	29.0	3
26	3	7	6 5	3	4
27	4	4.0	6 34	6	24.5
28	28.5	3	7 4	8	6
29	6	7	7 35	♌ 0.1	7
30	7	5.0	8 6	4	8
31	8	4	8 38	7	9
32	9	7	9 10	1.0	25.0
33	29.0	6.1	9 43	3	1
34	1	5	10 16	6	3
35	2	7.0	10 51	2.0	4
36	3	4	11 25	3	25.5
37	29.5	9	12 1	6	6
38	6	8.3	12 37	3.0	7
39	7	8	13 14	3	8
40	8	9.3	13 53	6	26.0
41	♉	8	14 32	4.0	1
42	0.1	10.4	15 12	4	2
43	3	9	15 53	7	4
44	4	11.5	16 35	5.1	26.5
45	6	12.2	17 18	5	7
46	8	8	18 2	9	8
47	1.0	13.5	18 48	6.3	9
48	2	14.2	19 35	7	27.1
49	4	9	20 23	7.1	2
50	6	15.6	21 13	6	4
51	8	16.4	22 4	8.1	6
52	2.0	17.3	22 57	6	8
53	2	18.3	23 52	9.1	28.0
54	5	19.3	24 48	6	1
55	8	20.4	25 46	10.1	3
56	3.2	21.6	26 46	7	5

23 H. 41 M. 39 S. — 355° 24′.7 — ♓ 25°

H.	11	12	1	2	3
Lat.	♈	♊	♋	♋	♌
°	°	°	° ′	°	°
22	28.9	3.4	5 1	29.0	24.9
23	29.0	7	5 29	3	25.0
24	1	4.0	5 57	5	1
25	2	3	6 25	8	2
26	3	6	6 54	♌ 0.1	3
27	4	5.0	7 24	4	4
28	29.5	3	7 54	6	25.5
29	6	6	8 24	9	6
30	7	6.0	8 55	1.2	7
31	8	3	9 26	5	8
32	9	7	9 59	8	9
33	♉	7.1	10 31	2.1	26.0
34	0.2	5	11 4	4	1
35	3	9	11 38	8	2
36	4	8.3	12 13	3.1	4
37	5	8	12 48	4	26.5
38	0.7	9.3	13 24	7	6
39	8	8	14 1	4.1	7
40	9	10.3	14 39	4	8
41	1.1	8	15 18	8	27.0
42	2	11.3	15 57	5.2	1
43	4	9	16 38	5	2
44	6	12.5	17 20	9	4
45	7	13.1	18 2	6.3	27.5
46	9	7	18 46	7	7
47	2.1	14.4	19 31	7.1	8
48	3	15.1	20 18	5	9
49	5	8	21 6	9	28.1
50	7	16.6	21 55	8.4	2
51	9	17.4	22 45	8	4
52	3.2	18.3	23 38	9.3	6
53	4	19.2	24 31	8	8
54	7	20.2	25 27	10.3	9
55	4.0	21.3	26 25	8	29.1
56	3	22.5	27 24	11.4	4

23 H. 45 M. 19 S. — 356° 19′.8 — ♓ 26°

H.	11	12	1	2	3
Lat.	♉	♊	♋	♋	♌
°	°	°	° ′	°	°
22	0.0	4.3	5 50	29.8	25.8
23	1	6	6 18	♌ 0.1	9
24	1	9	6 46	4	26.0
25	2	5.2	7 15	6	1
26	3	6	7 43	9	2
27	0.4	9	8 13	1.2	3
28	5	6.2	8 42	5	4
29	7	6	9 13	7	26.5
30	8	9	9 43	2.0	6
31	9	7.2	10 15	3	7
32	1.0	6	10 46	6	8
33	1	8.0	11 19	9	9
34	2	4	11 52	3.2	27.0
35	4	8	12 26	5	1
36	1.5	9.3	13 0	9	2
37	6	7	13 35	4.2	4
38	8	10.2	14 11	5	27.5
39	9	7	14 48	9	6
40	2.0	11.2	15 25	5.2	7
41	1	7	16 3	6	8
42	3	12.2	16 43	9	28.0
43	5	8	17 23	6.3	1
44	6	13.4	18 4	7	2
45	8	14.0	18 47	7.1	4
46	3.0	7	19 30	5	28.5
47	2	15.4	20 15	9	7
48	4	16.1	21 1	8.3	8
49	6	8	21 48	7	9
50	8	17.5	22 37	9.1	29.0
51	4.1	18.3	23 27	5	1
52	4	19.2	24 19	10.0	3
53	7	20.1	25 12	5	5
54	9	21.1	26 7	11.0	7
55	5.2	22.2	27 4	5	9
56	5	23.4	28 2	12.1	♍ 0.1

23 H. 48 M. 59 S. — 357° 14′.8 — ♓ 27°

H.	11	12	1	2	3
Lat.	♉	♊	♋	♌	♌
°	°	°	° ′	°	°
22	1.0	5.2	6 40	0.7	26.7
23	1	5	7 7	9	8
24	2	8	7 35	1.2	9
25	3	6.1	8 4	4	27.0
26	4	5	8 33	7	1
27	1.5	8	9 2	2.0	2
28	6	7.1	9 31	3	3
29	7	5	10 1	6	4
30	8	8	10 32	8	27.5
31	9	8.2	11 3	3.1	6
32	2.0	6	11 34	4	7
33	2	9.0	12 7	7	8
34	3	4	12 40	4.0	9
35	4	8	13 13	3	28.0
36	2.5	10.2	13 47	7	1
37	7	7	14 22	5.0	2
38	8	11.1	14 58	3	3
39	3.0	6	15 34	6	4
40	1	12.1	16 11	9	28.6
41	3	6	16 49	6.2	7
42	5	13.2	17 28	6	8
43	6	7	18 8	7.0	9
44	8	14.3	18 49	3	29.1
45	4.0	9	19 31	7	2
46	2	15.6	20 14	8.1	3
47	3	16.3	20 58	5	4
48	5	17.0	21 44	9	29.6
49	7	7	22 30	9.3	7
50	9	18.5	23 19	8	8
51	5.1	19.3	24 8	10.2	♍
52	4	20.2	24 59	7	0.1
53	7	21.1	25 52	11.2	3
54	6.0	22.1	26 46	7	5
55	3	23.1	27 42	12.2	7
56	6	24.3	28 40	7	9

	H. M. S.					H. M. S.					H. M. S.				
SID. T.	23 52 40				♓ 28°	23 56 20				♓ 29°	24 0 0				♈ 0°
ARC	358° 9′.9					359° 5′.0					360° 0′.0				
H.	11	12	1	2	3	11	12	1	2	3	11	12	1	2	3
Lat.	♉	♊	♋	♌	♌	♉	♊	♋	♌	♌	♉	♊	♋	♌	♌
°	°	°	° ′	°	°	°	°	° ′	°	°	°	°	° ′	°	°
22	2.0	6.1	7 29	1.5	27.6	3.0	7.0	8 19	2.3	28.5	4.0	7.9	9 8	3.2	29.4
23	1	4	7 57	8	7	1	3	8 46	6	6	1	8.2	9 35	4	5
24	2	7	8 25	2.0	8	2	6	9 14	8	7	2	6	10 3	7	6
25	3	7.1	8 53	3	9	3	8.0	9 42	3.1	8	3	9	10 31	9	7
26	4	4	9 22	5	28.0	4	3	10 10	4	9	4	9.2	10 59	4.2	29.8
27	2.5	7	9 51	8	1	3.5	6	10 39	6	29.0	4.5	6	11 27	5	8
28	6	8.1	10 20	3.1	2	6	9.0	11 9	9	0	6	9	11 56	7	9
29	7	4	10 50	4	3	7	3	11 38	4.2	1	7	10.2	12 26	5.0	♍
30	8	7	11 20	7	3	8	7	12 8	5	2	8	6	12 56	3	0.1
31	9	9.1	11 51	9	28.4	4.0	10.0	12 39	8	29.3	9	11.0	13 26	6	2
32	3.1	5	12 23	4.2	5	1	4	13 10	5.0	4	5.0	3	13 57	8	3
33	2	9	12 55	5	6	2	8	13 42	3	5	2	7	14 29	6.1	4
34	3	10.3	13 27	8	7	4	11.2	14 15	6	6	3	12.1	15 1	4	5
35	5	7	14 1	5.1	9	4.5	6	14 47	9	29.7	4	5	15 34	7	0.6
36	3.6	11.1	14 34	5	29.0	7	12.1	15 21	6.2	8	5.6	13.0	16 8	7.0	7
37	8	6	15 9	8	1	8	5	15 55	6	9	7	4	16 42	3	8
38	9	12.1	15 44	6.1	2	5.0	13.0	16 30	9	♍ 0.1	9	9	17 16	7	9
39	4.0	5	16 20	4	3	1	5	17 6	7.2	2	6.1	14.4	17 52	8.0	1.0
40	1	13.0	16 57	7	4	2	14.0	17 43	5	3	3	9	18 28	3	1
41	3	6	17 35	7.0	29.5	4	5	18 20	9	4	4	15.4	19 5	7	2
42	5	14.1	18 13	4	7	6	15.0	18 58	8.3	0.5	6	9	19 43	9.0	4
43	7	7	18 53	7	8	8	6	19 38	6	6	8	16.5	20 22	3	5
44	9	15.3	19 33	8.1	9	6.0	16.2	20 18	9.0	8	7.0	17.1	21 1	6	1.6
45	5.1	9	20 15	5	♍	2	8	20 59	4	9	2	7	21 42	10.0	7
46	2	16.5	20 57	9	0.1	4	17.4	21 41	7	1.0	5	18.3	22 24	4	8
47	4	17.2	21 41	9.3	2	5	18.1	22 24	10.1	1	7	19.0	23 7	8	9
48	6	9	22 26	7	4	7	8	23 8	5	2	9	7	23 51	11.2	2.1
49	8	18.6	23 12	10.1	5	9	19.5	23 54	9	4	8.1	20.4	24 36	6	2
50	6.0	19.4	24 0	5	7	7.1	20.3	24 41	11.3	1.5	3	21.2	25 22	12.0	3
51	3	20.2	24 49	9	9	4	21.1	25 30	7	7	6	22.0	26 10	4	4
52	6	21.1	25 39	11.4	1.1	7	22.0	26 20	12.1	9	9	9	26 59	8	6
53	9	22.0	26 31	9	2	8.0	9	27 11	6	2.0	9.2	23.8	27 50	13.3	8
54	7.2	23.0	27 25	12.4	4	3	23.9	28 4	13.1	1	5	24.8	28 43	8	3.0
55	5	24.0	28 20	9	5	6	24.9	28 59	6	3	8	25.8	29 37	14.3	1
56	8	25.1	29 18	13.4	7	9	26.0	29 55	14.1	5	10.1	27.0	♌ 0 32	8	3

NOTE:

As Mr. Dalton wrote in his introductory remarks, he did not include calculations beyond 56° N. Latitude as he did not think there would be need for such. However, he had second thoughts about this when he wrote a Postscript in 1903 (see page 5) when he gave instructions and formula for finding positions, both for northern latitudes, as well as for latitudes from the Equator to 22° Latitude.

The publishers of *Raphael's Tables of Houses* have been kind enough to allow us to include with this book, tables for 57° to 59° N which follow on the next pages.

TABLES OF HOUSES FOR Latitude 57° 9′ N.

H.	M.	S.	10 ♈ °	11 ♉ °	12 ♊ °	Ascen ♌ °	′	2 ♌ °	3 ♍ °
0	0	0	0	11	28	1	39	16	4
0	3	40	1	12	29	2	15	16	5
0	7	20	2	13	♋	2	52	17	5
0	11	1	3	15	1	3	28	18	6
0	14	41	4	16	1	4	5	18	7
0	18	21	5	17	2	4	41	19	8
0	22	2	6	18	3	5	17	20	9
0	25	42	7	19	4	5	53	20	9
0	29	23	8	20	5	6	29	21	10
0	33	4	9	21	5	7	6	22	11
0	36	45	10	22	6	7	42	22	12
0	40	27	11	23	7	8	18	23	13
0	44	8	12	24	8	8	54	24	13
0	47	50	13	25	9	9	30	24	14
0	51	32	14	26	9	10	6	25	15
0	55	14	15	28	10	10	42	26	16
0	58	57	16	29	11	11	18	27	17
1	2	40	17	♊	12	11	54	27	17
1	6	24	18	1	12	12	31	28	18
1	10	7	19	2	13	13	7	29	19
1	13	51	20	3	14	13	43	29	20
1	17	36	21	4	15	14	19	♍	21
1	21	21	22	5	16	14	55	1	22
1	25	6	23	6	16	15	32	1	22
1	28	52	24	7	17	16	8	2	23
1	32	38	25	8	18	16	45	3	24
1	36	25	26	9	19	17	21	3	25
1	40	13	27	10	19	17	58	4	26
1	44	1	28	11	20	18	34	5	26
1	47	49	29	12	21	19	11	5	27
1	51	38	30	13	22	19	48	6	28

H.	M.	S.	10 ♉ °	11 ♊ °	12 ♋ °	Ascen ♌ °	′	2 ♍ °	3 ♍ °
1	51	38	0	13	22	19	48	6	28
1	55	28	1	14	22	20	25	7	29
1	59	18	2	14	23	21	2	8	♎
2	3	8	3	15	24	21	39	8	1
2	7	0	4	16	25	22	16	9	2
2	10	52	5	17	25	22	54	10	2
2	14	44	6	18	26	23	31	10	3
2	18	37	7	19	27	24	8	11	4
2	22	31	8	20	27	24	46	12	5
2	26	26	9	21	28	25	24	13	6
2	30	21	10	22	29	26	2	13	7
2	34	17	11	23	30	26	39	14	8
2	38	14	12	24	♌	27	18	15	8
2	42	11	13	25	1	27	56	16	9
2	46	9	14	26	2	28	34	16	10
2	50	9	15	27	3	29	12	17	11
2	54	7	16	28	3	29	51	18	12
2	58	8	17	29	4	0 ♍	30	19	13
3	2	8	18	30	5	1	9	19	14
3	6	10	19	♋	6	1	47	20	15
3	10	12	20	1	6	2	27	21	15
3	14	16	21	2	7	3	6	22	16
3	18	19	22	3	8	3	45	22	17
3	22	24	23	4	9	4	24	23	18
3	26	29	24	5	9	5	4	24	19
3	30	35	25	6	10	5	44	25	20
3	34	42	26	7	11	6	24	25	21
3	38	49	27	8	12	7	4	26	22
3	42	57	28	9	13	7	44	27	23
3	47	6	29	10	13	8	24	28	23
3	51	16	30	11	14	9	4	29	24

H.	M.	S.	10 ♊ °	11 ♋ °	12 ♌ °	Ascen ♍ °	′	2 ♍ °	3 ♎ °
3	51	16	0	11	14	9	4	28	24
3	55	26	1	11	15	9	45	29	25
3	59	37	2	12	16	10	25	♎	26
4	3	48	3	13	16	11	6	1	27
4	8	1	4	14	17	11	47	1	28
4	12	13	5	15	18	12	28	2	29
4	16	27	6	16	19	13	9	3	♏
4	20	41	7	17	19	13	50	4	1
4	24	55	8	18	20	14	32	5	2
4	29	11	9	19	21	15	13	5	3
4	33	26	10	20	22	15	55	6	3
4	37	42	11	21	23	16	36	7	4
4	41	59	12	22	23	17	18	8	5
4	46	17	13	22	24	18	0	9	6
4	50	34	14	23	25	18	42	9	7
4	54	52	15	24	26	19	24	10	8
4	59	11	16	25	27	20	6	11	9
5	3	30	17	26	27	20	48	12	10
5	7	49	18	27	28	21	30	13	11
5	12	9	19	28	29	22	12	13	12
5	16	29	20	29	♍	22	55	14	13
5	20	49	21	♌	1	23	37	15	14
5	25	10	22	1	1	24	19	16	14
5	29	30	23	2	2	25	2	17	15
5	33	51	24	3	3	25	44	17	16
5	38	13	25	3	4	26	27	18	17
5	42	34	26	4	5	27	9	19	18
5	46	55	27	5	5	27	52	20	19
5	51	17	28	6	6	28	35	21	20
5	55	38	29	7	7	29	17	21	21
6	0	0	30	8	8	30	0	22	22

H.	M.	S.	10 ♋ °	11 ♌ °	12 ♍ °	Ascen ♎ °	′	2 ♎ °	3 ♏ °
6	0	0	0	8	8	0	0	22	22
6	4	22	1	9	9	0	43	23	23
6	8	43	2	10	9	1	25	24	24
6	13	5	3	11	10	2	8	25	25
6	17	26	4	12	11	2	51	25	26
6	21	47	5	13	12	3	33	26	27
6	26	9	6	14	13	4	16	27	27
6	30	30	7	15	13	4	58	28	28
6	34	50	8	16	14	5	41	29	29
6	39	11	9	16	15	6	23	29	♐
6	43	31	10	17	16	7	5	♏	1
6	47	51	11	18	17	7	48	1	2
6	52	11	12	19	17	8	30	2	3
6	56	30	13	20	18	9	12	3	4
7	0	49	14	21	19	9	54	3	5
7	5	8	15	22	20	10	36	4	6
7	9	26	16	23	21	11	18	5	7
7	13	43	17	24	21	12	0	6	8
7	18	1	18	25	22	12	42	7	8
7	22	18	19	26	23	13	24	7	9
7	26	34	20	27	24	14	5	8	10
7	30	49	21	27	25	14	47	9	11
7	35	5	22	28	25	15	28	10	12
7	39	19	23	29	26	16	10	11	13
7	43	33	24	♍	27	16	51	11	14
7	47	47	25	1	28	17	32	12	15
7	51	59	26	2	28	18	13	13	16
7	56	12	27	3	29	18	54	14	17
8	0	23	28	4	♎	19	35	14	18
8	4	34	29	5	1	20	15	15	19
8	8	44	30	6	2	20	56	16	19

H.	M.	S.	10 ♌ °	11 ♍ °	12 ♎ °	Ascen ♎ °	′	2 ♏ °	3 ♐ °
8	8	44	0	6	2	20	56	16	19
8	12	54	1	7	2	21	36	17	20
8	17	3	2	7	3	22	16	17	21
8	21	11	3	8	4	22	56	18	22
8	25	19	4	9	5	23	36	19	23
8	29	25	5	10	5	24	16	20	24
8	33	31	6	11	6	24	56	21	25
8	37	36	7	12	7	25	36	21	26
8	41	41	8	13	8	26	15	22	27
8	45	44	9	14	8	26	54	23	28
8	49	48	10	15	9	27	33	24	29
8	53	50	11	15	10	28	13	24	30
8	57	52	12	16	11	28	52	25	♑
9	1	52	13	17	12	29	30	26	1
9	5	53	14	18	12	0 ♏	9	27	2
9	9	51	15	19	13	0	48	27	3
9	13	51	16	20	14	1	26	28	4
9	17	49	17	21	15	2	4	29	5
9	21	46	18	22	15	2	42	30	6
9	25	43	19	22	16	3	21	♐	7
9	29	39	20	23	17	3	58	1	8
9	33	34	21	24	17	4	36	2	9
9	37	29	22	25	18	5	14	3	10
9	41	23	23	26	19	5	52	3	11
9	45	16	24	27	20	6	29	4	12
9	49	8	25	28	20	7	6	5	13
9	53	0	26	28	21	7	44	5	14
9	56	52	27	29	22	8	21	6	15
10	0	42	28	♎	22	8	58	7	16
10	4	32	29	1	23	9	35	8	16
10	8	22	30	2	24	10	12	8	17

H.	M.	S.	10 ♍ °	11 ♎ °	12 ♎ °	Ascen ♏ °	′	2 ♐ °	3 ♑ °
10	8	22	0	2	24	10	12	8	17
10	12	11	1	3	25	10	49	9	18
10	15	59	2	4	25	11	26	10	19
10	19	47	3	4	26	12	2	11	20
10	23	35	4	5	27	12	39	11	21
10	27	22	5	6	27	13	15	12	22
10	31	8	6	7	28	13	52	13	23
10	34	54	7	8	29	14	28	14	24
10	38	39	8	9	29	15	5	14	25
10	42	24	9	9	♏	15	41	15	26
10	46	9	10	10	1	16	17	16	27
10	49	53	11	11	1	16	53	17	28
10	53	36	12	12	2	17	29	18	29
10	57	20	13	13	3	18	6	18	♒
11	1	3	14	13	4	18	42	19	1
11	4	46	15	14	4	19	18	20	2
11	8	28	16	15	5	19	54	21	4
11	12	10	17	16	6	20	30	21	5
11	15	52	18	17	7	21	6	22	6
11	19	33	19	17	7	21	42	23	7
11	23	15	20	18	8	22	18	24	8
11	26	56	21	19	9	22	54	25	9
11	30	37	22	20	9	23	31	25	10
11	34	18	23	21	10	24	7	26	11
11	37	58	24	21	10	24	43	27	12
11	41	39	25	22	11	25	19	28	13
11	45	19	26	23	12	25	55	29	14
11	48	59	27	24	12	26	32	30	15
11	52	40	28	25	13	27	8	♑	17
11	56	20	29	25	14	27	45	1	18
12	0	0	30	26	14	28	21	2	19

TABLES OF HOUSES FOR Latitude 57° 9′ N.

H.	M.	S.	10 ♎ °	11 ♎ °	12 ♏ °	Ascen ♏ °	′	2 ♑ °	3 ♒ °
12	0	0	0	26	14	28	21	2	19
12	3	40	1	27	15	28	58	3	20
12	7	20	2	28	16	29	35	4	21
12	11	1	3	29	16	0 ♐	11	5	22
12	14	41	4	29	17	0	48	6	24
12	18	21	5	♏	18	1	25	6	25
12	22	2	6	1	18	2	3	7	26
12	25	42	7	2	19	2	40	8	27
12	29	23	8	3	20	3	17	9	28
12	33	4	9	3	20	3	55	10	♓
12	36	45	10	4	21	4	33	11	1
12	40	27	11	5	22	5	11	12	2
12	44	8	12	6	23	5	49	13	3
12	47	50	13	7	23	6	27	14	5
12	51	32	14	7	24	7	6	15	6
12	55	14	15	8	25	7	45	16	7
12	58	57	16	9	25	8	24	17	8
13	2	40	17	10	26	9	3	18	10
13	6	24	18	10	27	9	43	19	11
13	10	7	19	11	27	10	23	20	12
13	13	51	20	12	28	11	3	21	14
13	17	36	21	13	29	11	42	22	15
13	21	21	22	14	29	12	24	23	16
13	25	6	23	14	♐	13	5	25	18
13	28	52	24	15	1	13	46	26	19
13	32	38	25	16	2	14	28	27	20
13	36	25	26	17	2	15	10	28	22
13	40	13	27	18	3	15	53	♒	23
13	44	1	28	18	4	16	36	1	24
13	47	49	29	19	4	17	19	2	26
13	51	38	30	20	5	18	4	3	27

H.	M.	S.	10 ♏ °	11 ♏ °	12 ♐ °	Ascen ♐ °	′	2 ♒ °	3 ♓ °
13	51	38	0	20	5	18	4	3	27
13	55	28	1	21	6	18	48	5	28
13	59	18	2	22	7	19	33	6	♈
14	3	8	3	23	7	20	18	7	1
14	7	0	4	23	8	21	4	9	3
14	10	52	5	24	9	21	51	10	4
14	14	44	6	25	10	22	38	12	5
14	18	37	7	26	10	23	26	13	7
14	22	31	8	27	11	24	15	15	8
14	26	26	9	27	12	25	4	16	9
14	30	21	10	28	13	25	54	18	11
14	34	17	11	29	14	26	45	19	12
14	38	14	12	♐	14	27	37	21	14
14	42	11	13	1	15	28	30	23	15
14	46	9	14	2	16	29	23	24	16
14	50	9	15	3	17	0 ♑	18	26	18
14	54	7	16	3	18	1	13	28	19
14	58	8	17	4	18	2	10	♓	21
15	2	8	18	5	19	3	8	2	22
15	6	10	19	6	20	4	7	3	23
15	10	12	20	7	21	5	8	5	24
15	14	16	21	8	22	6	10	7	26
15	18	19	22	9	23	7	13	9	28
15	22	24	23	9	24	8	18	11	29
15	26	29	24	10	24	9	24	13	♉
15	30	35	25	11	25	10	32	15	2
15	34	42	26	12	26	11	43	17	3
15	38	49	27	13	27	12	55	19	4
15	42	57	28	14	28	14	9	21	6
15	47	6	29	15	29	15	25	23	7
15	51	16	30	16	30	16	44	26	8

H.	M.	S.	10 ♐ °	11 ♐ °	12 ♑ °	Ascen ♑ °	′	2 ♓ °	3 ♉ °
15	51	16	0	16	0	16	44	26	8
15	55	26	1	17	1	18	5	28	10
15	59	37	2	17	2	19	29	♈	11
16	3	48	3	18	3	20	55	2	13
16	8	1	4	19	4	22	26	4	14
16	12	13	5	20	5	23	58	6	15
16	16	27	6	21	6	25	35	8	16
16	20	41	7	22	7	27	15	10	18
16	24	55	8	23	8	28	59	13	19
16	29	11	9	24	9	0 ♒	47	15	20
16	33	26	10	25	10	2	40	17	21
16	37	42	11	26	11	4	37	19	23
16	41	59	12	27	12	6	39	21	24
16	46	17	13	28	14	8	47	23	25
16	50	34	14	29	15	11	0	25	26
16	54	52	15	♑	16	13	18	27	27
16	59	11	16	1	17	15	43	29	29
17	3	30	17	2	18	18	14	♉	♊
17	7	49	18	3	20	20	52	3	1
17	12	9	19	4	21	23	36	5	2
17	16	29	20	5	22	26	27	7	3
17	20	49	21	6	23	29	24	9	5
17	25	10	22	7	25	2 ♓	28	10	6
17	29	30	23	8	26	5	38	12	7
17	33	51	24	9	27	8	54	14	8
17	38	13	25	10	29	12	16	16	9
17	42	34	26	11	♒	15	43	17	10
17	46	55	27	12	2	19	13	19	11
17	51	17	28	13	3	22	47	21	12
17	55	38	29	14	5	26	23	22	14
18	0	0	30	15	6	30	0	24	15

H.	M.	S.	10 ♑ °	11 ♑ °	12 ♒ °	Ascen ♈ °	′	2 ♉ °	3 ♊ °
18	0	0	0	15	6	0	0	24	15
18	4	22	1	16	8	3	37	25	16
18	8	43	2	17	9	7	13	27	17
18	13	5	3	19	11	10	47	28	18
18	17	26	4	20	13	14	17	♊	19
18	21	47	5	21	14	17	44	1	20
18	26	9	6	22	16	21	6	3	21
18	30	30	7	23	18	24	22	4	22
18	34	50	8	24	20	27	32	5	23
18	39	11	9	25	21	0 ♉	36	7	24
18	43	31	10	27	23	3	33	8	25
18	47	51	11	28	25	6	24	9	26
18	52	11	12	29	27	9	8	10	27
18	56	30	13	♒	29	11	46	12	28
19	0	49	14	1	♓	14	17	13	29
19	5	8	15	3	3	16	42	14	♋
19	9	26	16	4	5	19	0	15	1
19	13	43	17	5	7	21	13	16	2
19	18	1	18	6	9	23	21	18	3
19	22	18	19	7	11	25	23	19	4
19	26	34	20	9	13	27	20	20	5
19	30	49	21	10	15	29	13	21	6
19	35	5	22	11	17	1 ♊	1	22	7
19	39	19	23	12	19	2	45	23	8
19	43	33	24	14	22	4	25	24	9
19	47	47	25	15	24	6	2	25	10
19	51	59	26	16	26	7	34	26	11
19	56	12	27	18	28	9	5	27	12
20	0	23	28	19	♈	10	31	28	13
20	4	34	29	20	2	11	55	29	13
20	8	44	30	22	4	13	16	30	14

H.	M.	S.	10 ♒ °	11 ♒ °	12 ♈ °	Ascen ♊ °	′	2 ♋ °	3 ♋ °
20	8	44	0	22	4	13	16	0	14
20	12	54	1	23	7	14	35	1	15
20	17	3	2	24	9	15	51	2	16
20	21	11	3	26	11	17	5	3	17
20	25	18	4	27	13	18	17	4	18
20	29	25	5	28	15	19	28	5	19
20	33	31	6	♓	17	20	36	6	20
20	37	36	7	1	19	21	42	6	21
20	41	41	8	2	21	22	47	7	21
20	45	44	9	4	23	23	50	8	22
20	49	48	10	5	25	24	52	9	23
20	53	50	11	7	27	25	53	10	24
20	57	52	12	8	28	26	52	11	25
21	1	52	13	9	♉	27	50	12	26
21	5	53	14	11	2	28	47	12	27
21	9	51	15	12	4	29	42	13	27
21	13	51	16	14	6	0 ♋	37	14	28
21	17	49	17	15	7	1	30	15	29
21	21	46	18	16	9	2	23	16	♌
21	25	43	19	18	11	3	15	16	1
21	29	39	20	19	12	4	6	17	2
21	33	34	21	21	14	4	56	18	3
21	37	29	22	22	15	5	45	19	3
21	41	23	23	23	17	6	34	20	4
21	45	16	24	25	18	7	22	20	5
21	49	8	25	26	20	8	9	21	6
21	53	0	26	27	21	8	56	22	7
21	56	52	27	29	23	9	42	23	7
22	0	42	28	♈	24	10	27	23	8
22	4	32	29	2	25	11	12	24	9
22	8	22	30	3	27	11	57	25	10

H.	M.	S.	10 ♓ °	11 ♈ °	12 ♉ °	Ascen ♋ °	′	2 ♋ °	3 ♌ °
22	8	22	0	3	27	11	57	25	10
22	12	11	1	4	28	12	41	26	11
22	15	59	2	6	29	13	24	26	12
22	19	47	3	7	♊	14	7	27	12
22	23	35	4	8	2	14	50	28	13
22	27	22	5	10	3	15	32	28	14
22	31	8	6	11	4	16	14	29	15
22	34	54	7	12	5	16	55	♌	16
22	38	39	8	14	6	17	36	1	16
22	42	24	9	15	8	18	17	1	17
22	46	9	10	16	9	18	57	2	18
22	49	53	11	18	10	19	37	3	19
22	53	36	12	19	11	20	17	4	20
22	57	20	13	20	12	20	57	4	20
23	1	3	14	22	13	21	36	5	21
23	4	46	15	23	14	22	15	6	22
23	8	28	16	24	15	22	54	6	23
23	12	10	17	25	16	23	33	7	23
23	15	52	18	27	17	24	11	8	24
23	19	33	19	28	18	24	49	8	25
23	23	15	20	29	19	25	27	9	26
23	26	56	21	♉	20	26	5	10	27
23	30	37	22	2	21	26	43	10	27
23	34	18	23	3	22	27	20	11	28
23	37	58	24	4	23	27	57	12	29
23	41	39	25	5	24	28	35	12	♍
23	45	19	26	6	24	29	12	13	1
23	48	59	27	8	25	0 ♌	11	14	1
23	52	40	28	9	26	0	25	14	2
23	56	20	29	10	27	1	2	15	3
24	0	0	30	11	28	1	39	16	4

Sidereal Time.			10	11	12	Ascen		2	3
			♈	♉	♊	♌		♌	♍
H.	M.	S.	°	°	°	°	′	°	°
0	0	0	0	11	28	1	58	16	4
0	3	40	1	12	29	2	35	16	5
0	7	20	2	13	♋	3	11	17	5
0	11	1	3	15	1	3	47	18	6
0	14	41	4	16	1	4	23	18	7
0	18	21	5	17	2	4	59	19	8
0	22	2	6	18	3	5	35	20	9
0	25	42	7	19	4	6	11	20	9
0	29	23	8	20	5	6	47	21	10
0	33	4	9	21	5	7	23	22	11
0	36	45	10	22	6	7	59	22	12
0	40	27	11	23	7	8	35	23	13
0	44	8	12	24	8	9	11	24	13
0	47	50	13	25	9	9	47	24	14
0	51	32	14	26	9	10	22	25	15
0	55	14	15	28	10	10	58	26	16
0	58	57	16	29	11	11	34	27	17
1	2	40	17	♊	12	12	10	27	17
1	6	24	18	1	12	12	46	28	18
1	10	7	19	2	13	13	22	29	19
1	13	51	20	3	14	13	58	29	20
1	17	36	21	4	15	14	34	♍	21
1	21	21	22	5	16	15	10	1	22
1	25	6	23	6	16	15	46	1	22
1	28	52	24	7	17	16	22	2	23
1	32	38	25	8	18	16	59	3	24
1	36	25	26	9	19	17	35	3	25
1	40	13	27	10	19	18	11	4	26
1	44	1	28	11	20	18	48	5	26
1	47	49	29	12	21	19	24	5	27
1	51	38	30	13	22	20	1	6	28

Sidereal Time.			10	11	12	Ascen		2	3
			♉	♊	♋	♌		♍	♍
H.	M.	S.	°	°	°	°	′	°	°
1	51	38	0	13	22	20	1	6	28
1	55	28	1	14	22	20	38	7	29
1	59	18	2	14	23	21	14	8	♎
2	3	8	3	15	24	21	51	8	1
2	7	0	4	16	25	22	28	9	2
2	10	52	5	17	25	23	5	10	2
2	14	44	6	18	26	23	42	10	3
2	18	37	7	19	27	24	20	11	4
2	22	31	8	20	27	24	57	12	5
2	26	26	9	21	28	25	35	13	6
2	30	21	10	22	29	26	12	13	7
2	34	17	11	23	30	26	50	14	8
2	38	14	12	24	♌	27	28	15	8
2	42	11	13	25	1	28	6	16	9
2	46	9	14	26	2	28	44	16	10
2	50	9	15	27	3	29	22	17	11
2	54	7	16	28	3	0 ♍	0	18	12
2	58	8	17	29	4	0	39	19	13
3	2	8	18	30	5	1	18	19	14
3	6	10	19	♋	6	1	56	20	15
3	10	12	20	1	6	2	35	21	15
3	14	16	21	2	7	3	14	22	16
3	18	19	22	3	8	3	53	22	17
3	22	24	23	4	9	4	32	23	18
3	26	29	24	5	9	5	12	24	19
3	30	35	25	6	10	5	51	25	20
3	34	42	26	7	11	6	31	25	21
3	38	49	27	8	12	7	11	26	22
3	42	57	28	9	13	7	51	27	23
3	47	6	29	10	13	8	31	28	23
3	51	16	30	11	14	9	11	28	24

Sidereal Time.			10	11	12	Ascen		2	3
			♊	♋	♌	♍		♍	♎
H.	M.	S.	°	°	°	°	′	°	°
3	51	16	0	11	14	9	11	28	24
3	55	26	1	11	15	9	51	29	25
3	59	37	2	12	16	10	32	♎	26
4	3	48	3	13	16	11	12	1	27
4	8	1	4	14	17	11	53	1	28
4	12	13	5	15	18	12	33	2	29
4	16	27	6	16	19	13	14	3	♏
4	20	41	7	17	19	13	55	4	1
4	24	55	8	18	20	14	36	5	2
4	29	11	9	19	21	15	18	5	3
4	33	26	10	20	22	15	59	6	3
4	37	42	11	21	23	16	40	7	4
4	41	59	12	22	23	17	22	8	5
4	46	17	13	22	24	18	3	9	6
4	50	34	14	23	25	18	45	9	7
4	54	52	15	24	26	19	27	10	8
4	59	11	16	25	27	20	9	11	9
5	3	30	17	26	27	20	51	12	10
5	7	49	18	27	28	21	33	13	11
5	12	9	19	28	29	22	15	13	12
5	16	29	20	29	♍	22	57	14	13
5	20	49	21	♌	1	23	39	15	14
5	25	10	22	1	1	24	21	16	14
5	29	30	23	2	2	25	3	17	15
5	33	51	24	3	3	25	46	17	16
5	38	13	25	3	4	26	28	18	17
5	42	34	26	4	5	27	10	19	18
5	46	55	27	5	5	27	53	20	19
5	51	17	28	6	6	28	35	21	20
5	55	38	29	7	7	29	18	21	21
6	0	0	30	8	8	30	0	22	22

Sidereal Time.			10	11	12	Ascen		2	3
			♋	♌	♍	♎		♎	♏
H.	M.	S.	°	°	°	°	′	°	°
6	0	0	0	8	8	0	0	22	22
6	4	22	1	9	9	0	42	23	23
6	8	43	2	10	9	1	25	24	24
6	13	5	3	11	10	2	7	25	25
6	17	26	4	12	11	2	50	25	26
6	21	47	5	13	12	3	32	26	27
6	26	9	6	14	13	4	14	27	27
6	30	30	7	15	13	4	57	28	28
6	34	50	8	16	14	5	39	29	29
6	39	11	9	16	15	6	21	29	♐
6	43	31	10	17	16	7	3	♏	1
6	47	51	11	18	17	7	45	1	2
6	52	11	12	19	17	8	27	2	3
6	56	30	13	20	18	9	9	3	4
7	0	49	14	21	19	9	51	3	5
7	5	8	15	22	20	10	33	4	6
7	9	26	16	23	21	11	15	5	7
7	13	43	17	24	21	11	57	6	8
7	18	1	18	25	22	12	38	7	8
7	22	18	19	26	23	13	20	7	9
7	26	34	20	27	24	14	1	8	10
7	30	49	21	27	25	14	42	9	11
7	35	5	22	28	25	15	24	10	12
7	39	19	23	29	26	16	5	11	13
7	43	33	24	♍	27	16	46	11	14
7	47	47	25	1	28	17	27	12	15
7	51	59	26	2	28	18	7	13	16
7	56	12	27	3	29	18	48	14	17
8	0	23	28	4	♎	19	28	14	18
8	4	34	29	5	1	20	9	15	19
8	8	44	30	6	2	20	49	16	19

Sidereal Time.			10	11	12	Ascen		2	3
			♌	♍	♎	♎		♏	♐
H.	M.	S.	°	°	°	°	′	°	°
8	8	44	0	6	2	20	49	16	19
8	12	54	1	7	2	21	29	17	20
8	17	3	2	7	3	22	9	17	21
8	21	11	3	8	4	22	49	18	22
8	25	19	4	9	5	23	29	19	23
8	29	25	5	10	5	24	9	20	24
8	33	31	6	11	6	24	48	21	25
8	37	36	7	12	7	25	28	21	26
8	41	41	8	13	8	26	7	22	27
8	45	44	9	14	8	26	46	23	28
8	49	48	10	15	9	27	25	24	29
8	53	50	11	15	10	28	4	24	30
8	57	52	12	16	11	28	42	25	♑
9	1	52	13	17	12	29	21	26	1
9	5	53	14	18	12	0 ♏	0	27	2
9	9	51	15	19	13	0	38	27	3
9	13	51	16	20	14	1	16	28	4
9	17	49	17	21	15	1	54	29	5
9	21	46	18	22	15	2	32	30	6
9	25	43	19	22	16	3	10	♐	7
9	29	39	20	23	17	3	48	1	8
9	33	34	21	24	17	4	25	2	9
9	37	29	22	25	18	5	3	3	10
9	41	23	23	26	19	5	40	3	11
9	45	16	24	27	20	6	18	4	12
9	49	8	25	28	20	6	55	5	13
9	53	0	26	28	21	7	32	5	14
9	56	52	27	29	22	8	9	6	15
10	0	42	28	♎	22	8	46	7	16
10	4	32	29	1	23	9	22	8	16
10	8	22	30	2	24	9	59	8	17

Sidereal Time.			10	11	12	Ascen		2	3
			♍	♎	♎	♏		♐	♑
H.	M.	S.	°	°	°	°	′	°	°
10	8	22	0	2	24	9	59	8	17
10	12	11	1	3	25	10	36	9	18
10	15	59	2	4	25	11	12	10	19
10	19	47	3	4	26	11	49	11	20
10	23	35	4	5	27	12	25	11	21
10	27	22	5	6	27	13	1	12	22
10	31	8	6	7	28	13	38	13	23
10	34	54	7	8	29	14	14	14	24
10	38	39	8	9	29	14	50	14	25
10	42	24	9	9	♏	15	26	15	26
10	46	9	10	10	1	16	2	16	27
10	49	53	11	11	1	16	38	17	28
10	53	36	12	12	2	17	14	18	29
10	57	20	13	13	3	17	50	18	♒
11	1	3	14	13	4	18	26	19	1
11	4	46	15	14	4	19	2	20	2
11	8	28	16	15	5	19	38	21	4
11	12	10	17	16	6	20	13	21	5
11	15	52	18	17	7	20	49	22	6
11	19	33	19	17	7	21	25	23	7
11	23	15	20	18	8	22	1	24	8
11	26	56	21	19	9	22	37	25	9
11	30	37	22	20	9	23	13	25	10
11	34	18	23	21	10	23	49	26	11
11	37	58	24	21	10	24	25	27	12
11	41	39	25	22	11	25	1	28	13
11	45	19	26	23	12	25	37	29	14
11	48	59	27	24	12	26	13	30	15
11	52	40	28	25	13	26	49	♑	17
11	56	20	29	25	14	27	25	1	18
12	0	0	30	26	14	28	2	2	19

Sidereal Time.			10	11	12	Ascen		2	3
			♎	♎	♏	♏		♑	♒
H.	M.	S.	°	°	°	°	′	°	°
12	0	0	0	26	14	28	2	2	19
12	3	40	1	27	15	28	38	3	20
12	7	20	2	28	16	29	14	4	21
12	11	1	3	29	16	29	51	5	22
12	14	41	4	29	17	0 ♐	28	6	24
12	18	21	5	♏	18	1	4	6	25
12	22	2	6	1	18	1	41	7	26
12	25	42	7	2	19	2	18	8	27
12	29	23	8	3	20	2	56	9	28
12	33	4	9	3	20	3	33	10	♓
12	36	45	10	4	21	4	11	11	1
12	40	27	11	5	22	4	48	12	2
12	44	8	12	6	23	5	26	13	3
12	47	50	13	7	23	6	4	14	5
12	51	32	14	7	24	6	42	15	6
12	55	14	15	8	25	7	21	16	7
12	58	57	16	9	25	8	0	17	8
13	2	40	17	10	26	8	39	18	10
13	6	24	18	10	27	9	18	19	11
13	10	7	19	11	27	9	57	20	12
13	13	51	20	12	28	10	37	21	14
13	17	36	21	13	29	11	17	22	15
13	21	21	22	14	29	11	57	23	16
13	25	6	23	14	♐	12	38	25	18
13	28	52	24	15	1	13	19	26	19
13	32	38	25	16	2	14	1	27	20
13	36	25	26	17	2	14	43	28	22
13	40	13	27	18	3	15	25	♒	23
13	44	1	28	18	4	16	7	1	24
13	47	49	29	19	4	16	50	2	26
13	51	38	30	20	5	17	34	3	27

Sidereal Time.			10	11	12	Ascen		2	3
			♏	♏	♐	♐		♒	♓
H.	M.	S.	°	°	°	°	′	°	°
13	51	38	0	20	5	17	34	3	27
13	55	28	1	21	6	18	18	5	28
13	59	18	2	22	7	19	2	6	♈
14	3	8	3	23	7	19	47	7	1
14	7	0	4	23	8	20	33	9	3
14	10	52	5	24	9	21	19	10	4
14	14	44	6	25	10	22	6	12	5
14	18	37	7	26	10	22	54	13	7
14	22	31	8	27	11	23	42	15	8
14	26	26	9	27	12	24	30	16	9
14	30	21	10	28	13	25	20	18	11
14	34	17	11	29	14	26	11	19	12
14	38	14	12	♐	14	27	2	21	14
14	42	11	13	1	15	27	54	23	15
14	46	9	14	2	16	28	48	24	16
14	50	9	15	3	17	29	41	26	18
14	54	7	16	3	18	0 ♑	36	28	19
14	58	8	17	4	18	1	32	♓	21
15	2	8	18	5	19	2	30	2	22
15	6	10	19	6	20	3	28	3	23
15	10	12	20	7	21	4	28	5	24
15	14	16	21	8	22	5	29	7	26
15	18	19	22	9	23	6	32	9	28
15	22	24	23	9	24	7	36	11	29
15	26	29	24	10	24	8	42	13	♉
15	30	35	25	11	25	9	49	15	2
15	34	42	26	12	26	10	58	17	3
15	38	49	27	13	27	12	10	19	4
15	42	57	28	14	28	13	23	21	6
15	47	6	29	15	29	14	39	23	7
15	51	16	30	16	30	15	57	26	8

Sidereal Time.			10	11	12	Ascen		2	3
			♐	♐	♑	♑		♓	♉
H.	M.	S.	°	°	°	°	′	°	°
15	51	16	0	16	0	15	57	26	8
15	55	26	1	17	1	17	17	28	10
15	59	37	2	17	2	18	40	♈	11
16	3	48	3	18	3	20	6	2	13
16	8	1	4	19	4	21	36	4	14
16	12	13	5	20	5	23	8	6	15
16	16	27	6	21	6	24	44	8	16
16	20	41	7	22	7	26	23	10	18
16	24	55	8	23	8	28	7	13	19
16	29	11	9	24	9	29	55	15	20
16	33	26	10	25	10	1 ♒	47	17	21
16	37	42	11	26	11	3	44	19	23
16	41	59	12	27	12	5	46	21	24
16	46	17	13	28	14	7	54	23	25
16	50	34	14	29	15	10	7	25	26
16	54	52	15	♑	16	12	26	27	27
16	59	11	16	1	17	14	52	29	29
17	3	30	17	2	18	17	24	♉	♊
17	7	49	18	3	20	20	3	3	1
17	12	9	19	4	21	22	48	5	2
17	16	29	20	5	22	25	42	7	3
17	20	49	21	6	23	28	42	9	5
17	25	10	22	7	25	1 ♓	49	10	6
17	29	30	23	8	26	5	3	12	7
17	33	51	24	9	27	8	23	14	8
17	38	13	25	10	29	11	49	16	9
17	42	34	26	11	♒	15	20	17	10
17	46	55	27	12	2	18	56	19	11
17	51	17	28	13	3	22	35	21	12
17	55	38	29	14	5	26	17	22	14
18	0	0	30	15	6	30	0	24	15

Sidereal Time.			10	11	12	Ascen		2	3
			♑	♑	♒	♈		♉	♊
H.	M.	S.	°	°	°	°	′	°	°
18	0	0	0	15	6	0	0	24	15
18	4	22	1	16	8	3	43	25	16
18	8	43	2	17	9	7	25	27	17
18	13	5	3	19	11	11	4	28	18
18	17	26	4	20	13	14	40	♊	19
18	21	47	5	21	14	18	11	1	20
18	26	9	6	22	16	21	37	3	21
18	30	30	7	23	18	24	57	4	22
18	34	50	8	24	20	28	11	5	23
18	39	11	9	25	21	1 ♉	18	7	24
18	43	31	10	27	23	4	18	8	25
18	47	51	11	28	25	7	12	9	26
18	52	11	12	29	27	9	57	10	27
18	56	30	13	♒	29	12	36	12	28
19	0	49	14	1	♓	15	8	13	29
19	5	8	15	3	3	17	34	14	♋
19	9	26	16	4	5	19	53	15	1
19	13	43	17	5	7	22	6	16	2
19	18	1	18	6	9	24	14	18	3
19	22	18	19	7	11	26	16	19	4
19	26	34	20	9	13	28	13	20	5
19	30	49	21	10	15	0 ♊	5	21	6
19	35	5	22	11	17	1	53	22	7
19	39	19	23	12	19	3	37	23	8
19	43	33	24	14	22	5	16	24	9
19	47	47	25	15	24	6	52	25	10
19	51	59	26	16	26	8	24	26	11
19	56	12	27	18	28	9	54	27	12
20	0	23	28	19	♈	11	20	28	13
20	4	34	29	20	2	12	43	29	13
20	8	44	30	22	4	14	3	30	14

Sidereal Time.			10	11	12	Ascen		2	3
			♒	♒	♈	♊		♋	♋
H.	M.	S.	°	°	°	°	′	°	°
20	8	44	0	22	4	14	3	0	14
20	12	54	1	23	7	15	21	1	15
20	17	3	2	24	9	16	37	2	16
20	21	11	3	26	11	17	50	3	17
20	25	18	4	27	13	19	2	4	18
20	29	25	5	28	15	20	11	5	19
20	33	31	6	♓	17	21	18	6	20
20	37	36	7	1	19	22	24	6	21
20	41	41	8	2	21	23	28	7	21
20	45	44	9	4	23	24	31	8	22
20	49	48	10	5	25	25	32	9	23
20	53	50	11	7	27	26	32	10	24
20	57	52	12	8	28	27	30	11	25
21	1	52	13	9	♉	28	28	12	26
21	5	53	14	11	2	29	24	12	27
21	9	51	15	12	4	0 ♋	19	13	27
21	13	51	16	14	6	1	12	14	28
21	17	49	17	15	7	2	6	15	29
21	21	46	18	16	9	2	58	16	♌
21	25	43	19	18	11	3	49	16	1
21	29	39	20	19	12	4	40	17	2
21	33	34	21	21	14	5	30	18	3
21	37	29	22	22	15	6	18	19	3
21	41	23	23	23	17	7	6	20	4
21	45	16	24	25	18	7	54	20	5
21	49	8	25	26	20	8	41	21	6
21	53	0	26	27	21	9	27	22	7
21	56	52	27	29	23	10	13	23	7
22	0	42	28	♈	24	10	58	23	8
22	4	32	29	2	25	11	42	24	9
22	8	22	30	3	27	12	26	25	10

Sidereal Time.			10	11	12	Ascen		2	3
			♓	♈	♉	♋		♋	♌
H.	M.	S.	°	°	°	°	′	°	°
22	8	22	0	3	27	12	26	25	10
22	12	11	1	4	28	13	10	26	11
22	15	59	2	6	29	13	53	26	12
22	19	47	3	7	♊	14	35	27	12
22	23	35	4	8	2	15	17	28	13
22	27	22	5	10	3	15	59	28	14
22	31	8	6	11	4	16	41	29	15
22	34	54	7	12	5	17	22	♌	16
22	38	39	8	14	6	18	3	1	16
22	42	24	9	15	8	18	43	1	17
22	46	9	10	16	9	19	23	2	18
22	49	53	11	18	10	20	3	3	19
22	53	36	12	19	11	20	42	4	20
22	57	20	13	20	12	21	21	4	20
23	1	3	14	22	13	22	0	5	21
23	4	46	15	23	14	22	39	6	22
23	8	28	16	24	15	23	18	6	23
23	12	10	17	25	16	23	56	7	23
23	15	52	18	27	17	24	34	8	24
23	19	33	19	28	18	25	12	8	25
23	23	15	20	29	19	25	49	9	26
23	26	56	21	♉	20	26	27	10	27
23	30	37	22	2	21	27	4	10	27
23	34	18	23	3	22	27	42	11	28
23	37	58	24	4	23	28	19	12	29
23	41	39	25	5	24	28	56	12	♍
23	45	19	26	6	24	29	32	13	1
23	48	59	27	8	25	0 ♌	9	14	1
23	52	40	28	9	26	0	46	14	2
23	56	20	29	10	27	1	22	15	3
24	0	0	30	11	28	1	58	16	4

Sidereal Time H.	M.	S.	10 ♈	11 ♉	12 ♋	Ascen ♌ °	′	2 ♌	3 ♍
0	0	0	0	12	0	2	57	17	4
0	3	40	1	13	1	3	33	17	5
0	7	20	2	14	2	4	8	18	6
0	11	1	3	15	3	4	43	19	7
0	14	41	4	17	3	5	19	19	7
0	18	21	5	18	4	5	54	20	8
0	22	2	6	19	5	6	29	21	9
0	25	42	7	20	6	7	5	21	10
0	29	23	8	21	7	7	40	22	10
0	33	4	9	22	7	8	15	23	11
0	36	45	10	23	8	8	50	23	12
0	40	27	11	24	9	9	25	24	13
0	44	8	12	26	10	10	0	25	14
0	47	50	13	27	10	10	36	25	14
0	51	32	14	28	11	11	11	26	15
0	55	14	15	29	12	11	46	27	16
0	58	57	16	♊	13	12	21	27	17
1	2	40	17	1	13	12	56	28	18
1	6	24	18	2	14	13	32	29	18
1	10	7	19	3	15	14	7	29	19
1	13	51	20	4	16	14	42	♍	20
1	17	36	21	5	16	15	18	1	21
1	21	21	22	6	17	15	53	1	22
1	25	6	23	7	18	16	28	2	22
1	28	52	24	8	19	17	4	3	23
1	32	38	25	9	19	17	40	3	24
1	36	25	26	10	20	18	15	4	25
1	40	13	27	11	21	18	51	5	26
1	44	1	28	12	22	19	27	5	27
1	47	40	29	13	22	20	3	6	27
1	51	38	30	14	23	20	39	7	28

Sidereal Time H.	M.	S.	10 ♉	11 ♊	12 ♋	Ascen ♌ °	′	2 ♍	3 ♍
1	51	38	0	14	23	20	39	7	28
1	55	28	1	15	24	21	15	7	29
1	59	18	2	16	25	21	51	8	♎
2	3	8	3	17	25	22	27	9	1
2	7	0	4	18	26	23	4	9	2
2	10	52	5	19	27	23	40	10	2
2	14	44	6	19	27	24	17	11	3
2	18	37	7	20	28	24	53	12	4
2	22	31	8	21	29	25	30	12	5
2	26	26	9	22	30	26	7	13	6
2	30	21	10	23	♌	26	44	14	7
2	34	17	11	24	1	27	21	14	7
2	38	14	12	25	2	27	58	15	8
2	42	11	13	26	3	28	36	16	9
2	46	9	14	27	3	29	13	16	10
2	50	9	15	28	4	29	51	17	11
2	54	7	16	29	5	0♍	28	18	12
2	58	8	17	♋	5	1	6	19	13
3	2	8	18	1	6	1	44	19	13
3	6	10	19	2	7	2	22	20	14
3	10	12	20	2	8	3	1	21	15
3	14	16	21	3	8	3	39	22	16
3	18	19	22	4	9	4	17	22	17
3	22	24	23	5	10	4	56	23	18
3	26	29	24	6	11	5	35	24	19
3	30	35	25	7	11	6	14	25	19
3	34	42	26	8	12	6	53	25	20
3	38	49	27	9	13	7	32	26	21
3	42	57	28	10	14	8	11	27	22
3	47	6	29	11	14	8	50	28	23
3	51	16	30	12	15	9	30	28	24

Sidereal Time H.	M.	S.	10 ♊	11 ♋	12 ♌	Ascen ♍ °	′	2 ♍	3 ♎
3	51	16	0	12	15	9	30	28	24
3	55	26	1	12	16	10	10	29	25
3	59	37	2	13	17	10	49	♎	26
4	3	48	3	14	17	11	29	1	27
4	8	1	4	15	18	12	9	1	28
4	12	13	5	16	19	12	49	2	28
4	16	27	6	17	20	13	30	3	29
4	20	41	7	18	20	14	10	4	♏
4	24	55	8	19	21	14	51	5	1
4	29	11	9	20	22	15	31	5	2
4	33	26	10	21	23	16	12	6	3
4	37	42	11	22	24	16	53	7	4
4	41	59	12	22	24	17	33	8	5
4	46	17	13	23	25	18	14	9	6
4	50	34	14	24	26	18	55	9	7
4	54	52	15	25	27	19	36	10	7
4	59	11	16	26	27	20	18	11	8
5	3	30	17	27	28	20	59	12	9
5	7	49	18	28	29	21	40	13	10
5	12	9	19	29	30	22	22	13	11
5	16	29	20	♌	♍	23	3	14	12
5	20	49	21	1	1	23	45	15	13
5	25	10	22	2	2	24	26	16	14
5	29	30	23	2	3	25	8	17	15
5	33	51	24	3	4	25	50	17	16
5	38	13	25	4	4	26	31	18	16
5	42	34	26	5	5	27	13	19	17
5	46	55	27	6	6	27	55	20	18
5	51	17	28	7	7	28	36	20	19
5	55	38	29	8	7	29	18	21	20
6	0	0	30	9	8	30	0	22	21

Sidereal Time H.	M.	S.	10 ♋	11 ♌	12 ♍	Ascen ♎ °	′	2 ♎	3 ♏
6	0	0	0	9	8	0	0	22	21
6	4	22	1	10	9	0	42	23	22
6	8	43	2	11	10	1	24	23	23
6	13	5	3	12	11	2	5	24	24
6	17	26	4	13	11	2	47	25	25
6	21	47	5	13	12	3	29	26	26
6	26	9	6	14	13	4	10	27	27
6	30	30	7	15	14	4	52	28	28
6	34	50	8	16	15	5	34	28	28
6	39	11	9	17	15	6	15	29	29
6	43	31	10	18	16	6	57	♏	♐
6	47	51	11	19	17	7	38	1	1
6	52	11	12	20	18	8	20	2	2
6	56	30	13	21	19	9	1	2	3
7	0	49	14	22	19	9	42	3	4
7	5	8	15	23	20	10	24	4	5
7	9	26	16	24	21	11	5	5	6
7	13	43	17	24	22	11	46	5	7
7	18	1	18	25	22	12	27	6	8
7	22	18	19	26	23	13	7	7	8
7	26	34	20	27	24	13	48	7	9
7	30	49	21	28	24	14	29	8	10
7	35	5	22	29	25	15	9	9	11
7	39	19	23	♍	26	15	50	10	12
7	43	33	24	1	27	16	30	10	13
7	47	47	25	2	28	17	11	11	14
7	51	59	26	2	29	17	51	12	15
7	56	12	27	3	29	18	31	13	16
8	0	23	28	4	♎	19	11	13	17
8	4	34	29	5	1	19	50	14	18
8	8	44	30	6	2	20	30	15	18

Sidereal Time H.	M.	S.	10 ♌	11 ♍	12 ♎	Ascen ♎ °	′	2 ♏	3 ♐
8	8	44	0	6	2	20	30	15	18
8	12	54	1	7	2	21	10	16	19
8	17	3	2	8	3	21	49	17	20
8	21	11	3	9	4	22	28	18	21
8	25	10	4	10	5	23	7	18	22
8	29	25	5	10	5	23	46	19	23
8	33	31	6	11	6	24	25	20	24
8	37	36	7	12	7	25	4	21	25
8	41	41	8	13	8	25	43	21	26
8	45	44	9	14	8	26	21	22	27
8	49	48	10	15	9	26	59	23	28
8	53	50	11	16	10	27	38	23	28
8	57	52	12	17	11	28	16	24	29
9	1	52	13	17	11	28	54	25	♑
9	5	53	14	18	12	29	32	25	1
9	9	51	15	19	13	0♏	9	26	2
9	13	51	16	20	14	0	47	27	3
9	17	49	17	21	14	1	24	27	4
9	21	46	18	22	15	2	2	28	5
9	25	43	19	23	16	2	39	29	6
9	29	39	20	23	16	3	16	30	7
9	33	34	21	24	17	3	53	♐	8
9	37	29	22	25	18	4	30	1	9
9	41	23	23	26	18	5	7	2	10
9	45	16	24	27	19	5	43	3	11
9	49	8	25	28	20	6	20	3	12
9	53	0	26	28	21	6	56	4	12
9	56	52	27	29	22	7	33	5	13
10	0	42	28	♎	22	8	9	5	14
10	4	32	29	1	23	8	45	6	15
10	8	22	30	2	24	9	21	7	16

Sidereal Time H.	M.	S.	10 ♍	11 ♎	12 ♎	Ascen ♏ °	′	2 ♐	3 ♑
10	8	22	0	2	24	9	21	7	16
10	12	11	1	3	24	9	57	8	17
10	15	59	2	3	25	10	33	8	18
10	19	47	3	4	26	11	9	9	19
10	23	35	4	5	26	11	45	10	20
10	27	22	5	6	27	12	20	11	21
10	31	8	6	7	28	12	56	11	22
10	34	54	7	8	28	13	32	12	23
10	38	39	8	8	29	14	7	13	24
10	42	24	9	9	29	14	42	14	25
10	46	9	10	10	♏	15	18	14	26
10	49	53	11	11	1	15	53	15	27
10	53	36	12	12	2	16	28	16	28
10	57	20	13	12	2	17	4	17	29
11	1	3	14	13	3	17	39	17	♒
11	4	46	15	14	3	18	14	18	1
11	8	28	16	15	4	18	49	19	2
11	12	10	17	16	5	19	24	20	4
11	15	52	18	17	5	20	0	20	5
11	19	33	19	17	6	20	35	21	6
11	23	15	20	18	7	21	10	22	7
11	26	56	21	19	7	21	45	23	8
11	30	37	22	20	8	22	20	24	9
11	34	18	23	20	9	22	55	24	10
11	37	58	24	21	9	23	31	25	11
11	41	39	25	22	10	24	6	26	12
11	45	19	26	23	11	24	41	27	13
11	48	59	27	24	11	25	17	27	14
11	52	40	28	24	12	25	52	28	16
11	56	20	29	25	13	26	27	29	17
12	0	0	30	26	13	27	3	30	18

Sidereal Time H.	M.	S.	10 ♎	11 ♎	12 ♏	Ascen ♏ °	′	2 ♑	3 ♒
12	0	0	0	26	13	27	3	0	18
12	3	40	1	27	14	27	39	1	19
12	7	20	2	27	15	28	14	2	20
12	11	1	3	28	16	28	50	3	21
12	14	41	4	29	16	29	26	3	23
12	18	21	5	♏	17	0♐	2	4	24
12	22	2	6	1	17	0	38	5	25
12	25	42	7	1	18	1	14	6	26
12	29	23	8	2	19	1	51	7	28
12	33	4	9	3	20	2	27	8	29
12	36	45	10	4	20	3	4	9	♓
12	40	27	11	4	21	3	40	10	1
12	44	8	12	5	22	4	17	11	3
12	47	50	13	6	22	4	55	12	4
12	51	32	14	7	23	5	32	13	5
12	55	14	15	8	24	6	9	14	6
12	58	57	16	8	24	6	47	15	8
13	2	40	17	9	25	7	25	16	9
13	6	24	18	10	26	8	3	17	10
13	10	7	19	11	26	8	42	18	12
13	13	51	20	12	27	9	21	19	13
13	17	36	21	12	28	10	0	20	14
13	21	21	22	13	29	10	39	21	16
13	25	6	23	14	29	11	18	22	17
13	28	52	24	15	♐	11	58	23	19
13	32	38	25	16	1	12	39	25	20
13	36	25	26	16	1	13	19	26	21
13	40	13	27	17	2	14	0	27	23
13	44	1	28	18	3	14	42	28	24
13	47	49	29	19	3	15	23	♒	25
13	51	38	30	19	4	16	6	1	27

Sidereal Time H.	M.	S.	10 ♏	11 ♏	12 ♐	Ascen ♐ °	′	2 ♒	3 ♓
13	51	38	0	19	4	16	6	1	27
13	55	28	1	20	5	16	48	2	28
13	59	18	2	21	6	17	32	4	♈
14	3	8	3	22	6	18	15	5	1
14	7	0	4	23	7	18	59	6	3
14	10	52	5	24	7	19	44	8	4
14	14	44	6	24	8	20	29	9	5
14	18	37	7	25	9	21	15	11	7
14	22	31	8	26	10	22	2	12	8
14	26	26	9	27	11	22	49	14	10
14	30	21	10	28	12	23	37	16	11
14	34	17	11	29	13	24	26	17	12
14	38	14	12	29	13	25	16	19	14
14	42	11	13	♐	14	26	6	21	15
14	46	9	14	1	14	26	57	22	17
14	50	9	15	2	15	27	49	24	18
14	54	7	16	3	16	28	43	26	19
14	58	8	17	4	17	29	37	28	21
15	2	8	18	4	18	0♑	32	♓	22
15	6	10	19	5	18	1	29	2	24
15	10	12	20	6	19	2	26	4	25
15	14	16	21	7	20	3	26	6	26
15	18	19	22	8	21	4	26	8	28
15	22	24	23	9	22	5	28	10	29
15	26	29	24	10	23	6	31	12	♉
15	30	35	25	11	23	7	37	14	2
15	34	42	26	11	24	8	44	16	3
15	38	49	27	12	25	9	53	18	5
15	42	57	28	13	26	11	4	21	6
15	47	6	29	14	27	12	17	23	7
15	51	16	30	15	28	13	32	25	9

Sidereal Time H.	M.	S.	10 ♐	11 ♐	12 ♐	Ascen ♑ °	′	2 ♓	3 ♉
15	51	16	0	15	28	13	32	25	9
15	55	26	1	16	29	15	40	28	11
15	59	37	2	16	♑	16	11	♈	12
16	3	48	3	17	1	17	35	2	13
16	8	1	4	18	2	19	1	4	15
16	12	13	5	19	3	20	31	6	16
16	16	27	6	20	4	22	5	9	17
16	20	41	7	21	5	23	43	11	19
16	24	55	8	22	6	25	24	14	20
16	29	11	9	23	7	27	10	16	21
16	33	26	10	24	8	29	1	18	22
16	37	42	11	25	9	0♒	57	20	24
16	41	59	12	26	10	2	58	22	25
16	46	17	13	27	11	5	6	25	26
16	50	34	14	28	12	7	19	27	27
16	54	52	15	29	14	9	40	29	29
16	59	11	16	♑	15	12	7	♉	♊
17	3	30	17	1	16	14	42	3	1
17	7	49	18	2	17	17	25	5	2
17	12	9	19	3	18	20	15	7	3
17	16	29	20	4	20	23	15	9	4
17	20	49	21	5	21	26	23	11	6
17	25	10	22	6	22	29	39	12	7
17	29	30	23	7	24	3♓	4	14	8
17	33	51	24	8	25	6	37	16	9
17	38	13	25	9	26	10	18	18	10
17	42	34	26	10	28	14	5	20	11
17	46	55	27	11	29	17	58	21	12
17	51	17	28	12	♒	21	56	22	14
17	55	38	29	13	2	25	57	25	15
18	0	0	30	14	4	30	0	26	16

Sidereal Time H.	M.	S.	10 ♑	11 ♑	12 ♒	Ascen ♈ °	′	2 ♉	3 ♊
18	0	0	0	14	4	0	0	26	16
18	4	22	1	15	6	4	3	28	17
18	8	43	2	16	7	8	4	♊	18
18	13	5	3	17	9	12	2	1	19
18	17	26	4	19	10	15	55	2	20
18	21	47	5	20	12	19	42	4	21
18	26	9	6	21	14	23	23	5	22
18	30	30	7	22	16	26	56	6	23
18	34	50	8	23	18	0♉	21	8	24
18	39	11	9	24	19	3	27	9	25
18	43	31	10	26	21	6	45	10	26
18	47	51	11	27	23	9	45	12	27
18	52	11	12	28	25	12	35	13	28
18	56	30	13	29	27	15	18	14	29
19	0	49	14	♒	29	17	53	15	♋
19	5	8	15	1	♓	20	20	16	1
19	9	26	16	3	3	22	41	18	2
19	13	43	17	4	5	24	54	19	3
19	18	1	18	5	8	27	2	20	4
19	22	18	19	6	10	29	3	21	5
19	26	34	20	8	12	0♊	59	22	6
19	30	49	21	9	14	2	50	23	7
19	35	5	22	10	17	4	36	24	8
19	39	19	23	12	19	6	17	25	9
19	43	33	24	13	21	7	55	26	10
19	47	47	25	14	23	9	29	27	11
19	51	59	26	16	26	10	59	28	12
19	56	12	27	17	28	12	25	29	13
20	0	23	28	18	♈	13	49	♋	14
20	4	34	29	19	2	15	10	1	14
20	8	44	30	21	5	16	28	2	15

Sidereal Time H.	M.	S.	10 ♒	11 ♒	12 ♈	Ascen ♊ °	′	2 ♋	3 ♋
20	8	44	0	21	5	16	28	2	15
20	12	54	1	22	7	17	43	3	16
20	17	3	2	23	9	18	56	4	17
20	21	11	3	25	11	20	7	5	18
20	25	18	4	26	14	21	16	6	19
20	29	25	5	28	16	22	23	7	20
20	33	31	6	29	18	23	29	7	21
20	37	36	7	♓	20	24	32	8	22
20	41	41	8	2	22	25	34	9	22
20	45	44	9	3	24	26	34	10	23
20	49	48	10	5	26	27	34	11	24
20	53	50	11	6	28	28	31	12	25
20	57	52	12	7	♉	29	28	12	26
21	1	52	13	9	2	0♋	23	13	27
21	5	53	14	10	4	1	17	14	28
21	9	51	15	12	6	2	11	15	28
21	13	51	16	13	8	3	3	16	29
21	17	49	17	15	9	3	54	16	♌
21	21	46	18	16	11	4	44	17	1
21	25	43	19	17	13	5	34	18	2
21	29	39	20	19	14	6	23	19	3
21	33	34	21	20	16	7	11	20	3
21	37	29	22	22	18	7	58	20	4
21	41	23	23	23	19	8	45	21	5
21	45	16	24	25	21	9	31	22	6
21	49	8	25	26	22	10	16	23	7
21	53	0	26	27	24	11	1	23	7
21	56	52	27	29	25	11	45	24	8
22	0	42	28	♈	26	12	28	25	9
22	4	32	29	2	28	13	12	26	10
22	8	22	30	3	29	13	54	26	11

Sidereal Time H.	M.	S.	10 ♓	11 ♈	12 ♉	Ascen ♋ °	′	2 ♋	3 ♌
22	8	22	0	3	29	13	54	26	11
22	12	11	1	4	♊	14	37	27	11
22	15	59	2	6	2	15	18	28	12
22	19	47	3	7	3	16	0	28	13
22	23	35	4	9	4	16	41	29	14
22	27	22	5	10	5	17	21	30	15
22	31	8	6	11	7	18	2	♌	15
22	34	54	7	13	8	18	42	1	16
22	38	39	8	14	9	19	21	1	17
22	42	24	9	16	10	20	0	2	18
22	46	9	10	17	11	20	39	3	19
22	49	53	11	18	12	21	18	4	19
22	53	36	12	20	13	21	57	5	20
22	57	20	13	21	14	22	35	5	21
23	1	3	14	22	15	23	13	6	22
23	4	46	15	23	16	23	51	7	22
23	8	28	16	24	17	24	28	7	23
23	12	10	17	26	18	25	5	8	24
23	15	52	18	27	19	25	43	9	25
23	19	33	19	29	20	26	20	9	26
23	23	15	20	♉	21	26	56	10	26
23	26	56	21	1	22	27	33	11	27
23	30	37	22	2	23	28	9	11	28
23	34	18	23	3	24	28	46	12	29
23	37	58	24	4	25	29	22	13	29
23	41	39	25	6	26	29	58	13	♍
23	45	19	26	7	27	0♌	34	14	1
23	48	59	27	9	27	1	10	15	2
23	52	40	28	10	28	1	46	15	3
23	56	20	29	11	29	2	21	16	3
24	0	0	30	12	30	2	57	17	4

Sidereal Time H.	M.	S.	10 ♈ °	11 ♉ °	12 ♋ °	Ascen ♌ °	′	2 ♌ °	3 ♍ °
0	0	0	0	12	0	3	31	17	4
0	3	40	1	13	1	4	6	17	5
0	7	20	2	14	2	4	41	18	6
0	11	1	3	15	3	5	16	19	7
0	14	41	4	17	3	5	51	19	7
0	18	21	5	18	4	6	26	20	8
0	22	2	6	19	5	7	1	21	9
0	25	42	7	20	6	7	35	21	10
0	29	23	8	21	7	8	10	22	10
0	33	4	9	22	7	8	45	23	11
0	36	45	10	23	8	9	20	23	12
0	40	27	11	24	9	9	54	24	13
0	44	8	12	26	10	10	29	25	14
0	47	50	13	27	10	11	4	25	14
0	51	32	14	28	11	11	39	26	15
0	55	14	15	29	12	12	13	27	16
0	58	57	16	♊	13	12	48	27	17
1	2	40	17	1	13	13	23	28	18
1	6	24	18	2	14	13	58	29	18
1	10	7	19	3	15	14	33	29	19
1	13	51	20	4	16	15	8	♍	20
1	17	36	21	5	16	15	43	1	21
1	21	21	22	6	17	16	18	1	22
1	25	6	23	7	18	16	53	2	22
1	28	52	24	8	19	17	28	3	23
1	32	38	25	9	19	18	3	3	24
1	36	25	26	10	20	18	39	4	25
1	40	13	27	11	21	19	14	5	26
1	44	1	28	12	22	19	49	5	27
1	47	49	29	13	22	20	25	6	27
1	51	38	30	14	23	21	1	7	28

Sidereal Time H.	M.	S.	10 ♉ °	11 ♊ °	12 ♋ °	Ascen ♌ °	′	2 ♍ °	3 ♍ °
1	51	38	0	14	23	21	1	7	28
1	55	28	1	15	24	21	36	7	29
1	59	18	2	16	25	22	12	8	♎
2	3	8	3	17	25	22	48	9	1
2	7	0	4	18	26	23	24	9	2
2	10	52	5	19	27	24	0	10	2
2	14	44	6	19	27	24	36	11	3
2	18	37	7	20	28	25	13	12	4
2	22	31	8	21	29	25	49	12	5
2	26	26	9	22	30	26	26	13	6
2	30	21	10	23	♌	27	2	14	7
2	34	17	11	24	1	27	39	14	7
2	38	14	12	25	2	28	16	15	8
2	42	11	13	26	3	28	53	16	9
2	46	9	14	27	3	29	30	16	10
2	50	9	15	28	4	0 ♍	7	17	11
2	54	7	16	29	5	0	45	18	12
2	58	8	17	♋	5	1	22	19	13
3	2	8	18	1	6	2	0	19	13
3	6	10	19	2	7	2	37	20	14
3	10	12	20	2	8	3	15	21	15
3	14	16	21	3	8	3	53	22	16
3	18	19	22	4	9	4	31	22	17
3	22	24	23	5	10	5	10	23	18
3	26	29	24	6	11	5	48	24	19
3	30	35	25	7	11	6	27	25	19
3	34	42	26	8	12	7	5	25	20
3	38	49	27	9	13	7	44	26	21
3	42	57	28	10	14	8	23	27	22
3	47	6	29	11	14	9	2	28	23
3	51	16	30	12	15	9	41	28	24

Sidereal Time H.	M.	S.	10 ♊ °	11 ♋ °	12 ♌ °	Ascen ♍ °	′	2 ♍ °	3 ♎ °
3	51	16	0	12	15	9	41	28	24
3	55	26	1	12	16	10	20	29	25
3	59	37	2	13	17	11	0	♎	26
4	3	48	3	14	17	11	39	1	27
4	8	1	4	15	18	12	19	1	28
4	12	13	5	16	19	12	59	2	28
4	16	27	6	17	20	13	39	3	29
4	20	41	7	18	20	14	19	4	♏
4	24	55	8	19	21	14	59	5	1
4	29	11	9	20	22	15	39	5	2
4	33	26	10	21	23	16	19	6	3
4	37	42	11	22	24	17	0	7	4
4	41	59	12	22	24	17	40	8	5
4	46	17	13	23	25	18	21	9	6
4	50	34	14	24	26	19	1	9	7
4	54	52	15	25	27	19	42	10	7
4	59	11	16	26	27	20	23	11	8
5	3	30	17	27	28	21	4	12	9
5	7	49	18	28	29	21	45	13	10
5	12	9	19	29	30	22	26	13	11
5	16	29	20	♌	♍	23	7	14	12
5	20	49	21	1	1	23	48	15	13
5	25	10	22	2	2	24	29	16	14
5	29	30	23	2	3	25	10	17	15
5	33	51	24	3	4	25	52	17	16
5	38	13	25	4	4	26	33	18	16
5	42	34	26	5	5	27	14	19	17
5	46	55	27	6	6	27	56	20	18
5	51	17	28	7	7	28	37	20	19
5	55	38	29	8	7	29	19	21	20
6	0	0	30	9	8	30	0	22	21

Sidereal Time H.	M.	S.	10 ♋ °	11 ♌ °	12 ♍ °	Ascen ♎ °	′	2 ♎ °	3 ♏ °
6	0	0	0	9	8	0	0	22	21
6	4	22	1	10	9	0	41	23	22
6	8	43	2	11	10	1	23	23	23
6	13	5	3	12	11	2	4	24	24
6	17	26	4	13	11	2	46	25	25
6	21	47	5	13	12	3	27	26	26
6	26	9	6	14	13	4	8	27	27
6	30	30	7	15	14	4	50	28	28
6	34	50	8	16	15	5	31	28	28
6	39	11	9	17	15	6	12	29	29
6	43	31	10	18	16	6	53	♏	♐
6	47	51	11	19	17	7	34	1	1
6	52	11	12	20	18	8	15	2	2
6	56	30	13	21	18	8	56	2	3
7	0	49	14	22	19	9	37	3	4
7	5	8	15	23	20	10	18	4	5
7	9	26	16	24	21	10	59	5	6
7	13	43	17	24	22	11	39	5	7
7	18	1	18	25	22	12	20	6	8
7	22	18	19	26	23	13	0	7	8
7	26	34	20	27	24	13	41	7	9
7	30	49	21	28	24	14	21	8	10
7	35	5	22	29	25	15	1	9	11
7	39	19	23	♍	26	15	41	10	12
7	43	33	24	1	27	16	21	10	13
7	47	47	25	2	28	17	1	11	14
7	51	59	26	2	29	17	41	12	15
7	56	12	27	3	29	18	21	13	16
8	0	23	28	4	♎	19	0	13	17
8	4	34	29	5	1	19	40	14	18
8	8	44	30	6	2	20	19	15	18

Sidereal Time H.	M.	S.	10 ♌ °	11 ♍ °	12 ♎ °	Ascen ♎ °	′	2 ♏ °	3 ♐ °
8	8	44	0	6	2	20	19	15	18
8	12	54	1	7	2	20	58	16	19
8	17	3	2	8	3	21	37	17	20
8	21	11	3	9	4	22	16	18	21
8	25	19	4	10	5	22	55	18	22
8	29	25	5	10	5	23	33	19	23
8	33	31	6	11	6	24	12	20	24
8	37	36	7	12	7	24	50	21	25
8	41	41	8	13	8	25	29	21	26
8	45	44	9	14	8	26	7	22	27
8	49	48	10	15	9	26	45	23	28
8	53	50	11	16	10	27	23	23	28
8	57	52	12	17	11	28	0	24	29
9	1	52	13	17	11	28	38	25	♑
9	5	53	14	18	12	29	15	25	1
9	9	51	15	19	13	29	53	26	2
9	13	51	16	20	14	0 ♏	30	27	3
9	17	49	17	21	14	1	7	27	4
9	21	46	18	22	15	1	44	28	5
9	25	43	19	23	16	2	21	29	6
9	29	39	20	23	16	2	58	30	7
9	33	34	21	24	17	3	34	♐	8
9	37	29	22	25	18	4	11	1	9
9	41	23	23	26	19	4	47	2	10
9	45	16	24	27	19	5	24	3	11
9	49	8	25	28	20	6	0	3	12
9	53	0	26	28	21	6	36	4	12
9	56	52	27	29	22	7	12	5	13
10	0	42	28	♎	22	7	48	5	14
10	4	32	29	1	23	8	24	6	15
10	8	22	30	2	24	8	59	7	16

Sidereal Time H.	M.	S.	10 ♍ °	11 ♎ °	12 ♎ °	Ascen ♏ °	′	2 ♐ °	3 ♑ °
10	8	22	0	2	24	8	59	7	16
10	12	11	1	3	24	9	35	8	17
10	15	59	2	3	25	10	11	8	18
10	19	47	3	4	26	10	46	9	19
10	23	35	4	5	26	11	21	10	20
10	27	22	5	6	27	11	57	11	21
10	31	8	6	7	28	12	32	11	22
10	34	54	7	8	28	13	7	12	23
10	38	39	8	8	29	13	42	13	24
10	42	24	9	9	29	14	17	14	25
10	46	9	10	10	♏	14	52	14	26
10	49	53	11	11	1	15	27	15	27
10	53	36	12	12	2	16	2	16	28
10	57	20	13	12	2	16	37	17	29
11	1	3	14	13	3	17	12	17	♒
11	4	46	15	14	3	17	47	18	1
11	8	28	16	15	4	18	21	19	2
11	12	10	17	16	5	18	56	20	4
11	15	52	18	17	5	19	31	20	5
11	19	33	19	17	6	20	6	21	6
11	23	15	20	18	7	20	40	22	7
11	26	56	21	19	7	21	15	23	8
11	30	37	22	20	8	21	50	24	9
11	34	18	23	20	9	22	25	24	10
11	37	58	24	21	9	22	59	25	11
11	41	39	25	22	10	23	34	26	12
11	45	19	26	23	11	24	9	27	13
11	48	59	27	24	11	24	44	27	14
11	52	40	28	24	12	25	19	28	16
11	56	20	29	25	13	25	54	29	17
12	0	0	30	26	13	26	29	30	18

Sidereal Time H.	M.	S.	10 ♎ °	11 ♎ °	12 ♏ °	Ascen ♏ °	′	2 ♑ °	3 ♒ °
12	0	0	0	26	13	26	29	0	18
12	3	40	1	27	14	27	4	1	19
12	7	20	2	27	15	27	39	2	20
12	11	1	3	28	16	28	15	3	21
12	14	41	4	29	16	28	50	3	23
12	18	21	5	♏	17	29	25	4	24
12	22	2	6	1	17	0 ♐	1	5	25
12	25	42	7	1	18	0	37	6	26
12	29	23	8	2	19	1	13	7	28
12	33	4	9	3	20	1	49	8	29
12	36	45	10	4	20	2	25	9	♓
12	40	27	11	4	21	3	1	10	1
12	44	8	12	5	22	3	37	11	3
12	47	50	13	6	22	4	14	12	4
12	51	32	14	7	23	4	51	13	5
12	55	14	15	8	24	5	28	14	6
12	58	57	16	8	24	6	5	15	8
13	2	40	17	9	25	6	42	16	9
13	6	24	18	10	26	7	20	17	10
13	10	7	19	11	26	7	58	18	12
13	13	51	20	12	27	8	36	19	13
13	17	36	21	12	28	9	14	20	14
13	21	21	22	13	29	9	53	21	16
13	25	6	23	14	29	10	32	22	17
13	28	52	24	15	♐	11	11	23	19
13	32	38	25	16	1	11	51	25	20
13	36	25	26	16	1	12	31	26	21
13	40	13	27	17	2	13	11	27	23
13	44	1	28	18	3	13	52	28	24
13	47	49	29	19	3	14	33	♒	25
13	51	38	30	19	4	15	14	1	27

Sidereal Time H.	M.	S.	10 ♏ °	11 ♏ °	12 ♐ °	Ascen ♐ °	′	2 ♒ °	3 ♓ °
13	51	38	0	19	4	15	14	1	27
13	55	28	1	20	5	15	56	2	28
13	59	18	2	21	6	16	38	4	♈
14	3	8	3	22	6	17	21	5	1
14	7	0	4	23	7	18	4	6	3
14	10	52	5	24	7	18	48	8	4
14	14	44	6	24	8	19	33	9	5
14	18	37	7	25	9	20	18	11	7
14	22	31	8	26	10	21	4	12	8
14	26	26	9	27	11	21	50	14	10
14	30	21	10	28	12	22	37	16	11
14	34	17	11	29	13	23	25	17	12
14	38	14	12	29	13	24	13	19	14
14	42	11	13	♐	14	25	2	21	15
14	46	9	14	1	14	25	53	22	17
14	50	9	15	2	15	26	44	24	18
14	54	7	16	3	16	27	36	26	19
14	58	8	17	4	17	28	29	28	21
15	2	8	18	4	18	29	23	♓	22
15	6	10	19	5	18	0 ♑	18	2	24
15	10	12	20	6	19	1	15	4	25
15	14	16	21	7	20	2	12	6	26
15	18	19	22	8	21	3	11	8	28
15	22	24	23	9	22	4	12	10	29
15	26	29	24	10	23	5	14	12	♉
15	30	35	25	11	23	6	18	14	2
15	34	42	26	11	24	7	23	16	3
15	38	49	27	12	25	8	31	18	5
15	42	57	28	13	26	9	40	21	6
15	47	6	29	14	27	10	52	23	7
15	51	16	30	15	28	12	6	25	9

Sidereal Time H.	M.	S.	10 ♐ °	11 ♐ °	12 ♐ °	Ascen ♑ °	′	2 ♓ °	3 ♉ °
15	51	16	0	15	28	12	6	25	9
15	55	26	1	16	29	13	22	28	11
15	59	37	2	16	♑	14	41	♈	12
16	3	48	3	17	1	16	3	2	13
16	8	1	4	18	2	17	28	4	15
16	12	13	5	19	3	18	56	6	16
16	16	27	6	20	4	20	28	9	17
16	20	41	7	21	5	22	5	11	19
16	24	55	8	22	6	23	45	14	20
16	29	11	9	23	7	25	29	16	21
16	33	26	10	24	8	27	19	18	22
16	37	42	11	25	9	29	14	20	24
16	41	59	12	26	10	1 ♒	14	22	25
16	46	17	13	27	11	3	21	25	26
16	50	34	14	28	12	5	34	27	27
16	54	52	15	29	14	7	54	29	29
16	59	11	16	♑	15	10	22	♉	♊
17	3	30	17	1	16	12	58	3	1
17	7	49	18	2	17	15	43	5	2
17	12	9	19	3	18	18	36	7	3
17	16	29	20	4	20	21	39	9	4
17	20	49	21	5	21	24	52	11	6
17	25	10	22	6	22	28	14	12	7
17	29	30	23	7	24	1 ♓	46	14	8
17	33	51	24	8	25	5	27	16	9
17	38	13	25	9	26	9	17	18	10
17	42	34	26	10	28	13	15	20	11
17	46	55	27	11	29	17	20	21	12
17	51	17	28	12	♒	21	30	22	14
17	55	38	29	13	2	25	44	25	15
18	0	0	30	14	4	30	0	26	16

Sidereal Time H.	M.	S.	10 ♑ °	11 ♑ °	12 ♒ °	Ascen ♈ °	′	2 ♉ °	3 ♊ °
18	0	0	0	14	4	0	0	26	16
18	4	22	1	15	6	4	16	28	17
18	8	43	2	16	7	8	30	♊	18
18	13	5	3	17	9	12	40	1	19
18	17	26	4	19	10	16	45	2	20
18	21	47	5	20	12	20	43	4	21
18	26	9	6	21	14	24	33	5	22
18	30	30	7	22	16	28	14	6	23
18	34	50	8	23	18	1 ♉	46	8	24
18	39	11	9	24	19	5	8	9	25
18	43	31	10	26	21	8	21	10	26
18	47	51	11	27	23	11	24	12	27
18	52	11	12	28	25	14	17	13	28
18	56	30	13	29	27	17	2	14	29
19	0	49	14	♒	29	19	38	15	♋
19	5	8	15	1	♓	22	6	16	1
19	9	26	16	3	3	24	26	18	2
19	13	43	17	4	5	26	39	19	3
19	18	1	18	5	8	28	46	20	4
19	22	18	19	6	10	0 ♊	46	21	5
19	26	34	20	8	12	2	41	22	6
19	30	49	21	9	14	4	31	23	7
19	35	5	22	10	17	6	15	24	8
19	39	19	23	12	19	7	55	25	9
19	43	33	24	13	21	9	32	26	10
19	47	47	25	14	23	11	4	27	11
19	51	59	26	16	26	12	32	28	12
19	56	12	27	17	28	13	57	29	13
20	0	23	28	18	♈	15	19	♋	14
20	4	34	29	19	2	16	38	1	14
20	8	44	30	21	5	17	54	2	15

Sidereal Time H.	M.	S.	10 ♒ °	11 ♒ °	12 ♈ °	Ascen ♊ °	′	2 ♋ °	3 ♋ °
20	8	44	0	21	5	17	54	2	15
20	12	54	1	22	7	19	8	3	16
20	17	3	2	23	9	20	20	4	17
20	21	11	3	25	11	21	29	5	18
20	25	18	4	26	14	22	37	6	19
20	29	25	5	28	16	23	42	7	20
20	33	31	6	29	18	24	46	7	21
20	37	36	7	♓	20	25	48	8	22
20	41	41	8	2	22	26	49	9	22
20	45	44	9	3	24	27	48	10	23
20	49	48	10	5	26	28	45	11	24
20	53	50	11	6	28	29	42	12	25
20	57	52	12	7	♉	0 ♋	37	12	26
21	1	52	13	9	2	1	31	13	27
21	5	53	14	10	4	2	24	14	28
21	9	51	15	12	6	3	16	15	28
21	13	51	16	13	8	4	7	16	29
21	17	49	17	15	9	4	58	16	♌
21	21	46	18	16	11	5	47	17	1
21	25	43	19	17	13	6	35	18	2
21	29	39	20	19	14	7	23	19	3
21	33	34	21	20	16	8	10	20	3
21	37	29	22	22	18	8	56	20	4
21	41	23	23	23	19	9	42	21	5
21	45	16	24	25	21	10	27	22	6
21	49	8	25	26	22	11	12	23	7
21	53	0	26	27	24	11	56	23	7
21	56	52	27	29	25	12	39	24	8
22	0	42	28	♈	26	13	22	25	9
22	4	32	29	2	28	14	4	26	10
22	8	22	30	3	29	14	46	26	11

Sidereal Time H.	M.	S.	10 ♓ °	11 ♈ °	12 ♉ °	Ascen ♋ °	′	2 ♋ °	3 ♌ °
22	8	22	0	3	29	14	46	26	11
22	12	11	1	4	♊	15	27	27	11
22	15	59	2	6	2	16	8	28	12
22	19	47	3	7	3	16	49	28	13
22	23	35	4	9	4	17	29	29	14
22	27	22	5	10	5	18	9	30	15
22	31	8	6	11	7	18	49	♌	15
22	34	54	7	13	8	19	28	1	16
22	38	39	8	14	9	20	7	1	17
22	42	24	9	16	10	20	46	2	18
22	46	9	10	17	11	21	24	3	19
22	49	53	11	18	12	22	2	4	19
22	53	36	12	20	13	22	40	5	20
22	57	20	13	21	14	23	18	5	21
23	1	3	14	22	15	23	55	6	22
23	4	46	15	23	16	24	32	7	22
23	8	28	16	24	17	25	9	7	23
23	12	10	17	26	18	25	46	8	24
23	15	52	18	27	19	26	23	9	25
23	19	33	19	29	20	26	59	9	26
23	23	15	20	♉	21	27	35	10	26
23	26	56	21	1	22	28	11	11	27
23	30	37	22	2	23	28	47	11	28
23	34	18	23	3	24	29	23	12	29
23	37	58	24	4	25	29	59	13	29
23	41	39	25	6	26	0 ♌	35	13	♍
23	45	19	26	7	27	1	10	14	1
23	48	59	27	9	27	1	45	15	2
23	52	40	28	10	28	2	21	15	3
23	56	20	29	11	29	2	56	16	3
24	0	0	30	12	30	3	31	17	4